THE PLATONISM OF MARSILIO FICINO

Published under the auspices of the

CENTER FOR MEDIEVAL AND RENAISSANCE STUDIES

University of California, Los Angeles

Publications of the

UCLA CENTER FOR MEDIEVAL AND RENAISSANCE STUDIES

1. Jeffrey Burton Russell, *Dissent and Reform in the Early Middle Ages* (1965)
2. C. D. O'Malley, ed., *Leonardo's Legacy: An International Symposium* (1968)
3. Richard H. Rouse, *Serial Bibliographies for Medieval Studies* (1969)
4. Speros Vryonis, Jr., *The Decline of Medieval Hellenism in Asia Minor and the Process of Islamization from the Eleventh through the Fifteenth Century* (1971)
5. Stanley Chodorow, *Christian Political Theory and Church Politics in the Mid-Twelfth Century: The Ecclesiology of Gratian's Decretum* (1972)
6. Joseph J. Duggan, *The Song of Roland: Formulaic Style and Poetic Craft* (1973)
7. Ernest A. Moody, *Studies in Medieval Philosophy, Science, and Logic: Collected Papers 1933-1969* (1975)
8. Marc Bloch, *Slavery and Serfdom in the Middle Ages: Selected Essays* (1975)
9. Michael J. B. Allen, *Marsilio Ficino: The Philebus Commentary, A Critical Edition and Translation* (1975)
10. Richard C. Dales, *Marius: On the Elements, A Critical Edition and Translation* (1976)
11. Duane J. Osheim, *An Italian Lordship: The Bishopric of Lucca in the Late Middle Ages* (1977)
12. Robert Somerville, *Pope Alexander III and the Council of Tours (1163): A Study of Ecclesiastical Politics and Institutions in the Twelfth Century* (1977)
13. Lynn White, jr., *Medieval Religion and Technology: Collected Essays* (1978)
14. Michael J. B. Allen, *Marsilio Ficino and the Phaedran Charioteer: Introduction, Texts, Translations* (1981)
15. Barnabas Bernard Hughes, O.F.M., *Jordanus de Nemore: De numeris datis, A Critical Edition and Translation* (1981)
16. Caroline Walker Bynum, *Jesus as Mother: Studies in the Spirituality of the High Middle Ages* (1982)
17. Carlo M. Cipolla, *The Monetary Policy of Fourteenth-Century Florence* (1983)
18. John H. Van Engen, *Rupert of Deutz* (1983)
19. Thomas K. Keefe, *Feudal Assessments and the Political Community under Henry II and His Sons* (1983)
20. John C. Shideler, *A Medieval Catalan Noble Family: The Montcadas, 1000-1230* (1984)
21. Michael J. B. Allen, *The Platonism of Marsilio Ficino: A Study of His Phaedrus Commentary, Its Sources and Genesis* (1984)

The Platonism of
Marsilio Ficino

A Study of His *Phaedrus* Commentary,
Its Sources and Genesis

by

Michael J. B. Allen

UNIVERSITY OF CALIFORNIA PRESS
BERKELEY   LOS ANGELES   LONDON

University of California Press   *u*
Berkeley and Los Angeles, California

University of California Press, Ltd.
London, England

Library of Congress Cataloging in Publication Data

Allen, Michael J. B.
  The platonism of Marsilio Ficino.

  Bibliography: p. 259.
  Includes index.
  1. Ficino, Marsilio, 1433-1499. Argumentum et
commentarius in Phaedrum. 2. Plato. Phaedrus. 3. Love.
4. Rhetoric, Ancient. I. Title.
B380.A9F573 1984   184   83-18187
ISBN 0-520-05152-1

Printed in the United States of America

1 2 3 4 5 6 7 8 9

303301

To BENJA

Nous eschellons ainsi de degré en degré.
—Montaigne, *Essais* 3.13

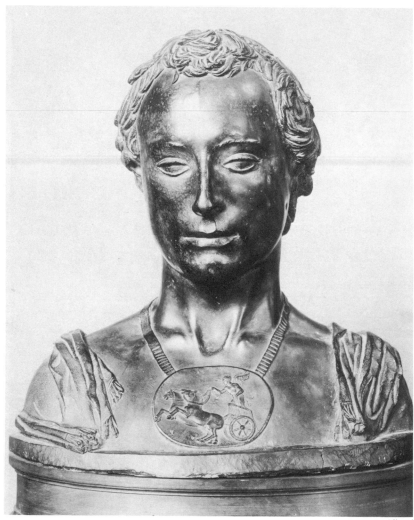

This is a bust in Florence's Museo Nazionale in the Bargello. It has been variously assigned, most notably to Donatello (and the 1440s) and more convincingly to a follower of Desiderio da Settignano (and the early 1470s). Around the sitter's neck hangs a disproprotionately large, ovoid cameo depicting a winged figure driving a two-horsed biga where the nearer— the left-hand—horse is rearing up rebelliously. The *Phaedrus's* myth is clearly in the very forefront of the artist's mind. This is made strikingly obvious when one compares it with reproductions of a classical cameo which was at one time listed in the inventory of Lorenzo de' Medici compiled in 1492. Though now lost, the classical cameo is generally supposed to have been the model for this one in the Bargello; but the reproductions of it show no disparity between the horses and depict the charioteer without wings. See Erwin Panofsky, *Renaissance and Renascences in Western Art* (Stockholm, 1960; reprint, New York, 1972), p. 189. Reproduced with the permission of the Museo Nazionale.

Contents

Preface

In 1496 the great Florentine Neoplatonist Marsilio Ficino (1433-
1499) published, along with some other Plato commentaries, an
incomplete commentary on Plato's *Phaedrus*. The culminating
attempt in a series of analyses, and written as late probably as
1493, it focused on one of the most memorable episodes in all of
Greek literature, the myth of the charioteer's ascent in the gods'
company to gaze upwards at the Ideas in the "supercelestial
place." Bar occasional citation, and a few appreciative but wholly
passing remarks by Giuseppe Saitta and Raymond Marcel,[1] the
Commentary has been almost completely neglected, however—
unhappily if not unaccountably so, given its difficulties, for it contains some of Ficino's latest and most speculative thought on Platonic theogony, mythology, and cosmology, on the metaphysics as
well as the psychology and epistemology of beauty, on the soul's
flight, descent, and immortality, and on the origins and nature of
the four divine madnesses, preeminently the poetic and the amatory.

The Commentary also betrays some fascinating misconceptions
of the *Phaedrus*, already a controversial text among Byzantine
scholars in quattrocento Italy. On ancient authority not dis-
counted till the nineteenth century, Ficino assumed it was Plato's
first dialogue, oriented towards the themes of youth, beauty, and
love, and also his most lyrical work. Like Solomon's Canticle
(which is at one point invoked), it was the song of a poet-theolo-
gian rather than the measured discourse of a philosopher. Convey-
ing religious mysteries in the dithyrambic language of possession,
it portrayed a demon-rapt and visionary Socrates caught up in an
enchanted grove by the spirits of noon and the river Ilissus, and by

---

1. Giuseppe Saitta, *Marsilio Ficino e la filosofia dell'umanesimo,* 3d ed. (Bologna,
1954), pp. 26, 28, 38, 52, 209; Raymond Marcel, *Marsile Ficin* (Paris, 1958), pp. 456-458,
533.

the beauty of Phaedrus,[2] the beloved also of Lysias and Plato. As Plato's first and most poetic work, it also anticipated his subsequent dialogues while bearing witness to his indebtedness to the ancient sages and particularly to his chosen teachers, the Pythagoreans.

In immediately obvious ways, naturally, Ficino's sense of responsibility to this text was different from a modern scholar's, since less attuned to the historical limitations of its language, theses, and underlying attitudes. But he was no less committed to an understanding of Platonic values, and to meeting and transmitting the challenge of one of the ancient world's most evocative and complex works of literary and philosophical art. In the process he exercised considerable originality.

Some, who have narrow criteria for defining a thinker, or who deem all Neoplatonists essentially the same,[3] dispute Ficino's claim to originality, though prepared perhaps to grant him special skills as a translator and academician. In this they fail, I believe, to appreciate his remarkable accomplishments as a builder of myth and symbol rather than of language or logic—his ability to deploy abstract ideas culled from a variety of sources, many of them arcane, as if they were metaphors, and to deploy them for paraphilosophical ends: apology, conversion, intellectual sublimity, and spiritual ecstasy.[4] His peers, if we consider their impact on the thought and culture of their respective ages, are Petrarch and

2. But Phaedrus did have thick legs! See Ficino's *De Amore* 6.18 (ed. Raymond Marcel as *Marsile Ficin: Commentaire sur le Banquet de Platon* [Paris, 1956], p. 236).

3. See the remarks by Paul Oskar Kristeller, "The Scholastic Background of Marsilio Ficino: With an Edition of Unpublished Texts," *Traditio* 2 (1944), 257-318 at 257-258: "The history of Platonism... must not be conceived as an endless repetition of identical doctrines, but rather as a continual adaptation and transformation of certain basic ideas. 'Platonism' is not a label... but a kind of general orientation." This essay was reprinted as chap. 4 in Kristeller's *Studies in Renaissance Thought and Letters* (Rome, 1956; reprint 1969), pp. 35-97; the quotation appears on p. 35.

4. See Ernst Cassirer, "Ficino's Place in Intellectual History," *Journal of the History of Ideas* 6.4 (1945), 483-501: having stressed the genuine independence of Ficino's thought and its essential, even systematic, unity, he warns us not to confuse "speculative thought with discursive thought" (p. 492) and insists that Ficino "poses his own questions and gives his own answers" (p. 483).

Frances Yates refers to the kind of knowledge that Ficino was striving to attain and transmit as "gnosis" in her *Giordano Bruno and the Hermetic Tradition* (London and Chicago, 1964; reprint, New York, 1969), pp. 44-45, 129.

Erasmus,[5] Rousseau and Johnson, Sartre and Jung,[6] rather than the conventional philosophers. Like theirs, his originality is impossible to define in terms of a single intellectual discipline. It depends not so much on achieving advances internal to that discipline as on articulating a profoundly compelling orientation—what Eugenio Garin has called a *forma mentis*[7]—towards both the objective and the subjective worlds, an orientation akin to the obviously unacademic, deeply emotional Platonism of a Piero della Francesca, a Michelangelo, or a Spenser, though presented in the philosophical cast and formulations of late Scholasticism.[8] Specifically it derived from the thoroughgoing syncretism of pagan and Christian elements he effected under the impulse of Plato, Plotinus, Proclus, the *Hermetica*, the Areopagite, Augustine, and Aquinas, to name only his primary wells of inspiration.[9] But this was allied with scholarly energy, acumen, and subtlety, an unusual breadth and profundity of learning, an abiding interest in magic, music, medi-

5. André Chastel, *Marsile Ficin et l'art* (Geneva and Lille, 1954), pp. 13-14: "Le jardin de Montevecchio, avec son *gymnasium* et ses statues antiques, devient vers 1490 un centre de pèlerinage où les Humanistes de Paris, d'Oxford et de Cologne, reliés aux Platoniciens de Florence, par de multiples échanges épistolaires, viennent se charger d'ambitions et de responsabilités nouvelles. Ces rapports de Ficin et de ses amis avec la jeunesse intellectuelle de l'Occident dessinent vers la fin du XVe siècle une sorte de réseau privilégié à l'intérieur de la culture de la Renaissance. Leur histoire... condensée dans l'énorme *Epistolarium* du Sage de Careggi... fournirait pour le XVe siècle un équivalent de ce que fut l'activité de Pétrarque au milieu du XIVe et d'Erasme au début du XVIe siècle."

6. Erwin Panofsky, *Renaissance and Renascences in Western Art* (Stockholm, 1960; reprint, New York, 1972), p. 187, speaks of Ficino's Neoplatonism achieving "a success comparable only to that of psychoanalysis in our own day." Indeed the noted Jungian, James Hillman, has argued, rather interestingly, that "Ficino was writing, not philosophy... but an archetypal psychology" and that he was "the formulator" for the quattrocento of its "central idea," the soul (*Re-Visioning Psychology* [New York, 1975], pp. 201-202).

7. Eugenio Garin, "Ritratto di Marsilio Ficino," *Belfagor* 6.3 (1951), 289-301 at 300; it was subsequently revised and republished in his *Medioevo e Rinascimento* (Bari, 1954; 2d ed., 1961), pp. 288-310, and entitled "Immagini e simboli in Marsilio Ficino." In its revised form the essay has been translated by Victor A. Velen and Elizabeth Velen in Eugenio Garin, *Portraits from the Quattrocento* (New York, 1972), pp. 142-160.

8. Chastel writes that "l'univers de Ficin est celui d'un poète et d'un visionnaire" and that Ficino "analyse de manière neuve les domaines obscurs de l'affectivité, de la connaissance poétique, et de l'éthique personnelle" (pp. 44 and 116). Consequently "les grands symboles qui dominent sa construction" effected "une révolution de la sensibilité" rather than a revolution of thought (pp. 116 and 123).

9. Eugenio Garin, *L'età nuova* (Naples, 1969), p. 284: "Il significato effettivo della sua opera, probabilmente, non deve ricercarsi nell'impalcatura sistematica della sua teologia, che non è né molto originale, né esclusivamente platonica. La sua importanza consiste nell'aver mediato temi diversi, e nell'avere ridotto entro una tradizione accogliente tutti i contrasti e tutti i fremiti pericolosamente rinnovatori."

cine, poetry, and mythology, as well as in philosophy and theology, and a continual inwardness, contemplativeness, and spirituality of gaze that make much of what he wrote peculiarly his own, imaginatively and aesthetically so if not always philosophically.[10] In the case of the *Phaedrus* Commentary he succeeded, almost single-handedly and after a series of meditations and analyses, in fashioning the response of an entire European epoch to the agonistic image of the Platonic charioteer.

I have tried to write a book that will serve in a minor way to complement Paul Oskar Kristeller's major study, *The Philosophy of Marsilio Ficino.*[11] While this surveyed Ficino's thought and work in its entirety, it was especially concerned with the more purely philosophical issues of the *Platonic Theology* and with the theses and argumentation of that huge and systematic masterpiece. By contrast I have concentrated on a single very different work where the preoccupations of Ficino's later years as a magus and an exegete of the highest Platonic mysteries (as well as a metaphysician and apologist) have come to the fore, and where a number of peculiar interpretational problems require elucidation.[12]

10. Garin and Chastel especially have drawn our attention to the critical role of beauty in Ficino's thinking. In his *L'età nuova,* p. 284, Garin refers to his "visione estetica del mondo," and notes in his *Lo zodiaco della vita* (Rome and Bari, 1976), p. 85, "Il mondo come opera d'arte, potrebbe essere il titolo di tutta la filosofia del Ficino—il mondo figurato, animato, vivente, degli astrologi e dei maghi." Chastel, in *Ficin et l'art,* insists that "l'émotion esthétique" (p. 32) and "l'exigence esthétique" (p. 18) underlie all Ficino's thought, being themselves a response to "la perfection esthétique" of the created world (pp. 57-58). He observes: "Il paraît donc indispensable de considérer le mouvement tout entier du Néo-Platonisme florentin *sub specie aestheticae*" (p. 49).

The most recent and comprehensive study of Ficino's *philosophy* of beauty is Werner Beierwaltes, *Marsilio Ficinos Theorie des Schönen im Kontext des Platonismus,* Sitzungsberichte der Heidelberger Akademie der Wissenschaften: Philosophisch-historische Klasse, Jahrgang 30, no. 11 (Heidelberg, 1980); see especially pp. 28-end.

11. Paul Oskar Kristeller, *The Philosophy of Marsilio Ficino,* trans. Virginia Conant (New York, 1943; reprint, Gloucester, Mass., 1964). The Italian edition, *Il pensiero filosofico di Marsilio Ficino* (Florence, 1953), was revised from the German original and is superior to the English in that the original quotations are given in Latin and two additional indices appear. The German original, *Die Philosophie des Marsilio Ficino,* was not published until 1972 in Frankfurt am Main; it includes the indices added to the Italian version and has a full, updated bibliography.

12. All analyses are keyed to my critical edition and translation of the Commentary and of other *Phaedrus*-related texts entitled *Marsilio Ficino and the Phaedran Charioteer* (Berkeley, Los Angeles, London, 1981). The following corrections should be noted: p. 1 μὲν; p. 31 n. 17 Trapezunzio; p. 33.14up *First*; p. 39.7up souls'; p. 41.7 *omit* 2 and 7; p. 41.23

However, though my specific aim has been to deepen our appreciation of one difficult if suggestive commentary and its attendant motifs and themes, I have attempted in the process to enhance our understanding in general of Ficino's Platonism, and of his indebtedness to the ancient Neoplatonic commentary tradition in which as a scholar he was so thoroughly and luminously immersed.

To do justice to these particular and larger aims, I have therefore approached Ficino's eight chapters of formal commentary from the viewpoint of certain primary themes. Thus my second chapter deals with Ficino's chapter 4 and the poetic madness; my third chapter with his chapters 5 and 6 and the soul's immortality; my fourth chapter with his chapters 7, 8, and 9 and the soul's ascent; my fifth chapter with his chapter 10 and the jovian cavalcade; and my sixth chapter with his chapter 11 and the cosmology of the *Phaedrus*. Consideration of Ficino's opening three chapters (which had served, incidentally, as an argumentum for his Latin translation of the dialogue) I have postponed until my ninth chapter, since they embodied, I discovered, an earlier and preliminary response to the charioteer myth, one that dated to the 1460s.[13]

Similarly, I had certain topics in mind as I cut a swath through the fifty-three summae which Ficino appended to his eleven chapters and which form an integral part of the *Phaedrus* Commentary in the first and all subsequent editions.[14] Some of the most interesting enabled me to explore in my first chapter the initiatory theme of Socrates' inspiration. Summae 23, 24, and 25, long enough to be commentary chapters in their own right, impelled me to take up in my seventh chapter some of Ficino's ideas on the soul's descent; and summae 26 to 33 led me to examine in my eighth chapter aspects of his philosophy of beauty and of love. Other summae, of course, I could treat as if they were additions to

---

contemperare; p. 41.25 p. 1488.2; p. 49.9 No. 3696; p. 49.10 Hain 13062; p. 85.9up declaramus; p. 149.8up anima; p. 167.13 Sed quidnam sibi; p. 220.3up infinite; p. 245.4up *Aeneid*; p. 248.18 *Days,* lines 120 ff.; p. 257.3up *filosofia*; p. 259.8up de Ficin; p. 259.7up *di Studi*; p. 261.25 1924-38; p. 92.8 motions; p. 93.7 *motiones* [em.].

For two revisions to the translation, see chap. 5, n. 61 and chap. 8, n. 33 below. For a few excellent suggestions by Patricia Vicari and John Warden, see their review, *Spenser Newsletter* 13.2 (1982), 29-34 at 33-34.

13. Allen, *Charioteer,* pp. 16-19, 21.

14. Ibid., pp. 23-25. Marcel, *Marsile Ficin,* p. 533, dismisses them, injudiciously, as notes.

his chapters of commentary proper, while the more perfunctory I could altogether ignore.

This strategy would surely have appealed to Iamblichus in that it effectively credits Ficino's Commentary with an implicit design. Starting with the setting and the numinous forces at work on Socrates, we move to the theory of the divine madnesses; to the nature of the soul's immortality; to its ascent to and participation in the jovian cavalcade; to its further ascent to the very summit of the intellectual realm; and thence to its subsequent descent, concluding with the overriding theme of beauty. At first glance, this might appear an overly logical arrangement for the seemingly disparate if elaborate material Ficino assembled on the *Phaedrus* for his 1496 volume. But I do not think it is. Not only does it do justice to Ficino's sense of the *Phaedrus*'s drama, the brilliant plotting of its scenes and sequences, the entrances and exits of its arguments and images, a drama to which his work on other dialogues had already made him sensitive; but we also have the evidence of a correspondingly systematic treatment of the dialogue by the ancient Neoplatonists familiar to Ficino from his translation of Hermias and from Proclus's *Theologia Platonica*.[15] For all its incompleteness, that is, I believe Ficino's Commentary has a structure that reflects the structure of the *Phaedrus* itself Neoplatonically conceived.

I have kept two historical surveys until last. Thus I treat of Ficino's attempts to allegorize the charioteer myth prior to his Commentary in my ninth chapter, and in my tenth of the nature of his indebtedness to various ancient commentators and to other authorities. These chapters could have appeared as prologues rather than as epilogues to the main study; but it seemed to me that an account of Ficino's earlier attempts and likewise of his departures from his predecessors' work could only come properly into focus after we had fully comprehended the scope of his authoritative achievement in the 1490s.

Rereading Pico's *Oration* on the night of a coppery lunar eclipse in 1982, I took wry note of an admonition there, "Profecto inge-

---

15. See chap. 10 below; also Allen, *Charioteer,* p. 10. For clarity's sake I shall henceforth refer to Proclus's work as the *Theologia Platonica* but to Ficino's masterpiece of the same title as the *Platonic Theology.*

nerosum est, ut ait Seneca, *sapere* solum *ex commentario.*"[16] If subject, for a while at least, to this "dishonorable" mode of knowing, I was rescued from many lesser errors by the counsel and correction of Professor Paul Oskar Kristeller; to this great master's kindness I owe a special and profound thanks. I am deeply grateful too for the scholarly and personal encouragement of Professor D. P. Walker, of John R. Miles, and of Professor Fredi Chiappelli; and also for the cheerful forbearance of Jeanette Gilkison, who typed and retyped reams over the elusive Los Angeles seasons, and of Nicholas Goodhue, who gave me scholarly assistance that went far beyond the duties of a copy editor.

This project was begun during a Guggenheim year, and I would like to thank the Foundation for its generous support at that time, as well as UCLA's Academic Senate for sundry small but welcome research grants since then. As close friends will testify, this book is not the product of some sequestered study, but of Benjamin's busy, burgeoning bedroom. My dedication is to him as he wheels his *biga* into the circus of the first grade, *ad astra pennatus.*

16. Ed. Eugenio Garin, *G. Pico della Mirandola: De Hominis Dignitate, Heptaplus, De Ente et Uno, e scritti vari* (Florence, 1942), p. 144. Pico is quoting from Seneca's *Epistle* 33.7.

THE STUDY

Chapter One: Socrates' Inspiration

For the ancient Neoplatonists the *Phaedrus*'s scattered allusions to the Nymphs haunting the banks of the Ilissus had betokened the special nature of Socrates' inspiration in his encounter at noon with the beautiful youth Phaedrus, the son of Pythocles. For instance, Proclus had written in his *Theologia Platonica* 1.4: "Having been enraptured by the inspiration that comes from the Nymphs, and having exchanged the activity of the intelligence (νοῦς) for divine madness, Socrates propounded a great number of secret doctrines throughout the dialogue. For his mouth was divinely inspired ... and everything he taught there was taught in a divinely inspired manner (as he explicitly notes himself). In fact, he makes the local or country divinities responsible for his madness."[1] While Ficino devoted a commentary chapter specifically to the general theory of the four divine madnesses, which Plato had adumbrated at 243E-245C, he used several of his summae to treat, directly or indirectly, of Socrates' submission to the influence of the Nymphs. And to more than just their influence; for he detected, again like the ancient commentators, the presence of other, more powerful divinities in a dialogue that was at once a dialectical exercise and a theological poem exhibiting, behind the personal art and invention, the unmistakable signs of impersonal, god-sent inspiration. Though his summae often merely hint at the possibilities, they do provide us with a sense of his subtle awareness of the *Phaedrus* as a Platonic hymn and a Platonic pastoral depicting an enraptured Socrates in an unfamiliar, numinous setting.

Scholars have frequently drawn our attention to the uniqueness of this setting.[2] Whereas Socrates is habitually presented to us in

1. Ed. and trans. H. D. Saffrey and L. G. Westerink as *Proclus: Théologie platonicienne,* 4 vols. to date (Paris, 1968, 1974, 1978, 1981), 1:17-18, glossing *Phaedrus* 238D1, νυμφόληπτος. Cf. Proclus's *Theologia Platonica* 3.22 and 4.5 (ed. cit., 3:78-79 and 4:18).

2. See, for example, Léon Robin, ed. and trans., *Phèdre* (Paris, 1933), pp. x-xii; Paul Vicaire, trans., *Phèdre* (Paris, 1972), p. 13; F. M. Cornford, *Principium Sapientiae* (Cambridge, 1952), pp. 66 ff.; W. K. C. Guthrie, *A History of Greek Philosophy,* vol. 4 (Cambridge, 1975), pp. 397-398, with further refs.

an urban or even a domestic context, dining at the table of an admirer or waylaying adolescents on their way to the agora, here he is portrayed as leaving Athens, on one of the few occasions in his life,[3] to stroll along the riverbank on a path that could still be traced in the twentieth century.[4] Initially he appears critical of the country: "trees and open country won't teach me anything whereas men in the town do" (230D).[5] At the far point of the walk Socrates does not succumb to rural charms as such but to the power of a recognizably sacred place, one which Ficino certainly would have compared to the enchanted grove in book 6 of the *Aeneid* and associated with the earthly paradises and enclosed gardens of medieval dream allegory and with their Renaissance counterparts, the Medicean parks and gardens at Careggi and Fiesole, at Poggio a Caiano, up in the Mugello or the Val d'Arno, retreats where he had himself savored the contemplative peace and tranquillity, the *otium,* of summer.[6] This distinction between the countryside at large and a specific sacred grove is not accorded much weight by modern *Phaedrus* scholars, for whom the setting is mainly a

3. The other occasions seem to have involved military duties and in one case a pitched battle: *Symposium* 219E-221A and *Apology* 28E—the expedition to Potidaea; *Symposium* 221AB, *Laches* 181B, 188E, and *Apology* 28E—the flight from the battle of Delium. Cf. Ficino's own *De Amore* 7.2 (ed. Marcel, p. 243).

Ficino did not espouse the view of one late Neoplatonist, probably a successor of Olympiodorus, that Plato rejected Athens as a setting for his dialogues after the death of Socrates "because he thought the Athenians unworthy to appear in his work," choosing, for instance, "the precinct of the Nymphs" for the *Phaedrus* (L. G. Westerink, ed. and trans., *Anonymous Prolegomena to Platonic Philosophy* [Amsterdam, 1962], pp. 32-33). Such a view would make little sense to someone, like Ficino himself, who believed that the *Phaedrus* was Plato's first dialogue; see Allen, *Charioteer,* pp. 8-9.

4. Robin charts such a walk (*Phèdre,* pp. x-xii) with something of the *ubi sunt* to his mood: "Aujourd'hui la source est obstruée, il n'y a plus d'ombrages, le lit de l'Ilissus n'est plus sillonné des filets d'une eau transparente, mais on a plaisir à faire avec le philosophe cette promenade dans un paysage dont il a si délicatement traduit la poésie" (p. xii). Today, fifty years later, one needs a smog mask.

5. Except where noted to the contrary, I shall use the translation by R. Hackforth, *Plato's Phaedrus* (Cambridge, 1952; reprint, 1972). For the Greek text I have used vol. 2 of the Oxford *Platonis Opera,* ed. John Burnet (n.d.).

6. For Ficino's sense of the propitiousness of gardens and certain sylvan scenes see especially his letter to Valori of 27 October 148[9] (*Opera,* pp. 893-894). See also Arnaldo della Torre, *Storia dell'Accademia Platonica di Firenze* (Florence, 1902), pp. 640-641; Chastel, *Ficin et l'art,* pp. 17 (nn. 14, 16, 19—on the *otium pastorale*), 23, 30-31, 147; André Chastel, *Arte e umanesimo a Firenze al tempo di Lorenzo il Magnifico,* trans. Renzo Federici (Turin, 1964), pp. 157 ff. (with further information on the Medici villas and their ambience); and Terry Comito, *The Idea of the Garden in the Renaissance* (New Brunswick, N.J., 1978), pp. 64-75 (on the *vis naturae*), 76-88 (on Ficino).

delightful but tangential concern. For the Neoplatonic Ficino it was necessarily otherwise, more particularly since he considered the *Phaedrus* Plato's first dialogue and thought it significant that Plato, like Vergil after him, should have commenced his philosophical career with a pastoral.[7]

At the end of their stroll Socrates and Phaedrus reach a sylvan shrine or sanctuary, a spot which, "judging from the statuettes and votive images" to be found there (230B), seemed consecrated to Achelous (a paradigmatic river-god), and to some of the Nymphs. These were presumably Dryads and Naiads, for summa 7 says they were spirits of wood and water who presided over generation and growth,[8] a theme close to the heart of the dialogue which will itself "generate" the subsequent dialogues even as it deals in part with the "generative" powers of beauty.[9] A bare quarter of a mile downstream, where worshipers crossed over to another sanctuary, Socrates recalls there is an altar dedicated to Boreas, the god of the north wind and ravisher of the Nymph Oreithyia (229B). Following Hermias, who identified Boreas with Socrates and the Nymph with Phaedrus, Ficino interpreted Boreas as the breath of inspiration ravishing a virgin soul (again the generation motif, this time by force).[10] The ravishment theme is

---

7. The importance of the *Phaedrus* for the history of the pastoral has been recognized for some time. See, for instance, Clyde Marley, "Plato's *Phaedrus* and Theocritean Pastoral," *Transactions of the American Philological Association* 71 (1940), 281-295, and Adam Parry, "Landscape in Greek Poetry," *Yale Classical Studies* 15 (1957), 3-29, esp. 16-29. Parry observes, "Plato, though never a pastoral writer in the strict sense, seems to have been its originator" (p. 29).

According to Richard Cody, Ficino was the figure responsible for establishing the *Phaedrus* as the model during the Florentine Renaissance for the pastoral eclogue (*The Landscape of the Mind* [Oxford, 1969], pp. 4 and 11). Though in need of considerable documentation, Cody's views are probably none too wide of the mark; cf. Comito, *Garden,* pp. 64-68, 76-88.

8. Hermias has a number of comments on the Nymphs (ed. P. Couvreur as *Hermiae Alexandrini in Platonis Phaedrum Scholia* [Paris, 1901; reprint, Hildesheim, 1971, with an *index verborum* by Clemens Zintzen], pp. 32, 53-56, etc.) and regards them as "divinities in the service of Semele's son, Dionysus, who preside over the act of rebirth" (p. 32). Ficino may also have turned to Porphyry's commentary on the *Odyssey* 13.102-112, 345, in the *De Antro Nympharum* 10-12 and passim. Cf. André Pézard, "Nymphes platoniciennes au paradis terrestre," in *Medioevo e Rinascimento: Studi in onore di Bruno Nardi* (Florence, 1955), 2:543-594 at 553; and Comito, *Garden,* p. 65.

9. Allen, *Charioteer,* p. 13.

10. Hermias, pp. 28-29; see also the commentary by P[ater] Amandus Bielmeier, *Die neuplatonische Phaidrosinterpretation* (Paderborn, 1930), pp. 33-34.

underscored by the story of Achelous, the lover of five Nymphs later metamorphosed into islands at the mouth of the river named after him.[11]

Ficino had already allegorized the details of Plato's depiction of the scene in his argumentum: the tall, spreading plane,[12] the flowering agnus castus,[13] the dappled shadows and the cooling breeze, the bubbling water and later the cicadas, in terms of the features he associated with the first Academy and its gardens and shrine dedicated to the nine Muses.[14] Though this specific allegorization may be subordinate to the general sense of a hallowed place, it nonetheless supplies us with a key to what the idea of an academy must have signified for Ficino. We know that he and his *conphilosophi* were bemused and at the same time obsessed by the notion of recapturing the spirit of the first Academy by imitating its day-to-day life, its setting and customs, its events and circumstances, as well as its intellectual program and religious practices. The Florentines' banquets and gatherings, their social rituals, courtesies,

At p. 29.2-4 ff. Hermias first derived Oreithyia's name from that of the Seasons (῟Ωραι) and noted that some call her "the generative power of the earth"; cf. Pézard, "Nymphes platoniciennes," pp. 563 and 574n. Porphyry's *De Antro Nympharum* 25-28 interprets *Boreas* to mean "the wind of amorous passion"; cf. Pézard, p. 552.

11. Hermias, pp. 32.9 ff.; cf. Ovid, *Metamorphoses* 8.547-9.88.

12. Hermias, pp. 32.7 ff.; also Bielmeier's comments, *Phaidrosinterpretation,* p. 78; and Cody, *Landscape,* p. 11.

Among Renaissance references to the Ilissus and its setting, see particularly Pico della Mirandola's remarks in his *Commento* on stanza 1 of Benivieni's *Canzona d'amore* (ed. Garin [see Preface, n. 16 above], p. 538): "Socrate... più volte, eccitato dalla beltà di Fedro, appresso al fiume Ilisso cantò li altissimi misterii di teologia". See also the letter of Pico's nephew, Giovanni Francesco Pico della Mirandola, to a friend, Lilius Gyraldus, which was printed with the 1513 Rome edition of a poem *De Venere et Cupidine Expellendis:* "Ad hunc ego lucum saepe cum diverterem, non philosophandi gratia, ut olim sub umbra platani propter Ilissum..." (sig. b iv[r]); this letter is quoted and discussed by Ernst H. Gombrich in his *Symbolic Images: Studies in the Art of the Renaissance,* 2d ed. (Oxford and New York, 1978), pp. 105-106, 223 n. 30.

13. Hermias, p. 32.16 ff., allegorizes the agnus castus bloom as Phaedrus's amenability to Socrates' instruction. For Pliny, on the other hand, the bush assuaged the assaults of love even as it symbolized fecundity (*Nat. Hist.* 24.9.38.59). Cf. Ficino's *De Vita* 3.12 (*Opera,* p. 547).

Other allegorizations by Hermias that Ficino did not refer to, however, include the identification of the river itself with birth (p. 27.21-23) and the reasons why Socrates went unshod and subsequently wet his feet (p. 27.24-28).

14. Diogenes Laertius, *Lives of the Philosophers* 4.1. See Franz Cumont, *Recherches sur le symbolisme funéraire des Romains* (Paris, 1942), chap. 4; Pierre Boyancé, *Le culte des muses chez les philosophes grecs* (Paris, 1937), esp. pp. 155-184, 249-297, 350; Harold Cherniss, *The Riddle of the Early Academy* (Berkeley, 1945), chap. 3.

and friendships, their lectures, readings, debates, and lyre recitals, their passing salutations and considered correspondence, were all modeled on the actual or putative example of Plato's original school.[15] Not least of these deliberately cultivated parallels was the garden or parkland setting. Plato enthusiasts raked the ancient notices and apocrypha for clues to its exact extent and situation, its statues, flora, and topography; and where they could find no sherds from the past, they felt at liberty to invent Platonically appropriate details. Since a modern academy almost invariably evokes images of rostra and desks, confined and sterile spaces, we tend to forget that its paradigm was a paradise ornamented with fountains, shrines, and statuary and dedicated to the Muses and their leader, Apollo.[16] Ficino's attempt to recover Plato involved therefore also recovering his mode of philosophizing: in live discussion and formal conversation, in feasts and banquets, in strolls through the coverts and groves of the grounds around the villas at Careggi and Fiesole, where one could subject oneself to the hidden genii of place and time and be caught up by a gust of borean wind to the realm of awesome abstractions.

But Ficino saw more to the setting than a type of academic sanctuary. Summa 7 comments on what we see as Socrates' wry contention at 238CD that "there seems to be a divine presence" in the place where they are sitting, and that, consequently, Phaedrus should listen in silence, emptied of "alien motions." Ficino notes that a place is "divine" when it is subject to higher "influences," those of the indwelling demons, genii, and local deities, and also of the greater divinities. In summa 39, for instance, he lists the gifts bestowed on Socrates beside the Ilissus: from Dionysus had come ecstasy, from the Muses poetry, from mercurial Pan eloquence, and from the Nymphs variety. In two summae he takes a further if somewhat hesitant step and suggests that Socrates was subject not only to a variety but to a definite sequence of inspira-

15. Della Torre and Chastel especially have explored this aspect of Florentine Neoplatonism in the works cited above; but see also Edgar Wind, *Pagan Mysteries in the Renaissance,* rev. ed. (New York, 1968), passim, and Michael J. B. Allen, "Ficino's Lecture on the Good?" *Renaissance Quarterly* 30.2 (1977), 160-171.

16. For the importance of Apollo in Plato's life see the refs. in Allen, *Charioteer,* p. 238 n. 1; to these might be added especially Hermias, p. 89.33.

tions: in summa 7 he observes that Socrates began his "hymn"
under the "more peaceful" influence of the Muses, but soon
yielded to the "bacchanals" of Dionysus; and in summa 10 he
actually postulates a threefold progression in Socrates' inspiration
when he writes that Socrates was moved first by the Nymphs to
carmina, then by Bacchus (Dionysus) to dithyrambs, and finally
by the power of a demon of Apollo. The sense of progression is
hinted at merely, but it raises the possibility that, had Ficino had
time to work up the summae into formal commentary chapters, he
might well have committed himself to the notion of an ascending
series of inspirations for Socrates and explored it systematically.[17]
It would have been in harmony with his general approach to the
dialogue and would also have served to amplify Proclus's rather
ambiguous statement that Socrates had "made the local or country divinities responsible for such madness (τοὺς ἐγχωρίους θεοὺς
τῆς τοιαύτης μανίας αἰτιώμενος)."[18]

In the light of Ficino's remarks in these summae, we should take
a closer look at his presentation in the *Phaedrus* of specific divinities. Lowest on the scale are the various kinds of demons, whom
Ficino, following Iamblichus and Hermias and what he took to be
Plato's own intention, saw symbolized by the cicada choir of both
230C and 258E-259D and alluded to in 279B's mention of "the
other gods dwelling in this place." The pieces he selected for translation from such Neoplatonists as Iamblichus, Porphyry, Syne-

17. Hermias offers us sufficient testimony that Iamblichus thought of the *Phaedrus*'s
structure in terms of the metaphysical ascent to, and then descent from, Beauty; see Bielmeier, *Phaidrosinterpretation,* p. 24; Bent Dalsgaard Larsen, *Jamblique de Chalcis:
Exégète et philosophe* (Aarhus, 1972), p. 366; and Allen, *Charioteer,* p. 10. Hermias also
observes that Plato had called upon a variety of styles in order to do justice to the dialogue's network of themes.

Neither Hermias, Proclus, nor Ficino seems to have entertained the notion that Socrates
submitted to the four divine madnesses in the order that he had himself dealt with them before turning to the immortality syllogisms. Had he done so, Socrates would then have become an inspired witness to the truth of his own classification of the madnesses. The
Phaedrus's several refs. to various deities suggested a more complex situation, as we shall
see.

18. *Theologia Platonica* 1.4 (ed. Saffrey and Westerink, 1:18.11-12). Cf. ibid., 4.5 (ed.
Saffrey and Westerink, 4:18) and 6.18 (ed. Aemilius Portus as *Procli Successoris Platonici
in Platonis Theologiam Libri Sex* [Hamburg, 1618; reprint, Frankfurt am Main, 1960],
p. 394); also *In Rempublicam* 6 (ed. G. Kroll as *Procli in Platonis Rem Publicam Commentarii,* 2 vols. [Leipzig, 1899, 1901], 1:180-182; trans. A.-J. Festugière as *Proclus: Commentaire sur la République,* 3 vols. [Paris, 1970], 1:200-202).

sius, and the Byzantine Psellus indicate Ficino's lasting fascination with demonology. He was well acquainted, moreover, with other primary ancient sources: sections in Plutarch, Apuleius, Varro (*apud* Augustine), and Calcidius, as well as the seminal texts in Plato (particularly the apocryphal *Theages* and the *Epinomis*), Plotinus (particularly the *Enneads* 3.5.5-6), and Augustine. The nature of his debts and own contributions is, however, a largely unresearched subject, despite the pioneering work by D. P. Walker on Ficino's conceptions of the "spirit" and of the demons;[19] and I shall confine myself, after a few introductory remarks, to the particular issues Ficino raises here.

He follows Proclus in arguing that the term "demonic" signifies the nature of all intermediate higher souls: those of ordinary men at the lower end of the scale right up to those of the planetary or star gods at the higher.[20] Closest to the star gods are the highest demons, sometimes referred to by the ancient Neoplatonists as angels.[21] Then come the ranks of demons proper. Finally come the

19. D. P. Walker, *Spiritual and Demonic Magic: From Ficino to Campanella* (London, 1958; reprint, Notre Dame, 1975), pp. 3-29, 44-53, and especially 46 ff. (with citation of some passages many in Ficino on the demons). See also Maurice de Gandillac, "Astres, anges et génies chez Marsile Ficin," in *Umanesimo e esoterismo: Atti del V Convegno Internazionale di Studi Umanistici,* ed. Enrico Castelli (Padua, 1960), pp. 85-109 at 107 ff.

Ficino's debts to the complex demonology of the great eleventh-century Byzantine Neoplatonist Michael Psellus have yet to be explored (for whom see K. Svoboda, *La démonologie de Michel Psellos,* Opera Facultatis Philosophicae Universitatis Masarykianae Brunensis, no. 22 [Brno, 1927]; and Perikles-Petros Joannou, *Démonologie populaire—démonologie critique au XIe siècle: La vie inédite de S. Auxence par M. Psellos,* Schriften zur Geistesgeschichte des östlichen Europa, no. 5 [Wiesbaden, 1971], introd.). We do, however, have some brief extracts which Ficino translated (paraphrased/adapted?) from Psellus's major treatise, *De Operatione Daemonum* (*Opera,* pp. 1939-1945); see Paul O. Kristeller, *Supplementum Ficinianum,* 2 vols. (Florence, 1937), 1:cxxxv—hereafter *Sup. Fic.*

Ficino's ideas on the demons were not always consistent (given the variety of his sources, this is hardly surprising). For instance, his remarks on the demonic body in his *Platonic Theology* 18.4 (ed. Raymond Marcel as *Marsile Ficin: Théologie platonicienne de l'immortalité des âmes,* 3 vols. [Paris, 1964-1970], 3:193-196; trans. Allen, *Charioteer,* pp. 230-234) are difficult to reconcile with similar observations in his commentary on Plotinus, *Enneads* 3.5.5-6 in his *Opera,* pp. 1715-1717.

20. Walker, *Magic,* pp. 46 ff., claims that in Ficino there are demons even higher than those attending the star gods: these would attend the pure intelligences or what Ficino will refer to here in his *Phaedrus* Commentary as the "supercelestial" gods (within, that is, the Plotinian hypostasis of Mind). Unlike lower demons, Walker says, they would have no bodies at all. I am skeptical of this claim and believe that for Ficino the highest demons are the decan—that is, the uranian—demons; see chap. 5, n. 51 below.

21. Ficino seems to have been especially sensitive to the problems of equating the Iamblichean and post-Iamblichean "angels" with the "angels" of Christianity; perhaps he re-

heroes, the souls of illustrious men who have achieved the demonic state.[22] The character and function of the last category is debatable. Sometimes Ficino seems concerned to differentiate its specifics, but at others he treats it merely as an aspect of demon or soul theory, being no more inconsistent in this respect than the ancient Neoplatonists.[23] A similar blurring of the demarcation line occurs at the upper end of the scale: on the one hand the highest demons are immediate companions and followers of the star gods and are thus almost gods; on the other hand Ficino often writes, as

---

called Augustine's strictures in the *De Civitate Dei* 8.13-22. A passage in the *De Amore* (6.3) sets up some important distinctions: "Ordinarily Dionysius the Areopagite [for instance, in the *Celestial Hierarchy* 9.257D-261B] uses the term angels for the governors of the lower world—that is, for the good [demons] who guard over us; and this is not at odds with what Plato has in mind. Moreover, what Plato names the gods and the souls of the spheres and stars we (in the manner of Dionysius) can call angels, meaning God's ministers. Again this is not contrary to Plato; for, as the tenth book of the *Laws* [896C-899D] makes clear, in no respect does he confine such souls to the limits of their spheres.... Between Plato and Dionysius, therefore, the disagreement is about terms rather than meaning" (ed. Marcel, p. 203; my translation). Cf. *De Amore* 6.4 (ed. Marcel, p. 204): "the seven gods who move the seven planets and whom we call angels." In this regard James Hutton reminds us that the distribution of the Dionysian hierarchies among the celestial spheres seems to begin with Dante and compares Ficino's *Opera*, pp. 19 and 973 f. ("Some English Poems in Praise of Music," *English Miscellany* 2 [1951], 23); see also Walker, *Magic*, pp. 46 ff., and John M. Dillon, *The Middle Platonists* (Ithaca, N.Y., 1977), pp. 171-174 (on Philo).

On other occasions, however, Ficino feels free to use the term "angels" to refer exclusively to the supercelestial gods (see n. 20 above) or to the supercelestial gods in addition to the celestial ones; see, for example, his *Platonic Theology* 13.2 and 18.8 (ed. Marcel, 2: 206 and 3:204). Thus Walker is not correct when he suggests that for Ficino the terms "good demons" and "angels" are synonymous (*Magic,* p. 45n).

22. Proclus distinguishes between "essential" demons ($\kappa\alpha\tau$ ' $o\dot{\upsilon}\sigma\dot{\iota}\alpha\nu$), which are never subject to error, and "conditional" demons ($\kappa\alpha\tau\dot{\alpha}$ $\sigma\chi\acute{\epsilon}\sigma\iota\nu$), which are human souls that have become demonic and can err and cause others to err (*In Remp.* 4 [ed. Kroll, 1:41.11-29; trans. Festugière, 1:58-59]). This is an important distinction that Ficino seems to have accepted, at least in part; see pp. 24 ff. below.

The notion that men, particularly good men, might become demons after death Ficino probably derived directly from Plato's *Cratylus* 398B and *Timaeus* 90A. It was, however, a Neoplatonic commonplace.

23. Following Proclus's *In Cratylum* 119 (ed. G. Pasquali as *Procli in Platonis Cratylum Commentaria* [Leipzig, 1908]), Ficino linked the notion of "heroes" to "Eros" in his *De Amore* 6.5 (ed. Marcel, p. 205) and glossed it to mean "lovers" (*amatorii*). In the same chapter he subdivides the heroes, who are third on the scale of rational souls, into three groups, those assigned to the elemental spheres of fire, of pure air, and of impure air, respectively.

D. A. Russell, in his *Plutarch* (London, 1973), p. 76, observes that it was Hesiod who first clearly distinguished between the various grades of rational beings by postulating the series: gods, demons, heroes, and men (*Works and Days* 122 ff.).

in summa 38, as if the minor or local gods were in fact demons, with other equally local demons under them. Despite this wide-ranging application of the term "demonic," however, Ficino usually employs the term "demons" to refer more narrowly to the beings situated between the heroes below and the gods above.

But where do the demons usually dwell? Ficino seems to have followed Apuleius and other Middle Platonists and most Neoplatonists in adopting the broadly Stoic view that the matter of the heavens was not a distinctly different, fifth essence, as Aristotle had hypothesized, but was the purest form of fire. At the same time he had to accommodate the notion of the aether, given the weight of the authorities, including Plato, who had testified to its existence. Swayed by the views of the *Epinomis,* of the *Timaeus* 58D, and of Calcidius's Commentary on the *Timaeus,* Ficino thinks of the aether as intermediate between the celestial fire and the ordinary air, as indeed the fiery form of air or the airy form of fire.[24] Several remarks in his own *Timaeus* Commentary are particularly revealing. In chapter 17 he lists the *ignis aethereus* as existing "under the Moon" and thus as intermediate between the *ignis coelestis* and the *aer* (*Opera,* p. 1445). In chapter 27 he distinguishes between the air closest to water, which is "thick" (*crassus*), "foggy" (*caliginosus*), and cold and is thus moved by the winds in sundry directions, and the air bordering on the sphere of

24. The *Epinomis* (which Ficino clearly regarded as an appendix to, or as the thirteenth book of, the *Laws*) refers to the aether as a fifth element at 981C, 984B-E, but only insofar as it succeeds fire and precedes air; cf. Ficino's epitome, *Opera,* p. 1527. The *Timaeus* at 58D defines the aether as "the brightest part of air" even as it postulates only four elements for the Demiurge to use as building blocks for the cosmos at 31B, 32BC, 40A, and 81E ff. (at 55C ff., however, it does introduce a fifth geometrical figure, the enigmatic dodecahedron, which Xenocrates, Albinus, and others subsequently equated with the aether as a fifth element). The *Cratylus* at 410B, incidentally, also introduces the aether as an element that "is always running in a flux about the air," though Plato treats it there after the air and before the earth.

For Calcidius's views, which were based on the *Epinomis* and not on Aristotle here, see his *In Timaeum* 178 (ed. J. H. Waszink as *Calcidius: In Timaeum,* Corpus Platonicum Medii Aevi, Plato Latinus, ed. R. Klibansky, vol. 4 [London and Leiden, 1962; 2d ed., 1975], p. 207). For various Middle Platonic views in general see Dillon, *Middle Platonists,* pp. 33, 49, 162, 170-171, 286, 315, 318n, etc.

The usual Neoplatonic view, following the Stoics and Plotinus (*Enneads* 2.1.2, 4, 6, 7; 6.7.11), was to assume that the aether was identical with the pure fire which was the stuff of the stars. They agreed with Aristotle, however, that it had a naturally circular motion.

the Moon (*aer vicinus Lunae*), which is clear, serene, and bright in
its motion, light, and heat and is thus moved on a circular path.[25]
While heaven itself is the "true fire" (*ignis verus*), the upper air,
thus ignited (*sic ignitus*), is called the aether (*Opera*, p. 1451). In
chapter 40 Ficino actually defines the aether as the *summus aer*,
"the upper air" (*Opera*, p. 1463^r), even though elsewhere he
seems to regard it as "the sublunar fire," the aethereal as distinguished from the celestial fire. The air is therefore divisible into
three categories: the upper air or aether, the middle or "pure" air,
and the lower "impure" air, vaporous and misty.[26]

With these distinctions Ficino could turn to the problem of characterizing the demons as the inhabitants of the air as a vast region
that stretched from the element of water up as far as the first planetary sphere, that of the Moon. For, in accordance with their commitment to the principles of continuity and plenitude, theorists
since antiquity had felt the necessity to people this region with
living beings of a higher order than birds, creatures essentially of
water and of earth.[27] While the highest demons were held to
accompany their gods, and to dwell in the celestial world of the
pure fire, most of the demons, given their intermediate station between gods and men, were usually supposed to dwell in the air and
thus in the air's three zones. Moreover, just as the highest demons
were held to possess bodies of the pure fire, bodies which the
ancient Neoplatonists had envisaged as envelopes, vehicles, or the
chariots Plato had alluded to in several dialogues, preeminently in
the *Timaeus* and the *Phaedrus*,[28] so the airy demons were held to

25. The notion of the two airs ultimately derives from the reference in the *Timaeus* 66DE
to "vapor"; see Dillon, *Middle Platonists*, p. 244.

26. In his *De Amore* 6.3 (ed. Marcel, p. 202), for instance, Ficino makes a triple distinction between the "aethereal fire located under the moon" (that is, the airy fire), the "pure
air," and the "cloud-laden air, that closest to the region of water." In his commentary on
Plotinus's *Enneads* 3.5.5 he even attributes this view to Plotinus (*Opera*, p. 1715). The end
of chap. 7 suggests that this is the theory he has in mind here in the *Phaedrus* Commentary
(ed. Allen, p. 101). On the other hand, to confuse matters, he had the Aristotelian view in
mind when writing the *Platonic Theology* 10.2 (ed. Marcel, 2:54-55), for there he presents
the sequence aether, fire, air. Clearly there were vagaries on his part.

27. See Plutarch, *De Facie in Orbe Lunae* (*Moralia* 920A-945E); also Dillon, *Middle Platonists*, pp. 172-174, 288, 318. Russell, *Plutarch*, pp. 73 ff., points out that Plutarch refers
to this "atmosphere" between the Earth and the Moon as "the meadows of Hades."

28. *Timaeus* 41DE, 44DE, 69C; *Phaedrus* 247B ff.; also *Phaedo* 113D and *Laws*
10.898E-899B. See Allen, *Charioteer*, pp. 250-251 n. 113; and chap. 4, nn. 28 and 29 below.

possess bodies formed of the various kinds of air in addition to purely fiery or celestial bodies. In theory, then, a demon of the lower or misty air possessed a vaporous body in addition to a body of pure air, another of the aethereal fire, and another of the celestial fire. Ficino was obviously unhappy with this Proclian multiplication of demonic bodies, however, and habitually thinks of the two fiery bodies as essentially one and the same, and only very occasionally acknowledges the feasibility of the distinction between the purely and the impurely airy bodies. He ends up, that is, with only two higher or demonic bodies: the celestial or aethereal (identified in his mind with the glorified body that is ours after the resurrection) and the airy (identified with the body we shall occupy in purgatory), the one being immortal, the other mortal but long-lived.[29]

Tradition also held that the lowest demons could be found inhabiting the zones of water and of earth, and even the subterranean zones as the guardians of precious stones and minerals. Such demons would still be airy beings, though their bodies, erect like ours, would be particularly cloudy in the case of the water demons, or smoky in the case of the earth demons, whose bodies contain, writes Ficino in his Plotinus Commentary, "a vapor as it were of the earth" (*quasi quendam terrae vaporem*).[30] Presumably, the

29. In summa 25 (ed. Allen, p. 169) he does, however, adopt the distinction between bodies made of the "pure" as contrasted to the "impure" air; see chap. 7, pp. 177 ff. below. For the "aethereal" body see Ficino's *Platonic Theology* 18.4 (ed. Marcel, 3:193-196; trans. Allen, *Charioteer*, pp. 230-235) and chap. 9, pp. 218 ff. below.

For the identification of the airy or aerial body with the one we occupy in purgatory, see Ficino's *Phaedo* epitome, *Opera*, p. 1392 (misnumbered as 1390 bis); likewise for the glorified body. See also Kristeller, *Philosophy*, pp. 195-196, 371, 390 ff., with other refs.

30. *Opera*, p. 1715. For the view that material demons have variously shaped bodies while the higher demons have wholly spherical ones, see Proclus's *In Cratylum* 35 and 72 and the comments by E. R. Dodds in his *Proclus: The Elements of Theology*, rev. ed. (Oxford, 1963), pp. 308, 309, 319. Ficino's comments in his own *Platonic Theology* 18.4 (ed. Marcel, 3:193-196; trans. Allen, *Charioteer*, pp. 230-235) suggest that he concurred with Proclus in this matter.

We should be alert to the distinction between corporeality and materiality. Like us, the demons are compounded of souls and bodies, though the latter may consist of extremely rarefied matter, the nonterrestrial matter of *spiritus;* see Ficino's *Opera*, p. 1715; Walker, *Magic*, pp. 46 ff.; and Giancarlo Zanier, *La medicina astrologica e la sua teoria: Marsilio Ficino e i suoi critici contemporanei* (Rome, 1977), p. 33 n. 60. At issue, ultimately, is the notion of incorporeal matter itself; see Kristeller, *Philosophy*, p. 39. Note that I shall try to observe a distinction between the specifically earthy and the more generally earthly demons and their demonic bodies.

subterranean demons would possess bodies contaminated with particularly dense smoke. However badly contaminated, however, all demons, with the possible exception of the very highest, were essentially airy beings occupying airy bodies, even though some of them habitually dwelt in the water and the earth.

In the *Phaedrus* Commentary Ficino is especially concerned with the status of all the demons as followers of the twelve world or celestial gods, whether or not they actually accompanied them like the higher demons. Each demon shared in the differentiating characteristics and powers of one of these leader gods, though in increasingly diminutive degrees, and presided over some part of that god's peculiar domain, be it a place, a human being, an animal, a plant, or an inanimate object. Each demon, major or minor, also bore its god's name, and thus references in the ancient poets to specific Olympians may often refer, so all the Neoplatonists argued and Ficino was to agree, to demons in their trains rather than to the gods themselves.[31] Generally, as the *Symposium* had emphasized at 202E, demons served to mediate between their own particular sovereign god and the lower world. Though able to ascend into the celestial realm to follow or accompany this god, they could also descend into the terraqueous world to do his or her bidding. Throughout the four sublunar spheres, though based if you will in the air, were therefore saturnian, jovian, martian, solar (or apollonian), venerean, mercurial, and lunar (or dianian) demons.[32] Additionally, there were vulcanian, junonian, neptunian, and vestal demons, the demons assigned to the deities presiding over the sublunar elements (the plutonian demons being confined, presumably, to the subterranean realms).[33] These lower

31. Proclus had insisted that all demons, however lowly, could bear on occasions their gods' names: e.g. *Theol. Plat.* 1.26 (ed. Saffrey and Westerink, 1:115.7-12); *In Alcibiadem* 72.12-74.10; 78.10-79.14; 158.3-159.5 (ed. L. G. Westerink as *Proclus: Commentary on the First Alcibiades* [Amsterdam, 1954]); *In Remp.* 6 (ed. Kroll, 1:91.11-19; trans. Festugière, 1:108); *In Timaeum* 3:204.23-32 (ed. Ernst Diehl as *Procli Diadochi in Platonis Timaeum Commentaria,* 3 vols. [Leipzig, 1903-1906; reprint, Amsterdam, 1965]; trans. A.-J. Festugière as *Proclus: Commentaire sur le Timée,* 5 vols. [Paris, 1966-1969]). Cf. E. Zeller and R. Mondolfo, *La filosofia dei Greci nel suo sviluppo storico,* pt. 3, vol. 6, ed. Giuseppe Martano (Florence, 1961), p. 163; also Allen, *Charioteer,* p. 243 n. 50.

32. See the *Phaedrus* Commentary, summa 30 (ed. Allen, *Charioteer,* pp. 180-185). For the separate and fascinating problem of whether for Ficino there are uranian demons, see chap. 5, n. 51 below.

33. Ficino's identification of Vesta with the earth, meaning, presumably, both element and world, would mean that the terrestrial demons were assigned to her (see chap. 5, nn. 56

demons could be found in all the elementary spheres according to a formula Ficino used in his *Apology* epitome, namely that in fire they appeared *ignea ratione,* in air *ratione aerea,* in water *ratione aquea,* and in earth, it would follow, *ratione terrena.* Ficino goes on to note that the watery demons preside over the life of pleasure, the airy demons over the life of action, and the fiery demons over the life of contemplation, "converting the discursiveness of our reason to contemplating things sublime" (*discursum rationis ad sublimiora contemplanda convertere*) (*Opera,* p. 1387).

Most Neoplatonists followed such Middle Platonists as Apuleius and Plutarch in acceding to the popular belief that some of the demons, especially the watery and terrene, were bad in the sense at least that they were subject to certain kinds of passion and thus to the disfigurement that passion brings. Proclus, for instance, entertained the notion that the "bad" demons were the souls of ex-men who had led impassioned, materialistic lives (though how these were to be distinguished satisfactorily from the category of "heroes" was another matter).[34] Xenocrates before them had warned us to beware their lust for cruel propitiations and sacrifices.[35] In addition to such Platonic authorities, and the ever-present sway of popular lore, Ficino had to accommodate also the "fallen" angels led by Lucifer in the Jewish and Christian traditions. These angels were the subject of numerous demonological

---

and 58 below). Pluto, as lord of the underworld, would be lord of all the subterranean demons. An extract Ficino translated from Psellus (*Opera,* pp. 1940-1941) postulates six kinds of demons: the fiery, airy, earthy (*terrenum*), watery or marine (*aquatile et marinum*), subterranean, and finally "the light-shunning, impenetrable, and wholly shadowy" (*lucifugum, imperscrutabile ac penitus tenebrosum*). The latter two kinds are never mentioned as such in Ficino's *Phaedrus* Commentary; but plutonian demons are mentioned in chap. 10, par. 13 (ed. Allen, *Charioteer,* p. 120), and they must be both "subterranean" and "light-shunning."

34. However, Proclus expressly denied that demons were intrinsically wicked in his *De Malorum Subsistentia* (ed. Helmut Boese in *Procli Diadochi Tria Opuscula* [Berlin, 1960], pp. 172-265 at 199 ff.), though acknowledging that not all demons were equally rational or liberated from matter (*In Alc.,* 68.3 ff. [ed. Westerink]; *In Crat.* 72, 121, 128; *In Remp.* 6 [ed. Kroll, 1:78.6 ff.; trans. Festugière, 1:95]). He had, of course, to accommodate Plato's *Laws* 10.896E ff. For the distinction between "essential" demons and "conditional" ones, see n. 22 above. See also de Gandillac, "Astres, anges et génies," pp. 98-100.

35. As quoted in Plutarch, *De Iside* (*Moralia* 360E-361C) and *De Defectu Oraculorum* (*Moralia* 417C). We should recall that Homer uses the adjective δαιμόνιος with no specific ethical connotations and had thus anticipated the argument that some demons could be malevolent, a view that was to be widely held by the Middle Platonists. See Dillon, *Middle Platonists,* pp. 31-32, 46-47, 317-320; Russell, *Plutarch,* p. 76.

treatises, chief of which were ten chapters, chapters 13 to 22, in the
eighth book of Augustine's *City of God,* a work that Ficino knew
intimately. Nevertheless, as a philosopher (as distinguished, say,
from a theologian, exorcist, or occultist), Ficino was primarily
concerned with the demon as a spiritual being who was intrinsically good.[36]

His authority here was Plotinus. For Plotinus had found it difficult to entertain the notion that any ensouled or spiritual being
could be evil; and he had devoted several years of his prime to vig-
orously attacking the Gnostics precisely on this point.[37] In Plotinus's metaphysical system Matter was the only "realm" that
approached the condition of being evil, and then only in the sense
that it was furthest removed from the One, the ultimate principle
of all reality, and therefore from what was synonymous with the
One, the Good.[38] There are tensions, of course, that have long
been recognized in Plotinus's thought, and one might argue that
the gradual loss of unity in the levels of being emanating further
and further from the One is in fact the gradual loss of goodness

36. In the *De Amore* 6.3 (ed. Marcel, pp. 202-203) Ficino deliberately confines himself to
this positive notion: "The Platonists do not attribute to the demons bodily passions; rather
they attribute to them certain feelings (*affectus*) of the soul, those with which, so to speak,
they love good men, hate bad men, and immerse themselves more ardently and concernedly
in the government of lower things, and especially human affairs. On account of this office
all these demons appear to be good. But some Platonists, along with Christian theologians,
have supposed (*voluerunt*) that others of them are bad. But our concern at the moment is
not with these bad demons at all." Cf. Pico, *Commento particolare* (ed. Garin, p. 539).

37. For instance, *Enneads* 6.4-5; 3.6; 4.3-5; 3.8; 5.8; 5.5; and 2.9 (the last four constituting originally, before the Porphyrian breakdown, a treatise in four parts). See R. T. Wallis,
Neoplatonism (London, 1972), pp. 39, 45, 82-85.

However, Plotinus does seem to have accepted the notion of a "bad" demon at *Enneads*
3.4.6 (and see too 2.1.6; 3.5.6-7; 4.3.18; 4.4.43); but here he is specifically concerned with
the problem of whether souls that enter into brute bodies still retain their demon. If they
do, he says, then it must be "an evil or foolish demon." Note that even here, in what is a
special case, "evil" is linked with, perhaps identified with, the notion of foolishness—that
is, ignorance. See Wallis, *Neoplatonism,* p. 71.

38. The apophatic theology of Proclus and of the pseudo-Areopagite, which even denies
the possibility of predicating goodness of the One, at least other than analogically, though
indebted to Plotinus, was not truly Plotinian. While Plotinus was prepared theoretically to
accept the impropriety of any kind of predication for the One (as in 6.9.3-4), in actual practice he always conceives of the One as the Good. Moreover, the Porphyrian arrangement
for the *Enneads* climaxes with the treatise (6.9) that argues for the identification of the two,
though, chronologically, this same treatise appears to be quite early (ninth in the sequence
of fifty-four). See Laurence Jay Rosán, *The Philosophy of Proclus* (New York, 1949), pp.
122-125.

and the gradual onset consequently of evil and not merely of non-being.[39] For Plotinus, however, the demons, even when they were obviously confined to the guardianship of a particular aspect of the material world, always represented the presence of rational Soul. They could not be accounted bad *in themselves:* in exhibiting a proprietary interest in and love for their particular domain they were exercising their divinely appointed task of providential care for inferiors. Were it not for the existence of such downward-flowing care, the Epicurean vision of an earth unvisited and unloved by the indifferent gods would be the authentic one. Unquestionably the demons may at times be bad *for us,* inasmuch as we permit them to distort our priorities and to be overly concerned with the domains under their tutelage. After all, even the higher saturnian or martian demons can afflict us with melancholy or choler if we succumb to their allurements or fail to avail ourselves of the requisite correctives or antidotes to their influences upon us —fail, that is, to temper them with jovian, apollonian, venerean, or mercurial virtues.[40] When approached correctly, however, such demons can serve as the proper guardians and guides to the intellectual or the active, martial lives.

Ficino seems to have responded with sympathy to Plotinus's optimism; for he focused upon the problem of evil demons in the *Phaedrus* only in the context of the notion of "the bait of pleasure" (*iocunda esca*), a figure with a long history that derives, in the Latin tradition, from Cicero but goes back ultimately to Plato himself.[41] Ficino had dwelt upon the notion in a series of apologues that had personified Pleasure and had eventually introduced her to the company of the Muses, the Graces, Mercury, and Apollo and then translated her to heaven, despite Pluto's machi-

---

39. See chap. 7, nn. 22, 23, and 24 below.

40. Ficino's great work on astrological and medical antidotes is the *De Vita;* see especially 3.23, 24 (*Opera,* pp. 566-568). Cf. Walker, *Magic,* chap. 1; Zanier, *Medicina,* pp. 5-60.

41. Cicero, *De Senectute* 13.44; Plato, *Timaeus* 69D. Of particular interest here is a letter Ficino addressed to Cavalcanti and dated 12 Dec. 1494 (*Opera,* p. 961.2). The following extract suggests he had the sirens of the *Phaedrus* and his own comments in the *Phaedrus* Commentary, and specifically those in summa 9, very much in mind; indeed the dates suggest that the letter and the summa may well have been written within weeks of each other: "Operae pretium est praeterea diligenter considerare platonicum illud in Phaedro de venefica mali daemonis astutia dictum. Daemon aliquis statim ab initi[o] vitiis quae plurimis

nations to keep her on earth.[42] But the local demons use pleasure in two ways, says Ficino in summa 9. While all of them "move our imaginations by means of their own imaginations, powers, and devices to believe in and to hope for future pleasure some day" in their provinces, and while "they seem to mix 'the bait of pleasure' with evils—that is, with our inclinations towards lower things—in order that they may detain us in this their province for a longer time," the good demons do so "so that the universal order may be fulfilled" (*ut universalis ordo expleatur, efficiunt*), but the bad ones "so that they may thwart it" (*ut officiant*). While this distinction certainly evokes the popular Gnostic-Christian notion of intrinsically evil (*improbi*) demons, it does so nevertheless against the backdrop of our involvement in the world of "fate"—a realm to which, as summa 9 says, we are "justly" bound for a time by the good demons until they help to release us from it. In short, the good demons eventually free us from our involvement in the lower world, whereas the bad, according to summa 35, detain us "by their traps and lures" in "bodily delight." The bad use pleasure like the Sirens' song to prevent us or to deter us from returning "to the port of [our] celestial home" (and Ficino is taking his cue

---

immiscuit voluptatem. Haec quidem ibi Socrates inquit admonens malorum daemonum praecipuum esse studium animas seorsum a coelesti patria in hoc exilio diutius detinere superni patris oblitas, longasque machinari moras illecebris oblectamentisque terrenis, quibus profecto, quasi poculis veneficae Circes soporiferisque Syrenum cantibus delinitae, nunquam aut certe tardius in coelestem patriam revertantur. Contra vero daemonicas insidias benefica providentia Dei statuit ducibus quidem his laetiferisque saporibus sapores amaros interim commisceri, ne ab eiusmodi voluptate, quam Timaeus malorum escam nominat, capiamur ut pisces ab hamo." Note that Ficino is again concerned with the "bad" demons in the *Phaedrus* solely in the context of "the bait of pleasure." Cf. too his letter to Braccio Martelli: "Quod quidem insidiante malo quodam daemone sub insolentioris voluptatis esca infeliciter accidisse Timaeus et Phaedrus et Dioti[m]a in academia testabuntur" (*Opera*, p. 867).

42. These appeared accompanying the first two drafts of the *Philebus* commentary (ed. and trans. Michael J. B. Allen as *Marsilio Ficino: The Philebus Commentary* [Berkeley, Los Angeles, London, 1975; reprint, 1979—N.B. this reprint contains several substantive corrections], pp. 10, 13, and app. II, pp. 446, 454-457, 464-467, 468-479). Later they were moved to the end of Ficino's tenth book of letters and dedicated to Martinus Uranius (alias Brenninger) (*Opera*, pp. 921 ff.). See also Wind, *Pagan Mysteries*, pp. 49-51.

In these apologues, and notably in the last, the demons are Jove's agents and are sent down to capture Pleasure and to bring her to heaven; they fail, as others like Minerva and Mars had failed, because they resorted to force rather than guile. The last apologue also specifically notes that they were martian and vulcanian demons—the attendants, that is, of the two gods "who were armed and very strong."

here from Plato's description at 259A of the cicadas' litany as a "bewitching siren-song"). Both kinds of demons are involved in the realm of fate and both utilize pleasure as a "bait," but the good finally liberate us, or at least help to liberate us, from this realm, while the bad endeavor to keep us tied to it so that they may "thwart" what Ficino calls "the universal order," the order presumably of God's higher providence.

Of particular interest are the personal demons, which Neoplatonism, following the *Timaeus* 90A-C, had occasionally identified with the highest part of our soul, our intuitive intelligence.[43] In commenting on the nine kinds of lives and the reasons for them in summa 30, Ficino argues that, since we are all members before birth of a train led by a particular god in the cavalcade of souls and thus partake of that god's peculiar powers and properties, we are duty-bound for the sake of our own happiness to ensure that we follow that god and his attendant demons.[44] He goes on to note that, although it may be permissible to change demons on occasion (though when exactly is never explored), we must nevertheless continue to follow a demon in the same class—a demon subject, that is, to the same patron deity as ourselves.[45] Usually we do not change demons at all and continue to follow the promptings of the

43. See Philip Merlan, "Theology and Demonology: Plato and Xenocrates," chap. 2, sec. G of Merlan's "Greek Philosophy from Plato to Plotinus," in *The Cambridge History of Later Greek and Early Medieval Philosophy,* ed. A. H. Armstrong (Cambridge, 1970), pp. 32-37 at 35. Cf. n. 22 above. In his *Apology* epitome (*Opera*, p. 1387) Ficino confronts this identification in the *Timaeus* by way of discussing Socrates' demon: "Sed numquid ipsum Socratis intellectum possumus daemonem nuncupare? Possumus certe. Nam Timaeus inquit Deum nobis supremam animi partem tanquam daemonem tribuisse." Ficino goes on, however, to insist that Plato and Socrates had a familiar higher demon that was different from the highest parts of their minds, and he suggests that perhaps we should call this familiar demon a good angel (*Opera*, p. 1388).

44. And of course to follow men and objects also associated with that god. For this theory and the related theory of synastry, see chap. 8, pp. 196-197 below.

In her *Bruno*, p. 35, Yates writes that in the Hermetic *Asclepius* "man has familiarity with the race of demons, *knowing that he is of the same origin*" (my italics).

45. In the *Phaedrus* Commentary Ficino does not specify whether the demon that one follows (and that a soul can change, says summa 30, "when it is itself radically changed") is *the* personal demon or merely *a* particular demon. I have the impression that the personal demon in Ficino belongs generally to the category of minor demons. Summa 30, however, is more concerned with relatively major demons, those who actually accompany the star gods and who preside over a number of souls. Again we should recall that the *Timaeus* 90A-C refers to the highest part of the soul itself as "a demon given by God to each man." Nowadays we suppose that Plato meant this only figuratively.

demon that has been ours from the beginning of this life. In Christian terms this is one's guardian angel, but it also partakes of some of the functions we now associate with the idea of a person's particular "genius."[46] For the notion of the personal demon-genius Ficino could easily have turned to the *Phaedo* (107D-108B, 113D), where Plato treats of the demon that is allotted to each man for his life and leads him to the place of judgment (though not necessarily of punishment) after death. But he specifically turned—as summa 9 proves—to the great myth of Er in the *Republic,* book 10 (617DE, 620DE), where Plato refers to the demon that each man actually chooses to be "the guardian of his life and the fulfiller of his choice."[47] Summa 9 defines such demons as "the leaders of chosen lives, of fate, and of chance," their specific function being to "detain souls in the provinces they have already chosen." To "detain," that is, but not permanently to confine. For while our physical, emotional, and what we now call our temperamental lives are subject to "fate," and thus to physical and astrological forces, our deliberative, intellectual, and intuitive lives are subject neither to fate nor to the local, personal, or higher demons, but rather to the dictates of providence.[48]

Since Plato makes no mention of a personal demon for Phaedrus, there was nothing to exercise Ficino's speculation here except insofar as it bore on the interesting topic of the "nine lives."[49] But

46. Apuleius is a significant figure in the history of demonology because of his decision to render the Greek term $\delta\alpha\iota\mu\omega\nu$ by the Latin term *genius.* In the process he introduced some of the indigenous Latin connotations of *genius* into the Greek term. Ironically, the notion of "genius" is still in a state of rapid semantic change while that of "demon" has all but ossified, as has that of "the guardian angel." Citing Ficino's *Opera,* pp. 1387, 1515, and 1636, Walker argues that "a guardian angel is the same as a familiar planetary demon" for Ficino (*Magic,* p. 47n); but this is only true in the sense that it is oriented towards a particular planet, like all demons, men, and indeed objects; it is not a planetary demon per se—that is, one actually accompanying a star god, a celestial demon.

47. Ficino was surely influenced here by Proclus's great commentary on the Er myth, *In Remp.* 16 (ed. Kroll, 2:96-359, specifically 271-273 [on 617DE] and 341-347 [on 620DE]; trans. Festugière, 3:39-316, specifically 229-231 and 299-305). Cf. Ficino's own epitome for the *Republic,* book 10 (*Opera,* pp. 1427-1438). Another major statement on the familiar demon occurs in his *De Vita* 3.23 (*Opera,* pp. 566-568).

48. Cf. Calcidius, *In Timaeum* 143-190 (ed. Waszink, pp. 181-214)—a major source; and Pico, *Commento* 2.24 (ed. Garin, pp. 516-517). For an important pioneering essay on the relationship between Fate and Providence in Ficino, see Marian Heitzman, "La libertà e il fato nella filosofia di Marsilio Ficino," *Rivista di filosofia neo-scolastica* 28 (1936), 350-371; 29 (1937), 59-82. See also Kristeller, *Philosophy,* pp. 297-300; and Charles Trinkaus, *In Our Image and Likeness,* 2 vols. (London, 1970), 2:474-487.

49. See chap. 7, pp. 174-179 below.

Plato does mention Socrates' "warning voice"—as elsewhere in his dialogues, particularly in the *Theages* and *Alcibiades I*—and this had been traditionally associated, following Apuleius and Plutarch, with Socrates' personal "demon." For Ficino, however, the issue was complicated by the remarkable distinction Porphyry introduces in his life of Plotinus, where in section 10 he tells the story of an Alexandrian sorcerer who had attempted to crush Plotinus with star spells but found his charms recoiling because Plotinus possessed "a mighty soul." Almost as a gloss on this episode, Porphyry introduces a second story: an Egyptian priest had visited Plotinus and wished to display his mediumistic powers by summoning up Plotinus's presiding demon in the Temple of Isis. "At the summons," Porphyry writes, "a Divinity appeared, not a being of the spirit (i.e. demon)-ranks, and the Egyptian exclaimed: 'You are singularly graced; the guiding-spirit within you is not of the lower degree but a God.'" Porphyry concludes that Plotinus did not possess an ordinary personal demon but rather "a Being of the more divine degree"—that is, a god.[50] This distinction was the subject of Plotinus's own treatise entitled "Our Tutelary Spirit" (*Enneads* 3.4). Socrates' demon, his "warning voice," was also of this higher divine kind, and we should identify it with the apollonian demon introduced by Ficino in summa 10: "perhaps the apollonian demon immediately enraptures him... with the result that he even exceeds the bounds of human behavior and thereafter treats of the divine love that excites us through some frenzy." We know from the *Apology* (23B) that Socrates thought of Apollo as his own Olympian god (οἰκεῖος θεός), and it is altogether appropriate that he should be attended at the climacteric of Apollo at noon by an apollonian demon,[51] though Plato provided no justifi-

---

50. I am using Stephen MacKenna's translation of Porphyry's *Life of Plotinus*, which prefaces his translation of the *Enneads*, 3d ed., rev. B. S. Page (London, 1962). The extracts are taken from section 10. For Ficino's Latin translation of this section, see his *Opera*, p. 1541.

51. Noon is traditionally a "demonic" period of transition. Cf. Hermias, pp. 217.22-218.17 (glossing *Phaedrus* 259D7-8) and 65.10 ff. (glossing 242A4); Augustine, *De Genesi ad Litteram* 4.29-30 (Migne, *PL* 34.315-316); and Pico, *Oratio* (ed. Garin, p. 128). See Nicholas J. Perella, *Midday in Italian Literature* (Princeton, 1979), and Reinhard C. Kuhn, *The Demon of Noontide: Ennui in Western Literature* (Princeton, 1976).

We should recall the importance for Ficino of the sun-scorched setting of Plato's *Laws*, the only work, apart from the *Letters*, where, Ficino says, Plato speaks *in propria persona*.

cation for its presence in the *Phaedrus* except for the reference at
242BC to "the familiar divine sign" that forbids Socrates to depart without first atoning for his having offended against love in
the course of his first speech to Phaedrus. A useful gloss here is
provided by Ficino's epitome for the *Apology* (*Opera,* p. 1387),
where he argues that Socrates' demon was apollonian and fiery
"because it lifted him to the contemplation of sublimities," and
fire demons, you recall, are the guardians of the contemplative
life. But he then adds, surprisingly, that the demon was also
"saturnian" "because, in a marvelous way, it abstracted the intention of Socrates' mind daily away from his body." It was not
"martian" too, however, because it was a revocatory demon,
never a provocatory one. Later in the same epitome Ficino
observes that it was on this account that Socrates was drawn
towards the *via negativa,* and that, possessed of such a demon to
the point of being himself demonic from birth, he was able to use
his higher aethereal senses in order to perceive his own demon, a
feat impossible for ordinary men (*Opera,* p. 1389). Even so, neither Socrates' "warning voice" nor his apollonian demon looms
very large in Ficino's analysis here; not unexpectedly so, given his
concern throughout the Commentary with Jove and with jovian
man.

While there are local gods—the Nymphs and river deities—there
are also local demons. These are all under the lordship of Pan and
are, according to summa 9, "distributed through the world's provinces" and allotted the guardianship of particular places and
objects. They account, says summa 38, "for the many differences,
both secret and important, among various places and things, especially the differences that have a bearing on our mental dispositions, behavior and morals, laws, fortunes, and authorities."
Along with the local gods, they mediate the powers and properties
of some one of the great ruling deities in the Olympian twelve, and
account, for instance, as summa 49 explicitly states, for the fact

For Ficino's views on the morning, see his *Phaedo* epitome (*Opera,* p. 1392) and *De Vita*
1.7, 8 (*Opera,* pp. 500-501); also 3.2, 4 (*Opera,* pp. 533, 535-536) on man as primarily solar.
Cf. Walker, *Magic,* p. 18.
    Note that the noonday demon Ficino is concerned with here is not an ordinary fire, that
is, vulcanian, demon.

that not only Naucratis but the whole of Egypt is subject preeminently to Mercury. Other places, as summa 38 observes, are solar
or lunar—that is, subject to Apollo or Diana.

Apart from the general question of the setting and its demonic
influences, the notion of local demons comes to the fore in
Ficino's interesting analysis of the myth of the cicadas at 259B-
D.[52] Despite Plato's reference at 259AB to their "bewitching siren-
song," and despite Ficino's allusion to this in summa 35, the Florentine views the myth entirely positively. Following Hermias, and
therefore presumably Syrianus and Iamblichus, Hermias's masters,[53] he identifies them with local demons, as summa 38 makes
clear, and also with "singers and interpreters"—a direct reference
to 262D. For it is to the local demons figured in the cicadas that,
summa 38 concludes, Socrates owes "the gift not only of invention but also of precise delivery" (*non solum inventionis sed etiam
elocutionis exacte munus*).

In summa 35, which is almost entirely devoted to allegorization
and interpretation, Ficino evocatively describes their noonday
vigil: "They stand by us overhead; they dispute together; meanwhile, they survey our deeds, condemning the bad and approving
the good, as observers of human affairs. . . . They receive gifts
from the gods and pass them on to us; they make the offices that
we perform known to the gods; they approach the Muses." Even
so, he obviously felt he was treading dangerous ground, for he
warns us beforehand, sensing the need for a flexible rather than a
rigid allegorical approach,[54] that "in part I follow in their [i.e.

---

52. Perceval Frutiger, *Les mythes de Platon* (Paris, 1930), pp. 233-234, argues that the
Theuth myth and the cicada myth are the only wholly original myths in Plato. For the cicadas see also Don Cameron Allen, *Image and Meaning* (Baltimore, 1960), pp. 83-86.

53. Hermias, pp. 212.29-216.19. Cf. Bielmeier, *Phaidrosinterpretation,* p. 28; John M.
Dillon, ed., *Iamblichi Chalcidensis in Platonis Dialogos Commentariorum Fragmenta* (Leiden, 1973), pp. 98-99, 255-256; and Larsen, *Jamblique,* p. 372.

54. Cf. Augustine's influential remarks on the need for a flexible, nonliteral approach to
interpreting ancient allegory in his *De Vera Religione* 1.50-51 and *De Trinitate* 15.9. Ficino
comments in his *De Amore* 4.2 (ed. Marcel, pp. 168-169): "Nam et Aurelius Augustinus
non omnia inquit, que in figuris finguntur, significare aliquid putanda sunt. Multa enim
propter illa que significant ordinis et connexionis gratia sunt adiuncta."

For Augustine's account of the deliberate "veiling" of the Platonic secrets that occurred
at the time of the Skeptical Academy of Arcesilaus and Carneades, and of their subsequent
rediscovery by Plotinus and his followers, see his *Contra Academicos* 3.17.37-19.42 and his
Epistle 118.17-33.

Hermias's and Iamblichus's] footsteps, but in part I deviate from them on the grounds of probability and reason'' (*partim vero probabili ratione prevaricor*).

Still, the cicadas are good demons, and are clearly linked, says summa 35, to the air: ''For these animals live by song—that is, by a certain sound, and via the sound by the drinking in of air; and after they appear to be dead, they are at last inwardly reformed. In the same way, the good airy demons live by song—that is, by contemplation and by the praise of divine things. They are satisfied with [or contained by] the air; and as easily as they seem to dissolve, so are they recreated inwardly by the perpetual drinking in of it.'' Note the air motif, already activated by the introduction of the Boreas myth. Specifically the cicadas are witnesses to the mystery of inner regeneration, regeneration effected by music and song, by the ''perpetual drinking in'' of air. Although, as summa 38 specifies, these airy demons are indeed ''local,'' they are not, states summa 35, ''natural'' demons but rather ''adventitious'' ones (*adventitii*). Previously I had taken this to mean that they had forgathered on the banks of the Ilissus as visiting demons specifically to preside over Socrates' noonday encounter with Phaedrus, keyed as it is to regenerative themes, to poetry and song, to contemplation and ''the praise of divine things,'' the very sustenance, summa 35 tells us, of the airy demons. But a passage in the *Apology* epitome sheds light on Ficino's intention here. He writes that ''some demons are naturally constituted so from the onset, while others are alien to that condition'' (*daemones alios naturales ab initio constitutos, alios peregrinos*) (*Opera*, p. 1387). ''Natural'' therefore designates those demons who were born demons from the very beginning; while ''alien'' designates those who acquired demonhood after living lives first as men. But *adventitii* might still be interpreted to mean demons ''who come from away,'' ''visiting'' demons, unless it could be conclusively proved that Ficino uses *peregrini* and *adventitii* as synonyms. A gloss in chapter 27 of Ficino's *Timaeus* Commentary provides just such a proof: ''Commonly we call those animals demonic who are either naturally so, or adventitiously so having once been men (*ex hominibus adventitii*), and who imitate their own sovereign planet in terms of both office and circuit; such demonic animals exist

similarly in the air, some of them as natural demons, some of them
—those who had once been men—as alien ones (*partim naturalia,
partim ex hominibus peregrina*)" (*Opera*, p. 1451.1). Thus *adventitii* here in summa 35 must mean that the cicadas were not born
but became demonic animals. As such—and this is after all consonant with Plato's tale of the poets' devotion to the Muses—they
became as "local" to the banks of the Ilissus as the god of the
river himself and the Naiads attending him.

Notable, in light of Ficino's comments in summae 11 and 35 on
the demons' critical role in the physiology of hearing, is the image
of the cicadas as the product, so to speak, of sound and song.
Though summa 11 had argued that a demon "may indeed frequently move the imagination, which is the universal sense,
through his own imagination, and can thus move it through the
sight and hearing alike," it had also argued that Socrates was
moved through the hearing, because he was "the most eager of all
for instruction and dedicated, as it were, to the hearing." Presumably, Ficino is confining himself—very much in the context of
"the warning voice"—to an analysis of Socrates in the *Phaedrus*.
For he was wholly familiar with Plato's portraits elsewhere, and
most prominently in the *Symposium*, of a Socrates dedicated to
sight rather than hearing as the faculty most adapted for perceiving outer beauty, and thus for setting us on the path towards the
inner beauty that is wisdom.[55]

But how does a demon mediate sound? Summa 11 briefly offers
us two surprising alternatives: "Either the demon takes the concept to be imagined and effectively extends it to, or generates it in,
the inmost hearing; or the demon himself in his own spiritual body
forms the sound by a certain marvelous motion, and with the same
motion strikes as a sound upon the spiritual body of Socrates.
When this vibrates, Socrates' inmost hearing is excited to the
same."[56] The first alternative assigns the demon the role of efficient cause; the second, that of actual material agent. In his fas-

---

55. See chap. 2, pp. 50-57 below.
56. According to Porphyry the demons have a body that is so malleable that it becomes
the object of their own imagination. See Dodds, app. II, p. 319; also Robert Klein,
"L'enfer de Ficin," in *Umanesimo e esoterismo: Atti del V Convegno Internazionale di
Studi Umanistici*, ed. Enrico Castelli (Padua, 1960), pp. 47-84 at 49 n. 8.

cinating study of the nature and status of music in Ficino's
thought, D. P. Walker observes that both music and the human
spiritus are living "kinds of air, moving in a highly organized
way." Since the ear contains air set deep within it, and since it is
"untroubled by ordinary aerial disturbances," sounds, "being
moving, animated air," must "combine directly with the *spiritus
aereus* in the ear."[57] A few pages later, he uses Ficino's own words
in the *De Vita* 3.21 to describe a view of music as "warm air, even
breathing, and in a measure living, made up of articulated limbs,
like an animal, not only bearing movement and emotion, but even
signification, like a mind, so that it can be said to be, as it were, a
kind of aerial and rational animal." He continues, "Musically
moved air is alive, like a disembodied human spirit."[58] In this last
phrase, Walker is recalling another sentence in the same chapter of
the *De Vita,* which reads, *Cantus... ferme nihil aliud est quam
spiritus alter,* and which to my mind Ficino meant literally: "Song
is almost nothing other than another spirit" (i.e. a demon, not a
human spirit).[59] Ficino clearly conceives of the demons as actually
being music or embodying it at least as it enters man's inner ear.
Thus he raises the possibility that we can "make" demons by
"making" music.[60] Be that as it may, the spiritual body of Soc-

57. *Magic,* pp. 6-8, citing Aristotle, *De Anima* 420A; Augustine, *De Musica* 6.5.10; and
Ficino, *Platonic Theology* 7.6.

58. *Magic,* p. 10.

59. *Opera,* p. 563. For this identification of *spiritus* here with a demon rather than the
vapor uniting soul to body, compare Ficino's *Platonic Theology* 10.7 (ed. Marcel, 2:82):
"Sonus ille est quasi quoddam animal constitutum ex aere fracto tamquam corpore atque
ex ipsa significatione tamquam anima"—note, however, that the subject is *sonus,* not
cantus.

60. Interesting in this regard are Lazzarelli's extraordinary comments in his "Hymn of
Divine Generation," the climax of the *Crater Hermetis* (Paris, 1505 but composed not long
before 1494), f. 78[r] ff., quoted and analyzed by Walker, *Magic,* pp. 64-72: "So the true
man makes divine souls, which he calls Atlantiad gods of the earth [Atlantiad meaning Her-
metic]" (p. 68). Unlike Kristeller, who sees Lazzarelli referring here simply to the rebirth
which a religious teacher achieves in his converted disciple ("Marsilio Ficino e Lodovico
Lazzarelli," *Annali della R. Scuola Normale Sup. di Pisa,* 2d ser., 7 [1938], 237-262 at 253
ff.), Walker claims that it was "a magical operation by which the master provided his disciple with a good demon. The operation consisted mainly of words sung in some special
manner. These sounds themselves became the demon: it is easy to understand how, if we
take literally Ficino's probably metaphorical description of the matter of song [and here
Walker cites the sentences again from *De Vita* 3.21 (*Opera,* p. 563)], ... Lazzarelli was not
summoning demons; he was making them. These man-made demons were, I think, conceived of as separated bits of the Holy Ghost or the Spirit of Christ" (pp. 70-71). But if we
bring our passage from the *Phaedrus* Commentary to bear and modify Walker's translation

rates vibrates in sympathy, and his inmost hearing vibrates in turn. Hence Ficino's insistence on the notion that the demon takes "the concept to be imagined" (*conceptum imaginabilem*), or what the summa eventually refers to as "the demon's reminder" (*demonicam admonitionem*)—i.e. the warning voice—and physically conveys it to Socrates' mind's ear. We are at the junction of musical theory and what we might call the theory of auditory intuition (rather than auditory hallucination).

Ficino takes the whole problem one stage further when he again introduces the notion that men, and most notably philosophers, eventually become airy demons themselves by shedding their earthy bodies in order to exist in their airy and aethereal ones alone.[61] For this implies that they can actually become sounds, can be "imaginable concepts." Presumably this signals the first stage in our ascent into pure intelligibility. The notion of "inspiration" here reacquires much of its original, literal meaning: as we breathe in air, we breathe in the very substance also constituting our demonic body (and of course the term δαιμόνιος in Greek itself means "inspired," as Plato makes especially clear in *Cratylus* 398C).

In Plato's fable, the cicadas upon their death report to their patrons, the Muses, informing them which men honor them and which Muse each man honors in particular (259C). Ficino does away with the notion of the insects dying, for they continue to live on air and song, transcending corporeal death as demons sleeplessly vigilant under the meridian sun while others drowse (259A). He also transforms the myth's initial premise that the cicadas were descended from men who had been so thrilled by the coming of the Muses and of music to the earth that they had continued singing, oblivious of their bodily needs, until, in Plato's words, "they actually died without noticing it" (259C). Subsequently the grateful Muses had granted their entomological offspring the boon of requiring no sustenance from birth to death. For Ficino's cicadas are, though airy demons, specifically agents of the Muses. Men

---

as I have suggested, then the revolutionary notion becomes Ficino's as well as Lazzarelli's. By 1494, that is, both had arrived (independently?) at a literal and not just a metaphorical description of demonic song. Cf. chap. 2, n. 63 below.

61. See n. 22 above and chap. 7, pp. 177 ff. below.

who have died to the world, in the *Phaedo*'s famous conceit (63E-68B), become such agents: having nourished their intellects alone and never permitted them to sleep, they can act now as demonic intermediaries between men and the greater, and not just the local, gods. Again, as we shall see, this has a bearing on the topic of the nine lives, and on the theory that the true philosopher has an "airy" body and is therefore a demonic being.[62]

The Muses are an important motif in Ficino's iconography, and his contemporaries' fascination with them is only paralleled perhaps by their comparable fascination with the Graces, the two motifs being frequently aligned.[63] Ficino took the unprecedented step (so far as I know) of making a representative Muse one of the primary Olympians in the jovian cavalcade.[64] He had commenced his *Phaedrus* Commentary by stressing Plato's debts to both the poetic and the venerean Muses,[65] and in summae 6, 7, and 39 he again attributes Socrates' poetic inspiration to them. For Ficino the most significant indicator of the part the Muses played in the life of Plato and his disciples was the fact that the Academy's garden contained their shrine: they were thus the first guardians of Platonic man.[66] Traditionally thought of as the daughters of Jove

---

62. See chap. 7, pp. 174-179 below.

63. In his fourth Pleasure apologue Ficino presents the following figure: "Phoebus captured Pleasure also with his lute, the Muses with songs and melodies (*cantilenis et modulis*), and the Graces with leaps and choral dances (*saltibus atque choris*). Having been enticed by them, Pleasure joined the singing Muses, and with outstretched hands she linked herself with the Graces who were gently dancing. So in singing and dancing she . . . was brought into heaven" (ed. Allen, *Philebus Commentary,* pp. 476-477; cf. n. 42 above). Cf. Cicero, *De Beneficiis* 1.3.

The Graces, who were traditionally three—Aglaia, Thalia, and Euphrosyne (though Pasithea sometimes figured as a fourth Grace: see Homer's *Iliad* 14.256-257)—frequently accompanied the Muses: see Frances A. Yates, *The French Academies of the Sixteenth Century* (London, 1947), pp. 84-85, 133. Ficino discusses their names in his *De Amore* 5.2 (ed. Marcel, pp. 181-182) but with some Orphic modifications. See Erwin Panofsky, *Studies in Iconology* (New York, 1939; reprint, 1962), pp. 168-169, and *Renaissance and Renascences,* p. 191n, where he observes that they "symbolized, howsoever defined, a triad of qualities . . . which make the soul capable of *amor divinus*"; also Chastel, *Arte e umanesimo,* pp. 272 ff.; Comito, *Garden,* p. 87; and Wind, *Pagan Mysteries,* pp. 39, 118 ff., 131.

For Ficino's favorite pun on the Graces and his villa at Careggi, see his *Opera,* p. 608.1 and 608.2.

64. *Phaedrus* Commentary, chap. 10 (ed. Allen, *Charioteer,* pp. 118-119). See chap. 5, pp. 133-135 below. She is almost certainly to be identified with Calliope; cf. n. 70 below.

65. *Phaedrus* Commentary, chap. 1 (ed. Allen, *Charioteer,* pp. 72-73).

66. See n. 14 above.

and of Memory, they inspire men peacefully, unlike Dionysus with his Bacchanalia, states summa 7; and they bestow on men, says summa 6, "grace and goodwill." Before the Muses' coming, observes summa 35, men were "uncultivated" (*rudes*); afterwards they had access to "harmonious contemplations" and could, if they listened attentively enough, die to the world as the first devotees had died. Socrates had himself invoked these "clear-voiced" deities at 237A with an etymological pun on the Ligurians, and also described Phaedrus or himself as their devotee at 259B.

Since the Muses' proper locale is with the gods of the celestial spheres to whom they are variously assigned, as Ficino observes in summa 35, Calliope can be supposed to accompany the World-Soul (identified astronomically with the *primum mobile*) or even to be the World-Soul because she is the eldest.[67] Urania, being the next eldest, is, or accompanies, "the first heaven" (astronomically the sphere of the fixed stars presided over by Uranus).[68] Ficino clearly hoped to avoid muddling his classificatory system by declining to dovetail the scheme of the nine Muses into the scheme of the nine lives at 248D-E. In allotting a representative Muse the task of mediating Jove's providence to intelligibles—along with her fellow divinities, Mercury, Apollo, Minerva, and Dionysus— his aim is not so much to make a cosmological point as to stress

67. In his *Ion* argumentum (*Opera*, p. 1283) and in his *Platonic Theology* 4.1 (ed. Marcel, 1:164-165), to which he specifically refers here, we find the following equations (though the *Platonic Theology* omits the first two): Jupiter is the Mind of God; Apollo is the Mind of the World-Soul; Calliope is the World-Soul; Urania is the soul of the sphere of the fixed stars; Polyhymnia is the soul of the sphere of Saturn; Terpsichore is the soul of the sphere of Jupiter; Clio is the soul of the sphere of Mars; Melpomene is the soul of the Sun's sphere; Erato is the soul of the sphere of Venus; Euterpe is the soul of the sphere of Mercury; and Thalia is the soul of the Moon's sphere (this Thalia is not, incidentally, the Grace Thalia). Cf. Chastel, *Ficin et l'art*, p. 137.

This arrangement is not the customary one as we find it in Gafurius, the Tarocchi cards, Giraldi, and so forth, which came via the Middle Ages from Martianus Capella, *De Nuptiis* 1.28. In this scheme Clio is assigned to the Moon's sphere while Thalia is left sitting on Earth, Calliope is assigned to Mercury's sphere, Terpsichore to Venus's, Erato to Mars's, and Euterpe to Jupiter's; that is, only Melpomene, Polyhymnia, and Urania are assigned the same spheres. See Jean Seznec, *The Survival of the Pagan Gods*, trans. Barbara F. Sessions (New York, 1953; reprint, 1961), pp. 124-125; Yates, *French Academies*, p. 133 n. 2; Chastel, *Arte e umanesimo*, pp. 261-264; also n. 68 below.

68. Ficino's scheme for the Muses has the major effect of elevating Calliope above Urania; but it introduces a new problem: if Calliope is the World-Soul (cf. Pico, *Commento* 1.11 [ed. Garin, p. 478]), what then to make of the more usual identification, both in the ancient Neoplatonists and in Ficino, of Jupiter, and even on occasions of Venus (and Venus/Juno), with the World-Soul? See also n. 70 below.

the centrality of Socrates' inspiration; for, as a lover of beauty, Socrates was, for a time at least, their medium, their seer. Though Plato had mentioned both Terpsichore and Erato at 259CD, and though Ficino mentions the latter in summa 6, it is the two eldest that preoccupy him in summa 35. For Plato had said at 259CD that they emit "the most beautiful sound" (*pulcherrima vox*); and Pythagoras had ascribed "the celestial concords" principally to them and made them responsible for the music of the spheres (which Ficino believed Pythagoras had actually heard).[69] Ficino glosses Plato's description of their song's theme as "the heavens and all the story of the gods and men" (259D) to signify that they preside over philosophy's two branches, metaphysics and natural science. Thus Calliope, the eldest (who was the mother, by Apollo and/or Oeagrus, of the poets Orpheus and Linus), becomes the Muse of hearing, hence of instruction in the mental "disciplines" and of "philosophical disputation."[70] Urania, the next eldest, becomes the Muse of sight and hence of astronomy (*aspectus celestium*).

Traditionally, the leader of the nine Muses is Apollo; and Ficino interpreted the noonday setting of the dialogue as testimony to his presence or to the presence of his demon, as we have seen. At the very beginning of his commentary Ficino had adverted to the legend (from Diogenes Laertius and others) that Apollo was Plato's actual father, and he had adopted the familiar Plotinian etymological definition of the god as the "not of many" and there-

69. *Phaedrus* Commentary, summa 35 (ed. Allen, *Charioteer,* pp. 196-197). Ficino's most obvious sources here were Hermias, p. 217.18 ff. and especially Macrobius, *In Somnium Scipionis* 2.1-4 (ed. J. Willis, 2d ed. [Leipzig, 1970]); perhaps too Porphyry, *De Vita Pythagorae* 30, and Iamblichus, *De Vita Pythagorae* 15. See S. K. Heninger, Jr., *Touches of Sweet Harmony: Pythagorean Cosmology and Renaissance Poetics* (San Marino, Calif., 1974), pp. 31, 100, 124, 178-187.

Recently Giovan Battista Alberti identified the MS of Macrobius that Ficino once possessed and lightly annotated, "Marsilio Ficino e il Codice Riccardiano 581," *Rinascimento,* 2d ser., 10 (1970), 187-193. He has also alerted us to the fact that the text of Ficino's Macrobius differs somewhat from the one now accepted as standard.

70. This is an unexpected role for Calliope, who is usually the Muse presiding over epic poetry. Apart from associating her with the World-Soul in the *Platonic Theology* 4.1 and the *Ion* argumentum (see nn. 67 and 68 above), he had also associated her in the *Ion* argumentum with the poet Orpheus and maintained that she was the Muse whose voice was the voice of all the spheres turning together. The *locus classicus* for the "symphony" of the Muses is Hesiod, *Theogony* 36-103; and, for Calliope especially, Macrobius, *In Somnium Scipionis* 2.3. See S. K. Heninger, Jr., *The Cosmographical Glass: Renaissance Diagrams of the Universe* (San Marino, Calif., 1977), pp. 136-138, 179.

fore as a type of the Neoplatonic One.[71] Nevertheless, rather unexpectedly perhaps, he only mentions him here twice: as one of the mediators of Jove's providence to intelligibles (as such, he is not a type of the One, but subordinate to Jove and his progenitors) and as patron of the apollonian demon who, summa 10 surmises, enraptures Socrates "perhaps" after Bacchus, the fellow deity with whom Apollo is frequently dialectically linked.[72]

Along with these gentler sources of inspiration, the Nymphs, the local demons and deities, the airy demons inhabiting the cicadas, the Muses, and Apollo himself, is the frenzied Dionysus, whom Ficino twice introduces to account for Socrates' references to dithyrambs, the poetic mode both of the god and of the Maenads, his followers.[73] Summa 7 describes Dionysus as the patron of the Nymphs, just as Apollo is the patron of the Muses;[74] this is unusual since this patronage is normally granted to Pan. Dionysus had been associated with the Nymphs, however, from childhood, for he had been nurtured by them on Mount Nysa (and specifically by the Hyades and Dodonidae) after Jove had transformed him into a kid to escape the wrath of Juno. It was these Nysaean Nymphs who had afterwards become the Maenads. Among the gods, Dionysus was famous as the "twice-born," or even, in the Orphic version of his nativity, as the "thrice-born" (from Persephone, from Semele, and finally from Jove himself).[75] A num-

71. The source for this etymology of *Apollo,* which Ficino refers to on a number of occasions, as for instance in the *Platonic Theology* 4.1 (ed. Marcel, 1:154-155) and the *Parmenides* Commentary, sixth hypothesis, chap. 1 (*Opera,* p. 1199^V), is probably Plotinus's *Enneads* 5.5.6; but he could have turned just as easily to a variety of other authorities, including Plutarch, *De Iside* (*Moralia* 381F) and *De E apud Delphos* (*Moralia* 388F) and Proclus, *Theologia Platonica* 6.12 (ed. Portus, pp. 377-378). His ultimate authority was, of course, Plato's complicated discussion of the god's name in his *Cratylus* 405A-406A; but Plato seemed apprehensive there of actually suggesting ἀπολῶν, even though he spoke of Apollo as "the single one" (406A).

72. Cody refers to "the essential pastoral myth of Apollo and Bacchus reconciled," which, he says, "is made explicit" in the *Phaedrus* when Socrates argues—"in shepherd's guise if ever cultivated man was—that the truest art is to live naturally" (*Landscape,* p. 12). In his *De Vita* 2.20 (*Opera,* p. 528) Ficino says the Sun is called Phoebus in the Spring and Bacchus in the Fall. See Chastel, *Ficin et l'art,* p. 47; and Wind, *Pagan Mysteries,* pp. 171-176, 196.

73. See Plato, *Laws* 3.700B; and Hermias, p. 55.16 ff.

74. *Homeric Hymn* 26: To Dionysus; cf. Plato, *Ion* 534A. Pico, however, has Bacchus as a leader of the Muses (*Oratio* [ed. Garin, p. 122]).

75. Orpheus, *Hymns to Dionysus* 29 and 51; *Homeric Hymn* 1: To Dionysus; Hermias, p. 54.34 ff.

ber of classical sources, most notably Ovid's *Metamorphoses*
3.261-315, tell the story of his being rescued from Semele's womb
just as she was being blasted to death by Jove's lightning bolt, and
then carried in his father's thigh till the due time of birth (though,
judging from a brief apologue he inserted into his Hermias translation, Ficino seems to have toyed with the notion that it might
have been in Jove's shank [*crus*]).[76] The double, or triple, birth
made him the natural choice for the god of regeneration, quite
apart from his other associations with Asiatic revelry, drunken-
ness, and female hysteria. Additionally he was Orpheus's god, and
Orpheus was his priest and teacher and even, according to some,
the inventor of the dionysian mysteries.

Ficino defines him as the god of "generation" (hence his leadership of the Nymphs) and of "regeneration"; for he sees Socrates
as initially concerned with generative love in the physical sense, by
virtue, if nothing else, of the impact of Lysias's speech. Hence
Socrates is under the influence of the Nymphs of wood (interpreted traditionally as prime matter, ὕλη)[77] and of water (the
medium of generation)—that is, of the plane tree and of the Ilissus. They are the first patrons of his theme, until the Muses preside over the poetic transformation of that theme into one of regeneration, rebirth, and spiritual renewal, the domain of Dionysus, who presides over our ability to transcend both sensibles and

76. MS Vat. lat. 5953, f. 170^r; see Michael J. B. Allen and Roger A. White, "Ficino's
Hermias Translation and a New Apologue," *Scriptorium* 35 (1981), 39-47 at 46-47.

77. The equation of "wood" with "prime matter" is inevitable in Greek, given the history of the word ὕλη; but it was schematized and glossed by Servius in his great commentary on the *Aeneid* and notably on the wood of 6.136 ff. (*In Vergilii Aeneidem VI*, f. 256^r).
See, for example, two glosses in Ficino's own *Philebus* Commentary, one on the wood
where Paris is pasturing his flocks just prior to his judgment on the goddesses, where *in
silva* is glossed as *in confusa elementorum materia* (ed. Allen, pp. 446-447), the other on the
wood in the *Aeneid*, where *per silvam immensam et antiquam* is glossed as [*per*] *mundi
materiam* (ed. Allen, pp. 448-449).

For Ficino another influential source would have been Calcidius's great commentary on
the *Timaeus*, notably chap. 123 on 40B: *Post enim chaos, quam Graeci hylen, nos siluam
vocamus, substitisse terram docet*; and chap. 268 on 47E: *hylen, quam nos Latine siluam
possumus nominare* (ed. Waszink, pp. 167.6-7 and 273.15-16). Raymond Klibansky notes
that a Calcidius MS in Milan (Ambrosian S14 sup.) bears the arms of Marsilio Ficino and
that "from a note in his hand it appears that he himself wrote it in 1454 at the age of twenty
—an interesting record of his early studies" (*The Continuity of the Platonic Tradition during the Middle Ages* [London, 1939; reprint, Munich, 1981], p. 30). A full description of
the MS was given by Kristeller in his *Sup. Fic.* 1:liv.

intelligibles.[78] When Socrates is about to speak of regenerative love, says summa 7, he is therefore seized by the Nymphs and by Dionysus. Having begun with relatively tranquil (*pacatioribus*) considerations under the Muses, he ends with the wilder, bacchanalian visions of the twice-born; for contemplations, writes Ficino, "pass on into frenzies."

The relationship between the roles of the Nymphs and the Muses may appear uncertain until we see them as representatives of the major contrasting but complementary divinities, Apollo and Dionysus. For all its brevity summa 10 provides us with an important clue: Bacchus inspires Socrates "mainly to dithyrambs," but the Nymphs inspire him to "songs" (*carmina*). Through the Nymphs Socrates "censures the intemperate lover," through Bacchus he "approves of the temperate." Consequently "he brings the young man forth again" (*regeneret*). Finally, since he has been rendered ecstatic (*excessus*) through Bacchus, "perhaps the apollonian demon immediately enraptures him (for Apollo is closest to Bacchus), with the result that he even exceeds (*excedat*) the bounds of human behavior (*mores humanos*) and thereafter treats of the divine love that excites us through some frenzy." Ficino not only refuses to see the two gods of illumination as rivals, he yokes them together as a pair. In the words of summa 14, all the divine madnesses are "mutually joined" (*invicem coniugati*),[79] since the "illuminating power" of Phoebus is yoked in the intelligible world to the related "inciting or producing and, as it were, heating power of Bacchus." In the illuminating power flourishes "the power for prophecy and poetry"; in the inciting, "the power for love and [priestly] prayer." As we shall see, Ficino is using a scheme for distributing the four madnesses that differs from the one he had explored in the fourth commentary chapter.[80] Summa 14 continues, "For light and heat refer to both Apollo and Bacchus. Furthermore, the Sun's power incites us via Mercury to the Muses [that is, to poetry], and via Venus to

---

78. *Phaedrus* Commentary, chap. 10 (ed. Allen, *Charioteer,* pp. 118-119). Interestingly, Plato's *Philebus* 61C describes Dionysus as a god who presides over "the ceremony of mingling."

79. Or, in the words of the summa's title, *invicem copulati.*

80. See chap. 2, pp. 47-50, 66-67 below.

love.'' Mercury's presidency over poetry and Venus's over love are made to subserve, in other words, the more fundamental division between Apollo's presidency over prophecy and Dionysus's presidency over worship and the hieratic art, even as Ficino leaves it to the astrologers (in this summa at least) to decide how the solar power can so signify. However, he does point to the profounder ramifications involving the relationship between the understanding, the will, and the four madnesses, which I shall deal with more fully below.[81]

Since Socrates assumes the roles of lover and priest as well as those of poet and prophet, he is seized by the dionysian ecstasy and moved to dithyrambic utterance, even though his personal god is Apollo. But the complementarity of the two gods is such that they form a unitary presence beside the smooth-sliding Ilissus, already crowned with the vocal reeds of the Naiads and of Pan. Thus Ficino could interpret Socrates himself as subject to the union of Dionysus and Apollo, as in a way an embodiment of that union. For we recall Alcibiades' delineation of the Silenian face with its satyr eyes and ears, amidst the drunken uproar and the lascivious melodies of Asiatic flutes, propounding the apollonian thesis that in truly ecstatic art all generic distinctions are subsumed.[82]

In short, the Nymphs and Pan, the demons and the Muses, Apollo and Dionysus, are all present or ambient in Ficino's interpretation of the *Phaedrus*. As numinous forces they preside over particular moments in Socrates' inspired unfolding of his hymn and its themes, passing as he does from tranquillity to Bacchanalia, from discursive reasoning to dithyrambic song and uranian vision. It is questionable whether Ficino would have committed himself to so schematic a progression as Iamblichus apparently entertained; but he undoubtedly understood Socrates as succumbing to a variety of inspirations that eventually led him to the heights of divine ''alienation.''

81. See chap. 2, pp. 50-51, 67 below.
82. Socrates is the Apollo in Dionysus, and therefore the living embodiment of the union between the gods. Cf. the verbal portraits and the attendant allegorizing in Ficino's *De Amore* 7.2, 16 (ed. Marcel, pp. 242-245, 260-262). On the related Marsyas-Apollo conflict and reconciliation, see Wind, *Pagan Mysteries,* pp. 171-176.

Though his role and functions are somewhat different from those of the deities treated above, one other god presides over the dialogue: Pan's father, Mercury. Ficino's principal statement is contained in summa 49, where he retells what was obviously one of his favorite Plato stories, the myth of Egyptian Theuth, identified elsewhere with the thrice-great Hermes, the supposititious author of the *Corpus Hermeticum*.[83] The story at 247C ff., like the enigmatic passage in Plato's seventh Epistle at 344CD, is clearly Pythagorean in its sentiments, for it decries writing and insists on the need for wisdom to be transmitted orally from master to pupil in order that it may remain alive.[84]

Ficino gives us an iconological description of Mercury, the legendary founder for the Neoplatonists of dialectic, ingenuity, and inventiveness, all the more intellectual skills. To his patronage he assigns arithmetic, geometry, astronomy, and the verbal accomplishments involved in writing and speaking,[85] as well as

83. In his *Philebus* Commentary 1.29 (ed. Allen, pp. 272-273), Ficino explicitly identifies the Egyptian Theuth with the Greek Hermes Trismegistus; cf. Cicero, *De Natura Deorum* 3.22, and Lactantius, *Div. Inst.* 1.6. Augustine's *De Civitate Dei* provided Ficino with a positive (18.29) as well as a negative (8.23) view of Hermes; see Yates, *Bruno*, pp. 6-16. Lactantius's account, however, was the one that prevailed.

Of the two works primarily associated with Hermes, Ficino translated all but the last (the fifteenth) treatise of the first work, which came to be known by the title of its first treatise as the *Pimander*. This was in 1463 immediately before his translation of Plato. The other work, the *Asclepius*, which had incurred Augustine's wrath in *De Civitate Dei* 8.13-26, had been translated into Latin in all probability by the fourth century A.D. By the ninth century, apparently, the Greek text had been lost and the Latin translation had come to be attributed to Apuleius; see Yates, *Bruno*, pp. 3n, 9-10. Ficino, like everyone else, accepted this attribution. The standard edition of the *Corpus Hermeticum* is by A. D. Nock and A.-J. Festugière, 4 vols. (Paris, 1945-1954); the major study is by Festugière, *La révélation d'Hermès Trismégiste*, 4 vols. (Paris, 1950-1954).

Kristeller has demonstrated, incidentally, that the two commentaries, one on the *Pimander*, the other on the *Asclepius*, included in Ficino's own *Opera Omnia* on pp. 1836-1871, are both in fact by Jacques Lefèvre d'Étaples (*Sup. Fic.* 1:cxxx-cxxxi and 97-98; also *Studies*, pp. 222 ff.). Yates accepted Kristeller's arguments with regard to the *Asclepius* but not, curiously, with regard to the *Pimander*, though the evidence is the same for both.

84. Ficino seems to have been concerned with Pythagoras less as a master of silence (see Wind, *Pagan Mysteries*, pp. 12n, 53n; Heninger, *Sweet Harmony*, pp. 23, 25, 37 n. 17) than as a propounder of oral wisdom—that is, as a master of the art of hermeneutics, of correct interpretation.

85. Mercury, we recall, is both the god of eloquence and the interpreter and guardian of secrets: he is thus at times the god of silence (in conjunction or otherwise with Harpocrates). A major text on Mercury for Ficino was Iamblichus's panegyric to the god at the opening of his *De Mysteriis* (ed. Des Places, p. 38), a text Ficino had himself translated/adapted (*Opera*, pp. 1873-1908); cf. Ficino's *Platonic Theology* 18.5 (ed. Marcel, 3:197). For an

"the most artful games" specified by Plato at 274CD as checkers and dice. He also assigns him all things Egyptian. Using the Orphic principles of enumeration described in commentary chapter 10, Ficino interprets Mercury and the mercurial according to different levels in the cosmic hierarchy. In his highest manifestation Mercury exists in Jove, his father; for Jove displays to the superlative degree the mercurial skills in his twin capacities as world-ruler and as world-leader.[86] The "greatest" Mercury—to draw on Ficino's own precise usage[87]—is therefore within the "greatest" Jove (as are the "greatest" Apollo, Dionysus, Mars, and so forth). Below this "greatest" Mercury in "greatest" Jove comes Mercury as a supramundane, wholly intellectual god.[88] Third comes the Mercury in "great" as opposed to "greatest" Jove—that is, in Jove as the world-leader and World-Soul. Fourth is the celestial Mercury, Mercury as the soul of the planet and its sphere. Fifth is the order of mercurial demons immediately subject to the planetary god, each of them entitled on occasion to be named Mercury, the lower, sublunar levels of this order are led by Pan. Sixth are mercurial humans, those possessed of peculiarly mercurial powers, skills, aptitudes, and attitudes, again each of them entitled on occasion actually to be named Mercury. Seventh and last come mercurial animals, plants, stones, and places, like the ibis, monkeys, keen-scented dogs, Naucratis, all of them specifically under the astrological influence of the planet Mercury as well as more generally under the sway of Mercury in his higher

---

interesting analysis of Mercury's Neoplatonic and Renaissance significance as *interpres secretorum,* see Wind, *Pagan Mysteries,* pp. 121-129, 196; also Chastel, *Ficin et l'art,* p. 140 n. 11. Of special note is Ficino's acceptance of the astrological notion, following Albumasar, that Mercury was the presiding deity of Christianity; see de Gandillac, "Astres, anges et génies," p. 89, and Garin, *Lo zodiaco della vita,* chap. 1.

86. For this distinction see the *Phaedrus* Commentary, chap. 10 (ed. Allen, *Charioteer,* pp. 114-115), and chap. 5, pp. 127-128 below. As world-ruler Jupiter could be equated with the Demiurge of the *Timaeus;* as world-leader, on the other hand, he was prime among souls, and therefore the World-Soul.

87. Ibid. "Greatest" Jupiter is the demiurgic world-ruler from the wholly intellectual/ intelligible realm; "Great" Jupiter is the world-leader and World-Soul; and Jupiter without an epithet is the soul of the sphere of the planet Jupiter. See chap. 5, p. 138 below.

88. For the critical distinction between the "mundane" and the "super/supramundane" deities (and their respective "heavens") see Allen, *Charioteer,* Headnote to Texts II, pp. 66-69; and chap. 10, n. 67 below.

manifestations. In short, summa 49 gives us a graph of the emanative descent of being as reflected in and keyed to a particular god, a god who could conveniently serve as a model for interpreting each of the other twelve Olympians.

Ficino goes on to note that Socrates' account at 247C ff. is both "allegorical" and "anagogical."[89] He means by this that we must not only allegorize Mercury in terms of the various "intellectual skills" but also interpret him anagogically in light of the seven levels of being: as a subhuman object, place, or living thing, as a man, a demon, a mundane god, a power or property in the World-Soul, a supramundane god, as "greatest" Jove himself. Thus the Theuth story acquires multiple meanings, and especially Theuth's encounter with Thamus. Though a man called Thamus actually reigned in Naucratis in Egypt, Socrates was also referring anagogically, Ficino says, to a mercurial divinity "in heaven or above heaven," meaning I take it the mundane or the supramundane Mercury. For at 274D4, as Ficino interpreted the unemended test, Plato had also mentioned the city's god and referred to him as Ammon—that is, as Jupiter.[90] Nevertheless, Ficino was alert to the problem that Socrates seems to identify Thamus and Ammon, at least in part. Thus he warns us in summa 49 that "Although Socrates' account seems to include Thamus and Ammon under the same person, reason in its precision distinguishes between them." That is, though Thamus may be a god, that is, Mercury, he is not the highest god, that is, Jupiter-Ammon. However, insofar as Theuth and Thamus both ultimately submit to Ammon, they both submit to the Mercury within Ammon, and thus to "great" Mercury; or even to "greatest" Mercury, to the supramundane Mercury or to the Mercury within the supramundane Jupiter. Whereas Ammon and Thamus stand for Mercury at the four highest of the seven levels, Theuth stands for him at the three lowest. The meet-

---

89. Cf. *Phaedrus* Commentary, chap. 10 (ed. Allen, *Charioteer*, pp. 110-111). See Des Places's note in his edition of Iamblichus's *De Mysteriis* on the two senses, the Chaldaean and the Neoplatonic, of ἀναγωγή (Édouard Des Places, ed. and trans., *Jamblique: Les mystères d'Égypte* [Paris, 1966], p. 86).

90. Most editors follow Postgate in emending θεὸν at 272D4 ("while the god himself they call Ammon") to θαμοῦν ("while they call Thamus Ammon"); so Hackforth, Hamilton, et al. As his 1484 *Platonis Opera Omnia* demonstrates, Ficino clearly wanted to adhere to the MS reading: *deumque ipsum ammonem* [*Graeci*] *vocant* (sig. b ii^v, col. 1).

ing between Theuth and Thamus in Ammon's city signifies the
dependence, therefore, of the lower on the higher; for, writes
Ficino, "inferior things are said to depend on their superiors in the
judging of inventions; and this is just." In particular the faculty of
invention must depend on the judgment, since the judgment is the
more outstanding (*praestantius*), pertaining as it does to our reason and understanding, while invention pertains to our natural
instinct and our powers of conceit, though both derive ultimately
from the mercurial powers in Jove. Invention, being the lower, is
granted to the mercurial man or demon called Theuth. As a man
he is endowed with the mercurial powers of eloquence and inventiveness. As a demon he serves as an intermediary and interpreter
between the gods and men: on the one hand by transmitting mercurial gifts to men, on the other by bringing men's "invention"—
that is, writing—to the court of the god-king Thamus for him to
submit it to his own and Ammon's judgment.

The Theuth story has a direct bearing on Socrates' preoccupation in the later sections of the *Phaedrus* with oratory, oratorical
inventiveness, and critical discrimination among orators. To
Ficino it suggested (insofar as we can tell from the scanty notes he
supplied for these sections) that Socrates was concerned to impress
upon Phaedrus the vital importance of acquiring living wisdom, as
against the written "opinion" of Lysias and the Sophists. Not that
Socrates condemns writing utterly, as Ficino warns us in summae
34, 50, 51, and 52. Still, we should not place too much confidence
in it; for "sublime matters" (*altiora*) must be entrusted to souls
who are worthy of them, not to sheets of paper (*cartis*), since writing is indeed only a kind of mercurial "game," say summae 51 and
52, even if it is "the most beautiful of all games."[91]

Though Mercury is keyed to the Theuth legend, he was for
Ficino an omnipresent deity. His inspiration may be different
from the other inspirational forces at work on and in Socrates, but
he too is a patron of the Muses and thus of the framework of argument, the dialectical progression, and the oratorical disposition
that Socrates supplies for his mythical hymn and the other satellite

91. In summa 51 (ed. Allen, *Charioteer,* pp. 212-213) he also identifies the written forms
of "doctrines" as "gardens of Adonis" that one cultivates "for the sake of flowers, not
fruits or produce."

myths. The structural "art" of the *Phaedrus* as well as its interpretation is, in short, his gift. Significantly, the Theuth story comes last in the dialogue's sequence of figurative episodes, and functions as an explanatory coda, a key to Socrates' strategies and intentions. If the apollonian demon had enraptured him during the palinode, the mercurial demon was also there as the divinity inspiring him both to eloquence of diction and to rhetorical inventiveness in the presentation of his material. As the sun crossed its zenith and the heat became less oppressive (279B), it was the mercurial rather than the apollonian demon, therefore, that presided over the later stages of the conversation, the "better agriculture" in summa 51's phrase, between Socrates and his beloved pupil.

Ficino notes with satisfaction in summa 53 that "just as he had from the beginning and elsewhere throughout the dialogue, so at the end likewise Socrates again atttributes all the power of invention and eloquence to the kindness of the gods (*deorum beneficio*)." And he continues, "Since the highest god often acts through intermediary gods and through those gods close to us, Socrates often mentions the local gods. Now he finally addresses his speech or prayer to them." Although "the highest god" is Jove, the world artificer, the focus at the conclusion of the summae is upon Mercury and upon his son Pan and his demons. For it is through his "kindness" especially that Socrates has been moved to discourse on Lysias's speech (263E). Thus Ficino sees Socrates turning at last to mercurial Pan—not to the capering satyr, but to the Theuth of the brooks and woodlands who "reigns everywhere under the Moon." Chief of all the sublunar deities, as his name indicates,[92] Pan is the sublunar counterpart of both the Mercury in great Jove, the leader of souls, and of the Mercury in "greatest" Jove, who inhabits the realm of pure mind. Having previously addressed a prayer to Love (257AB), so now the Pan-faced Socrates addresses a prayer to Pan that he may "become fair within" (279B),[93] wise like the ibis, like Theuth, like Mercury himself, the

92. *Cratylus* 408BC (cf. Proclus, *In Cratylum* 73). In his epitome for the *Cratylus, Opera,* p. 1313, Ficino has an interesting note on the "biform" Pan: "Pana Mercurii filium esse biformem, videlicet ob geminum sermonem, verum scilicet atque falsum. Nota ubi Pan ut homo pingitur sermonem verum significare; ubi vero ut brutum, falsum."

93. See B. Darrell Jackson, "The Prayers of Socrates," *Phronesis* 16.1 (1971), 14-37, esp. 23-30.

inventor and the judge of all pertaining not just to writing and speech but to intellectual, to interpretative understanding. We have moved from the panicky Pan in the train of Dionysus to the mercurial and even in a way to the jovian and saturnian Pan, the deity depicted so memorably and mysteriously by Ficino's contemporary, Luca Signorelli.[94] Just as Pan stands at the head of the various local spirits haunting the banks, the canopying willows, and the clear bubbling waters of the Phaedran setting, so he stands, anagogically, for the several deities inspiring Socrates from the local Nymphs to universal Jove.[95]

To conclude, for Ficino as for some of the later Neoplatonists in antiquity Plato had enveloped the *Phaedrus* not only in myth, allegory, prophecy, and poetry, but also in various manifestations of the numinous. A dialogue, a love poem, a series of prayers, and a theological vision, it bore witness both to the omnipresence of the gods and to the divine madnesses with which they enrapture those who die to the elemental world. Appropriately, therefore, Ficino turned to the theme of the divine madnesses in the first chapter of his commentary proper.

94. Cf. Vergil, *Georgics* 1.17 (*ovium custos*); *Homeric Hymn* 19: To Pan; and Orpheus, *Hymn to Pan* (i.e. Hymn 11). For Signorelli's picture, which was destroyed in the Second World War, see the fine analysis by Chastel, *Arte e umanesimo,* pp. 232-238, where he also deals with the particular significance Pan had for the Medici.

95. At this point, from the evidence of his own epitome for the *Alcibiades Minor* (*Opera,* p. 1134), Ficino was almost certainly recalling the story of Pan's death as described in the two most notable ancient sources: Plutarch's *De Defectu Oraculorum* (*Moralia* 418E-419B; see esp. the edition by Robert Flacelière, *Plutarque: Sur la disparition des oracles* [Paris, 1947], pp. 79-87) and Eusebius's *Praeparatio Evangelica* 5.17.206C-207B. Thus he would be reading Socrates' prayer to Pan here in the context of the various "pagan" or "Gentile" prefigurings of Christ's passion. Notable references during the Renaissance to Pan as Christ include Rabelais's *Gargantua and Pantagruel* 4.27-28, Spenser's *Shepherd's Calendar,* the May eclogue with E. K.'s gloss on "Great Pan," and Milton's "Ode on the Morning of Christ's Nativity," line 89.

Chapter Two: Poetic Madness

Since the first three chapters of the *Phaedrus* Commentary are the argumentum as it was initially printed at the head of the *Phaedrus* translation in the 1484 edition of Ficino's *Platonis Opera Omnia,* the fourth chapter begins the commentary proper. It opens with the signal statement that Ficino wishes to elucidate "some of this book's principal mysteries a little more fully," and first those which he has "neglected in the *Phaedrus* and not dealt with elsewhere," and which concern poetry and the other madnesses. "Mystery" is an important and complex term in Ficino's lexicon, for it bespeaks a conception of truth and of access to truth that is both abstract and figurative, classical and Renaissance, pagan and Christian.[1] He devoted much of his time and seemingly limitless energy as a commentator expatiating on the "marvelous mysteries" in Plato, Plotinus, and their predecessors and successors among the ancient theologians, poets, theogonists, and Platonic interpreters, and rejoicing in the parallels with those in the Bible, particularly in Genesis. Towards the end of the first chapter of the argumentum, for instance, he had compared the Pythagorean notion that some demon had made evil pleasurable to the mystery of the Edenic fall. Again, in the second chapter he had noted that the Pythagorean theory of the soul's descent through nine degrees was consonant with the Prophets' depiction of the nine angelic and demonic choirs. Then he had compared the story told by Pythagoras's reputed teacher, Pherecydes of Syros, of the

---

1. Wind, *Pagan Mysteries,* pp. 1-16, deals with the several meanings that the term already possessed in antiquity and also with the meanings it had for the Renaissance as it examined antiquity. For the terms in Ficino, see Chastel, *Ficin et l'art,* pp. 141-156. Of particular interest are Pico's comments in the proem to his *Heptaplus* (ed. Garin, p. 172): "Plato noster ita, involucris aenigmatum, fabularum velamine, mathematicis imaginibus et subobscuris recedentium sensuum indiciis, sua dogmata occultavit, ut et ipse dixerit in *Epistulis* neminem ex his quae scripserit suam sententiam de divinis aperte intellecturum, et re minus credentibus comprobaverit"; cf. his *Oratio* (ed. Garin, pp. 156 ff.) and *Commento particolare* (ed. Garin, pp. 580-581).

demons' rebellion under the titanic serpent, Ophioneus, to the biblical account of Satan's insurrection and rout.

But a mystery was more than the prefiguring of Christian doctrines concerning the first and last things, prefiguring best interpreted by the methods of Neoplatonic allegorizing. It could only be mediated by men divinely inspired, only transmitted to and understood by initiates in a state of ecstatic access to the gods. While the *Phaedrus* obviously contained many doctrinal mysteries concerning the soul's creation, sempiternity and fall, conversion, ascent and apotheosis, and concerning the natures and the cosmogonic and eschatological duties of the gods, it was also about the mediation process itself, about the mystery of these mysteries' transmission and comprehension. The four appointed mediators of mysteries were prophets, priests, poets, and lovers—the four faces of the truly Platonic philosopher.

Why then did Ficino start with the poetic madness at 245A, ignoring not only earlier doctrinal mysteries in the dialogue, such as the discussion of Socrates' familiar divine sign at 242BC and the Stesichorian palinode at 243AB, but also Plato's introduction of the first two recipients of divine madness, the prophets and priests? At first glance it seems an unexpected place to commence commentary even if Ficino had had no immediate intention of returning to the very beginning.

His opening phrases suggest deceptively limited goals. Currently he was not attempting to deal with all the dialogue's mysteries per se, merely with those that he still felt, in the 1490s, he had either "omitted" or "neglected" to some degree in his other works. But he had certainly not neglected the general theme of the divine madnesses, nor specifically of the poetic madness. A long chapter in book 13 of the *Platonic Theology* enlarges upon them, particularly the prophetic and hieratic madnesses, in the context of the theory of "vacation" or "alienation," as do sections in the *De Amore,* in the introduction to the *Ion,* and above all in the epistolary tract, *De Divino Furore.*[2] These and other writings furnish sufficient

2. *Platonic Theology* 13.2 (ed. Marcel, 2:201-222); *De Amore* 7.14 (ed. Marcel, pp. 258-260)—see below, pp. 208-210; *Ion* argumentum (in Ficino's *Opera Omnia,* pp. 1281-1284)—see below, p. 209, n. 9; and *De Divino Furore* (in the *Opera Omnia,* pp. 612-615). There is an English translation of the last in *The Letters of Marsilio Ficino,* 3 vols. to date

material (as I hope to argue on another occasion) for us to postulate a Ficinian poetics. Thus Ficino cannot mean by "neglected" that he had neglected the theme of poetry itself. He might have felt perhaps that he had neglected to consider Socrates sufficiently as a poet, or to place him in the tradition of the *prisci poetae*. However, I believe he commences at 245A because he intuitively felt that poetry and poetic inspiration provided the key to a proper understanding of the *Phaedrus*. It was Plato's first great poem, not just stylistically—and Ficino clearly admired in it what some ancient critics censured as overwriting—but because it sprang directly from his vision as a poet and was, in part at least, the outpouring of Plato's own poetic madness in addition to recapitulating that of Socrates.[3] The poetic mystery was paramount here, and our understanding of the other mysterious madnesses was dependent to a degree upon it. Until it had been analyzed, neither the contents nor the modality of the dialogue could be truly comprehended; for poetry was its seminal mystery, the controlling frame for an understanding of its doctrines. Thus the necessity of starting with 245A. Though third in the Platonic order of divine enthusiasts, the poet was the peculiar genius of this peculiarly poetic masterpiece.

Ficino initially suggests that the goal of poetic madness is twofold: instructing men in "the divine ways" or customs, and singing the divine mysteries. That is, instead of Horatian teaching and delighting, we have Orphic teaching and hymning. Plato's text reads differently: Socrates says poetry should "glorify the countless mighty deeds of ancient times for the instruction of posterity" (245A). Ficino's extrapolation, if not falsification, certainly constitutes a reinterpretation of this. For "the glorifying of ancient times" he substitutes "the singing" of present mysteries; for "the countless mighty deeds," "divine customs" and "divine mysteries"; and for the instruction "of posterity," instruction of those

---

(London, 1975, 1978, 1981), 1:42-48, by "Members of the Language Department of the School of Economic Science, London"—hereafter *Letters*; the three vols. are translations of books 1, 3, and 4, respectively.

    3. See Allen, *Charioteer*, pp. 8-14, plus accompanying notes.

who are alive and have ears to hear. In effect, contemplation has replaced activity, and the hymn of lyrical praise, epic recollection.

The Neoplatonic hymn, as sung by Orpheus, Musaeus, Homer, Iamblichus, Proclus, and Julian, and also by Plotinus in those corybantic rhapsodies which sometimes punctuate his meditation on a particular theme,[4] constitutes for Ficino and his contemporaries the archetypal poem, and therefore the touchstone for the theory and even arguably the practice of poetic inspiration.[5] The origins and history of this conception are problematic. But the twin authorities are on the one hand David the Psalmist and his double, Thracian Orpheus,[6] and on the other Plato himself, both in his recourse to hymnlike passages such as the *Phaedrus*'s own apostrophe to Beauty at 250B ff. and in his comments in the *Republic, Laws,* and elsewhere on divine poetry.[7] Plato's derogatory comments on profane poets in the *Ion,* the *Meno,* and especially the *Republic* Renaissance humanists had repeatedly explained away, following Proclus and Heraclides Ponticus:[8] partly

4. For example, *Enneads* 5.8.4, 10 (5.8 was a treatise of particular significance for Ficino and for his analysis of the *Phaedrus*'s myth; see chap. 10, pp. 234-238 below, and Chastel, *Ficin et l'art,* p. 154 n. 43). For the climactic nature of the rhapsodic passages in Plotinus, see Émile Bréhier, *The Philosophy of Plotinus,* trans. Joseph Thomas (Chicago, 1958), p. 27.

5. Walker, *Magic,* pp. 3-72 (on Pletho, Ficino, Diacceto, and Lazzarelli).

6. The most extensive treatment of Ficino's linking of David and Orpheus is D. P. Walker's *The Ancient Theology* (London, 1972), chap. 1, pp. 22-41 (this first appeared as an article in *Journal of the Warburg and Courtauld Institutes* 16 [1953], 100-120). Walker draws our attention to the famous opening chapter of Clement of Alexandria's *Protrepticus* (ed. Migne, *PG* 8.49 ff.), where the Greeks are exhorted to leave Orpheus's music for David's (p. 23n).

Cf. Ficino's letter to Pietro Dovizi da Bibbiena (*Opera,* p. 927) and his *De Vita* 1.7, 10 (*Opera,* pp. 500, 502); also Pico, Orphic Conclusion 4: "Sicut hymni Dauid operi Cabale mirabiliter deseruiunt, ita hymni Orphei opere vere licite et naturalis Magie" (Bohdan Kieszkowski, ed., *Giovanni Pico della Mirandola: Conclusiones sive Theses DCCCC* [Paris, 1973], p. 80). Kieszkowski's edition contains a number of errors, as José V. de Pina Martins points out in his *Jean Pic de la Mirandole* (Paris, 1976), chap. 3, pp. 43-82.

7. Plato's conceptions of poetry and poets have been the subject of continuous debate, but see particularly three studies by E. N. Tigerstedt: "The Poet as Creator: Origins of a Metaphor," *Comparative Literature Studies* 5.4 (1968), 455-488; *Plato's Idea of Poetical Inspiration,* Commentationes Humanarum Litterarum: Societas Scientiarum Fennica, vol. 44, no. 2 (Helsinki, 1969); and "*Furor Poeticus*: Poetic Inspiration in Greek Literature before Democritus and Plato," *Journal of the History of Ideas* 31.2 (1970), 163-178.

8. The *Quaestiones Homericae,* which the Renaissance attributed to Heraclides the philosopher (rather than to Heraclitus, a rhetorician of the first century A.D.), defend Homer against Plato's strictures by recourse to thoroughgoing allegory. Though the first edition did not appear until 1505, the work was widely distributed in manuscript. See Gombrich, *Symbolic Images,* p. 82.

by way of defending the high seriousness, and in Ficino's and Landino's case the Platonism, of Vergil (and of Dante); and partly by employing the allegorical method to moralize and even "theologize" Ovid and other ancient love poets, and so to defend them against the accusation of "profanity." Even now the *Phaedrus* presents a poetic facade with its "dithyrambic" style, its "palinodal" structure, and the self-definition of Socrates' second speech as "a mythical hymn." For Ficino it was Plato's Neoplatonic hymn par excellence, its combination of mythmaking and poetic ornament making it a supreme contribution to what he considered the quintessentially Orphic genre.

Socrates says the poetic madness "seizes a tender, pure soul" (λαβοῦσα ἀπαλὴν καὶ ἄβατον ψυχήν),[9] ἀπαλὴν and ἄβατον both suggesting a horse that has not yet been broken in and also chastity and delicateness, and ἄβατον suggesting in addition inaccessible places, mountainsides, streams, and groves, undefiled by the passing of man. Ficino's choice of Latin equivalents, *tener, mollis, intactus, immaculatus, vacuus,* though largely predictable, also suggests qualities Christianity has always associated with the soul: both the innocent, childlike ones enabling it to enter the kingdom of its Father as if it had never grown to sin, and also those characterizing the virgin Mother. The "tender, pure soul" is redolent of Christian associations that supply an added dimension to Socrates' conceptions of passivity and emptying (*vacatio*) and of the soul's need to reacquire such states via purgation and prayer.

The major difference in emphasis, however, results from the differing sources of poetic madness. While it is the Muses for Socrates (and indirectly their traditional patrons and leaders, Apollo and Dionysus, as we have seen), for Ficino poetic inspiration, like all authentic inspiration, comes directly and preeminently from God—*Animus igitur se ipsum formatu facillimum formatori deo subicere debet*—and secondarily from the divine Forms, the Platonic Ideas in God's mind. Underlying this entire conception is the complex notion of forming itself, with its implication that the poet is material or has material to be formed: "The poet's province is

9. The epithets Agathon uses to depict Love in the *Symposium* 195C-196A (νεώτατος ... νέος ... ἀπαλός ... ἀπαλώτατος ... ὑγρὸς τὸ εἶδος) are clearly in the forefront of Ficino's mind here; cf. Hermias, p. 98.4-5.

very wide, and his material is varied; so his soul (which can be formed very easily) must subject itself to God.''[10] The Latin is not precise enough to bear too close a scrutiny, for Ficino also raises the possibility that the potential poet might have already received "alien forms or blemishes." Whether we take these two as alternatives or in apposition, a number of difficulties emerge as soon as we try to dovetail them either into the general theory of disembodied Platonic Forms or into its Aristotelian counterpart. And Ficino does not provide us with enough argumentation to distinguish effectively between *alien* and *divine* forms. For all forms are divine in origin for a Platonist (imperfection being the result of inadequate participation in a form rather than something wrong with the form itself);[11] and they are alien only in that their absolute being is not in the soul—where they are merely imaged in formulae—but in God's mind. But these logical dilemmas are not peculiar to Ficino.

In elevating poetic madness from the particular context of being inspired by the Muses (theoretically by all nine, but by Polyhymnia and Erato in the first instance)[12] to the general context of being formed by God and by the divine Ideas (which are supremely active powers imprinting themselves on the passive human intelligence), Ficino makes it logically difficult for us to differentiate it from the other madnesses. The poet's degree of preparedness becomes a model, though perhaps the best one, for a soul's preparedness for God, who is, by definition, the ultimate and most

10. Ficino's Latin translation reads: *Amplissima enim est poete provincia omniformisque materia.* The notion of "omniform" matter raises a number of problems in light of the traditional distinctions between "form" and "matter"; hence my earlier decision to render *omniformis* as "varied." Clearly Ficino intends us to suppose that the poet's material is capable of receiving many or all "forms" Platonically conceived, or even of being itself a complex of such forms; it only has an analogical relationship, that is, to "normal" matter.

11. Among the Neoplatonists, apparently, only Amelius seems to have espoused the theory that there could be an "Idea" of evil; see Saffrey and Westerink, 1:153. Ficino treats of the whole question in his *Parmenides* Commentary, chaps. 8, 9, 11, 13, 14 (*Opera*, pp. 1140-1141), where he argues that there are no Ideas of singulars, parts, or artificial objects, or of evil or vile things. His guide here may well have been Albinus (Alcinous)—for whose formula see Dillon, *Middle Platonists*, pp. 28 and 281.

12. In his epitome of the *Ion* (*Opera*, pp. 1281-1284 at 1283) Ficino associates Polyhymnia with Saturn, i.e. with contemplation, and Erato with Venus, i.e. with love.

perfect inspiration. I postpone treatment of Ficino's grafting of the notion of *forming* on that of *rapture* or *seizure* until somewhat later in this chapter.[13]

The intriguing problem of establishing the correct relationship or relationships between the poetic madness and the other three divine madnesses, and, by extension, their mutual subordinations, preoccupies the second paragraph. The *Phaedrus* itself insists that the best, highest, and noblest madness is the amatory, "the greatest of heaven's blessings" (245BC, 249DE, 265AB). Even so, chronologically it treats it fourth after the prophetic, hieratic, and poetic. Ficino had reversed this sequence in his epistolary tract, *De Divino Furore*,[14] which was written before either his first draft of the *Phaedrus* translation or his *Phaedrus* introduction or commentary but presupposes nevertheless a knowledge of the dialogue, if not from the Greek at first hand, then from Bruni's partial 1424 translation.[15] The tract was addressed to Peregrino Agli and became a quattrocento favorite, to judge from the many manuscripts in which it and a contemporary vernacular version appear;[16] in many ways a key text for Ficino's ecstatics, it deserves independent study. The sequence of madnesses in the *Phaedrus* Commentary also differs from that outlined in Ficino's epitome for the *Ion* (presumably penned by the mid-1460s), and therefore from that outlined in the *De Amore* 7.14, which was written in 1468-1469 and which in this regard borrows directly from the epitome.[17] In

13. See below, pp. 58-61.
14. Marcel (in his ed. of the *De Amore*, p. 103) makes the inexplicable contention that, whereas the *De Amore* postulates four ascending madnesses, the *De Divino Furore* seems to argue that the poetic madness is sufficient by itself for the ascent. Anne Sheppard, in what is otherwise a particularly suggestive article, accepts this contention, "The Influence of Hermias on Marsilio Ficino's Doctrine of Inspiration," *Journal of the Warburg and Courtauld Institutes* 43 (1980), 97-109 at 101. See also n. 19 below.
15. Hans Baron, *Leonardo Bruni Aretino: Humanistisch-philosophische Schriften* (Leipzig and Berlin, 1928), pp. 125-128, 172; and Allen, *Charioteer,* pp. 5 and 30-31 n. 15. It went as far as 257C.
16. See Kristeller, *Sup. Fic.* 1:xciv. For information on Agli, see F. Flamini, *Peregrino Allio: Umanista, poeta e confilosofo del Ficino* (Pisa, 1893); della Torre, *Accademia Platonica,* pp. 552-553; and Kristeller, *Sup. Fic.* 2:322-323.
For the proem to the anonymous vernacular version, see ibid. 1:68-69.
17. See chap. 9, n. 9 below.

these two works the sequence runs: poetic, hieratic, prophetic, amatory.[18]

Clearly there are two basic paradigms: one where the poetic madness immediately precedes (or, in the reversed order of the *De Divino Furore,* follows)[19] the amatory; the other where the poetic —the lowest—madness is at the furthest extreme from the amatory—the highest—madness. In other words, we have the *Phaedrus*'s schema (with that in the Agli tract as its mirror image) as opposed to the *De Amore*'s schema (which was borrowed, it so happens, from the *Ion* epitome). The exact relationship between the hieratic and the prophetic madnesses is irrelevant at this point.[20]

Though the *Phaedrus* and the *Symposium* are complementary in that they both assign the highest value to the amatory madness and both put it last, Ficino is sensitive to the fact that in the two dialogues Plato was exploring different angles of the same problem. In commenting on the alternative sequences, he characterizes the *Symposium*'s as that which pertains "to the soul's restoration," but the *Phaedrus*'s as that which pertains "to the actual origin of madness." By the former, I take it, he means that as the soul moves upwards towards the divine, it first experiences the poetic madness, then the hieratic, then the prophetic, and finally, climactically, the amatory. But, essentially, this is a psychological pro-

18. See chap. 9, pp. 208-210 below for an analysis and further refs.

19. In his interesting if brief chapter on the *furores* in *Ficin et l'art,* pp. 129-135, Chastel fails to take account of the fact that the sequence of madnesses in the *De Divino Furore* is the reverse of that in the *Phaedrus* Commentary. In her *French Academies,* p. 82 n. 1, Yates states, rather misleadingly, that they both have the same sequence.

20. Chastel's chapter also includes a consideration of Ficino's letter to Pietro Dovizi da Bibbiena (*Opera,* p. 927) where Ficino writes that, whereas Lorenzo had been moved by the poetic and the amatory madnesses in his youth, he had been moved by the prophetic madness in his maturity, and by the hieratic in his later years. We would thus arrive at the ascending sequence: poetic and amatory, prophetic, hieratic. But I do not believe Ficino means us to take this as anything other than a compliment to Lorenzo. He had similarly praised him in the proem to the second version of his *Philebus* Commentary (ed. Allen, pp. 480-483) as a man who had gracefully avoided the horns of Paris's dilemma by admiring each of the three goddesses for her peculiar merits and thus winning the favors of all of them (cf. Kristeller, *Philosophy,* p. 358; and Wind, *Pagan Mysteries,* pp. 82, 197-198). In any event, the epistolary context here prevents us from taking it as a serious presentation of Ficino's views on the madnesses and their sequence; in equally relaxed circumstances he felt free to modify or invert traditional *topoi* and traditional mythological relationships, e.g. his letter to Naldi (*Opera,* p. 830). It certainly cannot be accorded the status that it receives in Chastel's analysis.

cess enacted in an individual as he rises through the various stages of inner ascent to personal union with the divine. By the latter, I take it, he is referring to the historical sequence in which the madnesses were mysteriously revealed to mankind through the course of time—the prophetic being granted first, and then, successively, the hieratic, the poetic, and finally the amatory. The amatory is the last revealed because divine Beauty is its goal and, as chapter 9 of the Commentary will make clear, "beauty is the last to proceed, as it were, in any god." But for that very reason "it is the first," the chapter continues, "to confront those ascending to that god" and is therefore, ultimately, "the most accessible" of the divine attributes. But to love God is the highest act possible for Ficino. Thus the amatory madness comes to occupy a paradoxical position: from one viewpoint it is the most accessible of the madnesses, being the desire for God's most accessible attribute; but from another it is the supreme, and therefore in a way the least accessible, madness, being the highest act open to man and indeed to angel. Interestingly, the individual's psychological progress through the madnesses does not reenact the race's historical progress: we do not commence with the prophetic, then move on to the hieratic, and thence to the poetic and the amatory.[21] For, once revealed, the amatory became the sovereign madness and wholly subsumed the other three: we recall the *Symposium*'s depiction of Love as both the youngest and the oldest of the gods. Thus Plato's mystery could be interpreted as adumbrating the central mystery of Christianity, the coming of the reign of love to supersede the reigns of nature and of law.[22]

In both the *Symposium*'s and the *Phaedrus*'s schemes the role of poetry was clearly subordinate. In terms of a person's ascent it

21. The race's progress could, of course, be viewed pessimistically: in the golden age we had need of prophecy alone; in the silver, of the hieratic art as a prelude to prophecy; in the bronze age, of poetry as a prelude to both; and in the iron age, of the amatory madness in addition to the other three. Such a view would dovetail neatly into Ovid's great myth and its analogues; but I cannot discover that Ficino ever entertained it, and it would be difficult to reconcile with Plato's insistence, in both the *Symposium* and the *Phaedrus*, on the supremacy of the amatory madness.

22. The supreme "Platonic" analysis of divine love for Ficino was to be found in the works of the Pseudo-Areopagite, as a letter to Orlandini (*Opera*, pp. 1425-1426) and his own commentaries (*Opera*, pp. 1013-1128) testify; see Michele Schiavone, *Problemi filosofici in Marsilio Ficino* (Milan, 1957), pp. 170-172.

marked the beginning stage only. In terms of mankind's acquisition of the various paths to mystical knowledge of the divine it came third after prophecy and priestcraft, and remained subordinate to them until the three together were eventually exceeded by love. Even so, it remained a factor in the other madnesses, being their medium of discourse and an integral aspect of their gradual unification of man, within himself and to the divine. Thus the *prisci theologi* were *prisci poetae* too:[23] they learned to embody the essence of their prophetic and hieratic visions, and eventually of their amatory visions also, in the language of poetry. Once the medium of divine poetry had been granted to man as the third madness, in a way all *theologi* became poets first and prophets, priests, and lovers subsequently.

Further complications ensue upon Ficino's decision to dovetail the *Phaedrus*'s sequence of madnesses into the hierarchy of major, or what he had referred to elsewhere as "knowing," faculties:[24] the intellect, the will,[25] hearing, and sight. His presentation of the hierarchical relationships between the first two faculties varies in the course of his career. Having commenced by arguing for the primacy of the intellect, he then espoused for a long period, perhaps as long as twenty years, the primacy of the will, though of will always conceived of as being in some form of close connection with, if not identical at times with, love. Ultimately he reverted, at least in part, to his earlier position under the impact, one assumes, of his close study of Plotinus during the 1490s.[26]

23. For an account of the *prisci theologi* and their theology, see Walker, *Ancient Theology,* especially pp. 1-131; also Charles B. Schmitt, "Perennial Philosophy: From Agostino Steuco to Leibniz," *Journal of the History of Ideas* 27 (1966), 505-532, especially pp. 507-511 with a full bibliography.

24. *De Amore* 2.2 (ed. Marcel, p. 147); cf. the *Philebus* Commentary 1.6 (ed. Allen, pp. 111, 539 n. 26, as emended in the 1979 reprint) and *Hippias* epitome (*Opera,* p. 1271).

25. Kristeller, *Philosophy,* pp. 257-258, argues that, technically speaking, the will is not a faculty, "an independent part of the Soul," but should be thought of rather as "the rational appetite or that part of the appetitive power which corresponds to the intellect." For this reason the *De Amore* 2.2 (see n. 24 above) had not included it in its list. Nevertheless, from the viewpoint of the argumentation here in the *Phaedrus* Commentary it is convenient to refer to it as a faculty.

26. For studies of Ficino's views on the intellect/will problem, see: Marian Heitzman, "La libertà e il fato," especially pp. 69-74; and Paul Oskar Kristeller, *Le thomisme et la pensée italienne de la Renaissance* (Montreal, 1967), pp. 106-125 (which resumes and enlarges on Kristeller's earlier analyses in his *Philosophy,* pp. 269-276, and in his "A Thomist Critique of Marsilio Ficino's Theory of Will and Intellect," *Harry Austryn Wolfson Jubilee Volume, English Section,* vol. 2 [Jerusalem, 1965], pp. 463-494); Sears Jayne, *John*

Notwithstanding these oscillations, and notwithstanding numerous theoretical and interpretational problems, it is clear that, whether inclining towards intellectualism or towards voluntarism in his own philosophical commitment, he never supposed that Plato had been anything else but an intellectualist, even in the *Symposium.* [27] Thus, in associating prophecy with the intellect and the hieratic art with the will, he makes a distinction that comes into proper focus only if later Christian conceptions of the priest and of the will are brought to bear. [28] Hence in claiming that the ancient poets were "admonished" by the prophets and the priests to worship the gods by way of celebration, prayer, intercession, and thanksgiving, he does not specify which admonition came from whom to which faculty. He merely observes that together the two guided and prepared the poets, presumably by way of their prophetic and hieratic madnesses as well as by rational and doctrinal instruction and advice. What they transmitted to the poets indeed was the pristine wisdom which God had given man both by way of special revelation to Moses and the Hebrew prophets and by way of general or natural revelation to the sages of other nations, Plato being the heir to both. [29]

In the process of linking love to sight and poetry to hearing, Ficino intends, as summa 35 makes clear, to subordinate sight to hearing. [30] Though this runs directly counter to the usual, and certainly the usually Platonic, subordination of hearing to sight, and

Colet and Marsilio Ficino (Oxford, 1963), pp. 56-76; and Allen, *Philebus Commentary,* pp. 35-48. Whereas Heitzman and Kristeller concentrate on texts where Ficino stresses the primacy of the will, Jayne and Allen do the reverse; all four scholars acknowledge Ficino's oscillations. See also n. 28 below.

27. See Schiavone, *Problemi filosofici,* pp. 135-145, and Allen, *Philebus Commentary,* pp. 43-45. For Landino's presentation of a debate between Ficino and others over the intellect and the will in book 2 of his *Disputationes Camaldulenses* scholars can now consult the austere edition by Peter Lohe (Florence, 1980).

28. For an analysis of Ficino's utilization of the Christian, i.e. the Augustinian, concept of the will, see Kristeller, *Philosophy,* pp. 256-288, esp. 257, and *Thomisme,* pp. 106-111. Cf. n. 26 above, and chap. 4, n. 8 below.

29. Ficino seems to have been especially intrigued by the notion that Plato was Moses "speaking Attic Greek"; see e.g. his *De Religione Christiana* 26 (*Opera,* p. 29), his *Concordia Mosis et Platonis* (*Opera,* p. 866.3), and his *Platonic Theology* 17.4 (ed. Marcel, 3:169). The sources were Numenius *apud* Clement of Alexandria, *Stromateis* 1.22, and Eusebius, *Praep. Evan.* 9.6.411A.

30. Several of his Venetian followers, including Bembo and Betussi, also upheld the primacy of the ear or at least the equality of the two senses; see Panofsky, *Renaissance and Renascences,* p. 185n, and *Studies in Iconology,* p. 148 n. 69, with further refs.

though it would seem to argue for love's subordination to poetry, it is less remarkable than it might first appear for the following reasons.

To begin with, Ficino is obviously not concerned with ordinary auditory sensa; for in the ordinary realm of perception sight was usually assigned the primacy precisely because, in summa 35's words, "we seem to see more than we hear in one act." Rather, he is concerned with a Socrates governed by his warning voice[31]—that is, in summa 11's terms, with a sage who is "most eager of all for instruction and dedicated, as it were, to the hearing," and whose present exposition treats of the medium of that instruction, the music and words of *carmen,* of poetic utterance.

Professor D. P. Walker has already explored the peculiar intensity of music's effect upon us. Of Ficino's argument in a letter to Canigiani[32] he observes that the Florentine "considered that visual impressions had a less powerful effect on the spirit than auditive ones."[33] The spirit is the key, for, being the junction or knot binding body to soul, it is precisely what is struck by sound or song. Aerial itself,[34] it is affected by air, and particularly by the air which song and sound, the letter says, "have broken up and tempered." Therefore musical sound, Walker concludes, being by its very nature akin to the human spirit, "seizes, and claims as its own, man in his entirety"; for it can move the spirit in a way impossible for visual images.[35] As his authorities here Ficino could turn to the *Timaeus* 67A and to the [Pseudo-]Aristotelian *Problemata* 30.27 and 29, where there is a discussion of music's importance in effecting emotional and moral change and in exciting in us various kinds of ethical response. In thus emphasizing the mobile nature of sound over and against the static nature of vision, Walker draws our attention to the uniqueness of hearing for Ficino, even as he recognizes Ficino's habitual acknowledgment of

---

31. See chap. 1, pp. 21-22, 25 above.
32. *Opera,* pp. 650-651, trans. in *Letters* 1:141-144. The letter is entitled *De Musica.*
33. *Magic,* p. 7.
34. And not in this instance fiery or aethereal; see ibid., p. 8.
35. Ibid., p. 9, quoting *Opera,* p. 1453, i.e. Ficino's commentary on the *Timaeus,* chap. 28 [*Concentus*] *per naturam, tam spiritalem quam materialem, totum simul rapit et sibi vindicat hominem.*

the supremacy of sight: indeed, "it is precisely because hearing is not the highest, most intellectual sense that it affects more strongly the whole of man."[36]

The highest music was, of course, the music of the spheres, which Pythagoras, according to summa 35, had actually heard (we must therefore suppose that other *prisci theologi* had heard it too). This is not the occasion to explore the history of this fascinating topic, nor even to trace the extent of Ficino's debt to its chief begetter for the Middle Ages and the Renaissance, Macrobius.[37] To hear the music of the spheres was to hear the harmonies of the *spiritus mundi,* the subtle aether that linked the World-Soul to the World-Body, the *anima mundi* to the *machina mundi.*[38] Such music could only be heard, however, by the inner ear, the ear in an ecstasy of auditory trance or rapture. The music we hear with the ordinary ear is merely an image of this supreme music. In this regard Kristeller has cited the *De Divino Furore:* "Through the ears the Soul perceives certain sweet harmonies and rhythms, and through these images it is exhorted and excited to consider the divine music with a more ardent and intimate sense of the mind."[39] Heard so intensely, such music can be heard no more except by the inner ear of the intelligence.

But ordinary music can similarly appeal to the intelligence when it accompanies a text: while the music works on the spirit, the words will reach beyond the *spiritus* to the *mens.*[40] But such *carmen* is exactly what Ficino is examining. We know from his Orphic lyre recitals that his own conception of a poem was essentially musical: he would chant or intone its words and then rise at

36. *Magic,* p. 7, citing also Ficino's *De Amore* 5.2 (ed. Marcel, pp. 179-182).

37. See chap. 1, n. 69 above. Ficino mentions Macrobius in his *Opera,* pp. 13, 35, 490, 740, 852, 899, 970, 1591 ff.

38. Yates, *Bruno,* pp. 68-69. The concept derived its authority, predictably, from Vergil's *Aeneid* 6.726. Walker, *Magic,* pp. 16-18, notes that whereas the benign planets have their particular kind of music, the malign planets—Saturn, Mars, and the Moon—only have "voices"; his source is Ficino's *De Vita* 3.21 (*Opera,* p. 563).

39. *Philosophy,* p. 308, citing *Opera,* p. 614, and comparing *Sup. Fic.* 1:54 ff.

40. Kristeller, *Philosophy,* p. 308: "But poetry is superior to music, since through the words it speaks not only to the ear but also directly to the mind"; Walker, *Magic,* pp. 9-10: "Hearing... powerfully affects the whole of us—the musical sound by working on the spirit, which links body and soul, and the text by working on the mind or intellect"; also pp. 21 and 26.

the climax to rapturous incantation, achieving an effect approximate to that of a religious rite.[41] The accompanying music was based, as we would expect, on what Ficino and his contemporaries believed to be Pythagorean—and therefore, given Plato's tutelage at the feet of various Pythagoreans, Platonic—principles of harmony. But the text too, in that it utilized the quantitative meters Ficino was familiar with in Greek and Latin poetry, also embodied Pythagorean-Platonic principles. True *carmen* united word to number, language to music, and both to mathematics. Accordingly, the highest *carmina* would approach the condition of the music of the spheres in that they wedded music, meter, and song to produce harmonies that pierced through the outward ear to strike upon the intellectual ear, the ear of the mind.[42]

But we must take the argument a step further. In voicing a text, the poet conjures up meanings and thoughts, denotations and connotations, that appeal directly first to the discursive reason and then at a sublimer level to the intuitive intelligence. I believe Kristeller and Walker are therefore correct to stress the superiority of the poet-musician to the mere musician. For he belongs with the prophets and the priests, men who have access to the Word and to the secret meanings of names.[43] Hence Pythagoras, we learn from summa 35, heard "the celestial concords" in the course of his life as a *philosopher.*[44] Even as he turned his gaze towards "celestials" —that is, looked up at the harmonious movements of the stars— he was "listening to [instruction] in the mental disciplines" and

41. Walker, *Magic,* p. 20: "Ficino's singing . . . was monodic, . . . expressive, effect-producing"; cf. p. 35.

42. Once one begins to use hearing figuratively—that is, as a way of talking about a mode of primarily intellectual comprehension—not only does the mutual relationship of hearing and seeing cease to be a real issue, but so does any distinction between them; for the intellectual ear and the intellectual eye are merely different ways of imaging the same thing. This figurative dimension may explain, or explain partially, Ficino's entertainment at different times of different theoretical positions with regard to the two senses. For the traditional distinction between sensible and intellectual sight, see Pico, *Commento* 2.9 (ed. Garin, pp. 497-498).

43. For a revealing passage on the power of particular names, see Ficino's *Philebus* Commentary 1.11, 12 (ed. Allen, pp. 134-145). For a Neoplatonist the ultimate authority on language, particularly the language of mythology, was of course the *Cratylus.* The is especially pertinent, given the prominence of mythological names and mythological epithets in the sacred poetry of antiquity, the very poetry with which Ficino is here concerned.

44. See Heninger, *Sweet Harmony,* p. 31; also chap. 1, n. 69 above.

concentrating upon "philosophical disputation." Ficino notes that while looking pertains to Urania, hearing pertains to Calliope. Calliope therefore must be the elder, for "listening seems older than looking in that in the end it teaches us things of greater antiquity (*antiquiora*) and more of them (*plura*)."[45] In sum, the inner ear of Pythagoras hears the music of the spheres precisely because it hears the voice of philosophy and learns and teaches according to its dictates. The line between the ear and the intellect has again blurred to the point of dissolution.

Hearing then is the province of the true, the Pythagorean-Platonic poet. The extent to which he can reenact the first stage of the Phaedran ascent, the journey up to the realm of the celestial gods by way of word and song and notably by hymning the gods' attributes and wondrous deeds, is the measure of his distance from the versifier whom Plato had condemned to the sixth life, the life which was inferior to the lives of athletic coaches, divinators, and men immersed in commerce and business. Having submitted to the instruction of prophets and of priests in preparation for the coming of the divine impulse, the poet is distinguished like them by his commitment to the life of purification, of prayer, and of intellection. As a *priscus theologus,* he is responsible with the prophet and the priest for the preservation and secret transmission of the *prisca theologia.*[46] Teaching through song, the divine poet teaches man through the outward and the inward ear to know God as the Good, but not yet to love Him as the Beautiful.

Even so, we should only subordinate sight to hearing if we are dealing on the one hand with the realm of ordinary sight,[47] and on the other with the highest kind of sound, with music allied with words as an image of the music of the spheres and as an instrument of knowledge. And this was precisely the situation that

45. See chap. 1, n. 70 above.
46. See Trinkaus, *Image and Likeness* 2:683-721, especially 712-721 on Landino (who, I believe, was more profoundly indebted to Ficino than Trinkaus suggests).
47. The *locus classicus* for the supremacy of ordinary sight over ordinary hearing is Horace's *Ars Poetica* 1.180-181: *segnius irritant animos demissa per aurem / quam quae sunt oculis subiecta fidelibus.* See Gombrich, *Symbolic Images,* pp. 144 and 208 n. 52. More pertinent for Ficino would have been Plato's comments on visual and aural perception in the *Timaeus* 45B ff., 47A-D and 67A ff.

existed prior to the revelation of the mystery of love, the mystery of the desire for the beautiful. But this desire, and therefore the amatory madness, is "usually" excited through the sight, writes Ficino, and we "naturally use" the sight "after" hearing, meaning by this, I take it, simply that the infant hears before it sees, but implying too that as individuals we learn to know before we learn to love. But mankind similarly learned to use its hearing before its sight—use the sight, that is, as a spiritual instrument. First it learned to approach the gods and the divine mysteries through the other "knowing" faculties: the intellect, the will, and hearing, and thus through prophecy, the hieratic art, and poetry. But it could use sight as a spiritual instrument only after it had learned how to use it in order to perceive, not ordinary visual sensa, but the beautiful and Beauty itself—use it, in other words, to ascend the ladder from sensible to moral to intellectual to intelligible beauty. Men could not master this art, however, until Socrates had revealed to them the secrets taught him by the Sibyl Diotima of Mantinea:[48] only when they had been instructed by him in the "discipline" of using their sight were they enabled to ascend from the beautiful in things to Beauty itself. Accordingly, writes Ficino, men learned to know God as the Beautiful, having already known Him as the Good. Whereas the intellect, the will, and hearing had given them the sublime knowledge of God's Goodness, it was sight that eventually granted them the special knowledge of His Beauty. Having already cherished (*dilectare*) Him, therefore, as the Good—cherishing being the response to the joy that knowledge of God's Goodness brings—men were henceforth endowed with the gift of loving (*amare*) Him as the Beautiful. For to love Beauty is to be filled with the desire, in accordance with the *Symposium*'s argumentation at 206E-207A, to attain Beauty and to be united with it, not just to know it: to be united with God in his Beauty, therefore, and not just to know Him in His Goodness.[49]

The acquisition of sight as a spiritual instrument that men could use to perceive the ultimate beauty of God's splendor brought with

---

48. *Symposium* 201D ff.; see also Ficino's *De Amore* 6.1, and his proem to the vernacular version (ed. Marcel, pp. 199-200 and 267). Ficino refers to Diotima as a "sibyl" in his *Philebus* Commentary 1.5 (ed. Allen, pp. 108-109).

49. See Kristeller, *Philosophy,* pp. 264 and 268-269.

it a new awareness of Beauty itself as one of God's highest but most accessible manifestations. Thenceforth the intellect, the will, and hearing, instruments already utilized to know God in His Goodness, were capable of also perceiving His Beauty, having been taught, as it were, by the sight. Accordingly they learned to love as well as to cherish. Thus, from being the least of the "knowing" faculties in the sense that it was the last to be utilized spiritually by mankind, sight became the teacher of its elders; and they became its pupils in mastering the mysteries of beauty and of love. Hence the appropriateness of Ficino's noting that the amatory madness is "usually" excited through the sight; usually, but not invariably or necessarily. For, having been apprenticed to the sight, the other faculties could now perceive and love beauty—that is, could now hear, will, and know the beautiful in all its manifestations as the image of God's splendor, of the Divine Beauty itself.[50]

At this juncture the sight clearly has ceased to be the lowest of the faculties and has become identical with the very highest act of the intellect, the intuitive and unitive vision of the Ideas. Literal sight has been transmuted into the intenser, the ideal seeing of figurative sight, the purest understanding of the mind's eye as it gazes on absolute beauty and concomitantly on absolute truth. From being subordinate to hearing, seeing has become the supremely intellectual act, the act of the unitary man in love with the Divine Being.[51] Thus it is altogether appropriate that the climax of the *Phaedrus*'s mythical hymn should depict a journey upwards to a point where the charioteers can *see* absolute Beauty in the supercelestial place far above them. It is a purely Uranian vision, one that we can no longer associate with Calliope, the Muse of hearing. Such a vision, in its transformation of the acts of hearing, willing, and knowing, is the object of all four of the divine madnesses, but preeminently of the madness of love, since Beauty and not Goodness or Justice or Temperance is its goal. To this, the

50. See chap. 8 below.
51. Hence Plato's constant recourse to the metaphors of sight and of light when speaking of the intellect and of intellectual understanding; indeed it is virtually impossible at times to disentangle the two. See n. 42 above.

youngest of the madnesses, the poetic madness becomes the least of handmaidens, an elder but decidedly an inferior. Nevertheless, Ficino feels that it deserves closer scrutiny, and in his third paragraph he turns to it again.

He had already attempted to graft the notion of *forming* on that of *rapture* or *seizure*. At 245A3-4 Socrates had briefly referred to the divine madness "seizing" the poet's soul and "stimulating it to rapt, passionate expression" (ἐγείρουσα καὶ ἐκβακχεύουσα κατά τε ᾠδὰς καὶ κατὰ τὴν ἄλλην ποίησιν), ἐγείρω meaning "to rouse," "waken," or "excite," and ἐκβακχεύω, "to incite to Bacchic frenzy." Traditionally such frenzy implied loss of individual, conscious control, the surrender of self to preternatural, demonic forces that could not be gainsaid and that used it as their docile medium. In stimulating the soul, they make it burst out in unfamiliar ways, respond "passionately" but uncharacteristically, "raptly" as an expressive instrument.[52]

Ficino's first paragraph had introduced other factors, notably the notion that the soul also received "form" and "purpose" in addition to the act of terrifying violence. Whereas the Greek simply connotes a temporary, even momentary possession leaving its medium stunned or partially impaired, Ficino's reconstruction in terms of being "formed by God" or by the divine Forms connotes inspiration of a more permanent and constructive kind: it substitutes for the transiency of ancient rapture an experience closer to religious conversion. But his third paragraph commences with a view of the poet's inspiration seemingly based on Plato's own. The man granted any kind of "spiritual possession" overflows his own humanity, his own human capacities: "raves, exults, and exceeds the bounds of human behavior." The models Plato himself calls to mind are the ancient accounts of oracular possession. In recent years considerable controversy has raged as to what Plato thought this was, and indeed as to what actually went on at Dodona and Delphi (and this is quite apart from any irony Plato

---

52. Particularly insightful here are Tigerstedt's *"Furor Poeticus"* and his *Plato's Idea of Poetical Inspiration.*

may have intended by his references).[53] On occasions Ficino was drawn to the problem of oracles, and, following Plutarch,[54] he habitually discussed them, along with prophecy and poetry, in the context of *vacatio* and *alienatio*. His most detailed treatment occurs in the *Platonic Theology* 13.2, where he dwells on the different kinds of alienation that men experience, and also on the common factor of their being swept up by an ineluctable force so that they stand outside themselves in ecstasy, in the literal sense of "exceeding" the bounds of human limitation.[55]

We must be aware at this point, I think, of the impact on Ficino of Plato's account of Socrates' "distractions"[56] and of Porphyry's account of Plotinus's four ecstasies and mystical alienations, his flights of the alone to the alone.[57] These, not philosophizing in the currently conventional sense of analyzing and systematizing propositions, nor even Aristotelian contemplation, constituted Ficino's notion of the Platonic goal—a goal he could parallel to St. Paul's

53. Some of the chief contributions have been: Pierre Amandry, *La mantique apollinienne à Delphes* (Paris, 1950; reprint, New York, 1975); Marie Delcourt, *L'oracle de Delphes* (Paris, 1955); H. W. Parke and D. E. W. Wormell, *The Delphic Oracle*, 2 vols. (Oxford, 1956); Robert Flacelière, *Devins et oracles grecs* (Paris, 1961); Wolfgang Fauth, "Pythia," in Pauly-Wissowa-Kroll, *Realencyclopädie der classischen Altertumswissenschaft* 24.1 (1963), 515-547 (531 ff. has a summary of previous views); and H. W. Parke, *The Oracles of Zeus: Dodona, Olympia, Ammon* (Oxford, 1967); idem, *Greek Oracles* (London, 1967).

54. The critical works are, of course, the *De Defectu Oraculorum* (*Moralia* 409E-438E) and the *De E apud Delphos* (*Moralia* 384D-394C). For a detailed study of Plutarch's views on oracles and related demonological matters see Guy Soury, *La démonologie de Plutarque* (Paris, 1942).

55. Ed. Marcel, 2:201-222, but especially 214-222, a section entitled *Septem Vacationis Genera;* cf. *De Amore* 7.3 (ed. Marcel, pp. 245-246). See Kristeller, *Philosophy,* pp. 216-217; and Chastel, *Ficin et l'art,* p. 44.

Chastel points out that *vacatio mentis* is not the same as *furor* and that it occurs, according to Ficino, in seven states: during sleep (as with Orpheus), during syncope (as with Hercules), during melancholy (as with Socrates), during temperamental equilibrium (as with Plotinus), during solitude (as with Zoroaster), during wonder or admiration (as with the Corybantes and with the priests of the Pythia at Delphi and of the Sibyl at Dodona), and as the result of "the chastity of a mind devoted to God" (as with Orpheus again, but also with St. John on Patmos, with Ezekiel in the valley of dry bones, and with Isaiah). Nevertheless, *vacatio,* like the notion of the ignorance of a poet, is a state of mind very closely related to *furor,* as Yates points out in her *French Academies,* pp. 128-129.

56. Particularly in the *Symposium* 175A-C; cf. Ficino's *Platonic Theology* 13.2 (ed. Marcel, 2:219-220).

57. *Vita Plotini* 23. Ficino's translation of this section can be found in his *Opera,* p. 1546. Also influential were Iamblichus's and Porphyry's lives of Pythagoras and Marinus's life of Proclus.

flight to the third heaven as described in 2 Cor. 12:2-4 (upon which he had written in 1476 a detailed commentary).[58] For the Pauline and Plotinian flights, and possibly subsequent mystical ecstasies in the medieval tradition (though Ficino never explicitly adverts to these), were at the heart of what he deemed the Platonic, and ultimately perhaps the Mosaic, vision, either of the Ideas or of the One and the Good ineffably beyond them. Whether Ficino experienced such mystical flights himself is difficult to ascertain, but he certainly believed in the absoluteness of their reality and in the possibility of a few men truly attaining them during this life for however brief a time. He customarily sought and, according to eyewitness accounts, effectively achieved trancelike, enraptured states during his Orphic lyre recitals when he intoned Platonic hymns apparently to the Sun;[59] contemporaries even viewed him as another Orpheus.[60] Ferrucci attempted, not altogether unsuccessfully, to capture the Ficinian rapture in the marble bust which now adorns the fourth bay of the south aisle of Santa Maria del Fiore.[61] Leaving the lyre recitals aside, however, it is understandable that the Florentine, given his adulation of Plato, should automatically assume the master had also experienced mystical ecstasies and so intimated in the dialogues. The *Phaedrus* was an obvious candidate with its enchanted setting and its central drama of being caught up in the train of a god and whirled upon the circuits of the pure intelligences.

In addition to the violence that is intrinsic to Plato's conception

58. *Opera,* pp. 697.2-706. The commentary took the form of a treatise addressed to Giovanni Cavalcanti in 1476 which Ficino entitled *De Raptu Pauli ad Tertium Coelum.* See Kristeller, *Sup. Fic.* 1:xcv; also Walter Dress, *Die Mystik des Marsilio Ficino* (Berlin and Leipzig, 1929), pp. 189 ff.

59. Walker, *Magic,* pp. 19, 23-24. Particularly memorable for the Italian humanists, though controversial, was the Emperor Julian's "Hymn to the Sun"; see Yates, *Bruno,* pp. 59, 63, 82, 153.

60. For example, Poliziano (*Opera Omnia* [Basel, 1553], p. 310; cf. Kristeller, *Sup. Fic.* 2:281), Lorenzo (*L'altercazione,* chap. 2: "Pensai che Orfeo al mondo ritornasse"), Pannonius (in Ficino's *Opera,* p. 871.2), and Naldi (in a poem published by Kristeller, *Sup. Fic.* 2:262-263). See della Torre, *Accademia Platonica,* pp. 589, 790; Kristeller, *Philosophy,* p. 22; idem, *Studies,* pp. 52-53; Chastel, *Ficin et l'art,* pp. 48, 175-176; idem, *Arte e umanesimo,* pp. 276 ff.; Walker, *Magic,* pp. 19-24.

61. For a description and an account of its commission, see Marcel, *Marsile Ficin,* pp. 580-582; also Chastel, *Ficin et l'art,* p. 48. A photographic reproduction appears as the frontispiece to the first volume of *Letters.*

of oracular possession, and as a logical consequence of the Neo-platonic notion of the soul's abandonment of *alien* forms in ecstasy, of its emptying itself of all that is foreign and corporeal, Ficino suggests by his phrasing in terms of being "formed by God" that divine madness also involves the recovery of "pure" forms. Though they may appear at first to be imposed from above, they are in fact uncovered within. For the sense of violence is ultimately illusory, and to yield to one's god is to rediscover one's internal, more authentic forms, to be converted to one's own divinity. Thus Apollo and Dionysus are not so much external spiritual forces as forces in our selves, enrapturing, liberating, and forming the self in its proper image after its lapse into the constricting limitations of alien forms.[62] The impersonality that we mistakenly ascribe to the numinous rapture is the product of our inadequate conception of our own personhood: it is the return in reality to our divine, excessive, ecstatic selves, purely and wholly formed in the image of God. This return is the experience of release from the forgetfulness of our antenatal condition induced by Lethe's waters, of remembering who we are and whence we came. Thus Ficino could harmonize the Platonic theories of anamnesis and of the Ideas with the experience of Neoplatonic ecstasy, and simultaneously reconcile them with Christian conceptions of the soul's return to its Maker. The result is syncretistic but not unsatisfactory and marks, I believe, an important new stage in the history of ecstatics.

Having described the general nature of divine madness, Ficino turns to deal with a specific aspect, again not in Plato, the recourse of all "madmen" to "heightened" utterance. "No madman," he writes, "is content with simple speech. He bursts forth into clamoring, songs, and poems (*in clamorem prorumpit et cantus et carmina*)."[63] In the preliminary moments of rapture any subject of

---

62. For an interesting Jungian approach to these matters, see Hillman, *Re-Visioning Psychology,* pp. 200-202, 210-211, 215; and James Hillman, "Plotinus, Ficino, and Vico as Precursors of Archetypal Psychology," in *Loose Ends: Primary Papers in Archetypal Psychology* (Irving, Texas, 1978), pp. 146-169 at 154-157. In the same vein, see Thomas Moore, *The Planets Within: Marsilio Ficino's Astrological Psychology* (Lewisburg, Pa., 1982).

63. See Yates, *French Academies,* p. 82; she renders *carmina* as "odes": "Therefore any *furor,* whether of prophecy, of religious mysteries, or of love, when it utters itself in songs

divine madness may indeed resemble the Delphic Pythia or the Dodonan Sibyl or Aeneas's Cumaean Sibyl writhing under the goad of Apollo; but the subsequent "release"[64] in the heightened utterance of poetry and song transforms the ecstatic subject, however partially or momentarily, into a poet. For all the divine madnesses, Ficino says, have recourse for their articulation to the poetic madness, since its poetry and song, its poetic song, "demand concord and harmony" (*exigit concentus harmonicos*). By this he means both metrical and musical organization, the observation and incorporation of Pythagorean mathematics and harmonies, and above all the structures of "well-composed" as opposed to ordinary "simple" speech[65]—the rhetoric, that is, of formal poetry with its deliberated figures and its measured cadences. In mythological terms Ficino claims then that every soul, when inspired by Apollo, Dionysus, or Venus, is also necessarily inspired by the Muses, of whom the three deities are perpetual companions and guardians. Given a unified theory of divine ecstasy and a synchronic rather than a diachronic approach, the divine poet, like the divine prophet, priest, or lover, is not so much a separate person as one of the manifestations or roles of any ancient theologian, one of the four faces of any *priscus theologus*. Accordingly, he too is a type of the charioteer,[66] struggling to im-

---

and odes, may be described as *poeticus furor.*" Walker, *Magic,* p. 21, translates it first as "songs" and then as "poetry." We should recall that Ficino defined *cantus* in his *De Vita* 3.21 (*Opera,* p. 563) as "almost nothing other than another spirit"; see chap. 1, p. 26 and nn. 59 and 60 above.

64. Ficino's Latin reads: *merito in furorem poeticum videtur absolvi.* Yates, *French Academies,* p. 82, misses the force of *absolvi videtur* altogether by rendering it as "may be described"; and the whole point of Ficino's argument, I believe, runs counter to the implications of Walker's translation, "any *furor . . .* since it leads to singing and poetry, can rightly be said to find its completion in the poetic *furor*" (*Magic,* p. 21). My own rendering, "justly seems to be released as poetic madness," emphasizes the more literal meaning of *absolvi.*

65. To gloss Ficino's reference here to *simplici sermone,* which Walker has rendered as "with ordinary speech" (*Magic,* p. 21), we must turn to his summa 48 (ed. Allen, *Charioteer,* 208-209; cf. p. 249 n. 96): *preterea compositis laudibus celebrare deos* ("we should celebrate the gods with praises that are well composed"). Interestingly, Walker subsequently refers us to a remark by Plotinus in his *Enneads* 4.4.38 to the effect that we can capture planetary influences by "prayers, either simple or sung with art" (οἷον εὐχαῖς ἢ ἁπλαῖς ἢ τέχνῃ ᾀδομέναις).

66. We should bear in mind that Ficino knew Parmenides' *Poema* with its presentation of the poet himself as a charioteer; and Leonardo Tarán has noted that by late antiquity it had become customary to read the *Poema*'s introduction in the light of the *Phaedrus*'s charioteer myth (*Parmenides: A Text with Translation, Commentary and Critical Essays* [Princeton, 1965], p. 18, citing Hermias, p. 122.19 ff.). See Allen, *Charioteer,* pp. 3, 29 n. 6.

pose the harmony of word and number on unruly steeds and using the poem as a word-chariot to ascend to apotheosis and to the vision of Beauty. This image of the poet as a charioteer is particularly striking in light of Ficino's belief in the priority and poeticalness of the *Phaedrus* itself.

The final paragraph serves as a transition. Ficino clearly intended to ignore the superficial paradoxes generated by Lysias's speech and by Socrates' first speech, for he has nothing to say on the passage at 245BC where Socrates tied them into his account of the divine madnesses. Instead, he prepared us for Plato's upcoming syllogisms at 245C-E by arguing that we cannot comprehend the role of love and beauty until we understand the soul's "condition" as an immortal being; and he warns us, by implication, to remember that Plato's myth treats of rational souls alone, divine and human. The issue of the soul's immortality bears not so much on its life after death as on its life before brith; for then it had the vision of absolute Beauty which now enables it to use sensible beauty "mysteriously" as a way of recalling its home and true divinity, and returning via this recollection to its native blessedness. In other words, past immortality is the condition for anamnesis which alone authenticates the mental processes of abstracting and idealizing from sensible beauty.

In praising the unique power of love (activated in us by the perception and recollection of beauty) to "restore" us to our homeland and to "unite" us with God, Ficino refers explicitly to St. Paul's celebrated passage in 1 Cor. 13:1-13 on God's greatest gift to man, charity ($\dot{\alpha}\gamma\dot{\alpha}\pi\eta$).[67] In so doing he seems to anticipate interpreting the *Phaedrus* in a more avowedly Christian manner than in fact he did—a manner which would not only stress the agapic dimensions of Socrates' elevation of the love madness over the others but also argue for Jove, the universal charioteer, as a type for Christ.[68] The *Platonic Theology* 18.8 had already identified the

67. Citing Ficino's letter to Filippo Controni (*Opera*, p. 632.2, trans. in *Letters* 1:92), Panofsky claims that Ficino "could not see any essential difference between the Platonic $\check{\epsilon}\rho\omega\varsigma$ and the Christian *caritas*" (*Studies in Iconology*, p. 140). For some finer distinctions, see Kristeller, *Philosophy*, pp. 263-269, and James A. Devereux, "The Object of Love in Ficino's Philosophy," *Journal of the History of Ideas* 30.2 (1969), 161-170.

68. The equation of Jove (if not specifically of the *Phaedrus*'s Jove) with God or the Son of God was to become a Renaissance commonplace. Particularly noteworthy, since it is contemporaneous with Ficino's final work on the *Phaedrus*, is a passage in Bartolommeo

Phaedrus's supermundane gods as the angels,[69] and the Phaedran fall through nine degrees is here explicitly compared to the Mosaic account.

Since Ficino's life's work was founded on his professional commitment to rational apology,[70] and to harmonizing Platonism with Christianity and asserting its religious and intellectual orthodoxy,[71] these parallels between the *Phaedrus* and certain Christian ideas and images—however farfetched they may first appear—should not be underestimated, and particularly in light of Ficino's own pointed advice at the conclusion of the Commentary's second chapter that we should interpret much of the dialogue, and notably the mythical hymn, just as we would the Canticle of Canticles, Solomon's mythical hymn to the vision of the bridegroom's absolute beauty and the ardent love it inspires in the bride, the human soul, collectively conceived of as the Church.[72]

---

della Fonte's *Poetics* of 1491: "besides Him, whose son the Gentiles call Jove, and we call Christ" (*praeter hunc autem cuius filium Iovem gentiles dicunt, nos Christum*) (ed. Charles Trinkaus in "The Unknown Quattrocento Poetics of Bartolommeo della Fonte," *Studies in the Renaissance* 13 [1966], 40-122 at 104; he also cites it in his *Image and Likeness*, p. 725). Ficino's own epitome for the *Ion* (*Opera*, p. 1283) equates Jove with the *mens Dei*. See also Seznec's *Survival of the Pagan Gods*, pp. 99n, 199-200, etc.

69. Ed. Marcel, 3:204: *cum diis supercaelestibus, id est angelis*; see chap. 1, n. 21 above.

70. Raymond Marcel, "L'apologétique de Marsile Ficin," in *Pensée humaniste et tradition chrétienne aux XVe et XVIe siècles* (Paris, 1950), pp. 159-168.

71. This went far beyond Augustine's assessment of Platonism as a propaedeutic, as a philosophy that had merely prepared him for the acceptance of Christianity. Rather, Ficino looked to the Areopagite and what seemed to him to be the perfect harmony of Christianity and Platonism. A comprehensive study of Ficino's indebtedness to the Areopagite, whom Ficino finished translating in 1492, has not yet been undertaken; but see Schiavone's various comments in his *Problemi filosofici*, pp. 65-67, 170-172, 193-194, 202-205, etc.

For Ficino's relationship to Augustine, see Kristeller, "Augustine and the Early Renaissance," now in *Studies*, pp. 355-372; and two recent studies by Alessandra Tarabochia Canavero, "Agostino e Tommaso nel Commento di Marsilio Ficino all'*Epistola ai Romani*," *Rivista di filosofia neo-scolastica* 65 (1973), 815-824, and "S. Agostino nella *Teologia Platonica* di Marsilio Ficino," ibid. 70 (1978), 626-646.

72. See Allen, *Charioteer*, p. 43 n. 59, for suggestions as to further parallels Ficino may have seen between the *Phaedrus* and *Canticle*. In her article, "Platone, Ficino e la magia," in *Studia Humanitatis: Ernesto Grassi zum 70 Geburtstag*, ed. Eginhard Hora and Eckhard Kessler (Munich, 1973), pp. 121-142 at 127, Paola Zambelli notes that Ficino makes mention in a letter to Cosimo subsequent to 1459 of his friend Lorenzo, the priest from Pisa (*Opera*, p. 615.2; trans. in *Letters* 1:48-49; see Kristeller, *Sup. Fic.* 2:349). At that time Lorenzo, who lived from ca. 1391 to 1465, had written, says Ficino, eighteen volumes of a commentary on Solomon's Canticle. He obviously admired this work: "Although I usually dislike prolixity, it does not seem to me that the work is too long, since I find hardly anything of importance in theology that he has not included within it." Indeed, Ficino justifies the commentary's length on the grounds that "the more intricate the knot which Solomon tied, the more the devices necessary to unravel it." Cf. Pico, *Commento particolare* (ed. Garin, p. 535).

Far from being a digression, and despite its thematic connections with such self-contained tracts as the *Ion* introduction, the Agli letter, and the "alienation" section in the *Platonic Theology,* this opening chapter of commentary proper is thus an absolutely fitting prolegomenon for the other seven chapters. It takes up the primary question posed by the dialogue, the question of modality. By underscoring the *Phaedrus's* poeticalness, Ficino goes beyond the point merely of being aware of the poetic nature of Socrates' inspiration: he accepts the dialogue itself as a work of the same kind as the poetic masterpieces of the Bible, requiring the same range and subtlety of interpretative response.[73]

Summae 13 and 14 cover the same section of text as chapter 4 (though the latter deals in effect with only one paragraph, 243E-245C), and there are several further points of note.

First, Ficino provides us with his sense of Socrates' strategy so far. At the beginning both Socrates and Lysias had inveighed against *incontinent* love, which drags the soul down into the body. Then Socrates had "secretly" praised *continent* love, which converts the soul to moral and to intellectual beauty; presumably this refers to Socrates' first speech and concerns what Ficino elsewhere designates the peculiarly "human" love. Finally in the mythical hymn Socrates embarks on the praise of *divine* love, which restores the soul to intelligible or ideal beauty.[74] Clearly Ficino is

73. Of course, the source of the *prisca theologia* (which is so designated by Ficino himself in his *De Christiana Religione,* chap. 22 [*Opera,* p. 25]) was the *Old Testament,* as Pico makes a point of emphasizing in his proem to the *Heptaplus* (ed. Garin, pp. 170-173). Its perfection in Plato therefore required of his interpreters a Mosaic understanding. Hence Ficino's insistence that the *Platonici*—that is, the later [Neo]platonists—had "used the divine light" of such Christians as St. John the Evangelist, St. Paul, Hierotheus, and Dionysius the Areopagite in order to interpret Plato (*Opera,* pp. 25 and 925.2). See Walker, *Ancient Theology,* pp. 81, 85 ff.; also chap. 1, n. 54 above.

74. On the complicated subject of Ficino's theory of the three loves and the two (three) Venuses, see Kristeller, *Philosophy,* pp. 110-114; Panofsky, *Studies in Iconology,* pp. 142-145; idem, *Renaissance and Renascences,* pp. 198-199; Wind, *Pagan Mysteries,* pp. 138-140 and 148; and Michael J. B. Allen, "Cosmogony and Love: The Role of Phaedrus in Ficino's *Symposium* Commentary," *Journal of Medieval and Renaissance Studies* 10.2 (1980), 131-153 at 148. The critical passages in Ficino are in his *De Amore* 2.7 and 6.5, 7, 8 (ed. Marcel, pp. 153-155, 205, 208-212), and in his commentary on Plotinus's *Enneads* 1.6 and 3.5 (*Opera,* pp. 1573-1578, 1713-1717).

Here Ficino clearly has in mind *amor divinus, humanus,* and *ferinus* (the last being defined as an insanity rather than a *furor*). Pico seems to have entertained the same division in his *Commento* 2.7 and 3.2-4 (ed. Garin, pp. 493-494, 524-531). Wind's depreciation of

thinking of a straightforward three-part progression that is totally
explicable in light of the theory of the three kinds or manifestations of beauty and the madness it inspires in those chosen by the
gods to transcend human limitations and the Aristotelian virtues
of temperance and prudence. For divine madness or alienation, he
says, remedies the severest afflictions and produces the most bene-
ficial goods.

Ficino next turns to the workings and to the symbolism of
Dodona and Delphi. Both oracles function similarly: the gods
respectively use jovian and apollonian demons, who in turn "perhaps" use jovian and apollonian men and instruments to deliver
oracular messages to the oak-crowned priestess or Sibyl at Dodona
and to the prophetess, the Pythia, seated on her tripod at Delphi.[75]
This account is predicated on the theory, later adumbrated in the
mythical hymn, that particular demons, men, animals, objects,
and indeed places are assigned to particular gods—in this case
Jove and Apollo—and are therefore peculiarly disposed by nature,
temperament, and training to mediate the special characteristics of
these gods. On the other hand, Ficino carefully notes that the two
oracles are kin (*cognati*), Apollo being directly subordinate to
Jove in that his "illuminating" power "ministers to" and "accompanies" Jove's "creative" power, creative in that Jove is the
World-Soul and therefore the architect, orderer, and preserver of
all life (246B and E) from whom proceed the other gods with their
more restricted spheres of influence. Thus Ficino succeeds in linking Dodona with Delphi and in placing both under the apollonian
aegis, either directly under Apollo or under the apollonian aspect
of Jove. None of this is in the Plato text.

Further modifications and additions to the commentary chapter
are introduced by summa 14. Ficino begins by insisting on the
interdependence, if not the complete interchangeability, of the
four divine madnesses; but he does so now by using the dialectically paired values of Apollo and Bacchus.[76] To Apollo is still
attributed the "illuminating" power as in the equation above with

Ficino in this regard (*Pagan Mysteries,* p. 139 and n. 31) is unwarranted, and should be
modified in the light of Panofsky's analyses in his *Studies in Iconology,* pp. 142-145 (which
Wind does not refer to).

75. See Michael J. B. Allen, "The Sibyl in Ficino's Oaktree," *MLN* 95.1 (1980), 205-
210; also Chastel, *Arte e umanesimo,* pp. 242 ff.

76. See chap. 1, n. 72 above.

Jove; while to Bacchus is attributed the power that "incites" and "heats." Thus the former is joined to the latter "in the intelligible world" and accounts for the interdependence of the divine madnesses. Since, however, Apollo is in charge of prophecy and poetry, the pairing with Bacchus means that the latter is responsible for prayer (priestcraft) and for love. At this juncture Ficino introduces two other deities as coworkers with Apollo and Bacchus, namely Mercury and Venus, the first presiding, remarkably, over poetry,[77] the second over love. In other words, the primary deities in the scheme, Apollo and Bacchus, are each given a subordinate companion, even though all are in turn subordinate penultimately to Apollo and ultimately to Jove. Ficino is calling upon the mythological relationships to plot the history of the divine madnesses and their temporal procession: from Apollo (prophecy) came Bacchus (the hieratic art), thence Mercury (poetry), thence Venus (love).

Next, Ficino utilizes the deities as coordinates for plotting the relationship between the intellect and the will, the intellect being assigned prophecy and poetry, the will, prayer and love. But prophecy and prayer constitute the primary opposites with sacred poetry as their common medium of expression and love as their common goal. Divine poetry, that is, has a special status as mediator, and Ficino notes that Plato "prefers it to prophecy" even as he banishes profane poetry altogether.[78]

In conclusion Ficino again admonishes us to be aware, as we enter on the charioteer myth, of the range of its applicability. For it refers not only to fallen, human souls, but to divine souls too, the souls of the great gods—those of the world spheres and their planets—and of their followers: the angels, the higher demons, and the heroes, all of whom we know through their manifested works, just as we know our own soul's nature through its affections for either temporal or eternal things. This caveat is especially necessary since the Socratic proposition Plato considers in his next section had been open since antiquity to radically divergent and even conflicting interpretations.

---

77. Since hermeneutics was the key to a proper understanding of poetry, Mercury, the god of interpretation, was also properly a god of poetry; see chap. 1, pp. 35-40 above.

78. An obvious reference to the *Republic* 2.379A ff.; 3.398A; 8.568B; 10.595A ff., 605A, 607A; etc.; and to the *Laws* 2.656, 660A-662B; 4.719A; 7.817D; 8.829D; 11.936A; etc.

Chapter Three: Immortality Proofs

Ficino's fifth and sixth chapters form a self-contained unit, and, like the corresponding sections in the *Phaedrus,* they so stand apart in tone, structure, and content from the lateral material that, at first glance, the contrast is striking. On the other hand, many of Plato's similarly dialectical passages accompany others of a more figurative or poetic cast and form an integral commentary upon them.[1] Though Ficino often refers to these *Phaedrus* sections quite independently of their Phaedran context on the assumption that their arguments had their own validity and could be set beside, even integrated with, similar arguments from other works,[2] and though they obviously form one of the main subsidiary attractions of the dialogue for him, he nevertheless remained conscious of their special status as Phaedran "proofs."[3] In his *Phaedo* epitome, for instance, he notes that one particular argument for the soul's immortality is reserved for the *Phaedrus* alone, namely that the soul is the principle of motion and thus moves perpetually and hence lives perpetually; it is so reserved because the *Phaedrus* is

1. Dialectic might normally suggest dialogue, but this is not invariably the case; see Frutiger, *Mythes de Platon,* pp. 19-28, esp. 26: "A la vérité, les deux choses se tiennent d'assez près; mais en s'éloignant de leur origine elles tendent à se différencier."

2. In the opening sentence to chap. 5 Ficino draws our attention specifically to his *Platonic Theology.* He has in mind such passages as 1.4; 5.1; 6.11, 12; and 9.4, 5 (ed. Marcel, 1:56-58, 174-175, 249-259; 2:18-44).

3. At 245C4 Socrates had introduced this section with the words: "Here then our proof begins (ἀρχὴ δὲ ἀποδείξεως ἥδε)."
Note that Ficino would have been acquainted with three Latin renderings of this entire syllogistic passage (245C-246A): in Calcidius's *In Timaeum* 57 (ed. Waszink, pp. 104-105), where it appears apropos of the *Timaeus* 37A-C; in Cicero's *Tusculanae* 1.23.53-54; and in Cicero's *De Republica* 6.25.27-26.28 (that is, the end of the *Somnium Scipionis*). He also knew Macrobius's commentary on the latter, *In Somnium Scipionis* 2.13-16. The passage in question corresponds to chap. 15 in Ficino's Latin translation of the *Phaedrus* (ed. Allen, *Charioteer,* pp. 52-53), but the various renderings seem to be mutually independent. Ficino would also have been familiar with Proclus's analyses in *The Elements of Theology,* props. 14-20 (ed. and trans. Dodds, pp. 16-23; with commentary, pp. 201-208), since at one point he had translated the work (see Kristeller, *Sup. Fic.* 1:clxiv-clxv and 1—the translation has not, however, survived).

concerned with all rational souls, divine as well as human, whereas the *Phaedo* is concerned solely with human souls.[4] Similarly, while Ficino's two commentary chapters might seem to fit without much modification into the opening chapters for instance of the *Platonic Theology,* where he also presented proofs demarcating and defining the soul's nature, functions, and immortality, they are in fact integral to his *Phaedrus* Commentary and are specifically concerned with what he saw as the metaphysical issues at the heart of the great myth of the charioteer. Lemmata and commentary alike cannot be detached, in the final analysis, from their larger context.

Ficino reverses Plato's sequence of ideas, presumably on the same grounds as Hermias: to improve the logic.[5] Thus treatment of the $\psi\upsilon\chi\grave{\eta}$ $\pi\hat{\alpha}\sigma\alpha$ crux is reserved for chapter 6, while chapter 5 deals with the syllogisms derived from the theses that the soul is self-moving and that it is the principle of motion.[6] Ficino's view—a traditional one—is that if the soul is the first entity to be moved passively, it must therefore be the first entity to move actively, the two movements being one in self-motion. Consequently it must be the source, cause, or principle ($\grave{\alpha}\rho\chi\acute{\eta}$) of all subsequent motion. The argument is based on two considerations: one, the assumption that although God is the prime unmoved mover in the sense that all things ultimately depend on Him, motion itself takes place in time and can only begin with an entity operating in time, an entity inferior to both God and the angels (or intelligences), who dwell beyond time in eternity; and two, the Aristotelian assumption that motion ($\kappa\acute{\iota}\nu\eta\sigma\iota\varsigma$) comprises not only local motion, but all change, growth, decay, intensification and remission, qualitative as well as

---

4. *Opera,* p. 1390: "Unum hoc in primis admonebimus, ne quis admiretur Socratem inter argumentationes ad immortalitatem animae pertinentes, praetermisisse hic illam, qua sola confidit in Phaedro: animam scilicet esse principium motionis, unde sequatur eam per se perpetuoque moveri semperque vivere. Id enim ideo factum est a Socrate, quoniam eiusmodi ratio non solum nostris, sed coelestibus etiam atque daemonicis animis est communis. In Phaedone vero rationes nobis magis propriae requiruntur."

5. Hermias, pp. 102-120 (ed. Couvreur); cf. Michael J. B. Allen, "Two Commentaries on the *Phaedrus;* Ficino's Indebtedness to Hermias," *Journal of the Warburg and Courtauld Institutes* 43 (1980), 110-129 at 120.

6. Chastel, *Arte e umanesimo,* p. 314, draws our attention to the significance and the originality of Florentine Platonism's constant emphasis on the soul as the source of all motion: *anima fons motus.* For one thing it stimulated interest in the enactment and the depiction of dance, particularly of dionysiac dance.

quantitative alteration, being born and dying.[7] Ficino further
assumes that the soul's true motion consists in life.

At this point we might have expected him to refer to the final
argument in the *Phaedo,* which we now see as being based on the
thesis that the soul cannot die because it participates in the Form
of Life (105C-107A).[8] However, Ficino interpreted this passage
very differently as concerned not with an ideal Form of Life but
specifically with the soul as a substantial form or idea of corporeal
life—the soul being the principle, the idea, of life and not a participant in an Idea of Life higher than itself. Whether or not he was
misinterpreting Plato is a separate question, but he was certainly
being internally consistent, as we shall see. In short, he does not
seem to have entertained the notion of an Idea of Life at all, and
he interpreted the *Phaedo* passage accordingly.[9] It is made to agree

7. Ernst Cassirer, *The Individual and the Cosmos in Renaissance Philosophy,* trans.
Mario Domandi (New York and Evanston, Ill., 1963), p. 174: "for Aristotle, movement
becomes the true foundation for a partitioning of the world." For life as motion, see Aristotle's *Physics* 8.1.250b14-15.

8. As Hackforth notes (*Phaedrus,* p. 68), the *Phaedo*'s argument seems to be based on
the tautological proposition that "so long as the soul exists it is alive"; cf. Frutiger, *Mythes
de Platon,* p. 138 n. 1, and Wallis, *Neoplatonism,* pp. 128 ff.

9. In his epitome to the *Phaedo* (*Opera,* pp. 1390-1395, specifically p. 1393), however,
Ficino did take up the problem: "Demum rationem disponit immortalitatis ex eo quod rationalis anima corpori praestet vitam, non ut accidentalis forma inhaerens corpori, sed ut
substantialis in se ipsa permanens, ex se formaliter vivens, quasi quaedam vitae corporalis
idea, atque per se efficienter corpus vivificans. Ideoque concludit animam non posse susci-
pere mortem, cum mors vitae opposita sit, anima vero et vitam propriam habeat et maneat
in se ipsa." ("Finally he establishes the immortality proof on the basis that the rational soul
gives life to the body. The soul is not like an accidental form adhering to the body but like a
substantial form which remains constant in itself and formally exists from itself; it is an
idea, so to speak, of corporeal life and through itself effectively bestows life on the body.
He therefore concludes that the soul cannot sustain death, since death is the opposite to
life, but the soul possesses its own life and remains constant in itself.")
We can gather from this that Ficino viewed the *Phaedo*'s argumentation, not in terms of
the Idea of Life in which a soul can and must participate, but rather in terms of a form that
the soul already possesses and gives to the body. That is, he is interpreting the passage very
differently from modern commentators by taking the *Phaedo*'s comments at 106D, "all
men will agree that God, and the essential form of life, and the immortal in general, will
never perish," to refer, not to an absolute "Idea of Life," but to the soul as the idea of its
own body's life (cf. Dillon, *Middle Platonists,* p. 137). As the principle of motion, soul is
the principle of life and cannot therefore participate in a higher idea of which it is itself the
principle. On the other hand, to thoroughly confuse matters, Ficino writes in his *Platonic
Theology* 5.13 (ed. Marcel, 1:208-209) that "since the rational soul is made without an
intermediary through the idea of life, it is a form which is always living by virtue of the
power of this its immediate origin; the irrational soul, however," etc. But compare his argument later in the same work at 9.5 (ed. Marcel, 2:31-37) that the soul is the principle of life!
In chap. 42 of his Commentary on the *Timaeus* he does briefly define the *crater* of 41D as

with the *Phaedrus*'s argument that the soul's true motion is life, and that since the soul is motion's source and principle, the soul must have perpetual motion, which is perpetual life. In rearranging Plato's argumentation, Ficino thus proceeds from the soul's self-motion, to its being the principle of motion, to its having perfect, perpetual motion, to its having perpetual life, which is the highest species of motion.

This is not the place to untangle the brave fallacies in this series of apparently logical steps, nor to trace them through Ficino's other writings back through the Scholastics, the Fathers, the Neoplatonists, and Cicero to the ancient Greek thinkers like Alcmaeon who first devised and combined them, nor, finally, to place them in the context of Plato's own thought. I wish merely to draw attention to some interesting Ficinian features. First we must be clear about his limited intentions. He is not commenting on all the intricate implications of Plato's proofs, but expanding on two themes: the theory of the soul's three powers and their three external and three internal motions; and the role of the irrational soul.

The soul's three powers are those of life, understanding, and desire. As almost every commentator on the charioteer myth has observed, there are some evident parallels to be drawn between its triplication and that in the *Republic* 4.435D and in the *Timaeus* 69C ff.;[10] and also between its attribution of motion to the soul

---

again "the idea of rational life" (*Opera,* p. 1463^V.2), but provides no further analysis. The topic awaits exploration.

For the important distinction between ἰδέα meaning the transcendent Idea, and εἶδος meaning the immanent form, see Seneca, *Letter* 58, sections 16-22, and Albinus (Alcinous), *Didaskalikos,* chaps. 4 and 10. Both were known to Ficino.

10. As Hackforth notes, "The problem of the tripartite soul is amongst the thorniest of all Platonic problems" (*Phaedrus,* p. 75); cf. Frutiger, *Mythes de Platon,* pp. 76-96. As evidence against the notion of tripartition are the *Phaedo*'s insistence on the simplicity of soul; the suggestion in the *Republic* 10.611D-612A that the true nature of the soul may be uncompounded; and a doubt raised in the *Timaeus* at 72D as to the tripartition explored earlier at 69C ff.

Ficino's views on these and other relevant passages have yet to be analyzed. Certainly he worked with the notion of the many parts or faculties of the soul—see, for instance, his reference to Plato's image of man's soul at *Republic* 9.588C-E as a therioanthropomorphic, many-headed assembly in his *Platonic Theology* 17.4 (ed. Marcel, 3:171)—but at the same time he maintained that the soul was one, united and eternal. See Kristeller, *Philosophy,* pp. 366-384.

and the *Laws'* attribution to the soul of desires, passions, and all the "motions" akin to them.[11] Though not choosing to elaborate on these parallels, Ficino sets up the distinctions between, and the mutual dependences of, the three powers under the primacy of the power of life. His stress on the latter automatically enhances the links between the motion proofs and the myth following upon them; for it is central to his conception of man's psychological unity, a unity graphically embodied in the overall figure of the charioteer. The vital power, as the prime power, has a sphere of operation effectively greater than those of the powers of understanding or desire and reaches down to embrace all the activities of both the rational and the irrational soul, including the broadly biological functions which we now attribute to the body and its chemistry but which were then classed as incorporeal. At the other extreme, as Soul's primary motion, the vital power is also Soul's primary differentiating factor, that which distinguishes it from the One and from Mind. For if life is the highest species of motion and Soul is the principle of motion, then we cannot attribute life—at least in the transitory form of becoming, being born, and dying—to Mind or to the One, which are the principles of being and understanding, and of unity and goodness respectively. We cannot even attribute to them Soul's perpetual life, though Mind has perpetual being and may, if we adopt the *Phaedo's* line of argument, possess within its own intellection the Idea of Life (though to do so would undermine the hypothesis that Soul is the principle of motion—that is, of life). By predicating rest as the goal of motion and therefore of life, Ficino can argue that Soul's highest motion, its highest life, is self-transcending and ultimately passes into the realm of Mind to become motionless, and therefore in a way lifeless, in transvital rest. The charioteer's flight is ultimately into tranquillity, motionlessly poised above all motion, all life, even all perpetual life in the realm of the intellectually existent alone. For the very concept of life is a limitation to which only souls and their inferiors are subject, though it be the perpetual life of the divine souls of the stars and the spheres. Higher than life is the being of

11. *Laws* 10.892A ff., 897A; cf. Hackforth, *Phaedrus,* pp. 75-76. *Laws* 10 was a favorite text of Ficino's; see his epitome, *Opera,* pp. 1515-1520.

the pure inanimate intelligences, the beings whom Iamblichus and his followers believed were the subjects of the Phaedran cavalcade, though in Ficino's view erroneously.[12]

Logical though this may appear, it came up against one great difficulty: the famous passage in the *Sophist* (248E-249D). The Eleatic Stranger asks, "But tell me, in heaven's name: are we really to be so easily convinced that change, life, soul, understanding have no place in that which is perfectly real [i.e. has perfect being]—that it has neither life nor thought, but stands immutable in solemn aloofness, devoid of intelligence? . . . But can we say it has intelligence without having life? . . . But if we say it contains both, can we deny that it has soul in which they reside? . . . But then, if it has intelligence, life, and soul, can we say that a living thing remains at rest in complete changelessness?" Since all three suppositions seem to be nonsense, the Stranger concludes, "In that case we must admit that what changes and change itself are real things [i.e. have being]."[13] The argument goes on to stress the need for there to be four categories of being under being: rest and motion, identity and difference (250B ff., 254 ff.), categories that were to play a major role throughout Neoplatonic analyses, including Ficino's own.[14] Two of the critical questions raised by the *Sophist* are thus: Can being be separated from life and understanding? and can Soul be separated absolutely from Mind?[15]

Armstrong among others has emphasized the importance of the notion of life to Plotinus's presentation of the intelligible world of Mind—that is, of Intellect thinking the Ideas. At 6.7.12.22-30 (cf.

---

12. See Allen, *Charioteer,* pp. 6-7, and chap. 10, pp. 243-251 below.

13. This is F. M. Cornford's translation in his *Plato's Theory of Knowledge* (London, 1935), p. 241, the bracketed glosses being my additions.

14. Ficino intended a major commentary for the *Sophist,* but in the event produced only a breakdown of the dialogue along with a few, though interesting, chapters of commentary, *Opera,* pp. 1284-1294. Notably, following the Scholastics, he subdivided being into being and existence, and thus arrived at a hexad of Platonic categories or "greatest genera," presuming, moreover, that this was what Plato had intended. The categories are central to the analysis in his *Philebus* Commentary 2.2 (ed. Allen, pp. 402-407).

In the *Enneads* 6.1-3 Plotinus had established the *Sophist's* categories as the five categories pertaining to the intelligible world, as opposed to the sensible world where Aristotle's ten categories pertained; see Dillon, *Middle Platonists,* pp. 50-51.

15. The Neoplatonists habitually linked this passage from the *Sophist* to the *Timaeus* 30CD, where Plato refers to the "all-complete animal" which Plotinus had subsequently identified as Mind. See Wallis, *Neoplatonism,* pp. 55, 65.

6.5.12.9) Plotinus writes, "in that world [of Mind] . . . everything is filled full of life, boiling with life." Armstrong comments, "Plotinus is always concerned to keep being, life and thought very closely linked in his descriptions of Intellect, to show it as a single reality which is at once the only perfectly real being, the fulness of life, and the perfection of intuitive thought which is identical with its object." He concludes, "Intellect for him originates from the Good as life. Being and thought are the self-determination and self-limitation of this life in its return to the Good, and are always living being and living thought. The World of Forms, the universe of real being, is a kind of spontaneous patterning of the flow of this inexhaustible life out from and back to the Good."[16]

So challenging are Plato's questions in the *Sophist,* and so persuasive are Plotinus's incorporation and transformation of them, that the later Neoplatonists predicated being, life, and understanding in that order as a triad that could be predicated as three aspects "of anything whatever" and that could be "applied to anything to which the verb 'to be' could be attached."[17] The reasons for this are twofold. First, they identified what we might call the Plotinian triad of Being, Life, and Understanding with references to the supreme Father's Existence (ὕπαρξις), Power (δύναμις), and Understanding (νοῦς) in a verse appearing in the *Chaldaean Oracles,* which Proclus (and Ficino) attributed to Zoroaster.[18] Thus

16. In *Cambridge History,* p. 246. See also Pierre Hadot, "Être, vie, pensée chez Plotin et avant Plotin," in *Les sources de Plotin,* Fondation Hardt, Entretiens sur l'antiquité classique, vol. 5 (Geneva, 1960), pp. 107-157.

17. A. C. Lloyd, "The Later Neoplatonists," in *Cambridge History,* p. 300. For Plotinus, life was sometimes, though not always, assigned the lowest station in the triad because of its association with Soul (contrast *Enneads* 6.6.8.17-22 and 6.6.17.35-43 with 6.7.17.14-16 and 6.7.21.2-6); see Wallis, *Neoplatonism,* p. 67. For the later Neoplatonists, however, it was definitively elevated to the second position in the triad—that is, elevated above understanding—on the grounds that just as being is prior to living, since not all that exists is alive, so living must be prior to understanding, since not all that lives thinks: see Proclus, *Elements of Theology,* props. 101-103 (ed. and trans. Dodds, pp. 90-93, with commentary on pp. 252-254), and *Theologia Platonica* 3.6 (ed. Saffrey and Westerink, 3:20-28); also Wallis, *Neoplatonism,* pp. 67, 124-125, 132-133, 156.

18. Ed. Des Places as frags. 3 and 4 (in Kroll, p. 12); cf. Proclus, *Theologia Platonica* 6.9 (ed. Portus, p. 365). See Wallis, *Neoplatonism,* p. 106, and Dillon, *Middle Platonists,* pp. 393-394.

For the status and history of the *Chaldaean Oracles* for Ficino and his contemporaries, see Karl H. Dannenfeldt, "The Pseudo-Zoroastrian Oracles in the Renaissance," *Studies in the Renaissance* 4 (1957), 7-30; also his "Hermetica Philosophica" and "Oracula Chaldaica" in *Catalogus Translationum et Commentariorum,* vol. 1, ed. Paul Oskar Kristeller

Plotinus's "Life" came to be understood as "Power,"[19] and Rosán, for instance, has argued persuasively that we should always render Proclus's ζωή accordingly.[20] Second, the later Neoplatonists (and Ficino) also saw the Plotinian triad corresponding to another fundamental triad in their metaphysics: permanence, procession, and reversion, with Life corresponding to procession.[21] In short, they and Ficino differentiated between the Power in absolute Being (the *Sophist*'s "Life," but not, note, the *Phaedo*'s "Idea of Life") and the primary power in Soul (the *Phaedrus*'s "life"). Insofar as it was integral to the basic ontological triad and its subdivisions and reflections at lower levels, Life was Power; but insofar as it was conceived of in the more usual sense—that is, in terms of motion, time, and space, or at least of motion and time—then it would derive from the principle of motion, Soul itself, and be the prime motion, animation.[22]

Next, Ficino utilizes the concept of freedom in the course of discussing the three powers, something that Plato does not deal with at all. Since the powers have three strictly internal spheres of activity or motion, they therefore have three areas of freedom and constraint: "Just as the power of understanding, when it ponders incorporeals, declares that a realm exists within itself which is free

(Washington, 1960), pp. 137-151, 157-164. The tentative attribution to Ficino himself of a Latin translation of the *Oracles* found in MSS Laurenziana Plut. 36.35 and Vaticana Ottob. lat. 2966 has now been called in question; see the 1981 dissertation of Ilana Klutstein-Roitman of Hebrew University, Jerusalem, entitled "Les traductions latines des Oracles chaldaïques et des Hymnes orphiques." We do know, however, that Ficino possessed a Greek MS copy (Riccard. 76) of the *Oracles,* along with the commentaries of Psellus and Pletho; see Dannenfeldt, "The Pseudo-Zoroastrian Oracles," p. 13 n. 36.

19. Lloyd, "Later Neoplatonists," pp. 309-310; Wallis, *Neoplatonism,* pp. 106, 116, 125, 132.

20. It has to be "Power," Rosán argues, "for only Soul is truly 'Life'" (*Philosophy of Proclus,* p. 109n; cf. p. 143); and he refers us not only to this *Phaedrus* passage (245C) but to the *Laws* 10.894B.

21. Cf. Plotinus, *Enneads* 6.7.36.12. See Lloyd, "Later Neoplatonists," pp. 299-300, 309, and Wallis, *Neoplatonism,* pp. 66-67, 132-133, with further refs.

22. While Ficino's position is obviously Neoplatonic in its orientation, the details remain to be explored by reference to such key texts as his *Parmenides* and *Sophist* Commentaries and his Commentaries on Plotinus. Future analysis will also need to explore his indebtedness to Proclus's various treatments of the problem.
Plotinus, *Enneads* 3.7.11.43-45, states that the life of Soul "is in transition from one phase of life to another," whereas the life of the Intelligible World, i.e. of Mind, is unchanging. See Wallis, *Neoplatonism,* p. 53; also Kristeller, *Philosophy,* pp. 128-129.

from the body, so the power of desiring, when it wishes for incorporeals and chooses many things that are contrary to the promptings of the corporeal condition, is demonstrating that free will exists. Similarly, a realm flourishes within the power of life (which is the foundation, as it were, of the other two powers); that is, the power of life brings forth from itself a certain vital act and effectual motion.''[23] The last freedom (of which the other two are reflections or imitations) constitutes the soul's ability to move itself of its own accord and to function as its own unconstrained principle of motion.[24] Ficino not only supposes a correspondence between the three kinds of freedom peculiar to the soul's three powers, he proceeds to argue that the soul is free from corporeal restraint and therefore from mortality because it is free to recognize, to choose, and to live the good life in its fullness and therefore in perpetuity. In seeking and exercising these incorporeal, internal freedoms, related as they are, the soul makes intellectual and moral choices by using its powers of understanding and desire. But enabling it to do so is its power of life, which must therefore be an incorporeal power. In other words, the soul passes from a recognition of its freedom intellectually to choose the good life and to improve itself by moral choice towards a recognition of the illusory nature of all corporeal restrictions and preeminently of mortality. But this passing is itself a kind of motion, the most fundamental, the most vital of all self-motions, the ultimate vindication of the hypothesis that motion, especially the motion of life itself, begins with Soul and has Soul as its principle. For it is the motion which assures our divinity, our becoming like to the gods in the phrase made famous for the Neoplatonists by the *Theaetetus* 176B.[25]

In adverting to the age-old distinction between the rational and the irrational soul in paragraphs 4 and 5, Ficino juggles with sev-

---

23. This is probably not to be equated with the *idolum,* for which see chap. 9, pp. 219-220 below.

24. For a full account of the soul's freedom, and especially the unique freedom it enjoys by virtue of its *ratio,* see Ficino's *Platonic Theology* 9.4; 10.6; 14.3-5 (ed. Marcel, 2:18-29, 76-79, 256-266). Here in the *Phaedrus* Commentary Ficino makes use of the notion of freedom in order to pursue his proof of the soul's immortality, not in order to examine freedom itself.

25. See Ficino's own epitome, *Opera,* pp. 1274-1281 at 1281.

eral problems.[26] All that is predicated of the soul per se is predicated of the rational soul, which the irrational soul then reflects or mirrors in some diminished way, Ficino says, since it is subject to the body. His own philosophical "set" towards the soul required a unitary concept, a whole with a diversity of functions rather than separable parts, or even the modalities, active and passive. The mirror analogy is not completely satisfactory here, in that the powers of knowledge and desire are now encompassed by a single superior power that functions passively rather than actively, a power that is itself opposed by an inferior power "which looks to vegetative activity and motion." This last, though subordinate to the other two powers, could only be a reflection of the vital power. But the irrational soul not only mirrors the rational, it is also "excited by natural influences" and "impelled by external objects." Thus it is moved, like the elements, by the World-Soul and by the soul of its particular sphere and, unlike the rational soul, by its own nature's "instinct" and by the "impulse" of external things. The hallmark of the irrational soul is therefore its instrumentality, passivity, and inability to move itself. It should not be confused, however, with the soul's *idol,* "the vital act" bestowed on the soul's celestial vehicle by the rational soul; and its introduction at this juncture can be attributed solely to the problems generated by the self-motion syllogisms, for it makes its first appearance, significantly, as "the irrational life subject to the body," not as a subdivision of the soul.

In chapter 6 Ficino deals with one of the most difficult cruces in Plato: the meaning of the phrase at 245C5, ψυχὴ πᾶσα ἀθάνατος.[27]

26. For an account of Ficino's psychology, and especially his views on the nature and function of the irrational soul, see Kristeller, *Philosophy,* pp. 364-388, esp. 370-371. Note that Ficino usually refers to the irrational soul in man as the *natura* or the *complexio vitalis* of the body, e.g., in the *Platonic Theology* 13.2 (ed. Marcel, 2:207 ff.). In beasts, however, the irrational soul seems to have consisted of the *natura* plus the *idolum;* see Kristeller, *Philosophy,* p. 385, and chap. 9, n. 31 below.

27. Cf. 246B6; the same grammatical relationship seems to be intended between ψυχὴ and πᾶσα. Note that Ficino only brought his translation of 245C5 into line with 246B6 when he devised his corrigenda (they were appended to the *Phaedrus* summae as printed in the 1496 *Commentaria in Platonem;* see Allen, *Charioteer,* p. 50); for he had originally rendered 245C5 as *anima omnis* and 246B6 as *omnis anima* (and they so appear in the 1484 and 1491 editions of his *Platonis Opera Omnia*). It is difficult to tell, however, whether this 1496 transposition really reflected a shift in his conception of Plato's argumentation.

Since antiquity, commentators have speculated as to whether Plato meant πᾶσα in a collective or a distributive sense—all soul / every soul is deathless—or both,[28] and, additionally, whether he intended to confine the meaning of soul to the rational soul.

Following Plotinus,[29] Ficino appears to opt for the collective sense; but he then proceeds to work with the conviction that, metaphysically conceived, every soul is potentially all soul, since every soul "has all the powers of the soul within itself" and "has, as it were, all souls within itself" and is therefore "so to speak" the universe. This is not an instance of Ficino failing to think his position through, but rather (and Hackforth makes a similar plea for Plato)[30] of his refusing to abide by the distinction for longer than the time required to make a limited point. For he is committed to a monistic conception of soul that impels him to short-circuit what would otherwise be mutually exclusive senses of πᾶσα. Hence he can use Plato's phrase to exalt the status and potentialities of the individual soul—every soul—as not merely part of the world or realm of souls, but as an entity mirroring and therefore "as it were" containing and being that world. Ψυχὴ πᾶσα ἀθάνατος comes to mean "each and every soul is immortal" when it is all and totally soul.

However, the crucial distinction for Ficino seems to be not so much between the collective and distributive senses as between all souls and all rational souls, Plato being at pains, as he sees it, to distinguish in his presentation of the *Phaedrus*'s myth between the two kinds of souls, the rational and the irrational, and to gear the charioteer allegory to the former. Ficino inherited and worked with a hierarchy of souls within the general category of "rational" souls: the World-Soul, the souls of the spheres and stars, the souls

28. See Frutiger, *Mythes de Platon,* pp. 130-134; Hackforth, *Phaedrus,* pp. 64-65; and G. J. de Vries, *A Commentary on the Phaedrus of Plato* (Amsterdam, 1969), p. 121. Particularly useful is Hermias's doxography of ancient views, pp. 102.10-114.27 (ed. Couvreur). Posidonius, for example, had espoused the collective sense of πᾶσα, Harpocration the distributive. Note that the argumentation at 246B6 seems to require the collective sense and that this would embolden those who favored the same sense for 245C5.

29. Plotinus explicitly invokes the argumentation at 245C in his *Enneads* 5.8.4.12-13, but he also refers to the critical phrase at 246B, "all soul has care of all that is soulless," on several occasions (3.4.2; 4.3.1, 7; etc.).

30. *Phaedrus,* pp. 64-65.

of spirits and demons, and the souls of heroes and of men. Though each of these is more circumscribed than its superiors in the hierarchy, each is one in essence with them and potentially equipollent. Accordingly, though Ficino habitually preserves the traditional steps in the hierarchy of rational souls, his obsession with the human soul compels him at times to talk of all higher rational souls as if they were actualizations of unrealized potentialities in the human soul. It depends on whether he is thinking in received terms or using them as a springboard for his own innovatory conceptions of man.

This oscillation is especially evident when Ficino again utilizes the concept of motion, which he sees as one of the dialogue's principal themes: "Here we have to remember that Socrates speaks not about every principle, but particularly about the principle of motion, the producer of all the species of motion." Motion, when keyed to the human soul rather than to all rational souls, is the critical factor in spiritual ascent. Ficino moves hesitantly. Midway through the first paragraph he had written, "any rational soul can be said to be the principle of motion . . . though not every rational soul is the first and universal principle of motion, as this is the office of the World-Soul." Thus lower rational souls are principles of motion—but of their own self-motion, not of all motion. However, he continues, any rational soul "can be said" to be the principle of all motion, as long as we understand this figuratively, or as referring to a state of potentiality. The distinction between the World-Soul and lower rational souls was clearly troublesome, for he returns in the next sentence to the more radical view: "any rational soul's power is so great that any one soul can in a way be the universe" when it "withdraws into its own fullness" and unfolds "all the varieties of motions and powers in itself." Finally, in the second paragraph, he simply speaks of the soul as "the fountain" of motion, and leaves it up in the air whether he is referring to the World-Soul or to the collective sense of all soul.

One outcome of thus emphasizing the concept of motion is to emphasize the soul's relationship to what is moved, its creative rather than contemplative relationship to the world. Rather than using motion to "prove" the existence of the prime mover, he uses it to prove the existence of the soul's powers; and he even goes so far as to suggest that the soul, in that it mirrors God's likeness, has a primarily creative relationship to the world. Thus, while the *Phaedrus* itself never suggests the applicability of its syllogisms to the proving of God's existence (though a later Aristotelian might utilize them to argue for the prime mover), it does provide Ficino with argumentation for analyzing the godlike nature of the soul.

To conclude this section Ficino argues that the soul is *ungenerated* on the grounds that generation is a species of motion, and that the soul, being the principle of motion, is therefore anterior to generation. While Plato only introduces the notion that the soul is ungenerated (ἀγένητόν) in his last sentence (246A1), for Ficino, understandably, it was implied all along because of the phrase ἀρχὴ δὲ ἀγένητον at 245D1 and Plato's subsequent use of γίγνομαι and its cognates. From the onset Christian thinkers had stressed the distinction between creation and generation, the authoritative formulation being Aquinas's *Summa Theologiae* 1.45.5. In his *Philebus* Commentary at 2.4 Ficino brings three critical distinctions to bear: "creating" pertains to God alone, for he works (*operatur*) without the Ideas and without matter, being Himself the author of both; "effecting" pertains to an intelligence, for, using both the Ideas and "a certain matter" (*ex materia quadam*), it effects in a motionless manner (*stabiliter efficit*); "generating" pertains to a soul, for, using "seeds" and "reasons" (*semina et rationes*) and a corporeal matter, it acts (*agit*) with motion and in time.[31] Note the different verbs and the introduction of both incorporeal and corporeal matter. Mind and soul were *created* by God and are sempiternal[32] as long as He so wills. But some things were also subjected by God to *generation*—to being the result, that is, of a temporary union between corporeal matter and certain reasons or seeds—and thus were enslaved to the motions of birth, maturing, and dying. The irrational soul may be such a generated

31. Ed. Allen, pp. 416-417. Cf. Proclus, *In Timaeum* 86E-90E (ed. Diehl, 1:282.27-296. 12; trans. Festugière, 2:129-148).

32. Incidentally, Ficino was certainly aware of the necessity at times of distinguishing between different aspects of "eternity" and of the importance of such distinctions in analyzing Plato's arguments at *Meno* 86A, *Laws* 10.904A, and above all *Timaeus* 28B, 37C-38B. For the latter he could turn not only to Calcidius's *In Timaeum* 105-106 (ed. Waszink, pp.

thing and so be mortal, though this too was a subject of dispute among the ancient Neoplatonists.[33] The rational soul, however, is liberated from corporeality and so from generation, though able to act upon the corporeal and thus to generate. The *Phaedrus* argues, therefore, that the soul is *ungenerated*[34] on the grounds that, since it has already been proved that the soul cannot pass out of being, it could not have once passed into being: it must have always been for all time from its creation, which, unlike the corporeal world's creation, did not take place in time but in eternity.[35]

Ficino introduces the Platonic theory of the Ideas in his third paragraph, but in the context of what Kristeller has designated the

---

154-155) but to Proclus's *Elements of Theology,* props. 52-55 (ed. Dodds, pp. 50-55, with commentary and further refs. on pp. 226-230) and *In Timaeum* 84E-86E (ed. Diehl, 1:276. 10-282.22; trans. Festugière, 2:121-129). In an article, "Notes platoniciennes de Marsile Ficin dans un manuscrit de Proclus, Cod. Riccardianus 70," *Bibliothèque d'humanisme et Renaissance* 21.1 (1959), 161-184 at 174, H. D. Saffrey reproduces a marginal note by Ficino which demonstrates his insight into Proclus's usage: "Sempiternitas [ἀϊδιότης] est duratio sine principio et sine fine, sive sit tota simul sive fluens. Huius species due sunt, id est eternitas [αἰών] et perpetuitas [χρόνος πρῶτος]: illa interminabilis simul tota, ista interminabilis fluens" (cf. ibid., p. 180).

The nature and consistency of Ficino's own usage and its debts to various Church Fathers await examination. For Pletho, who may have influenced him in this matter, see Milton V. Anastos, "Pletho's Calendar and Liturgy," *Dumbarton Oaks Papers* 4 (1948), 185-305 at 295-297.

33. In the Old Academy, for instance, Speusippus and Xenocrates accorded immortality to both kinds of soul, though this seems to be, according to Dillon, "a significant departure from Plato's doctrine" (*Middle Platonists,* p. 17n).

34. In the *Laws* 10.891-899 (an important section, to which Ficino often refers throughout his work) Plato has the Athenian use γένεσις and γίγνεσθαι of the soul, as Hackforth observes (*Phaedrus,* p. 67). This contradicts the *Phaedrus*'s assertion that the soul is ungenerated. Unlike later commentators, however, Ficino thought the two positions reconcilable, for in his epitome for *Laws* 10 (*Opera,* p. 1518) he argues thus: "Ubi vero Plato animam appellat motionem generationemque, intellige per modum causae, id est, proprium motionis generationisque principium."

35. Controversy had long raged between Christian Platonists and their detractors as to whether Plato believed in the eternity of the world, the key text being the *Timaeus* (and notably 28B and 41AB). For support Ficino could turn to Plutarch, Severus, and Atticus among the ancients, since they held—correctly, in Ficino's view, since it brought Plato into accord with Christian dogma—that Plato believed the world had been created in time and from preexisting matter and was not therefore eternal; see Ficino's *Timaeus* Commentary, chap. 13 (*Opera,* p. 1443), and Proclus, *In Timaeum* 87F-88F (ed. Diehl, 1:286.20-290.3; trans. Festugière, 2:134-139). Ironically, the majority of Middle Platonists and Neoplatonists in antiquity had almost certainly been correct in arguing that Plato, like Aristotle, believed in the world's eternity and had only used temporal terms in the *Timaeus* figuratively.

"primum in aliquo genere" theory[36]—namely that there is a prime
example of every species, exhibiting the characteristics peculiar to
that species to the highest degree, though deriving other characteristics and qualities from other paradigms; his example: the sun as
prime giver of light. This primum theory (which is owed in part to
Aquinas) is dovetailed into the all-embracing framework of the
Neoplatonic hypostases; the One or Good, Mind, and Soul, each
being the principle of the serially contracting primal activities of
being one, thinking, and moving. The framework enabled Ficino
(and he is not original in this) to deny the soul's mortality while
safeguarding its contingency. For the soul depends on the One for
unity and existence, on Mind for its intelligence, but on itself (or
on the World-Soul as the primal soul to which it is subordinate—
and the relationship between the two had always been problematic)
for motion, and preeminently for the motion constituting life
(though Ficino never actually says that the soul gives itself life as
contrasted with the being given it by God). Again, at the heart of
these notions is the distinction between creation and generation.

A notable corollary of both Plato's and Ficino's argumentation
is that if any self-mover—that is, soul—were destroyed, and not
just the World-Soul, then the whole of the universe—Plato says at
245E1 "what comes to be" (γένεσιν [MSS and Hermias]—that is,
τὰ γιγνόμενα), whereas Ficino says "all motion" and "every moving thing"—would stop and accordingly perish. Logically, this
stopping should mean stop moving or stop living, not stop being
or stop existing. Ficino restricts this stopping to the rational soul
on the grounds that the *Phaedrus* has clearly delimited its presentation to this soul: "If you could conceive of any one of the rational souls being destroyed," he writes in paragraph 6, "then you

---

We should bear in mind, however, that Christian Platonists could take gleeful satisfaction
from Aristotle's contrary assertion in his *De Caelo* 1.12 and 2.2 that Plato believed the
world had begun in time (even though Aristotle had then gone on to assail Plato for holding
such a belief; see Dillon, *Middle Platonists*, p. 7).

We might note parenthetically that the alignment of Severus here with Plutarch and Atticus could only have been known to Ficino via Proclus's *In Timaeum* 304B (ed. Diehl, 3:212.
8-9), and provides us with further evidence that he was familiar with the work.

36. *Philosophy,* chap. 9, pp. 146-170; also A. K. Lloyd, "Primum in genere: The Philosophical Background," *Diotima* 4 (1976), 32-36.

would be, necessarily, conceiving of the destruction of the rest of the souls''; and the future consequence ''of any soul thus perishing would seem, in a way, to be the downfall (*ruitura*) of the world's machine—that is, the corporeal machine.''[37] Note again the caveat ''in a way,'' for Ficino is not qualifying the logic of his deduction but alerting us to its figurative status as a hypothetical situation, conceivable but impossible. Note too Ficino's Christian argument, one at odds with Neoplatonism's system of mediated being, that all souls (those of the world, the spheres, demons, and all rational beings) are created by God ''without an intermediary'' and in the same mold, ''with similar proportions.'' The ontological hierarchy is retained, not by any logic interior to the system that has one kind of superior being ''create'' another inferior being, but in light of the external subordinations established by God—subordinations that simultaneously insure the integrity of each being's direct relationship to, and dependence on, the Creator, as contrasted with Plotinus's conception of the indirect or mediated dependency of all things on the One by way of Mind and Soul.[38]

But the soul's immortality—the eternity, that is, of the Phaedran charioteer—is not merely a consequence of arguing that Soul is the principle of motion: it is absolutely necessary to the sustaining of the world. Without the perpetuity, without the immortality of every soul (and we can see again that the initial distinction between the collective and distributive senses of πᾶσα must be abandoned eventually), the motion and therefore the life of the world would cease; and the relationship between the primary hypostases in either their original Plotinian or in their Christian-Plotinian interpretations would no longer pertain. Interestingly, Ficino introduces the term ''downfall'' (*ruitura*), with its Satanic and

37. Cf. *Platonic Theology* 5.15 (ed. Marcel, 1:215-222) citing at length from passages in Augustine's *De Immortalitate Animae*.
38. Cf. Ficino's *Platonic Theology* 10.7, 8 (ed. Marcel, 2:80-89). See Michael J. B. Allen, ''The Absent Angel in Ficino's Philosophy,'' *Journal of the History of Ideas* 36.2 (1975), 219-240 at 228-229; and Edward P. Mahoney, ''Metaphysical Foundations of the Hierarchy of Being According to Some Late-Medieval and Renaissance Philosophers,'' in *Philosophies of Existence, Ancient and Medieval*, ed. Parviz Morewedge (New York, 1982), pp. 165-257 at 188-192.

Edenic connotations, into a Platonic context strictly concerned with immobility.

Chapter 6's final paragraph is by way of a coda as it deals with an issue having only an indirect bearing on the immortality syllogisms: the nature of the One, the principle subsuming and transcending all other principles. Obviously Ficino feels this is not the occasion to launch into the metaphysics of this Plotinian hypostasis, as he has already considered it elsewhere: in the *Platonic Theology*,[39] in the *Philebus* Commentary,[40] and at great length in the *Parmenides* Commentary (to which he explicitly refers).[41] Plato does not suggest the issue at all by adverting to the Idea of the Good; and Ficino raises it only to note that we cannot argue from the nature of things subsequent to the One to the nature of the One itself, "the principle of principles." For the latter is wholly transcendent, and the only valid arguments are those from analogy and subject therefore to the limitations always accompanying analogy. While Ficino insists that all things ultimately depend on the One, he also insists that individual properties derive from different principles, and particularly motion from the soul. Furthermore, by referring to the *Parmenides,* he alerts us to the necessity at certain critical junctures of "placing" the *Phaedrus* in a larger Platonic context, and most immediately in the context of the third tetralogy, of which it is the junior member,[42] and the *Parmenides,* the sovereign dialogue of Neoplatonic metaphysics, the senior.[43] Only if we keep this tetralogy in mind can we begin to appreciate the profound significance for Ficino of the *Phaedrus.*

---

39. 1.6; 2.1 (ed. Marcel, 1:67-72, 73-75).

40. 1.4, 5 (ed. Allen, pp. 88-111).

41. Notably chaps. 2, 3, 41, 48, 49, 55-79 (*Opera,* pp. 1138, 1157-1158, 1163-1164, 1169-1189).

42. The two middle members of the tetralogy are the *Philebus* and the *Symposium;* see Allen, *Charioteer,* pp. 8, 48 n. 108. Dillon notes in his *Middle Platonists,* p. 184, that the notion of dividing Plato's works into tetralogies certainly predated Thrasyllus since Varro mentions it in his *De Lingua Latina* 7.37. Thrasyllus's breakdown—the one still adhered to for convenience sake—became the authoritative one, however; see Diogenes Laertius, *Lives* 3.49-62, a compiler to whom Ficino constantly refers.

43. See Michael J. B. Allen, "Ficino's Theory of the Five Substances and the Neoplatonists' *Parmenides*," *Journal of Medieval and Renaissance Studies* 12.1 (1982), 19-44 for details on the extraordinary status of the dialogue for Ficino and for further references.

At particular moments, as in this final paragraph of chapter 6, he sees the dialogue against a backdrop of metaphysical ideas of more comprehensive and intricate scope than those explicitly introduced by Socrates in the noontide colloquy. Had he had time, it is palpably the kind of situation he would have returned to to explore in a major speculative excursus.[44]

44. *Phaedrus* 245C-E is also covered by summa 15, but the summa is merely an efficient piece of summarizing that sticks closely to the syllogisms in hand and offers us only one interesting comment: "Since Socrates, like someone incited by frenzy, does not arrange the parts of the syllogisms entirely in order, let me briefly present them as follows." Ficino then proceeds to stress the primacy of the self-motion argument and to subordinate the argument that Soul is the principle of motion. Appropriately he sees both arguments as aspects of a single syllogism (whereas we usually accept Plato's breakdown into two); and he accurately perceives that Socrates has failed to set up the proofs in the correct order. The summa shows no Ficinian idiosyncrasies, though it shares in the general Neoplatonic conviction of Socrates' ongoing rapture, one that is already elevating him above the discursiveness of reason on a flight towards the simultaneity of intuitive vision.

Chapter Four: The Soul's Flight

Commentary chapters 7, 8, and 9 treat of 246A-E where Plato introduces his myth in order to explain the "idea" of the soul, having just proved its immortality. The myth is a comparison, Plato says, not a literal description, for "only a god could tell us" the truth about the soul, and even then "it would be a long story" (246A). Man, Socrates notes ironically, needs something briefer; and he proceeds to liken the nature of all souls to "the union of powers in a team of winged steeds and their winged charioteer," which Ficino translates as *Similis esto cognate potentie subalati currus* [later emended to *sub alti* (sic) *coniugii*] *et aurige*. The gods' steeds are "good and of good stock"—ἀγαθοὶ καὶ ἐξ ἀγαθῶν (246A8)—which Ficino translates literally as *boni sunt atque ex bonis,* thus opening up for metaphysical speculation the meaning of *ex bonis.* Another example of his literalism serving speculative ends is the emended word-order for *anima* and *omnis* in the sentence which finally stands as *Anima omnis totius inanimati curam habet* for reasons already discussed. For other significant word choices we should note *celum* for οὐρανός (and thus *caelius* for οὐράνιος), and *species* for εἴδεσι in the clause at 246B7 ἄλλοτ᾽ ἐν ἄλλοις εἴδεσι γιγνομένη (which Ficino translates as *alias videlicet alias sortita species*). These instances are sufficient, I think, again to alert us to the need for having Ficino's Latin translation, and its subsequent 1496 emendations, in front of us, as well as the Greek text. Not that we are likely to spot Ficino making many mistakes but rather that we can see how carefully he preserves the literal sense of certain key terms without producing a merely literal translation.

Chapter 7 is concerned with the idea of the soul and the metaphysical categories symbolized by the various parts of the chariot and charioteer. Chapter 8 concerns the relationship between, and occasional identity of, each separate soul and all soul as a class particularly in caring for the world and, in a sense, creating its own heaven or appropriate realm. It also deals with the soul's various bodies or chariots, beginning with the highest, the aethereal vehicle, and with the metaphysical process by which we not only descend into but in a way create corporeality if not matter as such. Chapter 9 concerns the goodness, wisdom, and beauty of the gods and their predication of truth. While thus devoted to a variety of topics, all three chapters are centered upon examining the "idea" of the soul in its pristine, godlike state and with the world or heaven it creates, sustains, or vitiates for itself. Hence my decision to deal with them together.

When Socrates depicts the idea of the soul, Ficino says at the beginning of chapter 7, we should be alert to the meaning of "idea." It can mean the supreme or "supernal" Form (though Plato never maintained the soul had such an Idea, for this was a development that came with his immediate successors in the Old Academy—particularly, as far as we can tell, with Xenocrates—and was accompanied by a host of problems).[1] Or it can mean the internal form or shape of a soul and the disposition of its powers (though not necessarily in the Aristotelian sense).[2] Surprisingly in a way, given his general commitment to Plato's theory of the Ideas, Ficino will not be concerned in this Commentary with the former.

1. In his *De Anima* 3.4.429a27 Aristotle alleges that Plato had described soul as the "place" ($\tau \acute{o} \pi o \varsigma$) of the Ideas: it received the Ideas into itself and somehow transformed them into mathematicals. See Dillon. *Middle Platonists,* pp. 6, 28-29; and Wallis, *Neoplatonism,* p. 20.

2. Of relevance here perhaps is a difficult passage in the *Enneads* (2.1.5) where Plotinus (following *Timaeus* 42D ff.) distinguishes between two souls: the Celestial or World-Soul that derives, along with our own souls, directly from the Creator God; and a "minor" soul, defined as its "image," which proceeds from the World-Soul, acts upon matter, and creates "the living things of earth." Man then is physically formed by the minor soul, "which is given forth from the divine beings in the heavens and from the heavens themselves," while his authentic inner self is the higher soul that sprang directly from God. While this supplies us with goodness ($\grave{\alpha}\rho\epsilon\tau\acute{\eta}$), Plotinus concludes, the minor soul merely provides our body with life.

Later commentators identify the minor with the irrational soul; but note its ambiguous or dual origin as either an image proceeding from the World-Soul or something proceeding from the gods in heaven or the heavens themselves.

Obviously Ficino had to reject the Apuleian notion that the World-Soul was the source of our higher souls, since he refused to identify the *Timaeus's* Demiurge with the World-Soul; see Dillon, *Middle Platonists,* p. 316. For Ficino's views on the *rationality* of the World-Soul, see chap. 5, pp. 127-128 below.

Even the latter can only be explored analogically, since true knowledge of the soul is reserved for the gods alone, perhaps as a result
of their seeing the Idea of Soul on one of their flights towards the
supercelestial place (though Ficino never raises this possibility).

To plot his analysis of Plato's comparison of the soul's idea or
shape to a charioteer,[3] Ficino introduces the five ontological categories he had discussed at length in the second book of his *Philebus* Commentary, categories which Plato himself had toyed with
towards the end of his career and notably in the *Sophist* 254D ff.
but which do not appear in the *Phaedrus*: essence or being, rest,
motion, identity, and difference.[4] At their head he adds unity. The
charioteer represents the intellect and therefore essence (the Neoplatonists, if not Plato, equating the two).[5] Thus the charioteer's
head or crown is the unity which crowns essence and which unites
the charioteer potentially, and indeed ultimately actually, with the
One, the principle or cause of all essence and being[6] (Ficino's second paragraph, however, introduces a further distinction, as we
shall see). The good horse, on the right side, is reason (*ratio*), both
the discursive reason that considers universals or species, and the
practical reason that examines particulars; it participates more in
rest and identity. The worse horse, on the left side, is the imagination "together with the nature (that is, the vegetative power)" and
also the appetite which is the companion apparently of both. Elsewhere in his works Ficino identifies the nature as a quality inherent
in the earthly body and calls it the "vital complexion" or "life"

---

3. Throughout this analysis Ficino seems to have only the *biga,* the two-horsed chariot,
in mind, though in the *Platonic Theology* 17.2 (ed. Marcel, 3:156-157; trans. Allen, *Charioteer,* pp. 228-230) he is also referring, obliquely, to the *quadriga,* the four-horsed. Additionally, following Plato, he seems always to equate the charioteer with the hero, though in
Homer of course they are frequently two separate persons.
4. 2.2, 3, and unattached chap. 3 (ed. Allen, pp. 402-409, 430-433). In 2.2 (ed. Allen, pp.
404-407) Ficino proceeds to distinguish between being and essence, and so arrives at six, not
five, categories. He also makes a fascinating attempt to accommodate the resulting six cate-
gories to the *Philebus*'s theory (ultimately of Pythagorean origin) of the limit ($\pi\acute{\epsilon}\rho\alpha\varsigma$) and
the infinite ($\check{\alpha}\pi\epsilon\iota\rho\rho\nu$): being, rest, and identity are associated with the limit, and essence,
motion, and difference with the infinite.
5. Since the first hypostasis, the One, was beyond being, Mind, the second hypostasis,
was the first being, the first existent; see n. 4 above.
6. For Ficino's doctrine of the unity, see Kristeller, *Philosophy,* pp. 250-251, 368-369.
Gombrich's rendering of this passage in his *Symbolic Images,* p. 217 n. 146, is incorrect.
Cf. Ficino, *De Amore* 7.13 (ed. Marcel, p. 257).

(sometimes he regards it as a kind of shadow cast on the body by the soul); in men it is the so-called irrational soul. The imagination, on the other hand, must represent the various powers intermediate between the *ratio* and the *natura,* powers which include the phantasy and sense perception.[7] For Ficino clearly intends the black horse to signify all the subrational powers of the human soul. In the case of fallen, incarnate souls, this worse horse participates more in motion and difference; but with the gods, and therefore with discarnate godlike souls, the motion and difference are "tempered," meaning presumably made equal in power to rest and identity.

Several things are noteworthy. Ficino talks of the "better" horse and the "worse"; but he insists, unlike Plato, that the latter is "less good" or "contrary" rather than fundamentally evil on the grounds that it prefers to follow the ontological elements of motion and difference, which are themselves "contrary" to those of rest and identity. The chariots of the gods also have this "worse" or "contrary" horse, the only difference being the greater "tempering" of the "contrary" elements, a tempering which in effect makes both the gods' horses "good and of good stock." Plato, however, never describes the worse horse in its risen state. At 253DE, in a passage that Ficino fails to reach in his full commentary but that colors every reader's memory of the myth, graphically he does depict a repulsive nag, one that Childe Roland might have encountered on his way to the dark tower. But Ficino consistently avoided this passage, not only, I believe, in order to present an optimistic view of man's opportunities for self-mastery, and to emphasize his kinship with the gods, but likewise because he was uneasy, as other comments demonstrate, about accepting a straightforward identification of the black steed with the appetite, or even with the imagination and nature (which have no bona fide reason for being in the gods at all, at least as we understand them).

---

7. See Kristeller, *Philosophy,* pp. 369-377 (and for the identification of the *natura* with the irrational soul, esp. pp. 370-371). For the knotty problem of the relationship between the *natura* and the *idolum,* which Ficino never mentions in the *Phaedrus* Commentary, see chap. 9, n. 31 below; and for the relationship between the imagination and the phantasy, ibid., n. 33 below. For a general background, see E. Ruth Harvey, *The Inward Wits: Psychological Theory in the Middle Ages and the Renaissance* (London, 1975).

As he suggests on other occasions, the "worse" horse, even in its fallen condition, would be better identified perhaps with another, more important and more complex faculty, the will, or with some aspect thereof.

One of Ficino's most obvious departures from Plato is his considerably greater emphasis on both the emotional and the volitional sides of man; and in this he was anticipated by the Areopagite and Augustine rather than the pagan Neoplatonists. It led him to move from a concept of the appetite, narrowly defined, to that of the will and the associated concept of love (ancient Greek has no term for "the will" as such; and though we find the notion in the New Testament, it does not emerge as a critical philosophical concept until Augustine).[8] In an earlier utilization of the myth in the *Philebus* Commentary (1.34), Ficino had got as far as identifying the black horse with the will's "ardor" even though the will itself he identified with one of the wings.[9] It is surprising therefore that the will does not appear at all in the *Phaedrus* Commentary (except for a brief and specialized instance in chapter 4 where "volition"—that is, "willing"—is said to be the province of the hieratic art). Perhaps its absence derives from the Commentary's late date; for the 1490s seem to have signaled Ficino's return to intellectualist positions, as I observed earlier. Plato's heightening of the contrast between the white and black steeds in subsequent paragraphs of the *Phaedrus* was of course a *donnée*. All that Ficino could do was to downplay it by dwelling on the black steed's rightful place in the chariots of gods and risen souls.

Interestingly, the genera of being are not schematically distributed by opposites. The white horse "participates"—and Ficino uses this word fully intending its technical meaning in Plato, namely "the participation of earthly realities in the eternal realities of the Ideas"—more in rest and identity and therefore less in motion and difference; the black horse either the reverse or equally. Both nevertheless participate in all four categories,

8. For some qualifications to this view see Albrecht Dihle, *The Theory of Will in Classical Antiquity* (Berkeley, Los Angeles, London, 1982), and Anthony Kenny, *Aristotle's Theory of the Will* (London and New Haven, 1979). Kristeller notes that Ficino seems to avoid speaking of the "evil" will (*Philosophy,* p. 66).

9. Ed. Allen, pp. 353-355.

though the figure requires that, in the final analysis, there be "more" rest and identity absolutely, since the black horse should have the opposing elements in equal measure, but the white horse more of rest and identity. This excess of rest and identity not only works against the notion that the horses represent movement, but also contradicts the notion of "tempering" that emerges as the ideal state of the two steeds viewed collectively, and where, logically one would have thought, the white steed should also have the four elements in equal measure. The problem is Ficino's, not Plato's, in that Plato makes no mention of the ontological categories and speaks merely of the horses being "good and of good stock."

Having commended rest, Ficino proceeds to concentrate on motion, as he is compelled to by the myth's exigencies—but on motion that is no longer, as in the previous chapter, the differentiating factor of the soul, its peculiar characteristic and glory. The horses particularly represent motion, and most motion is found in the black horse. But the horses, like their charioteer, also possess wings:[10] the chariot's motion is thus not horizontal but vertical, or perhaps on a rising parabola. The image is complicated and possibly recalls the apocalyptic four-winged cherub beasts from Ezekiel, chapter 1.[11] The primary complicaton is, in a way, Plato's

---

10. As Hackforth notes (*Phaedrus*, p. 69 n. 1), ὑπυπτέρου "winged" at 246A7 qualifies both the steeds (ζεύγους) and the charioteer (ἡνιόχου), as 251B7, πᾶσα γὰρ ἦν τὸ πάλαι πτερωτή, makes plain. Though Ficino's translation of the Greek sentence is ambiguous in his 1484 *Platonis Opera Omnia* (ed. Allen, *Charioteer*, p. 53), he certainly recognized this, as his analyses in chap. 7 and summa 33 testify (ibid., pp. 98-99, 188-191).

Failure to recognize the same, however, led Panofsky astray in his fine analysis of the medallion worn by the young man in the bust once attributed to Donatello in the Bargello (*Renaissance and Renascences*, p. 189n); see frontispiece and accompanying note above.

11. See Allen, *Charioteer*, p. 3; Heninger, *Cosmographical Glass*, p. 88; and D. P. Walker, "The Astral Body in Renaissance Medicine," *Journal of the Warburg and Courtauld Institutes* 21 (1958), 119-133 at 123.

Heninger points to the association occasionally made between the Merkabah chariot—derived as it is from Ezekiel's vision (Ezek. 1:16-28)—and a particular configuration of the sephiroth known as *Adam kadmon* and regarded often as "a microcosmic image of prototypical man." Pico is more likely to have stumbled on these associations than Ficino, whose knowledge of cabalistic lore and imagery was rudimentary at best; see Umberto Cassuto, *Gli Ebrei a Firenze nell'età del Rinascimento* (Florence, 1918), pp. 277-281.

Walker points out that the chariots of Ezekiel and Elijah were tentatively equated with the Neoplatonic astral body by Nicolaus Leonicus in a tract written around 1524, dedicated to Reginald Pole and entitled *Alverotus sive De Tribus Animorum Vehiculis* (in *Nicolai Leonici Thomaei Dialogi* [Lyons, 1542], pp. 102-103). See also n. 29 below.

attribution of wings to the charioteer; for it makes him potentially
independent of the chariot altogether in his ascent to heaven and
in effecting his own apotheosis. The formula of attributing wings
"preeminently" to the charioteer, in the next degree to the good
horse, and only in the last degree to the worse horse hardly serves
to clarify matters either. It suggests, indeed, and Ficino virtually
says this, that one set of wings, the charioteer's, could serve to
raise them all.

I postpone till later my consideration of the identification of the
chariot itself with the "celestial" body, sempiternal, spherical,
and swiftest of all the bodies a soul can possess. Ficino never
exploits or even explains, furthermore, the allegorization of the
two wheels as the last two stages in a non-Plotinian triad of procession, turning, and return.[12] What he does account for rather is
their dual motion: around their own axle, and forward on their
career.

Ficino returns to the charioteer's head in the last paragraph.
Since he needs another component in the myth to complete his
hierarchy of psychological faculties, he takes the unexpected step
of dividing the head into two aspects, a division reflecting the Neoplatonic separation of Mind from the One. Thus the twin heads
can represent the two activities attributed to the highest intelligence: joining with the One (earlier defined as "the universe's
principle") and, as the highest form of intellection, intuition of
the Ideas in the intelligible world. They are succeeded by the charioteer as intellect who understands by a process of intellection just
short of instantaneous intuition; then by the white horse as reason;
then by the black as imagination and the nature whose functioning
is slowest of all. Next, Ficino dovetails the charioteer image into
that of the world schema: the heads are equated with the twin
poles of the world or cosmic machine; the swiftest motion of
understanding with the diurnal motion of the fixed stars (the firmament) and thus with the motion imparted to them by the *primum mobile;* and the slower motion of discursive reasoning with

---

12. Wind, *Pagan Mysteries,* p. 38n, briefly suggested that there is a revealing difference
between the ancient triad of resting, procession, and return, and this "new" Renaissance
variation on it. This is a fascinating idea in need of further exploration.

the planets' motions. Here we have a subdivision: its more universal, contemplative motion resembles the circlings of the three major planets; its more particular and practical motion, those of the four minor ones. The even slower movement of the imagination, which Ficino refers to as a "period" rather than a "circuit," resembles the aether's motion.[13] Finally, the slowest motion of all, the period or functioning of the nature, resembles the more turbulent, though still essentially circular, "revolutions" of air and water. This set of equations between the charioteer image and the spherical movements of the cosmos is not just theoretical or illustrative. Ficino believed ardently in the validity of micro- and macrocorrespondences and in the justness of arguing from the one to the other, particularly as here from the psychological to the cosmological and the reverse. For it is the soul's powers which direct and sustain the cosmic spheres and are especially adapted to them. Though the charioteer myth is accessible to astrological analyses and apparently underwent such in antiquity, Ficino steers away from these and from cognate theosophical possibilities that might have stemmed from his earlier identification, already well worked out in the *Platonic Theology* at 18.4, of the chariot with the soul's aethereal vehicle.[14]

The truly signal contrast between Plato's introduction of the myth and Ficino's interpretation of it is the feeling for a carefully articulated and hierarchical metaphysical and psychological system which Ficino brings to bear. But this operates selectively in two respects. He almost invariably makes reference to the horses, wings, and head of the charioteer, rather than to the wheels, yoking, laming, and so on; and he always has in the forefront of his mind the chariot at the start of its career, when the note is one of confidence in the ability of human hands to hold and guide the reins, rather than the more powerful later image of the tumultuous struggle between man and beast. Despite the occasional bout of hypochondria and the stylish cultivation of melancholy,[15] both

13. See chap. 1, pp. 11-12 above.
14. Ed. Marcel, 3:193-196; trans. Allen, *Charioteer,* pp. 230-235. See chap. 9, pp. 218-220 below.
15. For an evocative portrait of Ficino as *il penseroso,* see Garin, "Immagini e simboli in Marsilio Ficino" (see Preface, n. 7 above); Eugenio Garin, *Rinascite e rivoluzioni* (Bari, 1975), pp. 108, 111.

befitting a celibate scholar interested in medicine and particularly
in the nature and aetiology of psychosomatic depression, Ficino
was temperamentally an optimist with the energy, productiveness,
and sustained effectiveness of the integrated achiever.[16] The expec-
tant charioteer hurtling upwards to realms beyond the planets and
the stars was an image he cherished and frequently resorted to; for
it corresponded, as perhaps no other did, to his basic emotional
and intellectual attitudes to life.

Summa 16 is an interesting addendum. Ficino introduces the
notion that motion and difference are the "worse" genera of
being, and that "of good stock" must therefore mean "from the
better genera," namely from rest and identity. Quite apart from
the fact that the whole notion of better and worse categories of
being itself raises a host of questions, the argument that the gods'
horses are all constituted from the better categories runs directly
counter to Ficino's earlier argument that the good horse has
"more" of rest and identity while the bad horse has them tempered in equal measure. Perhaps he sensed this, for he adds,
"rather, they have the same five genera possessed by all things but
which they possess in a more outstanding manner (*praestantius*)."
He notes, moreover, that our charioteer and horses "have a disordered and obvious contrariety" among the genera, since "they
can become bad at times," even though they possess the good
genera of rest and identity. It is difficult to see what "a disordered
and obvious contrariety" can mean here other than that the last
four genera of being must coexist in equal proportions so that the
better ones do not predominate. These few sentences, in short,
raise more problems than they solve.

In an earlier work, *Adversity's Noblemen: The Italian Humanists on Happiness* (New
York, 1940; reprint, 1965), pp. 37-38, Charles Trinkaus also dwelt upon Ficino's melancholy; but more recently in his *Image and Likeness,* pp. 482-498, he has emphasized the
more optimistic and affirmative strains.

16. This comes across most clearly in his exaltation of man and man's dignity; see
Eugenio Garin, "La 'dignitas hominis' e la letteratura patristica," *La Rinascita* 1.4 (1938),
102-146; Giovanni Gentile, "Il concetto dell'uomo nel Rinascimento," in his *Il pensiero
italiano del Rinascimento* (Florence, 1940), pp. 47-113 and especially 90 ff.; Kristeller,
Studies, pp. 261-286, 364 ff.; and Tigerstedt, "The Poet as Creator," pp. 470-474.

Ficino's most notable statements on man are probably those in his *Platonic Theology*
14.1-8 (ed. Marcel, 2:246-279); see Kristeller, *Philosophy,* pp. 117 ff.

We have such difficulty driving our chariots because our white steed is moved towards intelligibles, our black towards sensibles, where it declines to "generation." Whereas the divine souls can both contemplate intelligibles and "provide" for sensibles equally (*pariter*), and whereas we will be able to do the same when restored to our native land, in this life we cannot do both equally; hence our charioteership is difficult. Notice Ficino's switch from the concept of "generation" to "providing." As we shall see, the providential care the gods extend to the lower world lacks the element of appetitive desire present in the concept of "generation." To the contrary, "providing" is the third aspect of an orientation triad predicated both of gods, supramundane and mundane, and of men: looking upwards, selfwards, and downwards. While the latter means both guarding and protecting, it also implies caring for and sustaining in the paternalistic sense (as opposed to the erotic yearning and longing of the lower for the higher). This downward providential motion may meet the upward yearning of inferiors and indeed authenticate it, but in part it does represent a fall, a "providing" that can become "generation" if the soul cannot maintain the balance between it and contemplation. That is, there is no absolute qualitative difference between the two, but rather one movement that enters into two states.

The kinship between providing and generation can become near identity when we attribute both to the black steed by setting up the following set of equations: charioteer equals upward looking; white horse selfward looking; and black horse downward looking. Ficino does not actually make these equations, but he might well have done so, since the wings are by definition upward-moving powers and preeminently the charioteer's. In either case, the black horse is equivalent to, if not identical with, the agapic providential caring exercised by the gods over the world, or at least a fallen embodiment of it. Thus the gulf between the black horse as it struggles here to upset the chariot and as it pulls obediently in the traces of the gods accounts for its profoundly ambiguous nature in Ficino's analysis of the myth. While it drags us down, the only function it could possibly have in the chariots of the gods is to exercise the providential care that offsets the all-absorbing contemplation of the charioteer. It emerges not just as an integral

aspect of goodness but as the aspect most concerned with and
accessible to us. Ficino's goal is not its transformation into the
white steed, nor the postulation of a chariot drawn by two white
steeds alone.[17] For the black steed is as integral to the life of the
gods as the white or as the charioteer himself and serves to unite
both of them providentially to inferiors, creating thereby a unitary
reality where love flows downwards as well as selfwards and upwards in a perfect circle. The black steed is potentially, though it
may come as a shock to envisage it thus, a symbol for Christ, for
the incarnation of the Logos, the love in God that led Him to
create the inferior world in the beginning and to ensure its ultimate
salvation.

Chapter 8 confronts the problem of the individual's relationship
to the material cosmos and the soul's duties to the world. Along
with Plato, Ficino returns to the dictum at 246B6, "all soul has
care of all that is soulless or inanimate," and distinguishes again
between the universal responsibilities of the World-Soul and the
restricted zones of responsibility assigned to individual souls.
Despite the restrictions on the latter, the result for the world is that
everything is under the care of some one soul or other, as well as of
the World-Soul. But Ficino's next remarks are both more characteristic and more adventurous. He surmises that Plato's dictum
may also imply (and he sees it as plurisignation rather than the
offering of alternative meanings) that any rational soul can move
through all the world spheres in the course of time and "by
degrees" and thus escape the sublunar realm to which it has
hitherto been committed, and that it can also move into, or specifically "withdraw into," "the universal providence" in heaven, at
least occasionally. Such an interpretation harks back to some of
the propositions explored in the *Platonic Theology*.[18]

---

17. Nor, for that matter, the postulation in the case of sinners of a chariot drawn by two
black steeds alone.

18. For example, 2.13; 13.2, 3; 14.10; 18.10 (ed. Marcel, 1:124-126; 2:205-211, 225, 293-
296; 3:227-228). Among other works, Ficino was deeply indebted to Plotinus, *Enneads* 3.2,
3, and also to three treatises by Proclus which he knew in Latin translation: *De Decem
Dubitationibus circa Providentiam; De Providentia et Fato et Eo Quod in Nobis;* and *De
Malorum Subsistentia* (ed. H. Boese). See esp. Heitzman, "La libertà e il fato."

With its transcendental orientation, however, the *Phaedrus* does not serve as the best starting point for examining the soul's links with the material world, or, collaterally, with the immanental aspects of the Godhead. The polarities of transcendence and immanence both exerted their fascination on Ficino, while, simultaneously, he refused to be polarized. Even when transcendental material comes to the fore, he picks up passing phrases to offset it, to restore the balance. The chariot's flight is not only a mystical ascent from darkness into light but a cosmic ride through the hierarchy of being, inspired by love for the whole. The soul wishes not merely to flee to the One but to reach the One by way of a graduated ascent that takes her from one end of creation to the other and thus into all things.

Plato's phraseology suggests several possibilities. Ficino paraphrases "the soul . . . traverses the whole universe, though in everchanging forms," as "the soul has been formed [to move through all the world's spheres and eventually to withdraw into the universal providence], but to do so at different times and in different species." He steers clear of reincarnational and transmigrational possibilities, and postulates instead a sequence of states and corresponding duties, at least for the souls of men and inferior demons who must perforce commence by operating by means of time and space, in contrast with higher souls who operate timelessly and dimensionlessly and therefore changelessly. At first a lower soul inhabits the earth because it lives in the material body (species one).[19] Subsequently it inhabits higher, subcelestial spheres because it occupies a "purer"—what Ficino later calls an "airy"—body (species two).[20] Still later it seeks celestials in a celestial body

19. Ficino makes it clear that the earthy body is composed of all four elements and not just of water and earth. In his *Timaeus* Commentary, chap. 24 (*Opera,* p. 1449), Ficino enunciates the principle that each element is everywhere present *pro natura suscipientium:* thus all the elements are in heaven but in a heavenly way, as all celestial things are in the elements but in an elemental way. See Kristeller, *Philosophy,* p. 373.

20. As noted on pp. 12-13 above, this aerial body was sometimes subdivided into a body of pure air and one of misty or foggy air. The subdivision made possible a satisfactory accommodation between the resulting four bodies (the aethereal, the two airy, and the earthy) and the four elements. Thus the fiery or aethereal body was composed of the fiery aether; the purely airy body, of fiery aether and pure air; the misty body, of fiery aether, pure air, and vaporous air; and the earthy body, of all four elements together.

More often, of course, Ficino thinks in terms of only three bodies: the aethereal, the airy, and the earthy. He would certainly have known that Origen had espoused such a theory,

—that is, the fiery or aethereal body (species three); indeed, in returning to the planetary god that has exercised particular care over it, it acquires the power to live and act as if it were that god. Finally, having been restored completely "to the amplitude of its reasons, powers, and notions," the soul joins the World-Soul and receives its universal providence, not in a supracelestial body (since the concept of an individual body ceases to be meaningful above the celestial world) but in the great celestial body of the cosmos itself (species four).[21] Thus the soul is assured both of eternity and not so much of freedom *in* space as of freedom *from* space (just as eternity is freedom from time)—freedom, that is, from having to operate within either ontological category. We can see it is just a step away from the view of freedom customarily associated with Pico, the freedom to choose one's ontological kind, the freedom even not to be a soul (though Pico never saw the problem in these terms and did not therefore confront the many inherent contradictions).[22]

The notion that Jove bestows jovian qualities on things, Saturn saturnian, and so forth, has astrological implications that Ficino scrutinized in other works;[23] but in positing a universal providence that bestows every gift, including jovian and saturnian qualities, he bypasses the astrologers' differentiation of the various planetary activities. In devoting itself to any one planetary intelligence,

---

and also that Jerome had condemned him for it. See Klein, "L'enfer de Ficin," pp. 57-59, with further references. He also appears to reject the Proclian refinement that distinguishes between bodies of absolutely pure fire, the "astral vehicle," and those of fire mixed with air—that is, of aethereal bodies (as Ficino understood *aether* following the *Epinomis* and Calcidius; see chap. 1, n. 24 above). For him the aethereal body is the celestial body. Cf. Plotinus, *Enneads* 3.5.6.

21. That is, in the *spiritus,* not the *machina mundi;* see Yates, *Bruno,* pp. 68-69.

22. Pico's most celebrated statement on the soul's absolute freedom occurs in his *Oration on the Dignity of Man* (ed. Garin, pp. 102-109). However, as Garin, Kristeller, Yates, and others have pointed out, the statement consists in large part of a paraphrase of a passage in chap. 6 of the Hermetic *Asclepius* (ed. and trans. Nock and Festugière, *Corpus Hermeticum* 2:301-302). Nothing, incidentally, in Pico's subsequent writings entertains such an extreme view of human liberty or dignity; see especially Giovanni di Napoli, *Giovanni Pico della Mirandola e la problematica dottrinale del suo tempo* (Rome 1965), pt. 2, chap. 3. For some even severer reservations as to Pico's intentions in the *Oratio* itself, see William G. Craven, *Giovanni Pico della Mirandola: Symbol of his Age* (Geneva, 1981), pp. 21-45, and Henri de Lubac, *Pic de la Mirandole* (Paris, 1974), pp. 114-129.

23. Notably in the *De Vita.* Ficino's attitudes towards astrology vary; see chap. 7, n. 27 below.

the soul not only selects the gifts of that planet, but ultimately of that which governs all the planets, the universal providence which the World-Soul extends to its inferiors. The soul is thus free of the exterior constraints and necessities usually associated with the astrological world-view. Ficino might have been prepared to read into the charioteer myth, particularly at 247A and 252CD, much more astrology and astral lore than we think Plato himself intended or allowed, as did Plato's ancient commentators (to judge from Hermias's commentary and its sundry allusions to Iamblichus, Syrianus, Proclus, Harpocration, and others).[24] But his concern in these paragraphs is not with astrological necessity but with the gifts each planet bestows on man as a particular instance of the "providing" that celestial souls, like all souls, extend to their inferiors, animate and inanimate. Significantly, as chapter 11 demonstrates, the planets themselves are imaged as charioteers, not raining down baleful influences on man but leading him jubilantly towards the transcendent realm—leading him, moreover, in a cavalcade that cannot be allegorized in terms of the stellar conjunctions and oppositions that preoccupy the astrologer.

Paragraph 2 reverts to the former life of the soul in its integrity and universality, the possessor of both a speculative and a practical intellect which it exercises either in the universal manner proper to the World-Soul or in the more restricted manners proper to the planets. The soul is always envisaged as exercising providential care of some sort prior to its birth in a terrestrial body, and as doing so with the universal reason (*ratio*), the alternative name here for the practical intellect. In this prelapsarian state the rational soul is potentially all soul, as defined by the sixth chapter of the Commentary, since it still possesses the powers and knowledge proper to all soul: both its universality of acting on any or all of the created world, and its universality of desiring (*affectus*) the intelligible world, presumably also in its entirety. Though not the World-Soul, the rational soul performs the same office (extending universal providence) with the same faculty (the universal reason

---

24. See especially Hermias's doxography, p. 135.27 ff. (ed. Couvreur); cf. Dillon, *Iamblichi Fragmenta*, p. 251. See also P. Boyancé, "La religion astrale de Platon à Cicéron," *Revue des études grecques* 65 (1952), 312-350.

in its simplicity), though it can choose to operate in the more restricted ways of the Sun, Saturn, and so on.

The third paragraph interprets the notion of being winged or on the wing to mean that the soul exercises both its sublime activities to the highest degree, the wings themselves being precisely those powers that summon the soul to these activities. Consequently, it is the hampering of the wings, rather than the unruliness of the black steed, which signifies the soul's failure steadfastly to contemplate the whole, the "world's universal form," the world in its totality (rather than the Idea of the world—a concept alien to Ficino). Instead it begins to gaze too diligently on "a particular province" and "to love its life more ardently." This narrowing of gaze is attributed to the rational soul in its entirety, not to any one of its parts and faculties, and results from its allowing itself to be overruled by the attraction that its imagination and vital power or nature instinctively have for a particular province. The result "in a way" is that the soul "contracts" into the longeval airy body, and thus becomes a demonic or philosophical man. Finally it reaches the limit of contraction and acquires a terrestrial body with depth and grossness and, concomitantly, corporeal mortality (while remaining itself essentially immortal). Thus earthly man is man at his most contracted, at his least human.

For this graduated fall Ficino does not assign responsibility for the moment, and he will return to the question in later summae.[25] He is careful, however, not to blame the body but to praise it, at least indirectly, by postulating a hierarchy of bodies. In part he was influenced here by the Christian dogma of the body's resurrection on the last day, a dogma which predicates the body's as well as the soul's eventual perfection and immortality, but not necessarily its materiality. He was also influenced by Neoplatonic speculation on the soul's "garments," though this took him to the borders of heresy. The highest celestial body, the soul's ultimate chariot, is modeled from the fire constituting the heavenly spheres, Ptolemaically conceived—that is, from something infinitely purer than three-dimensional, gross matter, something on the verge of itself becoming immaterial, becoming soul. In a mundane god the

25. See chap. 7, pp. 166-173 below.

two are so compatible as to be virtually identical. On the basis of our understanding of the union between soul and corporeal body, we suppose such a "god" to be a soul with a fiery or aethereal body naturally and perpetually joined to it, though this supposition is entirely analogical, and Ficino warns us not to think of it as a union in our terms. Since the celestial body's power or potentiality to sustain life is commensurate with the soul's power actually to bestow it, the celestial body must be immortal. On the last day, therefore, or whenever we reascend to our natural states as mundane gods, we ascend with our celestial bodies; and these may or may not be, as I have already noted, our earthly bodies purified, or the essence of those bodies stripped of their accretion of earth, water, and air. Above the mundane are the supermundane gods, whom Ficino identifies, here as customarily, with the angels.[26] They have no bodies whatsoever, being pure intellects, not souls. Should we ever become angels, we would lose our celestial bodies therefore; but since there is no suggestion that we will or should ever lose our status as souls, we will never actually lose our "intimate" celestial bodies, the purest of our Phaedran chariots.

The celestial body's "wonderful readiness" for life determines not only its quality of life but even in a way its quantity, since the soul either is its life or else imposes it. It is unclear in the case of a fallen soul, however, whether the higher aethereal and airy bodies exist actually or potentially within or apart from the earthy body. Ficino has already introduced the term *spiritus* (*pneuma*) in paragraph 4, and we can determine the relationship between this important and traditional concept and the Phaedran chariot if we refer back to it, and also to a notable passage in the *Platonic Theology* (18.4) where the verse from the *Oracula Chaldaica,* "Don't soil the spirit, nor add depth to what is plane," appears again.[27] In

26. See chap. 1, n. 21 above. The mundane gods were often thought of as the lowest, the least angelic, of the angels.

27. Ed. Édouard Des Places, *Oracles chaldaïques* (Paris, 1971), p. 92, as frag. 104, with Psellus's commentary, p. 176; cf. frag. 158, pp. 104-105, with Psellus's commentary, pp. 162-164.

Bohdan Kieszkowski, in his *Studi sul platonismo del Rinascimento in Italia* (Florence, 1936), app., pp. 156, 161-163, draws our attention to some glosses by Pletho on frag. 104 and other verses, glosses preserved in MS Vat. Barberiniano greco 179, f. 16$^{\text{r-v}}$, and written

the preceding paragraph Ficino glossed "spirit" and "plane" to mean "the ever familiar celestial body"; and in the *Platonic Theology* he had referred the "spirit" to the *Timaeus*'s "vehicle" (and this has already been identified with the *Phaedrus*'s "chariot").[28] Thus "spirit" is clearly synonymous in Ficino's mind at this point with our highest body, the fiery or aethereal vehicle, though we might have expected it to signify, as it often does elsewhere, the next highest vehicle, the airy body.[29] Since his principal concern is

in the hand, along with accompanying Latin translations on ff. 16^V-17^V, of Francesco Patrizi. Pletho's gloss on this frag. 104 reads: "When he calls our soul's spirit and nearest vehicle a plane (*superficies*), he does not really intend it to be a plane, for it is a [three-dimensional] body; rather, he is emphasizing its extraordinary thinness." Of interest too is Pletho's next gloss on frag. 158, *Est idolo quoque locus in regione perspicua* (as translated by Ficino in his *Platonic Theology* 18.4 [ed. Marcel, 3:194]): "He is also correct to call that idol the soul's vehicle; with the soul it enters into the all-brilliant place, which again he also calls Paradise." Given Pletho's authority for Ficino in matters concerning the *Oracles,* he had probably read these glosses. See Dannenfeldt, "The Pseudo-Zoroastrian Oracles," pp. 9-15; Dillon, *Middle Platonists,* p. 395; Allen, *Charioteer,* pp. 240-241 n. 25, and p. 251 n. 118; see also chap. 9, nn. 30 and 31 below.

28. For a note on these terms and some of the scholarship see Allen, *Charioteer,* p. 250 n. 113. For Ficino see Robert Klein, "L'imagination comme vêtement de l'âme chez Marsile Ficin et Giordano Bruno," *Revue de métaphysique et de morale* 61 (1956), 18-39 at 22-30; idem, "L'enfer de Ficin," pp. 48 ff.; Kristeller, *Philosophy,* pp. 371-374; Walker, *Magic,* pp. 3-59, especially pp. 3-13, 38-40; Zanier, *Medicina,* pp. 24-29. Many aspects of the Neoplatonists' accounts of the "spirit," the "vehicle," and the various higher "bodies" await further study and clarification, as do Ficino's own theories and their indebtedness to ancient and Byzantine authorities. In particular we should beware of transposing Ficino's extensive and important account in his *De Vita* 3.1, 3, 4, 11, 20 (*Opera,* pp. 531-536, 544-546, 560-561) to other, very different contexts. See n. 29 below; also chap. 9, n. 28 below.

29. Kristeller, *Philosophy,* p. 373, argues, however, that *spiritus* for Ficino generally signifies the airy body: "Since the spirit is also called the 'vehicle of the soul,' it seems uncertain whether it is supposed to be distinct from the ethereal body. However, we must not be misled by verbal similarities. There is sufficient testimony to prove that Ficino clearly distinguishes the spirit from both the ethereal body and the earthly body"; cf. Klein, "L'imagination comme vêtement," p. 24. Kristeller then translates two passages from the *Platonic Theology:* from 17.2 (ed. Marcel, 3:154), "In like manner the Soul of man seems to behave with respect to its three vehicles: the ethereal, the air-like, and the composed body"; and from 18.4 (ed. Marcel, 3:195), "Many Platonists believe that the Soul uses three vehicles—the first, immaterial and simple, that is, celestial; the second, material and simple, that is, air-like; the third, material and composed, that is, made up of the four elements"; cf. Allen, *Charioteer,* p. 234. But neither citation determines the status of *spiritus:* they merely argue for the existence of an airy body intermediate between the aethereal (celestial) and the earthy (composed of all four elements).

Ficino was well aware of the medical tradition with its natural, vital, and animal spirits and frequently speaks of the *spiritus* or specifically the *spiritus aereus* to signify such spirits; see Walker, *Magic,* pp. 5-13, 38-39, and, for the ancients, G. Verbeke, *L'évolution de la doctrine du pneuma du stoïcisme à saint Augustin* (Paris and Louvain, 1945), passim, but especially pp. 77, 192, and 206. But he also speaks of the *spiritus* differently as "a certain mini-body, extraordinarily rarefied and dazzlingly bright" (*tenuissimum quoddam lucidis-*

with the ascent of man as a unitary being, his conception of the body is necessarily opposed both to the *Phaedo*'s presentation of it as the soul's prison (σῆμα) and to its denigration by certain Christian thinkers. Even the earthy body is not the soul's tyrannical keeper but a vehicle to which the soul gives motion and life. The body continually strives to receive, and yearns for, the gift of perpetual life, though it can ultimately accept this life only when it has reverted to its celestial or aethereal form.

Assuming that heaven has no matter (an assumption he does not usually accept), Ficino sets up in the penultimate paragraph the relationships first between the soul's "vital motion"—that is, its primary motion as life—and "dimension;" and next between its "understanding" and "light." The latter presupposes a complicated relationship between the process of understanding and the metaphysics of light, one which depends on the medieval-Renaissance theory of visual perception that has the eye send out a ray of light to illuminate an object; and Ficino will postpone treating it until his next chapter. The former is of immediate concern. "Heaven is so close to soul" that soul in its unimpeded, cyclical motion "proceeds as" and therefore "creates" its own heavenly sphere.[30] We should not confuse this type of creation with the absolute creation of all things by God; nevertheless it raises some unusual possibilities. Ficino is not merely tackling the problem of the relationship between soul and its sphere as formulated by Aristotle in the famous passage in the *Metaphysics* concerning the

---

simumque corpusculum) in the *Platonic Theology* 7.6 (ed. Marcel, 1:274) and elsewhere. That is, he often thinks of it as "of a nature more akin to light, fire, or the *quinta essentia* of the heavens, than to the air" (Walker, *Magic,* p. 8), and in such instances equates it with the *spiritus* that preoccupies St. Paul. Thus while the *spiritus* [*aereus*] is clearly associated in Ficino's mind with the airy body, the *spiritus* [*igneus*] is associated with the aethereal or celestial body. It is the context which must determine to which *spiritus,* i.e. higher body, Ficino is referring, and it is premature, I believe, to argue, as Walker does, that he is "somewhat inconsistent" in this matter (*Magic,* p. 13n). Here, for instance, the reference to the Zoroastrian verse—which also appears, incidentally, in the *Platonic Theology* 18.4, though three paragraphs prior to the passage Kristeller selected for citation—makes it quite clear that Ficino has the *spiritus igneus*—that is, the aethereal body—in mind and is identifying it moreover with the *Timaeus*'s vehicle and thus with the *Phaedrus*'s chariot. See also nn. 11 and 28 above.

30. It is difficult to determine here whether Ficino intends all the senses of soul; that is, should soul be capitalized and treated as the hypostasis, or should it be accompanied by the definite or the indefinite article?

fifty-five intelligences thought necessary to account for the manifest diversity of celestial motions and more particularly planetary motions.[31] Soul's vital motion moves through and thereby creates dimension or extension, and this motion parallels that of soul's understanding proceeding as light. One corollary Ficino draws from this theory is that, if you subtracted dimension from heaven, deprived heaven of its dimensionality (given the hypothesis that heaven is entirely immaterial),[32] you would be left simply with soul at rest, in stasis. Since soul as the principle of motion is never at rest, heaven always exists; but it exists as a modality of soul. Clearly, by "heaven" Ficino means something distinct from normal usage; but not entirely so, since his theory suggests not that heaven is a subjective state with no objective existence, but rather that it is coterminous with the very notion of soul.[33] Were soul to rest or cease to be soul and become pure intelligence (and this will never happen), then heaven would cease to be and we would have instead a superheavenly, a supramundane state or modality, itself dependent on our notion of what intelligence does or is, given its priority and superiority to soul.

At no point does Ficino clarify which particular concept of soul he is referring to. Since heaven is a unitary conception, he should mean all soul collectively or at least the World-Soul—in which case, from the viewpoint of an individual soul, heaven does have total objectivity in that it is the modality of all souls, not just of the individual soul. However, not only does Ficino's earlier argumentation in support of the ultimate interchangeability of each and all soul work against this, but so does his subsequent remark (in fact undermining the thesis of his previous sentence) that there is a "capacity" or power in heaven "to be formed" by the soul. This leads him in turn to equate "heaven" with each and every

31. *Metaphysics* 12.8.1073a ff. Cf. de Gandillac, "Astres, anges et génies," p. 101; Allen, "The Absent Angel in Ficino's Philosophy," pp. 230-232.

32. This is an entirely hypothetical situation. We should recall the distinction between corporeal and incorporeal matter; see Kristeller, *Philosophy,* pp. 39, 165, and, for the Plotinian doctrine of "intelligible matter," Wallis, *Neoplatonism,* pp. 20, 66, 117, 148-149, 166, 172.

33. We should be careful to distinguish between the special meanings Ficino attributed to the term "heaven" when analyzing the charioteer myth in the *Phaedrus* (see Allen, *Charioteer,* pp. 66-69) and those which he attributes here in this general analysis of soul, where it clearly refers to the realm of soul in motion and not to the realm of the intellectual gods.

"celestial vehicle" under its soul. That is, heaven (presumably *a* heaven) is a chariot now, not that which is created by a chariot's career. The larger problem of the relationship between one soul's vehicle or heaven and another's is left unresolved and indeed unformulated. The whole issue is not uniquely Ficino's since it comes with the Aristotelian theory of the intelligences having individual spheres. If heaven is soul in motion (however defined), "a sort of life from the soul extended outside," then the charioteer's career is both an upward return to heaven by lower rational souls, and simultaneously a creation of that heaven by higher rational souls ("heaven" now meaning the celestial spheres). Absolutely integral to these various notions is the assumption that the soul is the principle and cause of motion, and heaven is the result of this motion. Despite their brevity and vulnerability, however, Ficino's remarks are indicative of his philosophical idealism and of his obsession with the soul.

The final paragraph of chapter 8 briefly explores a corollary of the "extension" argument, namely that we can make legitimate parallels between the basic concepts of geometry and differing stages in the soul's descent from unity in the One to life in the elemental, the material body—a descent which is a creation simultaneously of descending ontological planes. If unity equals the One, then the point equals Mind; the line, Soul; the plane, Heaven; and the solid, the subcelestial World.[34] Kristeller has already demonstrated the importance of a hypostatic pentad for Ficino in emphasizing the role of Soul as the cosmic mediator, the "knot" of the universe.[35] But the pentad here is not the one employed in the opening books of the *Platonic Theology,* namely God (i.e. the

---

34. This series of parallels—derived in part from Plato's *Laws* 10.894A—was a philosophical commonplace that Platonists and Neoplatonists read into the *Timaeus* 32B and attributed ultimately to the Pythagoreans. It had drawn criticism and comment from Aristotle in his *De Caelo* 1.1.268a7-a28; *De Anima* 1.2.404b16-b24; *Metaphysics* 1.9.992a10-b18; 13.9.1085a7-b3; etc. See Dillon, *Middle Platonists,* pp. 5-6, 27-28, etc., for its subsequent history; and Heninger, *Sweet Harmony,* pp. 134 n. 16 and 196 n. 22, for references to various Renaissance treatments.

Ficino's sources would also have included Diogenes Laertius, *Lives* 8.25, and Plutarch, *De E apud Delphos* (*Moralia* 390D).

35. Notably in his *Philosophy,* pp. 106-108, 167-169, 266, 370, 384, 388, 400-401; but see Allen, "Ficino's Theory of the Five Substances," passim.

One), Angel (i.e. Mind), Soul, Quality, and Body.[36] Substituting for the last two (which never received much elaboration anyway) we now have Heaven and the subcelestial World; and though the World can be equated with Body, Heaven cannot be equated with Quality. Both pentads of course highlight the mean position of Soul. Just as the mathematical series derives from the evolution of the point from essence into existence into unidimensionality into bi- and then tridimensionality, so the ontological series arrives at Mind when essence is added to unity, at Soul when motion is added to Mind, at Heaven when Soul has "swollen" to a two-dimensional plane, and at elemental Body when Heaven has moved into three-dimensionality. Though Ficino is careful to introduce his usual qualifiers—"as it were," "sort of," "so to speak"—the force of the parallels is to underscore the continuous nature of the ontological series and thus Soul's potentiality to become the other hypostases, and particularly to fly downwards in its aethereal vehicle until it generates Body. Inevitably, the critical role of motion in the argumentation—it is built into the very nature of the chariot image—has the effect of highlighting Soul at the expense of the other hypostases.

Thus Ficino manages to transform Plato's enigmatic paragraph centered upon the image of the soul "shedding its wings" into a series of meditations on the soul's unique ontological position. In the process he focuses our attention on the flight itself rather than on the chariot's components; both the flight upwards, and then the swoop downwards, the result not so much of the loss or shedding of wings as of their temporary closing. This focus enables him to use the myth as a medium for exploring some of the basic concepts of his own variations on the Neoplatonic metaphysical system, and particularly those of the soul and its creative function as the universal "bond and copula." For the hurtling charioteer is eminently appropriate as a symbol for man: not the bare poor forked thing of Lear's despair but the truly cosmic animal, the amphibian horse-man-bird, the most powerful and compelling of heraldic and apocalyptic beasts.[37]

36. For example, 1.1; 3.2 (ed. Marcel, 1:39, 137 ff.). There are differing views as to why the pentad seems to be dominant only in the opening books.

37. Summa 17, which covers 246B-D, is extremely brief. Unlike the commentary chapter, however, it stresses the unknowability of the "immortal animal," the being composed of a soul and a celestial, i.e. aethereal, body.

Chapter 9 concentrates on the lemma at 246E1 that the divine nature is "beautiful, wise, and good," and directs our attention to the hierarchy governing the relationships between them; it also justifies the sequence in which Plato presents the epithets. Ficino had already treated aspects of the problem in his *Philebus* Commentary, where he deals, for instance, with the good's three attributes of sufficiency, desirability, and perfection.[38] But it constantly attracted him, partly, I conjecture, because it harmonized so well with the notion of searching the Platonic corpus for "vestiges" of the Trinity hidden there in philosophical form.[39] It also enabled him, conversely, to dovetail the fundamental problems of epistemology into a trinitarian metaphysical system. In exploring the connections between beauty, goodness, and truth (or wisdom), Ficino was thus directly drawn to the issue he found most pressing, the nature of man's divinity and of his knowledge of that divinity. Though discussion of at least two of the concepts, goodness and wisdom, owes something to medieval philosophizing on the transcendentals, *unum, bonum,* and *verum,*[40] Ficino's assumption of the problem in the midst of interpreting the charioteer myth was an independent decision and the result partly of his obsession with beauty (not, traditionally, one of the transcendentals). Even so, he had to expand on what are mere hints in Plato, transforming them into propositions again predicated on an articulated and comprehensive ontology, which was Plotinian in its essentials but which he had modified sufficiently to make uniquely his own.

The opening sentence attributes to the soul a power which "drags" it down towards sensibles, a power "simultaneously responsible" for imagining and vegetative functions. This power must be the black horse, though the whole context is concerned with the soul's *wings*—that is, with the elevating power in the soul's intellect or reason—and with the "binding" of that power. Whereas the two horses are mutually opposed, however, the wings

38. 1.30 (ed. Allen, pp. 290-297), glossing *Philebus* 20D.
39. See Chastel, *Arte e umanesimo,* p. 207; idem, *Ficin et l'art,* p. 146; Heninger, *Cosmographical Glass,* pp. 171-172; Walker, *Ancient Theology,* p. 14; Wind, *Pagan Mysteries,* pp. 241-255. Particularly interesting in this regard are Ficino's own *De Amore* 2.1 (ed. Marcel, p. 145) and *Platonic Theology* 4.1 (ed. Marcel, 1:162-163); and Pico's *Heptaplus* 6, proem (ed. Garin, pp. 308-311).
40. See Kristeller, *Philosophy,* p. 45, and chap. 8, pp. 185 ff. below.

are not opposed: they function either freely, with difficulty, or not at all. Since their "binding" is the result of the black steed's rebellion, we can ultimately oppose the black steed to the wing. Ficino's use of the traditional simile of the sun's power lifting dampness "which otherwise naturally descends" suggests on the other hand a natural opposition between the wing and all that it lifts: not only the black steed but the white steed, the chariot itself, and the charioteer. Notice, incidentally, that the wing is attributed indifferently to the intellect or to reason, though Ficino takes care throughout his writings to distinguish between the two faculties.

In lifting the intellect and reason, the wing lifts the soul "to love, contemplate, and worship the divine," in that order. Elsewhere, as in the *Philebus* Commentary,[41] these three actions are separated out and attributed to the two wings separately; but not here. In arguing that the soul may "participate" in the good via its understanding, Ficino means the immanent not the transcendent good, since the latter, called the absolute good, is by definition beyond all categories of predication, even strictly speaking of goodness itself but certainly of wisdom and beauty. By the immanent good we do not mean the One, Ficino says, but Mind, the second hypostasis, for that is "the essential and intelligible good," goodness in its being and knowability. The Phaedran flight ascends as far as Mind, but no farther. It is Mind, then, not the One, which can be legitimately described as simultaneously "good, wise, and beautiful" and moreover "present in"—that is, participated in by —all the gods, supramundane and mundane alike, under "the first god," meaning the first god in the intellectual realm, Uranus (though, as we shall see, Saturn presides over the intellectual realm in its entirety). By contemplating Mind as "the wise and beautiful good" any intellect, whether pure and separated or joined to a soul, is "nourished"—and Ficino has the pasturage of 248B7 rather than the nectar and ambrosia of 247E6 in mind.

To define the good's three attributes, paragraph 2 transposes the problem to another key by asking: In what way is a god, not Mind, "good, wise, and beautiful"? Since a god has a contemplat-

---

41. 1.34 (ed. Allen, pp. 353-355; trans. *Charioteer*, pp. 225-229). For a more detailed analysis see chap. 9, pp. 210-213 below.

ing intellect, we have in the epistemological process (1) the faculty itself, (2) the process of understanding, and (3) what is understood. By utilizing the Phileban formula (and his own previous commentary on it) that the good is "perfect, sufficient, and desirable," Ficino can make the following equations. What is understood—that is, the intelligible—is good; in the process of understanding the good, a god is wise; and a god's intellect is beautiful since it is "ablaze with the splendor of the Forms" or, in other words, participating totally in the intelligible Ideas as they first appear as Beauty. A god's goodness is less apparent, consequently, than his wisdom or beauty, since it exists as the intelligible enfolded in its unity and hidden within as "the essential and vital perfection" awaiting the process of understanding. We must remember that, as a Platonist, Ficino always thinks of the intelligible as active: hence his description of it here as "the fertile power and intelligible capacity" containing within itself all the Ideas and the light to contemplate them. I take it that Ficino is glossing "sufficiency," as the Phileban formula is clearly in the forefront of his argumentation, and he will return to the question of the good's "desirability" in his next paragraph.

A god is "wise," on the other hand, when his understanding "brings forth" almost in the literal sense the intelligible light (the Augustinian light of truth). The image once again is that of a light beam radiating outwards as contrasted with unradiated or concentered light.[42] In the process of radiating, a god's understanding inwardly "unfolds" the Forms in the good—that is, in the intelligible, in Mind (not, note, the forms as replicated in its own intellect, the *formulae idearum*).[43] A god's intellect is illumined by the light of truth which unfolds the Ideas internally so that it can understand them individually rather than as they are collectively enfolded and hidden in the unity of the good.

Finally, a god is "beautiful" when the unfolding of the Forms radiated by the light of truth has been completed and the unfolding process has thus reached its outermost limit.

---

42. Cf. Ficino's letter to Cavalcanti, his *De Sole,* and his *De Lumine* (*Opera,* pp. 825-826, 965-986). See Chastel, *Ficin et l'art,* pp. 103-104, and Yates, *Bruno,* pp. 119-120.
43. See Kristeller, *Philosophy,* pp. 236-243.

Ficino then returns to the order of the attributes in the lemma—
"the divine nature is beautiful, wise, and good," in order to jus-
tify Plato's making "beautiful" the first rather than the last term
in the series. Though last to proceed ontologically, beauty comes
first epistemologically: it is first to be understood by those ascending from earth. As the first and most apparent not only of a god's
attributes but of Mind's attributes in that it is the splendor of all
the Ideas, the splendor of truth's light, Ficino calls it the "clear-
est"; and to incorporate the epithets he mentions a little later from
the *Symposium* 195A-196B, "soft," "delicate," "charming,"
and "lovable."[44] Beauty is preeminently lovable in that it inspires
us with love for a god and the essential good and draws us to them
and to itself. As the first in the sense of the most accessible, the
most "splendid" of the divine attributes, it is understandably
therefore the theme of Plato's first dialogue.

In the beginning of the last paragraph, Ficino reverts to the
third term in the Phileban formula, desirability. Truth is good insofar as it flows out of the good as its light and, having irradiated
intellects with a vision of the intelligibles, leads them back to the
good—that is, to the intelligible realm. Truth is also wise in that it
enables intellects to know and intelligibles to be known. Finally, it
is also beautiful in that it endows both intellects and intelligibles
with "a marvelous splendor" and "fashions them with grace."
Thus truth partakes of the three attributes ascribed to the gods.
Notice, however, that it was only by concentrating on the third
term of the Phileban formula, desirability, that Ficino could pass
from consideration both of truth as the good's light and of beauty
as the "splendor" of that light to a consideration of the goodness,
wisdom, and beauty of a god and of the love he inspires. Truth is
preeminently desirable in that it is its splendid beauty alone which
enables a god to contemplate the good and thereby become good,
wise, and beautiful. Goodness, wisdom, and beauty must therefore be predicated primarily of truth (though ultimately of the
good) and only secondarily of a god. In effect we have not only
three attributes, but three hypostases: the good, truth, a god. This

44. Cf. Ficino's *De Amore* 5.2, 7 (ed. Marcel, pp. 179 ff., 190 ff.). Note, however, that
the *Symposium* supplies only three of the epithets.

triad has nothing to do with the major Plotinian triad of the One, Mind, and Soul, but serves rather to mediate between Mind and Soul.

Thus the ninth chapter affords an insight into Ficino's application of Plotinian principles on an *ad hoc* basis to the Plato text, his aim being to clarify the relationships between goodness, truth, and the gods. Plato, notably, does not mention truth here at all; and instead of the good or the intelligible world he talks of the "divine nature," meaning the nature of the gods.

Summa 18 is a summary allegorization of the wing as the lifting power innate to the intellect and reason, the power that can effectively (*efficaciter*) lift us, when it is freed, to the divine. There we shall enjoy perfectly the good, wise, and beautiful, which the wings can only prepare us for in this life, provided we do not give ourselves over to the contraries. These are specified as the bad, the ignorant, and the ugly, and they form a parallel inverse triad to the good, the wise, and the beautiful. The longing (*affectus*) for sensibles constitutes the bad; relying on sensation makes us ignorant; and sensation's source, matter, is ugly. These contraries "bind" the wing "so that it cannot immediately (*mox*) fly back to the heights after this life." This would seem to imply a period of purgation (later to be examined in terms of the nine lives) in which the refledging or strengthening of the wing takes place, the mention of "immediately" suggesting that the wing will take us back eventually. Plato, on the other hand, talks of the wings being "shed" (246C2), "falling away," and "being lost" (246D4-5), and of our plumage being "wasted" and "destroyed" (246E3-4) rather than merely "bound." Again, this connotes a much more pessimistic view of the possibility of man's achieving apotheosis than Ficino is willing to accept or to suppose Plato had accepted. Though a matter of detail, perhaps nowhere is the Florentine's optimism in the Commentary more apparent; for he has reinterpreted the lexical constituents of Plato's text, to the point, arguably, of deliberate misrepresentation.

Having dealt with the preliminary details of the charioteer allegory and the "idea" of the soul, Ficino turns to the most dramatic transition in the *Phaedrus,* Socrates' imperative, "And behold,

there in heaven, Zeus, the mighty leader, drives his winged team"
(246E4-5), the call to the theological mystery at the heart of the
dialogue. To be initiated into this mystery, however, we must first
understand to which Zeus Plato refers; and we can only arrive at
this after we have understood the basic principles of Platonic
"mythologizing" and the range of alternatives it offers us.

Chapter Five: The Jovian Cavalcade

Ficino's tenth chapter takes up a basic question: How can a Christian philosopher work with the deities of Greek mythology,[1] and particularly with Zeus, and remain faithful both to his monotheistic convictions and to what he sees as Plato's intentions? For Ficino the problem was perennial, since it involved his overall conception of the "theology" of classical antiquity, and of the "secret wisdom" transmitted by the ancient theologian-poets and above all by Orpheus. In discussing this chapter I am indebted to various general observations on Ficino's "poetic theology" by Gombrich,[2] Wind,[3] Chastel,[4] and Walker,[5] but I have started afresh with its assumptions and concentrated on its peculiar insights and difficulties. Clearly Ficino considered that a proper understanding of what the twelve Olympians could represent in different philosophical and theological contexts was a prerequisite for an understanding of the *Phaedrus*'s portrayal of the Olympian cavalcade. An erroneous reading here would vitiate one's response to the entire dialogue, even to Platonic theology itself.

He approaches Plato's reference to "the host of gods and demons" led by Zeus and "marshaled" into eleven companies with the traditional fourfold method of Christian allegorization as his initial model, since, he says, it pursues "one sense particularly

1. Like many of his predecessors and contemporaries Ficino often uses the Greek and Roman names of the gods indifferently—for example, Pallas and Minerva. Three points concerning his divine nomenclature deserve special note. Dionysius (*sic*) is his usual choice for the god Dionysus (Bacchus); Hermes is often punningly associated with Hermes Trismegistus; and Uranus is normally referred to as Celus, Celum, or Celius and linked with the first orientation in the three postulated by the Neoplatonists on the basis of Plotinus's analysis of the *Cratylus* 396BC (see chap. 6, n. 19 below).

2. Ernst H. Gombrich, "*Icones Symbolicae:* The Visual Image in Neoplatonic Thought," *Journal of the Warburg and Courtauld Institutes* 11 (1948), 163-192; reissued in a much amplified version in his *Symbolic Images,* pp. 123-191, 228-235.

3. *Pagan Mysteries,* passim, but esp. chaps. 1, 2, 4, 7, and 8.

4. *Ficin et l'art,* passim, but esp. pt. 3, pp. 118-171.

5. *Ancient Theology,* introd. and chaps. 1, 2, and 3.

here and another there.'' We should do the same for the *Phaedrus,*
interpreting it "according to the occasion." His point is analogical, for he does not mean us to interpret the dialogue literally,
morally, allegorically, and anagogically, but simply to utilize the
flexibility of interpretation natural to the medieval method.[6] That
he then discusses four ways of "augmenting [that is, enumerating]
the gods'''[7] is really incidental; for they do not correspond to the
ascending hierarchy of interpretation advocated by Christian theologians. By flexibility, however, I have something special in mind.
At first glance, Ficino does not appear to function with an internally consistent mythological system: no one deity or figure has a
fixed allegorical equivalency or set of equivalencies. An index to
his *Opera* would help us to locate his mythological references, but
not to understand what Jove or Narcissus or the Graces always
meant to him. Rather, it would point up the extraordinary diversity (possibly even the idiosyncrasy) of his work as the greatest of
Renaissance mythologists. We would be wrong to see this as the
outcome of a multifaceted, Cocteau-like sensitivity to the infinite
possibilities of reading classical myth. Though he rejected the
notion of any straightforward allegorical translation of items into
a mythological lexicon, he did believe, like Proclus (his ultimate
model), in the integrity of a mythological grammar, in the fixed-
ness of certain relationships between the items, whatever the values
ascribed them on particular occasions. Hence my reference to him
elsewhere as an algebraist:[8] the values in his mythological equations are changeable, but rules and procedures for converting and
solving them remain constant.[9] It is precisely this algebraic dimension that Ficino finds exemplified in the flexibility of medieval alle-

6. Cf. Chastel, *Ficin et l'art,* p. 146: "les quatre modes traditionnels lui semblent moins
utiles qu'une exégèse 'platonicienne' "; see also his *Arte e umanesimo,* p. 208.
7. Cf. Ficino's epitome for the *Cratylus* (*Opera,* p. 1311). Chastel was the first to point
out in his *Ficin et l'art,* p. 153 n. 29, that "augmenting" means enumerating here, not in-
creasing; that is, "la déduction des dieux à partir du principe métaphysique, c'est-à-dire
leur multiplicité en tant qu'elle exprime l'échelle de l'être au point de vue de la substance."
Gombrich, *Symbolic Images,* pp. 211-212 n. 95, and Panofsky, *Renaissance and Renascences,* p. 191, who follows him, both err in supposing that Ficino intended multiplying in
the conventional sense.
8. "Two Commentaries on the *Phaedrus,*" p. 122.
9. Hence Wind's reference to Ficino's "theory of permutations" (*Pagan Mysteries,* p.
128), though he finds it, quite unfairly, "singularly arid." See also Gombrich, *Symbolic
Images,* pp. 59-64: "There are no dictionaries in this language because there are no fixed
meanings.... the exegetic allegorist... always finds the meaning for which he searches,

gorization. His own term for it was to proceed "Orphically"— that is, as Orpheus himself supposedly proceeded in addressing hymns to the various deities in the classical pantheon. To proceed "Orphically" was the only way of accommodating polytheistic structures to the deep grammar of monotheism.[10]

The first method of "enumerating" the gods is to distribute them under the first three major hypostases in the Plotinian system, which Ficino also attributed of course to Plato: the One, Mind, and Soul. In effect this method only really needs the first three gods. The first and eldest god, whom Ficino refers to simply as "The Good" (not, note, as Uranus—a problem I shall discuss in a moment), is assigned to the One; his son, Saturn, to Mind— that is, to the "intelligible world" in its divided unity as both the first knower, the prime intellect, and the first known, the prime intelligible;[11] and his grandson, great Jove and heaven's leader, to Soul, and more particularly to the World-Soul.[12] Ficino reinforces

---

... There is something of a game in the technique employed" (pp. 59-60); and Chastel, *Ficin et l'art,* pp. 136-140: "la mythologie... est un immense poème qu'il faut savamment pénétrer" (p. 138).

10. Walker, *Ancient Theology,* pp. 22-41.

11. Ficino's source is ultimately Plotinus, *Enneads* 3.5.2. Cf. Pico's *Commento* 1.8, 9; 2.20 (ed. Garin, pp. 470-473, 511-512). Both would have known Boccaccio's "old" etymology *sacer nus* in the *Genealogia Deorum* 8.1 (ed. Vincenzo Romano as *Giovanni Boccaccio: Genealogie Deorum Gentilium Libri,* 2 vols. [Bari, 1951]).

12. Ficino's source is ultimately Plotinus, *Enneads* 5.1.7; 5.8.9, 10, 12, 13; etc.; and it, like Saturn's identification with Mind, became a Neoplatonic commonplace. We should note, however, that Plotinus had complicated the situation considerably by elsewhere identifying Zeus with Mind (e.g. 5.8.4.40-42) and even at one point with the One (6.9.7.20-26); see Wallis, *Neoplatonism,* p. 135. For Pico's identifications see n. 11 above. The relationship between Soul as the third of the Neoplatonic hypostases and the World-Soul was a subject of some controversy. For the ancient Neoplatonists the World-Soul, like all other souls, was itself a manifestation, though the prime one, of what we might call Universal Soul, the unparticipated third hypostasis; see Wallis, *Neoplatonism,* pp. 69-70. For Ficino, with his Christian assumptions, the distinction was naturally less clear, and he tends to identify the World-Soul with Soul and both with Jupiter; he stops short, however, of then identifying it with the Holy Ghost (since he also perceives the parallel of Jupiter with Christ!). The subject is in need of much further research; but for some preliminary observations on the World-Soul, see Chastel, *Ficin et l'art,* p. 42; idem, *Arte e umanesimo,* pp. 216-217; Eugenio Garin, *Studi sul platonismo medievale* (Florence, 1958), pp. 81-85; idem, *L'età nuova* (Naples, 1969), pp. 430, 433, 437; idem, *Lo zodiaco della vita,* pp. 81 ff.; Walker, *Ancient Theology,* pp. 37, 121. We should bear in mind that Ficino certainly knew book 3 of Proclus's commentary on the *Timaeus,* though the relationship between the two *Timaeus* commentators has yet to be examined; book 3 is wholly devoted to the World-Body and the World-Soul; see Rosán, *Philosophy of Proclus,* pp. 183-192, and n. 30 below.

METHOD 1: ENUMERATION ACCORDING TO SUBSTANCES
            (HYPOSTASES)

The ONE   (The Good or First or Demogorgon; sometimes referred to "unpla-
               tonically" as Uranus/Celius)

MIND/SATURN: the prime intellect and prime intelligible; he is called the first
               first world or heaven. Under him are:

               1. Uranus   ⎫
               2. Saturn   ⎬   The intelligible gods
               3. Jove   ⎭
               4. Mars   ⎫
               5. Apollo   ⎪
               6. Venus   ⎪
               7. Mercury   ⎬   The mixed gods
               8. Diana   ⎪
               9. Vulcan   ⎭
               10. Juno   ⎫
               11. Neptune   ⎬   The intellectual gods
               12. Vesta   ⎭

               This dodecade, led by Uranus but under the lordship of
               Saturn, constitutes the intellectual world, the second heaven.

SOUL/JOVE: the World-Soul, leader and lord of the dodecade of divine
               souls, known as the celestial, mundane gods, and of the
               demons, heroes and other divine souls following them. They
               are allotted the cosmic spheres thus:

               1. Uranus   that of the fixed stars
               2. Saturn   that of the planet Saturn
               3. Jove   that of the planet Jupiter
               4. Mars   that of the planet Mars
               5. Apollo   that of the planet Sol
               6. Venus   that of the planet Venus
               7. Mercury   that of the planet Mercury
               8. Diana   that of the planet Moon
               9. Vulcan   that of fire
               10. Juno   that of air
               11. Neptune   that of water
               12. Vesta   that of earth
               (13. Pluto   the subterranean world)

               This dodecade, again led by Uranus but under the lordship of
               Jove, constitutes the animate world, the third heaven.

his argument by alluding to the *Republic*'s Idea of the Good as it appears in books 6 and 7 (identified by the Neoplatonists automatically with the One), and to Socrates' fanciful etymology for the name Cronus in the *Cratylus* 396BC.[13] This seems simple enough.

However, the third paragraph introduces complications which derive from Iamblichus's elaboration of a distinction between the intelligible and the intellectual gods and from Proclus's postulation of a third class between them,[14] in terms of emanating and subdividing triads. These three categories of gods, all of whom are supramundane, "exist" between Mind, defined specifically as the prime intellect, and Soul, defined specifically as the World-Soul, the leader of the "sensible" world. Since they are under Mind, all these supramundane gods are commanded by Saturn. Ficino thinks it appropriate to turn to the traditional generational triad of Uranus-Saturn-Jove for the names of the three leaders of these gods. At first glance, we might suppose that, since twelve gods rule the twelve companies of supramundane gods, they would be divided into three tetrads led by Uranus, Saturn, and Jove. But Ficino tells us later, in chapter 11, paragraph 9, that they are divided into four triads, the first designated the intelligible gods, the next two the mixed gods, and the last the intellectual gods (though they are all referred to as a group as the intellectual gods).

13. The fortuitous similarity between the names Cronus and Chronos also played its part until eventually the two divinities were identified (e.g. in Cicero, *De Natura Deorum* 2.25. 64); see Panofsky, *Studies in Iconology,* pp. 73-74.

14. Whereas Plotinus had postulated a unitary intelligible realm, Iamblichus introduced a distinction between what he designated the intelligible (νοητός) and the intellectual (νοερός) orders of gods occupying that realm, a distinction accepted by Syrianus and Hermias. Proclus then converted this dyad into a triad by inserting the mixed—that is, the intelligible-intellectual—order between the other two. However, in apparent contradistinction to Iamblichus, Syrianus, Hermias, and Proclus, Ficino chose to refer to these two (or three) orders collectively, as well as to the lowest order specifically, as the "intellectual" gods (confusing as this might first appear).

Iamblichus's decision also had the effect of dividing the realm itself: for the Ideas must occupy the intelligible half and the intellectual gods, the intellectual half. We should always bear in mind, however, that since the "intelligible" realm of Plotinus precedes Iamblichus's and Proclus's subsequent distinctions within it, all Plotinus's references to that realm, and to the gods occupying it, must remain ambiguous in terms of those distinctions. In approaching the *Phaedrus,* Ficino could make use, therefore, of Proclus's innovations in order to adumbrate what he clearly regarded as a faithfully Plotinian analysis, one that was, ironically, quite different from Proclus's own. In his *Parmenides* Commentary, chaps. 94 and 95 (*Opera,* p. 1194[r-v]), Ficino takes care to reject any "substantive" difference between the two orders. See chaps. 6 and 10 below.

The three unequal groups are not led by Uranus, Saturn, and Jove respectively, since, Ficino says, they are first, second, and third in the "class" of intellects under Mind and thus constitute the first triad of the dodecade. Consequently the three subordinate triads are subdivisions of Jove.

Though Saturn is assigned the supramundane realm in its entirety, since it consists exclusively of the three kinds (but four triads) of intellectual gods, Uranus is the first intellect in that realm. That is, the ranking, Uranus-above-Saturn-above-Jove, is always observed even though the ontological level in question may be assigned in its entirety to Saturn (as in the case of Mind) or to Jove (as in the case of Soul). If this seems confusing, we should bear in mind that Ficino is not working either here or later with the familiar Olympian twelve as he himself enumerates them in the *Platonic Theology* 4.1 when talking of the zodiac: that is, Pallas, Venus, Phoebus Apollo, Mercury, Jupiter, Ceres, Vulcan, Mars, Diana, Vesta, Juno, and Neptune.[15] The fact that the ancients often disagreed as to who were to be numbered among the actual twelve—Dionysus for instance came and went—is irrelevant here, since Ficino is treating rather of the twelve gods he thought Plato had identified, most notably in the *Timaeus* and the *Epinomis,* not with the zodiacal signs but with the twelve cosmic spheres.[16] These spheres and their deities consist of: Uranus as the fixed stars; and then Saturn, Jupiter, Mars, Apollo, Venus, Mercury, and Diana as their respective planets—the Ptolemaic seven, though not necessarily in the Ptolemaic order;[17] and finally Vulcan as fire, Juno as

15. Ed. Marcel, 1:153. Cf. Ficino's epitome for the *Laws* 5 (*Opera,* p. 1502) and his *De Amore* 5.13 (ed. Marcel, p. 198). This enumeration is of course that of the Roman pantheon with its equal number of gods and goddesses. Interestingly, Hermias records (p. 136. 10-17 [ed. Couvreur]) that at least one ancient interpretation of the *Phaedrus* adduced the zodiac; cf. Hackforth, *Phaedrus,* p. 74. For the zodiacal twelve in general and for Ficino's debt to Manilius see Carol V. Kaske, "Marsilio Ficino and the Twelve Gods of the Zodiac," *Journal of the Warburg and Courtauld Institutes* 45 (1982), 195-202.

16. *Timaeus* 38B-41A; *Epinomis* 986AB, 987B-D. Cf. Calcidius, *In Timaeum* 178 (ed. Waszink, pp. 206-207).

17. In this pre-Copernican era the order of the seven planets was much debated, and Ficino was familiar with at least five different theories, including, incidentally, the Copernican under another name:

1. The Ptolemaic, or more properly the Chaldaean, espoused by most of the Pythagoreans and by Aristotle: Moon, Mercury, Venus, Sun, Mars, Jupiter, Saturn;

2. The Platonic: Moon, Sun, Mercury, Venus, Mars, Jupiter, Saturn;

3. The Porphyrian: Moon, Sun, Venus, Mercury, Mars, Jupiter, Saturn;

air, Neptune as water, and Vesta as earth.[18] We may call this, for convenience sake, the astronomical dodecade, and Ficino uses it for both the supramundane intellects and later for the "visible" gods, the celestial souls.[19] In this dodecade Uranus, not Jove, is

---

4. That attributed to Philolaus of Crotona, and espoused too by Aristarchos of Samos and then by Copernicus: Sun, Mercury, Venus, Earth with the Moon circling around it, Mars, Jupiter, Saturn.

5. The Egyptian, but also espoused by Vitruvius, Martianus Capella, Macrobius, and Bede: Moon, Sun with both Mercury and Venus circling around it, Mars, Jupiter, Saturn. This theory effectively reconciles the Ptolemaic with the Platonic.

Ficino's principal authorities would have been Calcidius, *In Timaeum* 72, 73, 97 (ed. Waszink, pp. 119-122, 148-150); and Macrobius, *In Somnium Scipionis* 1.19. Ficino specifically mentions the Egyptian order in his *De Sole* 6 (*Opera*, pp. 968-969).

Usually—that is, in nonastronomical contexts—Ficino is happy to accept the Chaldaean-Ptolemaic order, as for instance in his *De Amore* 6.4 (ed. Marcel, p. 204), where he lists the gifts of the planets, or in his *De Vita* 3.21 (*Opera*, p. 562), where he lists the objects and faculties under the sway of each planet and is especially concerned to emphasize the median position of music and its deity, the Sun (see Walker, *Magic*, p. 21). Indeed his fascination with the metaphysics of light and its source the Sun, particularly as manifested in his tracts the *De Sole* and *De Lumine* of 1492 and 1493, often led him into positions that were not easily reconcilable with any of the astronomical orders, or with the subordination of Apollo to Jupiter and Saturn if not to Mars.

Nevertheless, as an ardent and diligent Platonist, he was swayed by the *Timaeus* 38C-E, which explicitly locates the Sun immediately after the Moon. Ficino makes specific reference to this passage in his own *Timaeus* Commentary, chap. 35 (*Opera*, p. 1461[r].1) and adds that the mathematician "Geber" had proved Plato correct (this is Abū Mūsā Jābir ibn Hayyān; see P. Kraus, ed., *Jābir ibn Hayyān: Essai sur l'histoire des idées scientifiques dans l'Islam* [Paris and Cairo, 1935], and Garin, *L'età nuova*, pp. 395, 400). Cf. also chap. 17 of his commentary on the *Republic*, book 8 (*Opera*, p. 1424.2). Renaissance commentators came to associate Ficino with the Platonic order or with its Porphyrian variant; see, for instance, Sir Edward Sherburne, app. III: "Of the Cosmical System," affixed to his translation of Manilius's *The Sphere* (London, 1675), p. 131, citing Father Riccioli's *Almagestum Novum* (Bologna, 1651), 9.3.

Ficino's differing positions await further exploration; but see Heninger, *Cosmographical Glass*, pp. 58-59, 66-79, for the various Renaissance theories; A. E. Taylor, *Commentary on Plato's Timaeus* (Oxford, 1928), pp. 192-193, for Plato's position; and Yates, *Bruno*, pp. 152 and 213 (quoting Bruno).

There is insufficient evidence in the *Phaedrus* Commentary to determine which order—the Chaldaean, the Platonic, or the Porphyrian—Ficino had in mind. Given the predominantly mythical and theological dimensions of the dialogue for him, dimensions that had astrological but not really astronomical implications (though of course the two are often difficult to distinguish prior to the Enlightenment), it was probably the Chaldaean. It is this universally familiar order that I have adopted therefore when enumerating the planets in this study. Since Ficino makes no attempt to exploit any particular planetary pairing such as Diana with Apollo or Mars with Jupiter, determining his position here—even supposing one could do so—would be of little significance.

18. Note that Pluto, as god of the underworld, is not included among the twelve Olympians and is not therefore in the jovian cavalcade.

19. This paralleling of the two dodecades seems to be without Neoplatonic precedent; notably so, given Ficino's acquaintance with Proclus and with Hermias. It may be another example of his using their distinctions to produce a much simpler though still Neoplatonic interpretation of the *Phaedrus*'s myth.

always the highest of the gods by virtue of his identification with
the highest sphere, that of the firmament of the fixed stars. Thus
the first rank of intellectual gods has to consist of Uranus's followers, though all the intellectual gods are by definition primarily
Saturn's.

Below the supramundane gods or intellects (and Ficino uses
"supermundane" and "supramundane" indifferently) come the
mundane gods and souls (mundane in the sense of belonging to the
created cosmos).[20] That is, Ficino now subdivides the third Plotinian hypostasis, Soul, assigned in its entirety to Jove and led by him
as the World-Soul. Under this Jove is ranked the same astronomical dodecade, but now it signifies the cosmic spheres, the spheres
of the animate world which constitute the realm of Soul, again
with Uranus leading. An obvious consequence of such a procedure
is that Saturn and Jove become ambivalent: they are both kinds
and degrees. They signify the second and third highest realms or
hypostases in their entirety, and at the same time individual ranks
within each realm (the One transcends all distinctions, and the two
lowest realms, Quality and Body, are not at issue here).

Ficino next identifies Soul as the third hypostasis with the
World-Soul, since both contain all subsequent souls, and he has
Plato's authority in the *Philebus* 30D for calling Jove the World-
Soul.[21] Since Jove has both intellect and soul to the highest degree
simultaneously, he can mediate between Mind and its intellectual
gods and Soul and its celestial or animate gods, the souls of the
world spheres. Ficino makes it clear that he is talking of only
twelve spheres because Plato talks of twelve, and that Plato, Aristotle, and he himself would all be quite willing to accept more than
twelve spheres (and thus presumably go along with the multiplication of spheres that marked the final pre-Copernican phase of
Ptolemaic astronomical speculation); he leaves room, that is, for

20. Note that "mundane" refers to both corporeal and animate beings, men or the planetary gods, while "supramundane" refers to either the intellectual gods or the intelligible
Ideas. Ficino is adapting (and not adopting) Proclus's distinction between "cosmic" (and
"encosmic") and "hypercosmic." Note too, however, that the distinction between "celestial" and "supercelestial" is even more complicated, given the special meaning of the term
"heaven" in the *Phaedrus*'s myth. See Allen, *Charioteer,* pp. 66-69, and chaps. 6 and 10,
n. 67 below.
21. See n. 12 above.

the inclusion if need be of the crystalline[22] or other intermediate spheres. Ficino has no problem, incidentally, with the question of whether Jove's cavalcade in the *Phaedrus* does or does not include Vesta (Hestia), since he sees Plato including her even as he deliberately sets her off as the deity who stays at home, figuratively speaking.[23] Following the twelve celestial gods and the spheres they govern, and attributed variously to them, are the particular greater and lesser gods, the higher demons and the heroes as detailed in Iamblichean and Proclian "theology."

Thus method 1 uses the names of the astronomical dodecade to explore the divisions and subdivisions of Neoplatonic ontology. While theoretically able to include any number of deities, in actuality it uses the same sets of three and twelve over and over again, each time assigning them different values while retaining their mutual proportionality.

The second method distributes the gods among the Platonic Ideas,[24] the species as they exist absolutely in the intelligible world or heaven—that is, as they exist in the Plotinian Mind as signified by Saturn. This distribution might presuppose a hierarchy within the realm of Ideas with Uranus perhaps as the Good, Saturn as Truth, Jove as Beauty, and so forth. But Ficino neither makes these explicit identifications nor postulates a precise number of Ideas and therefore of gods. His last sentence suggests, moreover, that he is thinking particularly, if not exclusively, of the Ideas of the planetary and elemental spheres rather than of abstract conceptions or of other living or material things. For he adds the curious note that in the old days to swear by natural objects, "animals,

---

22. Sometimes known as the *coelum aqueum;* see Heninger, *Cosmographical Glass,* p. 177. Cf. Dante, *Convivio* 2.6. If postulated at all, usually the crystalline sphere is beyond the sphere of the fixed stars, designated the *firmamentum,* and prior to the *primum mobile* and the empyrean; but Ficino sometimes equates it with the *primum mobile,* as in his *De Christiana Religione,* chap. 14 (*Opera,* p. 19). Cf. Pico, *Commento* 2.15 (ed. Garin, p. 506), and *Heptaplus* (ed. Garin, pp. 230-231).

23. See pp. 140-141 below and nn. 56, 58, and 59 below.

24. Cf. *De Amore* 5.10 (ed. Marcel, p. 195): *Sic ergo angeli illius in deum dilectio, partim antiquior est ideis que dii dicuntur, partim etiam iunior.* In his *Commento* 2.13 (ed. Garin, p. 503), Pico singles out the method of Parmenides as the one that "always calls the Ideas gods"; and he notes that Venus is "that splendor and grace which proceeds from the variety of those Ideas."

METHOD 3

THE ONE

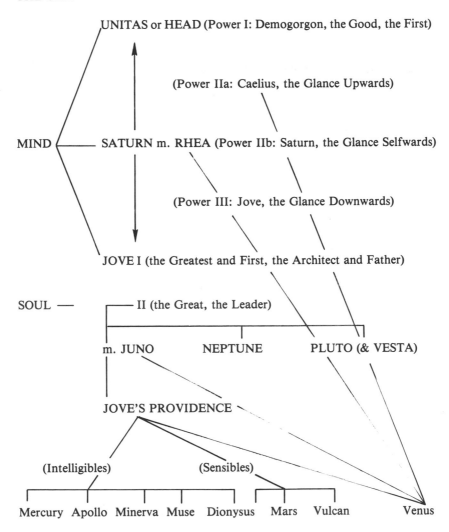

UNITAS or HEAD (Power I: Demogorgon, the Good, the First)

(Power IIa: Caelius, the Glance Upwards)

MIND ———— SATURN m. RHEA (Power IIb: Saturn, the Glance Selfwards)

(Power III: Jove, the Glance Downwards)

JOVE I (the Greatest and First, the Architect and Father)

SOUL ——   —— II (the Great, the Leader)

m. JUNO   NEPTUNE   PLUTO (& VESTA)

JOVE'S PROVIDENCE

(Intelligibles)   (Sensibles)

Mercury Apollo Minerva Muse Dionysus Mars Vulcan   Venus

trees, and lower things," was in effect to treat them as divine as long as men had their Ideas in mind, not their material embodiments; and this suggests he is thinking of the Ideas as described in the *Timaeus* rather than in the *Republic* or the *Phaedrus* itself.[25] As the brevity of commentary would indicate, Ficino never really cared to utilize method 2, partially perhaps because it would have involved him in an analysis of Plato's theory of Ideas, their number and mutual subordination. His treatment of Venus might have been better suited here than in method 3.

Method 3 receives much more extended treatment, so much so that one is led to speculate whether Ficino had several sources at hand besides Proclus and Hermias, possibly the work of Pletho or another Byzantine. Initially he speaks of enumerating the gods by using "more extensive and more general properties than the species." This might suggest he means intelligible genera, but in fact he means the fundamental "powers" exemplified to their highest degree in Mind—that is, the powers of the hypostases themselves, or at least of the hypostases below the One. In terms of the charioteer myth, if the divine Mind has a head, already defined as the unity, then this would be the first "power" or "property," and we could use the name of the very first god for it (and Ficino offers as alternatives "The Good," "Demogorgon," and "The Absolute First"). The succeeding clause, *consequenter autem quod in secundo vel tertio primum nominare placuerit,* is difficult, but I take it to mean simply, "But consequently I would prefer first to name what is in second or third place." Ficino has already clearly felt some reluctance actually to *name* the first god, since Plato does not call upon any name from Olympian mythology but refers to the One, simply by way of abstract definitions, as "The Good," "The Absolute First" (and "Demogorgon," of course, derives from Boccaccio, not from the ancient Platonic tradition).[26] We can thus understand his concluding remark in paragraph 12 that, "wherever I may perhaps have said that the first principle is called

25. That is, they are the Ideas of things and beings rather than those of abstract concepts such as Goodness, Justice, and so forth; see Allen, "Cosmogony and Love," p. 151n.
26. This is a rare instance of Ficino being indebted directly to Boccaccio's *Genealogia Deorum.*

Sky [i.e. Uranus], I have been talking in a sense that is not the Platonic one."[27] While Saturn can signify Mind, and Jove Soul, Uranus apparently cannot signify the One, even though he is both Saturn's and Jove's progenitor, and can signify the first intellect in Mind and the first soul in Soul as the first Olympian in the astronomical dodecade. This whole argument runs counter to the tenor of Ficino's account of method 1, described in the first and second paragraphs, though there too we remember he had declined to use Uranus as the name for the One. Since Uranus cannot be used "Platonically" for the One, he cannot obviously be used for the direct reflection of the One in the charioteer model, the unity. This said, Ficino abandons the notion of the unity and its power or property in order to concentrate on "what is in second or third place"; and he could have added "fourth," for his concern now is to "name" the three powers that orient any of the mediate hypostases to each other, instead of "uniting" them with the One.

For this orientation triad he turns to the *Cratylus* at 396BC, where Plato, at least as the Neoplatonists interpreted him, refers to Uranus as the upward-regarding power, Saturn as the selfward- or inward-regarding power, and Jove as the downward-regarding power.[28] Thus Ficino's insistence later in paragraph 12 that Uranus is not the universe's first principle—that is, the One—since he looks up at something higher than himself (which the One need never do). That is, Uranus is the upward-regarding power in the second (or third and presumably in subsequent) hypostases, not a hypostasis itself. The same pertains for the Ideas that concern method 2. The orientation triad symbolizes how each hypostasis and therefore presumably, *mutatis mutandis,* how each Idea regards or is related to its superiors, peers, and inferiors. If restricted to Soul, the triad functions in terms of motion, but not so with Mind. Ficino uses it, however, as an integral formula that we may predicate of absolutely everything except of course the two

27. This does not prevent him from referring to Sky (Uranus), following Plotinus and Cicero, as *summus ille deus,* as in the *De Amore* 2.7 and 6.7 (ed. Marcel, pp. 154, 208). See chaps. 6, n. 19, and 10, n. 10 below.

28. Cf. Plotinus, *Enneads* 5.8.13, and Ficino's *Philebus* Commentary 1.26 (ed. Allen, pp. 246-247) and *Cratylus* epitome (*Opera,* p. 1311).

extremes, the One and Matter, which share in only two of the orientations, though not the same two. Confusingly, at first glance anyway, it may also be predicated of the three gods who themselves symbolize its three aspects. Thus we may talk of the upward or uranian, the selfward or saturnian, and the downward or jovian "motions" or "regardings" (to use Ficino's more usual term) of Uranus (when he stands for the first in a subordinate series), of Saturn, and of Jove, as well as of all the other deities, demons, heroes, men, and things subject to them. As an orientation triad, that is, it designates the most fundamental set of relationships inherent in any hierarchy, the relationships of any one step in that hierarchy to itself and to those above it and below. Unlike other Platonic absolutes, however, which are found at their best and most paradigmatic when they first occur and which gradually lose their identity and efficacy as more and more subsequents intervene, this triad remains a universally applicable formula predicable equally of the prime hypostases and of individual entities. What happens when the downward regarding comes to predominate and the internal balance of forces is consequently upset is the subject of my seventh chapter.

Though he likewise leaves it to paragraph 12, Ficino introduces one other important criterion for understanding what he sees as Plato's deployment of myth in describing the fundamental powers of Mind, and therefore of Soul too, and of individuals. This criterion derives from the principle, attributed to Orpheus, that "all the gods are not only located in Jove, as both the world-architect and the World-Soul [and he will elaborate on this distinction presently], but also in any one god." By virtue of Jove's triple relationship to all the deities in the Greek pantheon—that is, to his progenitors, to his brothers and sisters, and to his sons and daughters and their subsequent offspring—Jove is present in every deity and they in him. This series of filial, fraternal, and paternal relationships is itself reflective of and corresponds to the *Cratylus's* orientation triad. Though exemplified to the highest degree in Jove, the Orphic principle is not confined to him but is universally applied. Not only are all the gods in Jove and he in them, but all the gods are in each god and each in all, not just by virtue of their membership in the Olympian family, but absolutely. For Ficino, therefore, as for Proclus before him, Orpheus's hymns to various deities were secretly addressed to each and every deity, to all in one and one in all. Their polytheism was just a tough rind concealing the sweet fruit of monotheism, as Orpheus's Universal Hymn, which served both as a prologue to the *Hymns* and as the poet's palinode, seemed to state expressly.[29] Admittedly, it is difficult in practice to see much point in discussing the minervan powers of Priapus, or the vulcanian of Hebe. Nevertheless it is precisely his profound understanding of and commitment to the Orphic principle that makes Ficino the most significant theoretician of myth in his epoch. And it has the unexpected effect of making Jove the archetypal counter, the key to the solution of all mythological equations.

Of the two intellectual powers or understandings in the prime intellect, the first is subdivided and can be described both as uranian insofar as it regards the Good or the One above it, and then as saturnian insofar as it regards itself. The second power is wholly jovian insofar as it "regulates all in the manner of an architect and father." These three aspects of Saturn's two intellects as it were, the contemplative and active, are then replicated for Jove as the prime soul. But this immediately creates the necessity for two Joves. So Ficino turns to elaborate on what he sees as the authentically Plotinian (and thus by extension Platonic) doctrine of the twin Jove,[30] a doctrine more central to his interpretation of ancient

29. For the importance of this palinode to Renaissance Neoplatonists, see Walker, *Ancient Theology,* pp. 25-35, and, on the related question of Jove as the one God, pp. 35-41. At p. 27 Walker refers us in particular to Augustine's *De Civitate Dei* 4.11, to Bessarion's *In Calumniatorem Platonis* 3.5 (ed. Ludwig Mohler in his *Kardinal Bessarion als Theologe, Humanist und Staatsman,* 3 vols. [Paderborn, 1923-1924], 2:233), to Pico's Orphic Conclusion 3 (ed. Kieszkowski, p. 80), and to Ficino's letter to Uranius of 9 June 1492 (*Opera,* pp. 933.2-935.2). We should note Ficino's own reference here (ed. Allen, *Charioteer,* p. 119) to his *De Sole* (*Opera,* pp. 965-975, especially pp. 970-971).

In the light of the emendations suggested by Martins, *Jean Pic de la Mirandole,* pp. 62 and 79, Pico's conclusion should read: "Nomina deorum, quos Orpheus canit, non decipientibus demonum, a quibus malum et non bonum prouenit, sed naturalium uirtutum, diuinarumque sunt nomina, et uero Deo in utilitatem maxime hominis si eis uti sciuerit mundo distributarum."

30. Cf. Ficino's observations as edited by Saffrey, "Notes platoniciennes," p. 176: "*Iuppiter,* ut dicit Plotinus libro secundo de dubiis anime [4.4.10], significat duo: aliquando intellectum opificem, aliquando animam mundi; et dicit quod ille intellectus vocatur *Iuppi-*

thought and indeed to his own poetic theology than even the *Symposium*'s analysis of the twin Venus and her twin Cupid.[31]

When designated in superlative terms as "the greatest" and "the very first," Jove (who always symbolizes the downward-regarding power in the orientation triad) is being considered, Ficino argues, in the light of his architectonic and regulatory powers as the father caring for and governing the world, as the Demiurge of the *Timaeus*,[32] as, in other words, the downward regarding of Saturn. But when simply designated as "great" Jove, he embodies the inspirational and guiding powers, the upward regarding, that we associate with a leader; he is no longer the jovian power in Mind, but Soul dominated by its uranian power. We thus have a hierarchy of powers orienting the hypostases, Mind and Soul: the uranian, saturnian, and jovian powers of Saturn, and then the same of Jove. Since a Platonist can use a proper noun in adjectival positions, we thus have a Uranus in Saturn, a Saturn in Saturn, a Jove in Saturn (Jove "the greatest and first"), and a Uranus in Jove, a Saturn in Jove, and a Jove in Jove (Jove "the great"). Since the One is beyond rational analysis and cognition, the mediatory steps whereby it emanates into Saturn or Mind are ineffably mysterious; but such is not the case with the steps from Mind to Soul, from Saturn to Jove. Hence the latter transition becomes the first, and therefore the paradigmatic, instance of cosmic mediation cognizable by man: Jove's ability to become and be Saturn symbolically represents Soul's ability to become Mind and

---

ter opifex, *Iuppiter pater*, anima autem mundi dicitur *Iuppiter dux*." In addition to the *Enneads* 4.4.10, see 3.5.8 and 4.4.9; see too Proclus, *In Timaeum* 297C ff. (ed. Diehl, 3:190 ff.) and Plutarch, *Quaest. Plat.* 9.1.1007F (i.e. frag. 18). For commentary see Dillon, *Middle Platonists*, p. 27; Wallis, *Neoplatonism*, p. 135; Zeller-Mondolfo, *Filosofia*, p. 157; Rosán, *Philosophy of Proclus*, p. 167; and Walker, *Ancient Theology*, pp. 35-41. Walker refers us to the Orphic fragments 21, 21A, 167, and 168 (ed. Kern). We should note that the distinction in question is not between Jupiter as planet and as World-Soul, but rather between Jupiter as the World-Soul and as the lowest aspect of the second hypostasis, Mind. See n. 12 above.

31. See pp. 130-132 below.

32. Cf. Proclus, *In Timaeum* 93A-97D (ed. Diehl, 1:303.24-319.21; trans. Festugière, 2: 156-177); *Theologia Platonica* 5.12 ff. (ed. Portus, pp. 268 ff.). See Zeller-Mondolfo, *Filosofia*, pp. 155-158. We should bear in mind the traditional etymologies for Jupiter stemming from the *Cratylus* 396AB's "the God through whom all creatures always have life": for instance in Cicero, *De Natura Deorum* 2.25.64 (*iuvans pater*), and in Boccaccio, *Genealogia Deorum* 2.2 (ed. Romano, 1:70).

the individual soul's ability to become a disembodied intellect.[33] Jove is the link between the two ontological realms of Mind and Soul, necessarily participating in both and mediating between them to establish a continuum between thought and life. "Greatest" Jove is a solitary figure, the Demiurge and judge, united with his progenitors, Uranus and Saturn, and his mother Rhea. "Great" Jove by contrast is the leader and guide of his own family: his two brothers, his sister-wife, and his eight children, and their offspring in turn. Since method 3 is concentered on Jove, it has a central bearing on the *Phaedrus,* where Jove is the critical mythological figure, not Uranus or Saturn, though the hypostases they represent are both, Ficino says, "secretly" presupposed in the dialogue, and he refers to Plato's sixth letter at 323D.[34] Moreover, the method is concerned with powers, the three primary orientation powers and their ramifying subdivisions. It is not concerned with a dodecade, neither with the astronomical nor with the traditional Olympian in any of its variations. Thus it can embrace an almost limitless number of deities by simply subordinating them in multiplying triads, all deriving ultimately from the leader of the gods. Here, for reasons that will become obvious, Ficino concen-

33. The problem of satisfactorily distinguishing between Soul at its highest and Mind at its lowest was a perennial one that had its origins in Middle Platonism; see Dillon, *Middle Platonists,* pp. 211-214; Wallis, *Neoplatonism,* pp. 33-34, 52-53, 81-82, 119-120. For Ficino, I have argued, it had the unexpected consequence of undermining the ontological status of Angelic Intellect ("The Absent Angel," pp. 233 ff.). See nn. 12 and 30 above.

34. For the significance of the sixth letter for Ficino see his epitome, *Opera,* pp. 1533-1534. The critical lines in Plato read: τὸν τῶν πάντων θεὸν ἡγεμόνα τῶν τε ὄντων καὶ τῶν μελλόντων, τοῦ τε ἡγεμόνος καὶ αἰτίου πατέρα κύριον ἐπομνύντας (323D). In his 1491 Venice edition, *Platonis Opera Omnia,* Ficino translates them as follows: "testando deum rerum omnium ducem presentium et futurarum: ac ducis et cause patrem dominum" (f. 332ʳ, col. 2). The epitome glosses them thus: "Ubi enim ait omnium ducem praesentium atque futurorum, mundi animam vult intelligi, quae utpote principium motus res omnes a futuro in praesens, a praesenti in praeteritum temporali ratione perducit. Ubi vero patrem dicit et dominum, summum deum ipsumque bonum significat; sed mediam into duo haec mentem quandam divinam videtur inserere, quando dum repetit *ducis* subiungit *et causae.* Nam apud Platonem saepe rex significat ipsum bonum, causa vero mentem, dux denique animam." ("For when Plato says 'the leader of all present and future things,' he means us to understand the World-Soul, which, as the principle of motion, guides all things from the future into the present, from the present into the past, in the temporal manner appropriate to the reason. But when Plato says the father and lord, he means the highest god, the Good itself. Inserted between the two, however, is apparently a certain divine Mind, for when he repeats 'of the leader' he adds 'of the cause' too. In Plato the king often signifies the Good itself, the cause signifies Mind, and the leader, Soul.") (*Opera,* p. 1533.)

trates on Rhea, Neptune, Pluto (and Vesta), Juno, Mercury, Apollo, Minerva, the Muse, Dionysus, Mars, Vulcan, and Venus. Though this happens to add up to twelve deities (if we exclude Vesta), it corresponds neither with the Phaedran twelve, who are, as we saw earlier, the astronomical dodecade, nor with the Olympian, the zodiacal, twelve.

Neptune and Pluto, being his brothers, are both immediate subdivisions of Jove's powers. Neptune is defined as "the active, moving power"—that is, the capacity to complete Jove's work—and also as what imparts this same active, moving power to "effects," meaning presumably that it makes Jove's completed work efficacious or active in turn.[35] Pluto and Vesta (the two are equated here in terms of their powers—logically so, since the one presides over the subterranean, the other over the terrene) are Jove's power to come to rest and to impart rest (*firma proprietas atque firmans*).

Juno, by contrast, is the member of another triad of powers involving herself, Rhea her mother, and Venus as her sister rather than as her (step-)daughter. All three signify in various ways what Ficino calls "the quickening" or "vital" power. Rhea is the vital power in the intelligible world of Mind, of Saturn; she is thus the potentiality for Soul—that is, the first manifestation or "quickening" of life as opposed to being or thought. Hence both the saturnian and jovian understandings "lie upon her," the first as husband-lover, the second as child.[36] Juno is her immediate offspring, the quickening and life-giving power in Jove. Juno's status is dual also, since she is Jove's sister and his wife, and reflects her husband-brother's dual status as "greatest" and "great." As such we might have expected Ficino to be more concerned with her and her allegorical possibilities. But Plotinus had already identified her

35. Cf. Pico, *Commento* 1.10 and *Heptaplus* 1.3 (ed. Garin, pp. 475-477, 214): [*Neptunus*] *apud Platonicos pro ea virtute accipitur quae generationibus praeest* (p. 214).

36. Plato refers to Rhea in the *Cratylus* 401E-402B and the *Timaeus* 40E-41A: in the *Cratylus* she is associated with the Heraclitian doctrine of eternal flux (see Ficino's *Cratylus* epitome, *Opera,* p. 1312); in the *Timaeus* she is called the daughter of Oceanus and Tethys, themselves the children of Earth and Heaven; cf. Plotinus, *Enneads* 5.1.7 (where she is the realm of flux). In Proclus, however, she is associated with potential life, *Theologia Platonica* 5.11 (ed. Portus, pp. 265-267); see Zeller-Mondolfo, *Filosofia,* p. 157; and also nn. 43 and 44 below.

with one of the twin Venuses in the *Symposium* (180DE), and
Ficino was obligated to follow him.[37]

Of critical significance were the two contrasting accounts of
Venus's parentage and birth: the Homeric account depicts her as
the daughter of Jove and a mortal woman, Dione;[38] the Hesiodic
depicts her as the Anadyomene, sprung from the seed of the cas-
trated Uranus, and therefore as Jove's aunt.[39] Further complicat-
ing matters is Plotinus's curious decision when discussing the episode to equate Uranus with Saturn and to treat them both together
as her father; in the process, of course, she also becomes Jove's
sister.[40] These alternative accounts endowed her not only with the
same kind of ambivalent status as Juno's, the sister-wife, but also,
given her traditional attributes and especially those granted her by
Lucretius, with an allegorical potential second only to Jove's.[41]
Drawing heavily on his own previous analyses in the *Symposium*
Commentary and the *Platonic Theology,* Ficino therefore di-
gresses to treat of a twin Venus who can "correspond" to a twin

37. *Enneads* 3.5.8. Ficino does not deal with this or its adjacent sections (3.5.7-9) in his
own Plotinus Commentary (*Opera,* p. 1717) since he had already treated them at length in
his *Symposium* Commentary 6, esp. chaps. 7-10 (ed. Marcel, pp. 208-223).

38. *Iliad* 3.373-425; 14.187-221; 23.185-187; *Odyssey* 4.259-264; 20.67-78. Panofsky,
both in his *Studies in Iconology,* p. 142, and in his *Renaissance and Renascences,* p. 199,
erroneously equates Dione here with Juno. From Ficino's viewpoint it is essential that this
Venus should be the result of a union between a god and a human being.

39. *Theogony* 178-206. Cf. Ficino's *De Amore* 2.7; 6.7 (ed. Marcel, pp. 153-154, 209-
210); and his *Philebus* Commentary 1.11 (ed. Allen, pp. 136-139).

40. *Enneads* 3.5.2: "To us Aphrodite is twofold; there is the heavenly Aphrodite, daughter of Ouranos or Heaven; and there is the other the daughter of Zeus and Dione, this is the
Aphrodite who presides over earthly unions; the higher was not born of a mother and has
no part in marriages, for in Heaven there is no marrying. The Heavenly Aphrodite, daughter of Kronos [Saturn]—who is no other than the Intellectual Principle—must be the Soul
at its divinest... following upon Kronos—or, if you will, upon Heaven, the father of Kronos—the Soul directs its Act towards him and holds closely to him" (trans. MacKenna).
Cf. Ficino's commentary, *Opera,* p. 1714.2: [*Plotinus*] *Christianae trinitatis in hoc mysteri-
um imitatus;* cf. also Pico, *Commento* 1.8-9; 2.11, 18-20; 3.1 (ed. Garin, pp. 470-473, 499,
509-512, 521-524). Failure to advert to this passage and to recognize its critical importance
for both Ficino and Pico has led some scholars astray: Gombrich, for instance, in his *Symbolic Images,* p. 218 n. 155, was led to translate *Celio* as *Chronos.* See chap. 6, n. 19 below.

Note that Pico, in his *Commento* 2.11 (ed. Garin, p. 499), specifically objects to Ficino's
decision in the *De Amore* 2.7 (ed. Marcel, pp. 153-155) to interpret Venus as a "power" in
the soul or mind, and insists on interpreting her as beauty itself, the end cause and object of
the power of love.

41. In a poem by one of Ficino's friends, Bonincontri, Venus is actually identified with
the Virgin Mary (in B. Soldati, *La poesia astrologica nel Quattrocento* [Florence, 1906], p.
191); see Gombrich, *Symbolic Images,* p. 63.

Jove.[42] In support he refers to what he sees as Plotinus's decision to identify Venus both with the World-Soul (Jove or, perhaps more strictly speaking, junonian Jove)[43] and with Juno's counterpart in Mind, Rhea.[44] Just as we may think of Jove as "greatest" in Mind, or merely as "great" when he is the World-Soul or Soul, so we may think of Venus, his aunt-sister-daughter, as accompanying him in either aspect. Accordingly, she supplants Juno as Jove's corresponding female power; or, to put it another way, under one at least of her aspects she is Juno. In the second paragraph of summa 30 Ficino calls the planet Venus Jove's sister and Jove's spouse, and identifies her totally with Juno as "the fortune of heaven." This dual deity, Venus-Juno, is called Juno in that as a wife, an inferior, she "abundantly sustains Jove's gift"; but she is called Venus in that as a sister, an equal, she is seen in her own right as the goddess of "love and generation." In brief, the Homeric Venus is also Juno, while the Hesiodic Venus is wholly and independently Venus.

Even more significant is the identification of Venus with Jove. In postulating a contemplative saturnian intellect versus an active jovian intellect, Ficino first suggests that Venus is the power striving for beauty in both these intellects—in which case we could talk of a venerean Saturn, or Venus in Saturn, and a venerean Jove, or Venus in Jove, the one contemplating beauty, the other striving to imitate it. But he then recalls the Venus-versus-Cupid/Eros/Desire distinction accorded such prominence in the *Symposium,* and this leads him to suggest that Venus is the beauty itself in both the saturnian and jovian intellects, and that Cupid is therefore the

42. Eventually, as Ficino's *De Amore* 6.5, 7 (ed. Marcel, 205, 208-210) makes clear, we must accept three (or even more) Venuses (and thus Loves—see chap. 2, n. 74 above). This is logical enough once we accept the Orphic theology Ficino brings to his analysis of Jove; but the resulting complexities account for the disagreement between Ficino and Pico—and their modern commentators—as to who was the "second" Venus.

43. *Enneads* 3.5.3-5. Insufficient notice has been taken of this arresting Plotinian identification, one that enhances the stature of Venus and therefore of Beauty. It is even more arresting than Plotinus's identification of Venus with Juno at 3.5.8, or, at least as Ficino read it, with Rhea at 3.5.2 (see n. 44 below).

44. Plotinus nowhere identifies her as the Juno-in-Mind; for this is a notion that stems from Proclus (see Rosán, *Philosophy of Proclus,* pp. 66, 154, 165n). But again Ficino was almost certainly thinking of the *Enneads* 3.5.2, and of its enigmatic identification of Uranus with Saturn as the father of the heavenly Aphrodite; see nn. 36 and 40 above.

power contemplating or imitating it—in which case we could talk of a cupidian Saturn and cupidian Jove, or even of a cupidian Venus in Saturn and cupidian Venus in Jove. However, the beauty or Venus contemplated in the intelligible world of Saturn—which Ficino defines as "the completely unfolded series of the Ideas"— Ficino subdivided into three, to correspond to her three aspects (presumably, given the correspondence theory, this triadic division is replicated at lower ontological levels). As "grace" or absolute beauty, beauty is Venus. As "splendor," in the Augustinian sense of being seen by others, beauty is Apollo. And as "power"—that is, as exercising power over those others—beauty is Pallas Athena.[45] We thus end up with an unusual triad for Venus as beauty: Venus, Apollo, and Pallas. Though Ficino sees this triad as compatible with the dyad, Venus as "ideal" grace and Venus as "vital power," he makes no attempt to reconcile it with the triad he had experimented with earlier, Rhea, Juno, and Venus.

Having thus digressed to treat of one of the most important if plurisignative members of Jove's family, Ficino next turns to seven of Jove's children. Apollo and Pallas now symbolize something quite distinct from Venus and her attributes or powers, referring rather to Jove's providence, his downward-regarding power, which regulates "sensibles and intelligibles equally." Significantly, Ficino does not deal with the distinction between the animate and intelligible worlds, but with our perception of sensibles as opposed to our comprehension of intelligibles. Since he speaks of Jove's providence as "regulating," we might assume initially that he intends the higher Jove. But he is concerned with specifically human perception and comprehension here, and so with activities within the realm of Soul; we are thus dealing with the lower or "great" Jove. His analyses of Apollo, Minerva, Mer-

---

45. In the *Cratylus* 407B Plato allegorizes her both as "the divine intelligence" and as "she who knows divine things"; this led Varro and others to equate her with Plato's Ideas (*apud* Augustine, *De Civitate Dei* 7.28). Cf. Pico, *Commento* 3.4 (ed. Garin, p. 529), and Cabalistic Conc. 10 (ed. Kieszkowski, p. 84 [corrected by Martins, *Jean Pic de la Mirandole*, p. 79]: "quod ab Orpheo Pallas, a Zoroastre materna mens, a Mercurio Dei filiu[s], a Pythagora sapiencia, a Parmenide sphera intelligibilis nominatur"). See Gombrich, *Symbolic Images*, pp. 69-72; Kristeller, *Philosophy*, pp. 358-359; Walker, *Ancient Theology*, p. 39; and, more generally, R. Wittkower, "Transformations of Minerva in Renaissance Imagery," *Journal of the Warburg Institute* 2 (1938-39), 194-205.

cury, the Muse, Dionysus, Mars, and Vulcan are concerned, accordingly, with the subdivisions of great Jove, as was the case with Neptune and Pluto, and in part at least with Juno and Venus.

In adumbrating the powers of the Olympians ruling over intelligibles—that is, over the process of human intellection of intelligibles—Ficino puts Mercury first as the "bestower" of the capacity for inquiry; Apollo second as the bestower of the capacity potentially to comprehend intelligibles; Minerva third as the bestower of the capacity actually to comprehend them; the Muse fourth as the bestower of the harmony which prepares the understander to comprehend the harmony of what he understands; and Dionysus fifth as the twice-born god who bestows on man the capacity to transcend what he understands even as he enables him to transcend the objects of his loving. With sensibles, on the other hand, Mars bestows on us the potential capacity to perceive them, and Vulcan the actual perception of them. Again Dionysus bestows on us the capacity to transcend these perceptions, just as he had the capacity to transcend our comprehension of intelligibles.

The introduction of both Dionysus and the Muse is interesting in the light of a passage in the *Platonic Theology* (4.1) where Ficino attributes to the souls of each of the eight celestial spheres and to the World-Soul a Muse and a Dionysus under one of his cognomina: for instance, to the soul of Mars's sphere he attributes Bacchus Bassareus and Clio; to the World-Soul, Bacchus Eribromos and Calliope.[46] The whole scheme is ascribed to Orpheus (his source being *Hymns* 45-54): "In Orpheus, then, a Bacchus is in charge of each of the Muses; and this shows that their powers are

---

46. Ed. Marcel, 1:164-165. In the *Ion* epitome (*Opera*, pp. 1283-1284), which was written several years before the passage in the *Platonic Theology*, Ficino had merely identified each of the Muses with a sphere as follows: Urania with the fixed stars', Polyhymnia with Saturn's, Terpsichore with Jove's, Clio with Mars's, Melpomene with Sol's, Erato with Venus's, Euterpe with Mercury's, Thalia with Luna's, and then Calliope with the musical concord (*vox*) to which they all contributed. With them he associated Musaeus, Pindar, Hesiod, Homer, Thamyras, Sappho, Ovid, Vergil, and Orpheus, respectively. By identifying Calliope as the combined harmony of the spheres he successfully reconciled nine as the number of the Muses with eight as the number of the spheres. Cf. chap. 1, n. 67 above. Interestingly, Ficino also seems to have entertained the notion of identifying the nine Muses with the nine hypotheses that constituted for him and for other Neoplatonists the second part of the *Parmenides;* see his *Parmenides* Commentary, sixth hypothesis, chap. 1 (*Opera*, p. 1199^V.2).

inebriated by the nectar of divine knowledge. Thus the nine Muses
with their nine Bacchi abandon themselves to frenzy around one
Apollo—that is, around the splendor of the invisible Sun."[47] As
the daughter of Jove and the goddess of memory, Mnemosyne, the
Muse is not of course one of the traditional Olympians; but as representative of all nine Muses, she must be introduced in the context of a discussion of Jove's providence over intelligibles, a providence which, in the language of Platonic and subsequent medieval
epistemology, harmonizes the knower and the known. There is no
need for Ficino to identify her specifically as Calliope (the muse of
the World-Soul—that is, of Jove); and though she occupies a midway position in a hebdomad of deities symbolizing the subdivisions of Jove's "ample providence," this in itself seems of no significance.[48] Her traditional companions are Mercury and Apollo;
and Orpheus was sufficient authority for Ficino to associate her
also with Dionysus. Her companionship with Minerva, however,
is best explained in the light of the last excerpt of ten affixed to the
earliest manuscript of his *Philebus* Commentary.[49] This presents
us with a fable about Pleasure and describes how she was eventually induced to abandon earth for heaven after a series of fruitless
attempts to abduct her thither, including one in which she had
actually thwarted Minerva by penetrating her shield. She was eventually wooed into heaven by Mercury, Apollo, the Muses, and the
Graces, and then, Ficino says, was "transferred to" or perhaps

47. That is, Apollo is the invisible sun here while Melpomene and Bacchus Trietericus are
powers in the soul of the sphere of the visible sun. In the *Ion* epitome on the other hand,
since Calliope was the World-Soul, Apollo becomes the World-Soul's intellect, *mens
animae mundi* (*Opera*, p. 1283). Elsewhere, as we have seen (see chap. 1, n. 71 above),
Apollo often symbolizes the One itself. He shares, in short, in the diverse meanings that the
sun had come to assume for a commentator indebted to both the astrological-astronomical
and the Neoplatonic traditions; moreover, like those of other plurisignative deities in a Pro-
clus-inspired mythology, his various roles are often mutually irreconcilable. Of interest in
this respect are Ficino's notes on Julian's "Prayer to the Sun" in the Riccardiana's MS 76;
see Kristeller, *Iter Italicum* 1:184. These have been edited by Eugenio Garin in "Per la
storia della cultura filosofica del Rinascimento," *Rivista critica di storia della filosofia* 12.1
(1957), 3-21 (though the MS is identified incorrectly as greco 79). See also Garin's chapter
on the Copernican revolution and Renaissance solar mythology in his *Rinascite e rivoluzioni*, pp. 255-282.
48. For hebdomads in Proclus, however, see Rosán, *Philosophy of Proclus*, p. 97.
49. Ed. and trans. Allen, pp. 472-479. Proclus in his *Theologia Platonica* 6.11 (ed. Portus, pp. 372 ff.) had linked Athena with Core. There seems to be no connection, however,
between Proclus's Core and Ficino's Musa.

"changed or translated into" Minerva, her old enemy (*ad Minervam translata est*), translation being the province of Dionysus. Hence "we can only attain complete pleasure in the presence of divine wisdom." Thus the Muses ended up accompanying Minerva as transcendent intellectual pleasure. Ficino's choice of five gods to preside over man's intellectual functions is therefore entirely appropriate, though the inclusion of the Muse and of Dionysus may at first seem strange.

As far as I can tell, this particular scheme for allegorizing both the fundamental orientation powers and the subdivisions of Jove's downward-regarding, providential power, owed nothing specifically to Iamblichus, Hermias, or Proclus, though it is obviously Proclian in spirit;[50] and the decision to approach the *Phaedrus* in terms of both the *Cratylus's* orientation triad and Orphic theology was probably Ficino's own, particularly given his profound and passionate conviction that the *Cratylus* and the *Hymns* were both concerned with naming the Platonic powers. The presence of great palinodes in both the *Hymns* and the *Phaedrus* must have been an additional factor in his decision to read the one in the light of the other.

Method 4 takes up the exhortation in paragraph 12 that we should remember to enumerate all the divinities present in any one god and particularly those demonic beings present in the twelve cosmic spheres under their respective leader gods. For examples of this method at work, Ficino specifically refers us to his introduction to the *Cratylus* (*Opera,* p. 1311) and to his tract *On the Sun* (*Opera,* pp. 965-975); but it is based, as he freely acknowledges, on the practice of the three great late Neoplatonists, Iamblichus, Syrianus, and Proclus, though he avoids discussing their particular demonic categories here (perhaps because of the potential confusion with the dionysian orders of angels). Since all these demonic beings are attached to Jove's cavalcade (whether this now includes Vesta is not clear) and named after its leader gods, there are many demonic Joves, Junos, Neptunes, and so on, and also demonic

---

50. See Allen, "Two Commentaries on the *Phaedrus,*" pp. 121-123; also Zeller-Mondolfo, *Filosofia,* pp. 21-24, 159-162, 198n.

Saturns and presumably Uranuses (though Ficino makes no mention of what must be the dreadful thirty-six decan demons).[51] The
"office" of all these demons is to administer the universal or
"ample" providence of Jove as Soul after it has been distributed
among the twelve celestial gods of the spheres, in the manner
described in method 3, each demon performing different offices
under the presidency of its own particular deity. Ficino obviously
felt this was not the occasion to present a demonology (he had
done so at length if unsystematically on several occasions, though,
despite the pioneering work of D. P. Walker, many of its central

51. Origen, *Contra Celsum* 8.58-59, suggests Celsus thought of them as aethereal gods.
The major work on the decans is by W. Gundel, *Dekane und Dekansternbilder,* Studien der
Bibliothek Warburg, no. 19 (Glückstadt and Hamburg, 1936); see especially p. 280. But see
also Festugière, *La révélation d'Hermès Trismégiste* 1:115 ff.; Garin, *L'età nuova,* pp. 418,
429, 436-437; and Yates, *Bruno,* pp. 36-37, 45-48, 53, 55-57, 64, 70, 72.
    Yates defines the thirty-six as "the decans, or divisions of ten degrees into which the 360
degrees of the circle of the zodiac are divided" (pp. 36-37). A full list, along with the zodiacal signs to which they belong, occurs in the *Picatrix* 2.11 (and we now have epistolary evidence that Ficino was well acquainted with this magic handbook, originally composed in
Arabic but known to Ficino and the Renaissance in a Latin translation). Other sources
would have been Albumasar and Peter of Abano, both of whom Ficino cites by name in his
De Vita 3.18 (*Opera,* pp. 556 and 558)—that is, in the same chapter where we find his solitary reference to a decan image: "in the first face of Virgo is a beautiful girl, who is seated
with twin ears of corn in her hand and nursing a child" (*Opera,* p. 556). Yates observes that
Ficino "seems to avoid decan images, concentrating almost entirely on planet images" (p.
72).
    We should note that the decan demons are not the twelve zodiacal signs themselves, nor
the traditional thirty-six constellations, the two together making up the forty-eight "universal" signs; see Manilius, *Astronomica* 4.294-307, and Firmicus Maternus, *Mathesis* 2.4,
4.22. Rather they are the thirty-six "faces" of the zodiacal signs, and the thirty-six constellations are their images. Attending each decan demon are ten other lesser demons, one for
each of the 360 degrees in the full circle. At the end of summa 22, Ficino says that the actual
number of higher demonic souls is, however, "computed secretly," and I take this to be an
oblique reference to the thirty-six decan demons and to the hosts at their command. In the
De Vita 3.18 he notes cautiously that, in addition to the zodiacal signs and constellations
that everyone can see, "there are multitudes of forms which are not so much seen as imagined and which the Indians, Egyptians, and Chaldaeans perceived in, or at least supposed
distributed through, the faces of the signs," the beautiful girl in Virgo being an example
(*Opera,* p. 556). Cf. Pico, *Heptaplus* 2.5 (ed. Garin, pp. 238-241), and Garin, *Lo zodiaco
della vita,* p. 84.
    My supposition here is that Ficino is deliberately avoiding any reference to "uranian"
demons because they would have to be the decan demons he was always anxious, it seems,
not to discuss. This supposition is reinforced by the fact that Hermias in glossing *Phaedrus*
246E4 specifically introduces the δεκαδάρχαι θεοί (p. 136.14 [ed. Couvreur]; see Dillon,
Iamblichi Fragmenta, p. 251), and Ficino would have been well aware of this since he had
by now carefully translated all of Hermias's commentary (see Allen and White, "Ficino's
Hermias Translation and a New Apologue").

aspects remain to be explored).[52] The very mention of method 4, however, does underscore his awareness of the demonological dimensions of the *Phaedrus* and should alert us particularly to those of the setting and of the Theuth and cicada myths.

One startling outcome of this method should be to heighten our sense of the array of alternatives open to Ficino whenever he came upon a god's name in Plato, in the Neoplatonists, or for that matter in the poetic theologians who preceded Plato, the *prisci Platonici*. For the name might well signify neither a Plotinian hypostasis, nor its power, nor a Platonic Idea, nor any of their immediate subdivisions, but a relatively lowly demon charged with a circumscribed office. This is another factor that suggests that the compilation of a mythological index to Ficino's writings would be a complex if useful task.

With these four methods, Ficino has covered the range of possibilities of allegorizing the pagan gods "Platonically"—that is, as the Neoplatonists and as Plato himself had putatively allegorized them. The methods, unlike the four of Christian allegorization, are generally mutually exclusive: we may go from one to the other "as the occasion demands," but no lemma can be allegorized all four ways since it does not possess the plurisignative nature of Scripture. Disagreement may of course arise as to which sense Plato intended in a particular context; but that is a different matter, requiring not only expertise and experience in reading Plato, but, as Ficino observes in several places, a proper mental and spiritual set, a proper preparedness for illumination as to which sense pertains. In their entirety, the four methods enabled him to dovetail the many Platonic and pre- and post-Platonic references to the gods in the philosophers into his own Christian-Platonic system. In doing so, he infused new life into the pagan myths and instilled a new sense for the Renaissance of their utmost seriousness.

---

52. Ficino's most notable work on demonology consists of his translations-adaptations of Porphyry, Proclus, Synesius, and Psellus and his commentary on certain passages in Plotinus; see *Opera*, pp. 1715-1717, 1908-1928, 1934-1937, 1939-1945, 1968-1978. There are comments, however, throughout his work. The great Christian demonologist is of course the Pseudo-Areopagite, whose treatises Ficino knew intimately, angelology being, for a Neoplatonist, a branch of demonology. For further refs., see chap. 1, n. 19 above.

Of the four, Ficino clearly favors two: enumeration in terms of the hypostases and of the powers intrinsic to these hypostases and their subdivisions. Method 4 is in essence an extension of method 3 and utilizes the same principles. The odd one out, at first glance, is method 2. It could be a particular application of method 1 were it not for the perennially difficult problem of deciding whether there can be Platonic Ideas of all, or at least of all the lower, Plotinian hypostases. On the other hand, it could also be part of method 3 in that Ficino, as a Platonist, always saw the Ideas in terms of the powers they exerted, though Plato himself had talked of them primarily as entities. In other words the Ideas occupied an uneasy status somewhere between the notion of the substances or hypostases and the notion of their powers. We might argue indeed that Ficino is only employing two fundamental methods: allegorization in terms of substance and of power. Hence his concentration on the dodecade for the one and on the Orphic theology of Jove for the other. However, since his translation of the lemma at 246E4 reads, *Magnus utique dux in celo Iupiter...*, we should interpret the Phaedran Zeus not only as a power but as leader of the cavalcade of celestial gods and souls in the animate realm. Zeus is not, as we noted before, the Iamblichean and Proclian leader of the intellectual gods in the realm of Mind, for he would then be described as *maximus atque primus*. On the other hand, the fact that Plato writes *magnus Jupiter,* and not simply *Jupiter* without an epithet, means for Ficino that he is speaking of the World-Soul, not simply of the planet Jupiter.

Before turning to the final chapter of commentary proper, let me briefly consider some related topics in summa 19, which deals with 246E to 247A. First, Ficino postulates two chariots for Jove, since as the World-Soul he is the first to move and be moved: an internal chariot, which is winged, and the external chariot of the world, the universal "machine," which is moved by the internal chariot as the body by the soul. There is no mention here, surprisingly, of two or four horses. The internal chariot is winged in that Jove devotes himself to the divine (*divinis incumbit*) even as he governs the world. Subsequently summa 20 will define this chariot as composed of "the internal discursive powers," which "simul-

taneously contemplate and provide equally";[53] and chapter 5 of
the commentary has already determined they impart the motions
of life, understanding, and desire.[54] But why, given these three
motions, does summa 19 now speak of the chariot's two motions
of conversion—presumably the motion of the wheels revolving on
their axes and the forward motion of the chariot and the wheels
themselves—and key them to the *Timaeus* 40AB? The *Timaeus*
reads: "And the Demiurge assigned to each [of the stars] two
motions: one uniform in the same place, as each always thinks the
same thoughts about the same things; the other a forward motion,
as each is subjected to the revolution of the same and uniform."[55]
The answer lies, I take it, in Ficino's decision to stress the "activation" (*exercere*) of the two final "motions" in the adapted Neoplatonic triad of proceeding, turning, and returning (and in the
corresponding triad of life, understanding, and desire). In terms
of the *Cratylus*'s orientation triad, that is, he is concentrating on
the "quickening" (*citare*) of the selfward, saturnian regarding,
and of the upward, uranian regarding. While the internal chariot
does indeed provide—look down in the jovian regard for inferiors
—this is not a motion of "conversion," of turning and returning,
but rather the contrary motion of proceeding into the external
world, of imparting movement to the external chariot. But such
providing and proceeding must be accompanied by the two
motions of conversion if the sublime souls are to remain unfallen,
to retain immaculate their wings.

Following Jove as World-Soul come the twelve leaders of the
host (*exercitus*), including of course Jove as leader of the planet
Jupiter. The leaders imitate Jove's twin motions of conversion
even as they imitate his third "processional" motion in the providential moving of their external chariots, the celestial and elemental spheres. The host itself consists of the souls of "stars" (the
individual stars in the firmament of the fixed stars under Uranus)
and of higher demons (note once again Ficino's concern that we

53. Ed. Allen, *Charioteer,* pp. 152-153.
54. Ibid., pp. 86-89.
55. The translation is F. M. Cornford's in his *Plato's Cosmology: The "Timaeus" of Plato Translated with a Running Commentary* (London, 1937), p. 118. Ficino may well have had Plotinus's *Enneads* 2.2.2 in mind also, since it refers to this passage.

differentiate between the higher and the lower, local demons); it too imitates Jove's three internal movements. Though this situation may seem clear enough, it should alert us to the two levels of allegorization Ficino resorts to to interpret the meaning of a god's "chariot" in Plato's dialogues. These we might call the astronomical and the theological levels, the first referring to the external chariots of the gods' aethereal (or, in the case of the demons, airy or lower) bodies, the second to the internal chariots of the three discursive powers in their souls.

The summa also elaborates on the role of Vesta, whom Plato at 247A1-2 mysteriously keeps behind in the dwelling place of the gods (ἐν θεῶν οἴκῳ)—she is, after all, the goddess of hearth and home[56]—instead of "advancing," "leading," "rousing," and "following" like the others in the dodecade; for Plato specifically mentions *eleven* as the number of those advancing after Zeus (247A1).[57] The sequence of what Ficino has already defined as "internal" motions implied by the verb "to follow" (246E6) is from a poetic viewpoint less appropriate for Vesta (and the contrast is not absolute, but a matter of degree). Thus, Ficino says, Plato temporally excludes her from the procession upwards and

56. Her centrality is mentioned in line 30 of *Homeric Hymn* 5: to Aphrodite (cf. *Hymns* 24 and 29: To Hestia); and Plato's *Cratylus* 401B-D describes her as "the essence of things" (glossed by Ficino in his epitome thus: "memento deam Vestam significare essentiam formarum separatarum divinorumque stabile fundamentum, ideoque Vestae ante alios deos sacrificare priscos consuevisse," *Opera*, p. 1312; cf. his epitome for *Laws* 5, *Opera*, p. 1502, *fons essendi*). See too Plotinus, *Enneads* 5.5.5; and Calcidius, *In Timaeum* 178 (ed. Waszink, pp. 206-207)—an actual gloss on the *Phaedrus* passage in question (246E-247A)—"Solam siquidem Uestam ait manere in sua sede, Uestam scilicet animam corporis uniuersi mentemque eius animae moderantem caeli stellantis habenas iuxta legem a prouidentia sanctam. Quam legem saepe diximus esse fatum serie quadam consequentiarum atque ordinem sancientem." In chap. 122 (ed. Waszink, p. 166) Calcidius had equated her with *terra*, again citing the *Phaedrus* 247A and following Roman tradition (see, for instance, Ovid's *Fasti* 6.267).

Though Vesta is always one of the Olympians in the Roman pantheon, we should recall that in Homer Hestia is not even a goddess; see Hackforth, *Phaedrus*, p. 73n.

57. Since the astronomical dodecade has Uranus and Saturn, Ficino has to account for the two Roman Olympians not included in that dodecade, Minerva and Ceres. Of Ceres he makes no mention whatsoever in the *Phaedrus* Commentary, but in his *De Vita* 3.19 (*Opera*, p. 559) he equates her with Vesta, "that is, the earth." Recognition of this equation, which is in fact an aspect of a Venus-Ceres-Vesta triad, enables us to solve, incidentally, one of the problems that puzzled Yates in her analysis of the world talisman, the *figura mundi*, described in the *De Vita* chapter; see her *Bruno*, pp. 73-76. For Minerva, see pp. 132-135 above.

regards her as the leader who rules over a "stable mass."[58] In point of fact—if we disregard, that is, "the poetic license"—Vesta does have "internal" motions, an internal chariot, and can be numbered among those who "follow" Jove; and this internal chariot, likewise, moves her external chariot, the stable mass of the earth, though the movements of the latter are "more hidden" than those of other external chariots (Ficino may have earthquakes in mind). She is responsible too for providing these hidden motions "in a fixed order"—that is, by exercising the same providence that is divinely enjoined upon her as upon the other gods but which they enact "with a more manifest motion." Ficino does not explain how Vesta can be satisfactorily allegorized as the soul of earth or the Earth when Plato has her remain in the gods' dwelling place as the solitary keeper of their hearth.[59]

While the souls of the stars and other divine souls control their external chariots as easily as Jove, and while they are still within the intellectual heaven, they too share in the vision of "many blissful spectacles" and "the ways to and fro."[60] Now the objects of

---

58. We recall that Ficino had already associated (though not identified) her with Pluto insofar as they were both "fixed and fixing" powers (*firma proprietas atque firmans*) in the Commentary, chap. 10, par. 6. Though she is the soul of the Earth and he of the under-earth, Hades, and they are both therefore earth deities, she is one of the Olympians and takes part in the Phaedran cavalcade, while he has no part in it at all, being lord of the realm to which the human charioteers descend when their wings are broken and the black steeds have successfully rebelled against them; see chap. 7 below.

In this regard Ficino seems to have changed his mind, or entertained some flexibility, for in his *De Amore* 1.3 (ed. Marcel, pp. 139-140) he had interpreted Pluto to mean the "idea" of earth, as Vulcan was of fire, Juno of air, and Neptune of water. But this cannot be Pluto's role here, given Plato's introduction of Hestia.

59. Of significance perhaps is Ficino's acquaintance with the Pythagoreans'—and most notably Philolaus's —identification of Vesta with the universe's central fire; see, for instance, his *De Lumine* 9 and 14 (*Opera,* pp. 979, 983-984). Philolaus is said to have called this fire "the hearth of the universe and the dwelling place of Jove, and the mother of the gods, and the altar and measure of nature" (Stobaeus, *Eclogue* 1.21); it was also known as the "guardhouse" of Zeus (Aristotle, *De Caelo* 293b4). For this theory see Garin, "Per la storia della cultura filosofica del Rinascimento," p. 3; and Zanier, *Medicina,* p. 50.

Of no significance, however, is the even more intriguing and complicated theory that Vesta was the Counter-Earth, for which see Heninger, *Sweet Harmony,* pp. 127-128, with further refs.

60. Hackforth, *Phaedrus,* p. 73n, notes that διέξοδοι at 247A4 is "commonly used for the orbits of heavenly bodies," but Ficino's sensitivity to the special meaning of "heaven" in the *Phaedrus*'s myth compels him to assume that these "orbits" are in the intellectual, not the lower, the animate, realm.

this vision are not yet the Ideas, the intelligibles,[61] for they will be seen later in the supercelestial place beyond the intellectual heaven, but rather two manifestations of these Ideas at a lower level: as they are witnessed "with a motionless gaze" or with a gaze that "moves around."[62] This distinction among the intellectual "sights" presumably parallels the distinction Ficino will later make between the Ideas themselves, the head Ideas and their "consequent" or "subsequent" Ideas, those seen in the course of the circuit around a head Idea.[63] Moreover, the "motionless" gaze suggests a perception where the *mens,* the intuitive intellect, dominates; while the gaze that "moves around" suggests a perception where the *ratio,* the discursive reason, also plays a part, albeit subordinate. For the intellectual realm is precisely the realm we perceive with the intellect when it is accompanied by the reason, as chapter 11, paragraph 5 of the Commentary will make clear.

In addition to contemplating these "intellectuals,"[64] each god, before envisioning the intelligibles themselves, also at 246E5-6 "provides" (in Greek ἐπιμελέομαι and διακοσμέω, meaning liter-

---

61. If we look at summa 19 in isolation, we might momentarily take *spectacula* to refer to the Ideas themselves; and a casual glance at summa 28's definition of the Ideas as *beata spectacula* might seem to confirm this impression. We must turn to Ficino's Latin translation of the dialogue, however, for clarification. At 250C3 (the lemma behind summa 28's definition) Ficino uses *beata spectacula* to render εὐδαίμονα φάσματα, "blessed spectacles." At 247A4-5, on the other hand, which is the passage treated by summa 19, he renders Plato's πολλαὶ μὲν οὖν καὶ μακάριαι θέαι τε καὶ διέξοδοι ἐντὸς οὐρανοῦ by *permulta igitur beataque ut qui spectacula discursusque intra celum existunt*—"therefore within the heaven there are many blessed spectacles *as it were* and ways to and fro." That is, he is pointing up the distinction between the *spectacula,* the φάσματα, themselves and the sights below, the θέαι, which resemble them—"spectacles as it were" (*ut qui* being the crucial qualification). By choosing to use *spectacula* to render both φάσματα and θέαι, however, he seems to be emphasizing the fact that the one images the other. Having failed to unravel this subtlety earlier, I tried to reconcile the *spectacula* referred to in summae 19 and 28 by mistranslating the critical clause in summa 19: it should read, "then they happily gaze on those divine things shining above in the intellectual heaven" (*Charioteer,* p. 150).

62. That is, Ficino does not take θέαι τε καὶ διέξοδοι as a hendiadys, as does Hackforth, *Phaedrus,* p. 70n. Cf. chap. 6, p. 162 below.

63. Cf. summae 21, 24 (ed. Allen, *Charioteer,* pp. 156-157, 162-163); also *Platonic Theology* 17.3 (ed. Marcel, 3:159; trans. Allen, *Charioteer,* p. 230). See chap. 7, pp. 171-173 below.

Again, the distinction would be paralleled at even lower levels.

64. Cf. summa 22 (ed. Allen, *Charioteer,* pp. 158-159): "[anima] a principiis exemplaribusque celum subit iterum procedens scilicet ad intellectualia contemplanda; ex intellectualibus autem ad se ipsam et que proprie ad anime naturam pertinent contuenda, idque est redire domum."

ally, for someone nurtured on the *Cratylus,* "to go through the cosmos").[65] For a god, that is, the contemplative and providential offices complement instead of impede each other as in fallen man. Since the gods know no envy—and Ficino interprets this famous dictum to mean that they always overflow with goodness to all things—any human soul or lower demonic soul who has the will and the ability (*vult atque potest*) can suddenly or immediately (*subito*) follow the gods and partake of their happiness. Rather surprisingly, however, Ficino then goes on to gloss the formula at 247A6-7, ἔπεται δὲ ὁ ἀεὶ ἐθέλων τε καὶ δυνάμενος, which he had translated as *sequitur autem semper volens et potens,* to mean "is called above again by the gods," thereby shifting the responsibility for pursuing the ascent from man to the gods, at least in part. But this is a rare lapse of faith in the individual's godlike powers. Ficino now turns to the nature of the ascent itself.

65. *Cratylus* 396A-B; cf. Ficino's *Philebus* Commentary 1.26 (ed. Allen, pp. 246-247).

Chapter Six: The Phaedrus's Cosmology

This, the most metaphysical chapter in Ficino's Commentary, attempts to interpret the charioteer myth in terms of Neoplatonic ontology and cosmology and thus to establish the design of the soul's ascent, the stages in its flight from the sense world to the intelligible world, if not to the transcendent goodness of the One. In treating of the soul freely joining the flight of the jovian cavalcade, and voyaging with it up through the dome of the intellectual heaven to gaze beyond towards the furthest "heaven," the intelligible world of the Ideas in what Plato calls "the supercelestial place," it treats of the individual soul as Jove himself, the supreme charioteer, and of Jove's ascent within the saturnian realm almost as high as Saturn, the prime intellect or Mind.

Ficino does not confine himself to one section of the text, but assumes familiarity with all the material from 247A to 247E and even beyond, while concentrating on a handful of key terms and phrases: the summit of the arch or dome, the notion of a world or heaven, the world's back, the supercelestial place, twelve as the number of the company, and so on. But one senses that he found the material so rich and suggestive that he could have continued discussing its implications almost indefinitely; for this was the core of the *Phaedrus*'s mysteries, the initiatory vision, before Plato turned back to the crippling of the wings, the Icarian fall, and the vicious insurrection of the black steed.

Below the Good or One, which cannot be referred to properly as a "world" since it cannot be understood either perceptually or intellectually and is beyond even the Ideas themselves (and Ficino uses the hallowed metaphor of the Sun for it), are four worlds or realms which Ficino also calls "heavens" on the authority of the *Timaeus* (28B, 30C-31B). The first realm or "heaven"—the super-heavenly place of the myth[1]—is the intelligible world of the pure

---

1. That is, in terms of the *Phaedrus*'s myth it is the "superheavenly" place, while in terms of the *Timaeus*'s definition of a "world" or "realm" it is a "heaven."

Forms, the series of the Ideas as they exist in Mind and are Mind, the prime intellect and prime intelligible as one. This realm is perceptible by the intellect alone, beyond the reach of reason entirely, and is imaged as the world of pure, unclouded light (the light proceeding from the Sun as the Good). Next is the intellectual realm of the Ideas as they exist in the pure intellects subordinate to Mind and under its sway. This is perceptible primarily by the intellect but with the aid of the reason and is imaged as the world of participated or clouded light or color; it is the realm, as we have seen, of the intellectuals. Third is the animate realm of the forms as they exist both in the World-Soul or in Soul and in the divine souls under it (in other words, Ficino is not differentiating between Soul and souls as he had between Mind and minds). This world is perceptible primarily by the reason but with the aid of the intellect— that is, the primacy of the two faculties is reversed from that pertaining to the second realm—and is imaged as the world of shape or three-dimensional extension. Finally comes the corporeal world of the forms as they exist in Body, the World-Machine; and, since this is the realm of perceptual rather than mathematical qualities, it is perceived by the imagination and senses.[2] We thus have a pentad: the One, Mind, Minds, Soul with souls, and Body. Though this pentad is clearly either a latent hexad if we separate, or a tetrad if we collapse, the singular and plural terms, the *Phaedrus's* myth itself compelled Ficino to maintain the distinction between Mind and minds but to treat of Soul and souls together. For the jovian cavalcade traverses the realm of minds, the intellectual realm, but not the realm of Mind, the intelligible realm.

Ficino calls the two higher realms, the "supermundane" worlds or heavens and the two lower the "mundane." One might suppose that the distinction between "supercelestial" and "celestial" would parallel this, but the *Phaedrus's* critical reference to the intelligible world as "the supercelestial place" forced Ficino to interpret the next, the intellectual, world as "the celestial place" (that is, heaven), and the two lower, the animate and sensible, worlds as "the subcelestial place."[3] When not keyed to this spe-

2. There is no entire realm, apparently, that is perceived by the reason alone (*ratio simplex*).

3. Thus he can observe in his *Parmenides* Commentary, chap. 60[1] (*Opera*, p. 1175.2): "Ibi [in Phaedro] enim per locum sub coelo sensibilem vel ad summum animalem designat naturam; per locum vero coelestem, intellectualem; per supercoelestem, intelligibilem."

cific schema of places, however, "celestial" refers to the animate star gods, and "supercelestial" either to the intellectual gods or to the Ideas above them. Thus we can speak of "celestial" gods in the "subcelestial" place of their animate realm, and of "supercelestial" gods in the "celestial" place of their intellectual realm. In seeking to account for this anomaly, Ficino notes that for Plato "heaven" may often signify the highest goal for each realm as well as, in the *Timaeus's* sense, the realm itself. Thus "heaven" comes to mean the animate realm for sublunar beings, the intellectual realm for the celestial animate gods (the "heaven" which dominates the *Phaedrus's* myth), and the intelligible realm for the intellectual gods. Could we entertain the notion of calling the One a world too, then it would be the "heaven" for the intelligible realm of Mind; but since we cannot do this legitimately, we cannot call it a "heaven," and the highest possible "heaven" is therefore the intelligible realm of the Ideas in the hypostasis, Mind.

The human soul also has four worlds which are the four series of the universal forms, but these worlds do not correspond exactly to the hypostatic realms, since they exist in the vegetative nature (and are thus perceived by the senses), in the imagination (now distinct from the senses), in reason, and in intellect.

The four realms make up the universe, which, as its name connotes, is unified, is one. The links binding them together are in each instance the highest and lowest members mediating the transitions. From the viewpoint of both the *Phaedrus* and the *Symposium,* Beauty (which Ficino identifies in paragraph 6 with Truth, Wisdom, and Being as we perceive them) is at the apex of the universe since it exists, formally, as the crown and splendor of the intelligible world, the beauty of Mind itself. Beyond Beauty and therefore beyond Mind, but transcending the universe altogether because transcending being and intelligibility, is the One, the "hypostasis" beyond all predications, light in its enfolded, unradiated, unsplendored essence. When Socrates says, therefore, that the mundane gods climb to heaven, he means that the celestial

---

("In the *Phaedrus* Plato means by the place beneath heaven the sensible, or at its height the animate, nature; by the celestial place, the intellectual nature; and by the supercelestial place, the intelligible nature.") See Allen, *Charioteer,* pp. 66-69.

souls ruling the animate realm ascend by virtue of their intellects into their heaven, the intellectual realm, which they comprehend with their intellects (with the aid of reason). But, since as the highest souls they also possess pure intellects (intellects that transcend reason and are capable of perceiving the intelligibles themselves), these mundane gods can also ascend to the very limits of the intellectual heaven and gaze upwards at the furthest "heaven" of all, the heaven that the intellectual beings also gaze up to, the intelligible heaven or world of Mind, in the supercelestial place, supercelestial because beyond the heaven which—in terms of the *Phaedrus's* myth—is the intellectual realm.

Unlike the *Parmenides,* however, the *Phaedrus* does not explore, Ficino says, the possibility of the ultimate ascent from Mind to the One.[4] As intellectual souls rather than pure intellects, the mundane gods must rest content with a vision of the intelligibles— usually individually but at supreme moments possibly in their totality as Beauty, or as present in one of the head Ideas. That is, they must rest content with the Beauty of Truth (which is simultaneously the prime intellect and the prime intelligible) or, to hark back to his discussion of the third method of allegorizing the gods, with venerean Saturn, Venus in Saturn.

Ficino next proceeds to chart the topography of the penultimate world, the intellectual realm in the pure intellects below the prime intellect—that is, in the saturnian beings below Saturn as Mind (one of these is Saturn as a leader intellect, we should recall, just as Jupiter is a leader soul as well as Soul!). At 247A-C Socrates describes the mundane gods as climbing "the steep ascent even as far as the summit of the arch that supports the heaven"—in Ficino's translation *in celestem circunferentiam proficiscuntur iam ascendentes.* Having attained this summit or dome, they come forth and "stand upon the back of the heaven"—*cum ad summum pervenerint, extra progresse in celi dorso consistunt;* and im-

---

4. That is, the ascent of our one, our *unitas,* to the absolute One; cf. Kristeller, *Philosophy,* pp. 250-251, 368. However, Kristeller underestimates the importance of this essentially Plotinian notion for Ficino or at least for the later Ficino when he argues that such an ascent "is not a particular act distinguished from contemplation, but merely an attribute of the contemplative act itself" (p. 251). Ficino was always conscious of higher ecstasies, I believe, than the contemplative, as his love theories testify. See Beierwaltes, *Marsilio Ficinos Theorie des Schönen,* pp. 38-42; also chap. 9, n. 13 below.

mediately "the revolving heaven carries them around, and they look upon the regions without"—*ibi constitutas circunferentia ipsa circunfert atque ille intuentur que sunt extra celum.* This passage depicts the celestial gods (who already exist as our heaven, the animate heaven looked up to by the sublunar world) as climbing upwards through the three concentric regions of the intellectual realm which is their heaven: first to the concave region beneath the dome, then up to the dome itself at its highest point (variously translated as *summum, profundum,* and *circunferentia*), and finally out upon the convex region "on the back" of the dome. From this position on the back of the intellectual heaven they can gaze upwards at the Ideas in Mind, in the supercelestial place, which is the intelligible, the superheavenly heaven. Since Mind is "universally the universe" insofar as it has no particular category of mind, soul, or body under it but all things existing corporeally, animately, or intellectually, it is the paradigmatic world or heaven and contains all the worlds or heavens. At the same time, since it is closest to the One and is itself one to the highest possible degree (*maxime*), it is the universe in its unity. However, we can only talk of this prime universe, of this supercelestial place, in metaphors: best of all as unfolding, radiant, or splendored light blazing down upon the regions of the intellectual dome.[5]

Assigned to the three regions of the dome are the lowest, middle, and highest orders of intellectual or saturnian beings, who together make up the intellectual realm. They are led by twelve intellects with the same names as the twelve gods of the astronomical dodecade[6]—the number twelve, Ficino says, being "appropriate" for the leaders of both hosts, the intellectual and the animate.[7] These supermundane beings (whom Ficino and the Neoplatonists also call gods) are not grouped as we might first expect into three tet-

5. For this traditional, ultimately Augustinian, distinction between the three kinds of light, see chap. 4, p. 109 above, and chap. 8, pp. 186-187 below.

6. Ficino makes no attempt to refer to the intellectual gods by using the names of deities in the pre-Jovian dynasties familiar to him from Hesiod's *Theogony*: Iapetus, Theia, Hyperion, and so forth, the exceptions being Uranus, Cronus, and Rhea.

7. Despite his earlier disclaimer that the actual number of the spheres had not yet been determined and that Plato had settled on twelve for convenience' sake (chap. 10, par. 4), Ficino, like the ancient Neoplatonists, found the number twelve numerologically very significant, as he makes especially clear here in chap. 11, par. 9 (see Allen, *Charioteer*, pp. 243-244 n. 55, with further references).

rads occupying the concavity, dome, and convexity of the realm, but into four triads, the first being closest to the intelligible realm, the last to the animate, and the other two mediating between them.[8] Since we know the names and hierarchy of the gods in the celestial dodecade, we can perhaps deduce the members of this supercelestial dodecade: Uranus, Saturn, and Jupiter probably constitute the first triad; Mars, Apollo, and Venus, the second; Mercury, Diana, and Vulcan, the third; and Juno, Neptune, and Vesta, the fourth.[9] Ficino chooses to work in triads rather than tetrads because he can then retain the Uranus-Saturn-Jove unit intact, and think of the others again as three subdivisions of Jove.

With an eye perhaps to Hermias's doxography,[10] Ficino has some suggestions for interrelating and not just paralleling the animate and intellectual dodecades.[11] Perhaps the members of the higher dodecade are intellects ruling over and providing for the souls of the lower. Or perhaps, in responding to this providential ruling, the souls themselves turn to their corresponding intellects in order "to worship and imitate them with all their might."[12] Or perhaps each of the twelve intellects gazes up at those Ideas or "models" in the intelligible world which principally concern both itself, its soul, and the souls, spheres, and inferiors within them directly subordinate to it. Ficino's iteration of "perhaps" and his note at the beginning of paragraph 9 that all this "appears to be

8. In his *Parmenides* Commentary, chap. 94 (*Opera,* p. 1194.3), Ficino speaks of *three* tiers of gods in the intellectual, and similarly in the animate, realm. He may, however, be thinking simply in terms of the intelligible, the mixed, and the intellectual categories.

9. Again, I am assuming that Ficino was following the Chaldaean rather than the Platonic or Porphyrian order (see chap. 5, n. 17 above); and I am also assuming that he intends the planetary and not the zodiacal twelve. In postulating the same set of deities for both the mundane and the supermundane dodecades, Ficino perforce rejected Proclus's hypercosmic-encosmic twelve; see Saffrey, "Notes platoniciennes," pp. 171-172; also Allen, *Charioteer,* pp. 34-36; and chap. 10 below.

10. *In Phaedrum,* pp. 135-136 (ed. Couvreur); cf. Dillon, *Iamblichi Fragmenta,* p. 251.

11. Ficino seems to be unique in arguing for a simple parallelism between the intellectual and the celestial dodecades of gods implied by the *Phaedrus* Neoplatonically interpreted; for Proclus, his prime authority in this respect, had argued for a much more complicated arrangement, most notably in his *Theologia Platonica* 4.4-26 (ed. and trans. Saffrey and Westerink, 4:17-78). Interestingly, he may have been under Proclus's sway still when he composed the last book of his own *Platonic Theology* and especially in chap. 8 (ed. Marcel, 3:204; trans. Allen, *Charioteer,* p. 236). See chap. 9, pp. 220-221 below.

12. According to Rosán, *Philosophy of Proclus,* p. 179n, Proclus had ultimately rejected the notion that there might be "hypercosmic souls" ($\dot{v}\pi\varepsilon\rho\kappa\dot{o}\sigma\mu\iota\alpha\iota\ \psi\upsilon\chi\alpha\dot{\iota}$) on the grounds that we would be able to characterize them with greater detail and precision if they existed.

credible'' should alert us to the fact that he is presenting us with opinions, not dogmas. The following paragraph tells us why. Some ancient interpreters had argued that in the *Phaedrus* Plato had intended to depict the ascent of the supramundane, not the mundane, gods; and Ficino has the views of Iamblichus, Syrianus, Hermias, and Proclus in mind.[13] But others, though Plotinus is the only one we now know about, had argued that it was the mundane (in the *Enneads* 5.8.10, 12, and 13).[14] Ficino thinks this last the ''probable'' reading.

Apart from the authority of Plotinus, he finds grounds for rejecting the supramundanist interpretation in Plato's choice of the word ''animal'' (ζῷον) at 246C5 and D1. ''Animal,'' he writes, describes the composite structure of soul and body in a mortal being from which we have to analogize to describe a god. At 246C7 Plato says that our fancy forms a picture for us (πλάττομεν from πλάσσω) of someone ''whom we have never seen nor fully conceived'' but whom we can only imagine as an immortal ''animal'' possessing ''a soul and body united for all time.'' Since Plato had attributed charioteers, chariots, horses, and the two internal and one external motions to the gods, along with the companionship not only of Vesta but also of demons and even of human souls, Ficino argues that he must have pictured them as beings with souls and bodies, however aethereal, and thus as ''animals'' as defined by Socrates. In short, however much analogy may be at work here, Ficino sees Plato as describing the beings in the jovian cavalcade of the mundane gods, and not of the supramundane, purely intellectual gods who would ride (if such a verb of motion could be deemed appropriate) in the saturnian cavalcade.

Perhaps the most powerful, if unstated, argument for the mundanist view is Ficino's assumption that the dialogue is primarily concerned with soul in terms of *motion* and that it is its flight

13. See Allen, *Charioteer,* pp. 6-7, 244-245 nn. 56, 58, 59, with further references; also chap. 10 below.
14. In these sections Plotinus is clearly conceiving of Zeus as the ''manifested'' god—that is, as the World-Soul. Cf. *Enneads* 4.3.7 and 4.8.2; also Ficino's own commentary (though disappointingly brief) on all these sections in his *Opera,* pp. 1734.2, 1754.8-1755, 1769. See chap. 7, n. 20, and chap. 10, pp. 234 ff. below (in the latter I include Ficino's 1492 Latin translation of the *Enneads* 5.8.10, given its critical importance for his understanding of Plotinus's view of the *Phaedrus*).

which is bodied forth by the charioteer myth, not the unimaginable, motionless ascent of pure intellect. Given Ficino's lifelong obsession with the soul, its nature, immortality, powers, and freedoms, it is predictable he would be attracted by the Plotinian rather than the Iamblichean and Proclian interpretation, and especially since a cavalcade of pure intellects would have to be in effect angels,[15] and he was committed to the notion that the *Phaedrus*'s myth is preeminently concerned with man. As it is, the jovian cavalcade of souls including human souls ascends through the ranks of angels anyway, and shares with them, however momentarily, their intuitive vision of the Ideas in the mind of Christ.

Ficino's last paragraph of formal commentary is again concerned with Plato's several references to "heaven" through 247A-C: "there are many spectacles of bliss and ways to and fro within heaven (*intra celum*)" (A4-5); "the immortal souls . . . come forth and stand upon heaven's back (*in celi dorso*)" (B7); and "straightway the circumference carries them around and they look upon the regions outside heaven (*extra celum*)" (C2). ficino is vehemently opposed to those who interpret "heaven" in these instances to mean the "sky" we see daily,[16] presumably the spheres of air and fire; for it is absurd to suppose the mundane gods should have to contemplate both "the images of the spectacles of bliss and the ways to and fro" within our sky (let alone the spectacles themselves) in order to receive blessedness, when we as fallen souls cannot receive blessedness thence. Furthermore, they exist far above our sky, and should they turn to contemplate it, they would have to look backwards instead of upwards—look backwards, moreover, at the manifestation of something for which they already know "the causes and reasons." Looking back at the subcelestial air would imply, Ficino says, that their wings had been crippled or lamed, a condition foreign to the gods. It is equally absurd to suppose the mundane gods are carried around "on the back of our sky," since they are the source and principle of all celestial

15. This is exactly what he had assumed it was when writing his *Platonic Theology* 18.8 (ed. Marcel, 3:204; trans. Allen, *Charioteer,* p. 236); see chap. 9, p. 221 below. For the relationship between the terms "angel" and "god" see chap. 1, n. 21 above.

16. Ficino was almost certainly indebted here to Proclus's *Theologia Platonica* 4.5 (ed. Saffrey and Westerink, 4:18-22), which proffers a similar set of refutations.

motions and cannot be moved by any one sphere's motion. If they looked up at the intelligible Ideas in the supracelestial, supra-heavenly place from the position of being carried around on the air's or fire's dome or back, then their gaze would be bypassing their own animate realm and also the intellectual realm; and this is inconceivable. Finally Ficino argues against supposing there are four triads of divine souls distributed across the convex, dome, and concave of our elemental sky. With this series of objections he dismisses in effect an erroneous interpretation of the jovian ascent at the opposite pole from the supramundanist, an interpretation we might call intramundanist, materialist, or even Stoic.

We should turn for confirmation that the "heaven" of these lemmata is the intellectual heaven to the Cratylean formula, where Uranus is the gazing upwards towards the supernal Ideas. For Uranus is both the first intellect of the intellectual dodecade (as his mundane counterpart is the first soul of the animate dodecade) and also the whole class of intellects when they look upwards (even though ontologically this class is under Saturn). So, Ficino concludes, the mundane gods under Jove as World-Soul, having ascended the three regions of the intellectual heaven (those occupied by the four trinities of intelligible, mixed, and intellectual gods), are at last carried around on the outside of its back and gaze upwards in a uranian vision at the fourth and highest realm of Mind in the supercelestial place. While rejecting the supramundanist interpretation of the Phaedran cavalcade, Ficino can therefore still agree with the supramundanist interpretation of "heaven" in these critical lemmata at 247A-C as referring to the intellectual realm. He returned, that is, to what may have been and what he certainly thought was the pre-Iamblichean position propounded by Plotinus.[17]

17. Both Ficino and the later ancient Neoplatonists could invoke Plotinus's authority here, and particularly the later sections of 5.8, because of the profoundly figurative nature of his thought and expression, at the opposite remove from the academic precision of Proclus. Plotinus's realm of Mind had been divided into the intelligible and the intellectual by Iamblichus, out of which division Proclus had established the triad of intelligible, intelligible-and-intellectual, and intellectual; for Ficino, however, it retained much of its original unity, though he was familiar with and employed the later distinctions as we have seen. That is, he was striving, I believe, to rediscover the Plotinian interpretation of the *Phaedrus,* one that he supposed was much simpler than the Iamblichean or Proclian and

It is signal that Ficino should end his commentary on a uranian note; for underlying his conception of the charioteer from the beginning has been another central tenet of Orphic theology: namely that when the poets talked of Uranus begetting Saturn and Saturn begetting Jove and each deposing his predecessor violently in turn, they were secretly speaking of the emanation of the Plotinian hypostases, a process which is destined to reverse.[18] Thus Jove

---

therefore more easily accommodated to Christianity. In terms of the Iamblichean distinction, Ficino interpreted the *Phaedrus* as referring to the "intellectual" heaven or realm. He made it the home of Proclus's three kinds of intelligible, mixed, and intellectual gods (though for Proclus himself it was the home of the lower two triads of mixed gods alone) and located it below the intelligible or superheavenly place of the pure intelligibles, the Ideas (though Proclus had assigned this place to the first triad of mixed gods). In terms of Plotinus's metaphysics, however, he realized that the "intellectual" heaven and the superheavenly place, the higher intellects and the Ideas, were all aspects of the unitary realm of Mind. Cf. Proclus, *Theologia Platonica* 4.5, 23 (ed. Saffrey and Westerink, 4:21, 68-69); with Dillon's analyses, *Iamblichi Fragmenta*, pp. 251-253. See chap. 10, pp. 250 ff. below.

18. The best introduction to the Neoplatonists' account of Uranus's castration, familiar to them from Hesiod's *Theogony* 168-192, is in Wind's *Pagan Mysteries*, pp. 133-137. Wind notes that the castration is "of one type with the dismemberment of Osiris, Attis, Dionysus, all of which signify the same mystery to the neo-Orphic theologians: for whenever the supreme One descends to the Many, this act of creation is imagined as a sacrificial agony, as if the One were cut to pieces and scattered. Creation is conceived in this way as a cosmogonic death, by which the concentrated power of one deity is offered up and dispersed..." (p. 133); similarly with the enchainment of Saturn. Of critical importance here are Plotinus, *Enneads* 5.8.13, and Proclus, *Theologia Platonica* 5.3-6, 36 (ed. Portus, pp. 252-258, 324-326), *In Crat.*, p. 64.15-27 (ed. Pasquali), and *In Timaeum* 295B ff. (ed. Diehl, 3:183 ff.).

Wind continues, "it follows logically that resurrection from death must appear as a destructive force.... By the same logic the myth of Saturn eating his children was greeted as a promise of redemption, the Many returning to the One, a reversal of primeval 'dismemberment'" (p. 135n). Cf. Hesiod, *Theogony* 453-467; and Plotinus, *Enneads* 5.1.7.

Apart from Hesiod, Plotinus, and Proclus, Ficino's sources might have also included Cicero, *De Natura Deorum* 2.24.63-25.64; Plutarch, *De E apud Delphos* (*Moralia* 388F-389A); Macrobius, *In Somnium Scipionis* 1.12; and Boccaccio, *Genealogia Deorum* 3.23.

Ficino refers to these twin motifs in his *De Amore* 5.12 (ed. Marcel, p. 197); in his *Philebus* Commentary 1.11 (ed. Allen, pp. 138-139); and in his Plotinus commentaries on 5.1.7 and 5.8.13 (*Opera*, pp. 1758.2, 1769.6). But his most explicit statement on these matters (overlooked by Wind) is contained in his gloss on the *Cratylus* (*Opera*, p. 1312): "Memento ...nomina deorum masculina significare in divinis actum efficientem, foeminina vero potentiam capientem; praeterea quod coelum suo motu generet tempus consumens, continueque consumat, imago quaedam est referens deum Coelium et Rheam atque Saturnum filios devorantem. In his autem Coelius est essentia ipsa divina, Rhea eiusdem vita, Saturnus mens eiusdem. Saturni filii ideae sunt rerum, intelligentia divina intra se genitae, quae sicut producuntur a mente ita et reducuntur in mentem, eas in se, ut ita dixerim, absorbentem." ("Remember that with the names of the gods the masculine signify act as it effects actions in divine matters, the feminine signify potency as it receives such actions. Moreover, in that heaven by its own motion generates and continuously consumes consuming time, so it is an image for the god Heaven and Rhea and Saturn devouring his children. For

must become Saturn who must become Uranus (who must perhaps become Demogorgon, though this is an impenetrable mystery, given the transcendence of the One as absolute). The ultimate charioteer is therefore uranian Jove, Jove as Uranus, the son as father and even as the father's father, the triune God.[19] The con-

---

here Heaven is the divine essence, Rhea its life, and Saturn its intelligence. Saturn's sons are the universal Ideas borne by the divine understanding within itself: as they are produced from the intelligence, so are they led back into it, and the intelligence, so to speak, swallows them up into itself.'') Again Ficino must have had Plotinus's *Enneads* 5.1.7 and 5.8.13 in mind.

Cf. Pico, *Commento* 2.18, 20 (ed. Garin, pp. 509-512).

19. Again this would make Uranus equivalent to the One, if not to God the Father; for Ficino was of two minds as to whether the Platonists or even Plato had adumbrated the mystery of the Christian Trinity (compare, for instance, the conflicting positions in his *Opera*, pp. 956 and 1533.4). He also had to confront several profoundly enigmatic if not mutually irreconcilable texts on the meaning of Uranus—that is, Heaven.

First there were the *prisci theologi*, Hesiod and Orpheus. The *Theogony* depicts the cosmic succession as beginning with Chaos, who was succeeded by Earth (Gaea), Tartarus, and Love. Chaos next brought forth Night and Erebus, while Earth gave birth to Heaven, Hills, and Sea. From an incestuous union between Earth and her son, Heaven, proceeded Oceanus, Rhea, Cronus, and a number of other deities. And so on. Whether we take these deities to signify actual beings or merely abstractions, the fact remains that Heaven is two generations away from the primordial Chaos, and is the son, before he is the husband, of Earth. Ficino had apparently translated the *Theogony*, since he mentions it in a letter to Uranius (*Opera*, p. 933.3), though it has not survived (see Kristeller, *Sup. Fic.* 1:clxiv); and he was interested in the prominence Hesiod received at the start of Phaedrus's speech in Plato's *Symposium* at 178B (see Allen, "Cosmogony and Love," pp. 138 ff.).

In the Orphic genealogy the succession is simpler; it runs: Phanes, Night, Heaven, Cronus, Zeus, and Dionysus. Cf. Orphic frag. 107 (ed. Kern); Hermias, p. 152.15 ff. (ed. Couvreur); Proclus, *In Crat.* 105 (ed. Pasquali, pp. 54-55) and *In Timaeum* 3:168.15 ff. (ed. Diehl). Once again, however, Heaven is third. See chap. 10, pp. 246 ff. below.

Next, there was the *Cratylus's* influential definition of Uranus as "the upward looking" at 396BC, the definition that Ficino constantly refers to throughout his works and almost invariably here, e.g. in chaps. 10 and 11 (see Allen, *Charioteer,* pp. 115, 119, 129).

Finally, among what Ficino considered the primary texts there was the difficult passage in Plotinus's *Enneads* 5.8.13 (for Ficino's own rendering, see chap. 10, p. 237 below). As his commentary heading makes clear, Ficino regarded this as concerned with the three hypostases, the One, Mind, and Soul, symbolized by Uranus, Saturn, and Jupiter, respectively: *Intellectus divinus, qui et Saturnus cognominatur castrat Coelium, id est, ipsum bonum* (= *Opera*, p. 1769.6); similarly with 5.5.3 and Ficino's note, *Opera*, p. 1763.6. On the other hand, he had to account for 3.5.2, where Plotinus had presented Venus as the daughter of both Uranus and Saturn as if they were one and the same (see chap. 5, n. 40 above).

All of these texts, and others, received extensive Neoplatonic commentary, which Ficino was undoubtedly familiar with in part, though the whole issue awaits exploration. A guideline to the subtlety and breadth of his understanding is provided by his *Cratylus* epitome, however: "Prima quidem nominum positione Coelius significat animam sphaerae stelliferae, Saturnus sequentis sphaerae animam, Iupiter vero tertiae. Secunda vero positione Coelius significat deum, Saturnus angelicam mentem, Iupiter mundi animam atque coelestem. Tertia Coelius Dei ipsius significat foecunditatem, Saturnus eius intelligentiam, Iupi-

templative flight ascends in the *Phaedrus,* therefore, as far as a uranian vision of the Ideas as Jove obeys the Uranus in himself.

Interestingly, Ficino now arrives at the point of having to set bounds to the scope of the *Phaedrus* and to assess its limitations. The dialogue does not treat of the return of all things to the One, to Demogorgon, or even of the flight into the intelligibles in the fourth and highest heaven, though in paragraph 4 Ficino had indeed talked of the gods "proceeding" thither. Effectively, it leaves us on the threshold of the final ascent of the cavalcade of mundane gods from their transient position in the third, the intellectual, realm to the fourth realm above. We can thus see why, following Neoplatonic precedent, Ficino subordinated the *Phaedrus* to the *Parmenides,* to the *Sophist,* and even to the *Timaeus* in a letter he wrote to Niccolò Valori and used as the proem to his 1496 volume, the *Commentaria in Platonem.*[20]

In discussing the disposition of his commentaries in that volume, he places first those on the two metaphysical dialogues, which treat of the one universal principle and of being and non-

---

ter beneficam voluntatem omnibus providentem. Quarta Coelius in quolibet numine aspectum ad superiora designat, Saturnus respectum ad semetipsum, Iupiter prospectum inferioribus providentem." ("If the names [of the gods] are used in one context, Heaven signifies the soul of the sphere of the fixed stars; Saturn, the soul of the next sphere; Jupiter, the soul of the third. In a second context Heaven signifies God; Saturn, the angelic intelligence; Jupiter, the soul of the world and the celestial soul. In a third context Heaven signifies the fecundity of God Himself; Saturn, God's understanding; Jupiter, the generosity of God's will, which provides for all. In a fourth context Heaven in any deity signifies the gaze upwards towards superiors; Saturn, the regard that looks inwards; Jupiter, the glance downwards that provides for inferiors.") (*Opera,* p. 1311; cf. *Philebus* Commentary 1.26 [ed. Allen, pp. 246-247].)

Uranus, in brief, at various times can signify: the soul of the firmament, God Himself, God's fecundity, or the gaze that looks upwards. Though the divine poets like Hesiod and Homer, however, had employed all four senses, and the Neoplatonists—that is, the *Platonici antiqui*—had followed them, Ficino's remarks in chapters 10 and 11 of the *Phaedrus* Commentary suggest that he considered Plato's own usage more circumspect; in particular, he feels, Plato had declined to use Uranus to signify the One, that is, God, though Plotinus had not hesitated to do so subsequently. Thus in the *Phaedrus* Uranus as "the upward looking" is taken to signify either the first of the intellectual gods or the first of the celestial gods (and as such is the soul of the outermost sphere of the fixed stars): see Allen, *Charioteer,* pp. 113, 115, 119, 129; and chap. 5, n. 27 above. Cf. Pico, *Commento* 1.8-9 and 2.20 (ed. Garin, pp. 470-473 and 511-512). Pico argues that God may be called Uranus and that Uranus may stand for anything that is first or preeminent in its class ("Celio è significativo d'ogni cosa prima ed eccellente sopra l'altre" [p. 470]).

20. Now to be found in his *Opera,* p. 1136.2.

being; and then the commentary on the *Timaeus,* which treats of the animate and physical worlds. The commentary on the *Phaedrus* is fourth since it mixes divine matters with natural and human matters (*divina cum physicis humanisque permiscet*). Last is the commentary on the *Philebus* since it mixes them all together in a way. Ficino notes that he has dealt with the *Phaedrus* before the *Philebus* because it disputes of divine matters at greater length (*ob longiorem videlicet divinorum disputationem*) and because the madness inspiring it is more divine than that inspiring the *Philebus.* However, since another important commentary, the *Symposium's,* had already been published in an earlier volume and did not need to be included here, Ficino seems to be intellectually justifying (though on good Neoplatonic grounds) what was probably an originally pragmatic decision to publish the material at hand in 1496. Admittedly, the *Phaedrus's* principal concerns, despite the great gift of madness inspiring it, were not so metaphysically far-reaching as those of the *Parmenides* or the *Sophist,* two other "theological" dialogues. But in other ways it was closer to Ficino's heart, since its mysteries were specifically concerned with the mundane gods with whom man is ontologically and epistemologically most closely allied, the gods whom he can actually join in a vision of that "place beyond the heavens of which no earthly poet has sung and none shall worthily sing" (247C3-4), the realm of intelligible being. The *Phaedrus* in short takes us to the very limits of what we might call contemplative theology. To go beyond it we would have to depart on the unitive Plotinian flight "of the alone to the alone," of man's unity to the transintelligible One—the valediction, fittingly, of the *Enneads,* and the secret concern of Plato's supreme masterpiece, the *Parmenides.*[21]

Though Ficino abandoned his formal commentary at this point, three related summae give us valuable insights into Ficino's interpretation of other details concerning the uranian vision.

Summa 20 deals with the ascent of the mundane gods to the heights of contemplation proper to the supermundane gods, this being likened at 247A8 to both a feast and a table: "feast" insofar

---

21. See Allen, "Ficino's Theory of the Five Substances," *passim;* and n. 4 above.

as it reflects the generosity of the givers, "table," the capacity of the receivers. Other details dovetail into the cosmology outlined above; but Ficino adds that, since the mundane host is composed of souls, it must, unlike pure intellects who understand motionlessly, understand the intelligibles by moving perpetually around them. Hence the references at 247C1, "and the circumference carries them around," and at 247D4-6, "until heaven's revolution brings the soul back full circle; and while she is borne around, she discerns Justice itself," etc. Thus we have three descending degrees of contemplating the intelligibles: first, intellectual contemplation, which is motionless (pure intuition)—the mode of the separated supramundane intellects; second, eternally discursive or ratiocinative contemplation, revolving unceasingly around the intelligibles —the mode of the higher, divine souls; and third, temporally discursive or ratiocinative contemplation, reaching only intermittently, "in certain intervals of time," towards the intelligibles— the mode of lower souls. That Plato had endowed the Phaedran gods with chariots *in motion* (in terms of both wings and wheels) is additional evidence for supposing that he intended the dodecade to be mundane, the chariots themselves being defined as "the internal discursive powers"—that is, powers that operate the discourse, the discursiveness of reason.[22] However, the zenith in the flight of the cavalcade is the convexity of the dome constituting the intellectual heaven. While the metaphors of flight and ascent are inappropriate for the intuitional contemplation of the intelligibles by the supramundane gods, they can still apply to the mundane gods. Thus, when Ficino talks in chapter 11, paragraph 4, of the intellects of the mundane gods proceeding (*progrediuntur*) to

22. We should bear in mind that Ficino's conception of discursiveness (*discursus* or *discursio*) is tied to his conception of the reason (*ratio*) as a faculty of the soul that passes in time sequentially from one thought to the next. The intellect (*mens*) by contrast intuits nontemporally and nonsequentially. The chariot, suggesting as it does both time and motion, is an ideal image for the soul governed primarily by its *ratio*; but it is an intrinsically inadequate, because paradoxical, image for the pure apprehension of the *mens,* or even for the soul primarily governed by its *mens,* what we might call the angelic soul. See Kristeller, *Philosophy,* pp. 378-382.

Wallis, *Neoplatonism,* pp. 52-53, notes that Aquinas had made a careful distinction in his *Summa Theologiae* 1a.14.7 between "discursive" meaning "reasoning from premises to conclusion" and "discursive" meaning the "simple transition from one object to another." While human thought is discursive in both these senses, the thought of divine souls is discursive in the second sense alone, and this is what Ficino primarily has in mind.

the intelligible heaven, he means to imply that, while the pure intellects contemplate that realm motionlessly (*stabiliter intelligere*), intellects joined to souls continue to circle around the intelligibles discursively: divine souls perpetually, human souls intermittently (*per quedam temporum intervalla*). But the next summa, as we shall see, suggests that the mundane gods too can share, at least potentially, in the "motionless" glance.

Glossing 247CD, summa 21 is close to being a chapter of commentary. It deals with one of the most difficult of all the interpretative problems posed by the dialogue: what do the souls see and how, when they gaze upwards towards the supercelestial place? Again we must bring Neoplatonic metaphysics to bear. The intelligible world is primary, though above it is still the One. As such it is the realm of the Platonic Ideas, and notably of the three Plato specifically mentions here, Temperance, Justice, and Knowledge, together constituting Truth, which the *Republic* had defined, says Ficino, as "the light that proceeds from the Good and is diffused through both intellects and intelligibles."[23] I shall postpone treating of the special problems raised by Ficino's introduction of Beauty as Truth's "splendor" until a later chapter,[24] as it marks, in a way, the climax of the dialogue, if not of the commentary.

As is traditional in Christian Neoplatonism, Truth exists preeminently in the prime intellect, which is the prime intelligible and is equated here with the supercelestial place, because it is "the first complex (*complexio*) of Ideas" (with the root meaning, "to fill to completion," to the fore). As "the first, universal, and perfect essence," this complex is intuited directly by intellect alone and is beyond the scope of the senses and imagination, and even of simple reason (*ratio simplex*)—that is, reason without the cooperation of the intellect in any way. Primarily it is intuited in a supermundane intellect and then in a mundane intellect, that of a celestial soul. A celestial soul can attain this intelligible realm, however, only when wholly governed by its intellect (just as it can

23. Ficino is referring in general to the *Republic* 6.508A-509B and 7.517BC; cf. his chap. 9 (ed. Allen, *Charioteer,* pp. 108-109).
24. See pp. 188-189 below.

attain God Himself only when wholly governed by its higher unity).

In glossing 247C7-8's lemma, which he had translated as, "Truth uses the soul's pilot or governor alone, namely the contemplating intellect," Ficino notes, with both Platonic and Augustinian arguments in mind, that the intelligible realm (i.e. Truth) epistemologically is the active agent which "uses" a passive intellect; it is not a passive realm apprehended by an active intellect. Divine as well as human souls have innate formulae of the Ideas,[25] which they must turn to (*convertere*) for any kind of genuine knowledge (*scientia*); but for the supreme knowledge (*scientia consummata*) this turning is not enough, for Truth's light must reveal the Ideas to them. In other words, the formulae are Truth's "instruments" for "using" souls and for transporting them to the Ideas. Ficino implies nevertheless that this possession by Truth does not occur until we have turned to the formulae: preliminary epistemological activity must precede the contemplative goal of passivity that must in turn precede activation by Truth.

In terms of the charioteer myth, the celestial gods, whose habitual and peculiar mode of apprehension, since they are souls, is through discursive reasoning (*cogitatio... id est discurrens illa cognitio*), must "be nourished" by the supramundane gods and by "inviolable knowledge." A soul, whether celestial or human, is so "nourished" when the supramundane gods illumine its cogitation and it is brought by them to contemplate the prime intelligible, which it loves at first sight as Beauty.[26] Then, as it contemplates it more attentively, it sees it as Truth, or rather as Truths or as the Ideas; for it can see the Ideas of all entities in the one entity, Truth. Thus, from gazing upwards, the soul—whether celestial or human—is both "nourished" and "perfected," and attains, as postulated also in the *Philebus,* the compound felicity of vision and of joy (Plato says merely that it is nourished and prospers).

---

25. See Kristeller, *Philosophy,* pp. 236-242, 248; Allen, "The Absent Angel," pp. 235-237.

26. In Christian terms this would involve the angels, in some measure at least, in the soul's acquisition of true knowledge and ultimately of ecstasy. But Ficino was loath to attribute too great a power over man to the angels; see Allen, "The Absent Angel," pp. 233-239.

Finally, Ficino comments on the lemma at 247D2 *intuita per tempus* (in Greek ἰδοῦσα διὰ χρόνου). The celestial souls must not be supposed to contemplate as we do, since we are subject to "cessation," to intervals of not looking. But as souls they must still contemplate in temporal succession and perform their circuits (*circuli, circuitus*) in time, whereas supramundane intellects perform their circuits in an instant (*momento*), not just individually but collectively. Both mundane and supramundane intellects, however, commence from and return to a summit (*summitas*), which, we learn later from summa 24, is the Idea at the head (*caput*) of a particular circuit, and thus perfect their journey round that circuit —that is, round other Ideas "subsequent" to the head Idea.[27] While the head or principal Idea is intuited instantaneously both by the supermundane gods and by the mundane gods accompanied by human souls, the subsequent Ideas are perceived differently. Whereas the supermundane gods intuit them in the same instantaneous manner and at the same time as they intuit the head Idea, the mundane gods and the souls under them examine them rationally and therefore discursively. Yet the myth implies for Ficino, as it had for the ancient Neoplatonists, that the mundane gods and souls are in the train of the supermundane gods, and therefore that both kinds of vision, the intuitive and the discursive, are taking place both in and out of time. In short, there are a number of problems here which derive from the paradoxes inherent in the Platonic theory of the Ideas and of the hierarchy among them. When Plato writes, however, that "the heaven's revolution brings the soul back full circle" (247D4-5), Ficino paraphrases it as "that celestial circumference above the visible heaven rules this circling in the soul," and takes it to mean that the fastest circling of all, that of the pure supramundane intellects (who constitute the dome which is the intellectual heaven), controls the slower circling through time which is that of the intellects joined to souls, until

27. Presumably these "subsequent" Ideas are the same as the "consequent" Ideas of summa 24. I take it that they are the subdivisions of a "head" Idea that we arrive at via *diairesis,* the process of dialectical division. One might assume that they are genera and species respectively, but Ficino's analyses of the relationship between these two concepts elsewhere militates against this (see in particular his *Philebus Commentary* 1.13-14, ed. Allen, pp. 144-161).

they both return to a supercelestial Idea at the head or summit of a circuit.

Ficino warns us that "intellectual souls," by virtue of their being souls, not pure intellects, must exercise their powers both of contemplating and of rejoicing (contemplating the truth of any or all Ideas, and rejoicing in its or their beauty and goodness) by means of motion, since motion is "a natural property" of the soul and necessarily pertains to its essence. Yet, since "intellectual souls" are intellectual in power (*proprietate*), they can also partake via their intellects of a motionless intuiting (*intuitum quendam stabilem*), which is properly the possession of the pure, separated intellects, even though this intuiting is beyond the understanding by motion (*mobilem intelligentiam*), which is properly their own. Thus divine souls—though this seems to undercut some of Ficino's previous distinctions—can simultaneously intuit the Ideas and understand them discursively:[28] they are both in flight and yet they can hover at the summit of that flight in a motionless, timeless, flightless moment.

In summa 22 Ficino completes his analysis of the ascent of liberated souls in the train of Jove. As others have been, he is struck by Plato's limiting himself, effectively, to just three Ideas: Justice, Temperance, and Knowledge; for these "principally lead to felicity and most pertain to beauty." Following Plato, he glosses Knowledge as neither like that knowledge "begotten" from "notions" which we possess strictly as rational souls, nor like the knowledge of formal causes and reasons (*formales rationes*) which we possess in our soul's intellect; nor at the other extreme is it the knowledge of "what we commonly call entities (*entia*) . . . for it does not look at natural things as [its] objects." Rather, it is "the unbegotten, simple, and essential power, essence itself," whose object of regard is its own essence. In the prime entity, which is Mind, it is

28. Ficino seems concerned, that is, to retain movement even at this apex of the epistemological ascent in order to underscore his interpretation of the *Phaedrus's* myth as being concerned with souls and not merely with pure minds. This seems to contradict his statement in chap. 11, par. 5, of the commentary proper that "the intelligible world is perceived by the intellect alone" (ed. Allen, p. 123). Of interest here is S. E. Gersh's Κίνησις ἀκίνητος: *A Study of Spiritual Motion in the Philosophy of Proclus* (Leiden, 1973).

"the true knowledge," the model (*exemplar*) and cause of all other knowledge. Hence in regarding Justice, Temperance, and Knowledge, a divine soul regards all that truly exists, all the Ideas, as the authentic entities (as opposed to what we "commonly" call entities), and is subsequently nourished by them. Thus it comes to possess not only contemplative vision but the nourishment of joy: it both sees and tastes (*gustat*). Having seen the Ideas, the principles and models of all entities "commonly so called," and having seen them in the supercelestial place of the prime intellect, the soul straightway turns back towards the dome of the intellectual heaven: first to contemplate intellectuals,[29] and then to gaze upon itself and on things proper to itself alone. This second stage of the descent, Ficino says, is what Plato means by his phrase "returning home."

Unlike our fallen souls, however, divine souls do not thereby "abandon" the goal of their circuit, the Ideas, which they continue to contemplate with their highest powers, their pure intellects. Nor do they relinquish the contemplation and cogitation of the intellectuals with their middle powers, their intellects and their reasons,[30] even as they exercise their lowest, their providential and rational, powers in "returning home," referred to here as consideration.[31] All three are exercised simultaneously even as they circuit; for souls, of necessity, must also turn to the intellectuals, and

29. As noted above in chap. 5, pp. 141-142, these refer presumably, not to the intellectual gods themselves, but rather to the contents of their realm—that is, to the Ideas at their first level of diminishment or participation as "formal causes or reasons." It will be recalled that the *Phaedrus* 247A4 refers both to the many blessed sights (θέαι) and to the ways to and fro (διέξοδοι) and that this division would itself reflect for Ficino the division in the higher, the purely intelligible realm, between "head" Ideas and their "subsequents."

30. "Contemplation" of the intellectuals is not quite the same as the "cogitation" of them; whereas "contemplation" signifies an act performed primarily by the intellect and secondarily by the reason, "cogitation," as summa 21 has noted, is "the process of acquiring knowledge discursively," and this might suggest that reason is now the dominant faculty. But chap. 11, par. 5, of the Commentary has keyed such a reason-dominated perception to the perception of the animate, not the intellectual, realm. Hence we are dealing with finer, more Proclian, distinctions in that "cogitation" is still an intellect-dominated act, but one in which reason is playing a larger role than it does in "contemplation." The objects of "contemplation" and "cogitation" respectively are probably the θέαι and διέξοδοι; see n. 29 above.

31. As summa 22 defines it, "consideration" on the part of a god seems to be equivalent to "exercising" its own property in order to provide for worldly things. Ficino does not juxtapose "cogitation" with "consideration," so the relationship between them is not clear; but "consideration" is surely lower. For a god it would be the act where reason be-

then to exercising their lowest powers. The result is a strange distortion. Ficino allegorizes the image of the charioteer "stopping his horses at the stable" as the intellect filling the lower powers, "through which [its] providence is enacted," with the goods derived from contemplation, and also nourishing them at "the memory and preservation of divine things" both with "the food of ambrosia" (insofar as the charioteer stops them in their causes and goods) and with "the drink of nectar" (insofar as he both strengthens and excites them to overflow downwards providentially).[32] In doing so, Ficino treats the stopping more as a kind of climax than as an anticlimactic epilogue—under the influence perhaps of previous analyses of "ambrosia" and "nectar" (which at one time he seems to have confused with the pasturage in the meadow of truth).[33] In short, it is not the uranian intuitive ecstasy of the charioteer's gazing at the intelligibles nor the saturnian contemplation of the intellectuals that constitutes the figure's conclusion, but rather the jovian activity of rational providing.

Plato's introduction of the notion of a descent "home" to the stable, and his substitution of ambrosia and nectar for the sublime pasturage of the Ideas themselves, bring with them, however, an implied fall. In postulating not only the circling of a divine soul around an Idea's subsequents and back—a conceptual process enough in itself to account for a god's motion—but also a move-

---

gins to dominate as it does in our flawed perception of the animate world. Cf. Marian Heitzman, "L'agostinismo avicennizzante e il punto di partenza della filosofia di Marsilio Ficino," *Giornale critico della filosofia italiana* 16 (1935), 295-322, 460-480; 17 (1936), 1-11, at 460; and Ficino's distinctions in his proem to his Commentary on St. Paul, *Opera,* p. 425: "Ratio autem triplex quasi coelum triplex esse videtur: infima quidem practica rerum humanarum privatarumque et publicarum gubernationi et providentiae dedita; superior autem ratio mundanum ordinem physica facultate considerans; suprema denique ratio, sive mens, res divinas altiores mundo theologica ratione contemplans." See n. 30 above.

32. James B. Wadsworth, "Landino's *Disputationes Camaldulenses,* Ficino's *De Felicitate,* and *L'altercazione* of Lorenzo de' Medici," *Modern Philology* 50.1 (1952), 23-31 at 25, has argued that the distinction between the ambrosia and the nectar is of "fundamental importance" for Ficino in that "they are the symbols of the two very distinct terms of the debate" over the primacy of the intellect or the will. See chap. 9, pp. 211-212 below. Cf. Hesiod, *Theogony* 639-642; Aristotle, *Metaphysics* 3.4.1000a12-17; Plotinus, *Enneads* 3.5.9; Hermias, pp. 156.17-157.3 (ed. Couvreur); Proclus, *Theologia Platonica* 4.5 (ed. Saffrey and Westerink, 4:46-47); and Pico, *Oratio* (ed. Garin, pp. 120-123), and *Commento* 2.13 (ed. Garin, pp. 503-504).

33. See Allen, *Charioteer,* Texts IV, Excerpts 1, 2, and 3, pp. 218-229; also chap. 9, pp. 224-225 below.

ment that spins out of that circling altogether in a descending parabola that returns "home," Plato presented Ficino with an insoluble problem. From a Christian viewpoint "home" must be, not the jovian manger, but the uranian contemplation of intelligibles and even of the One, of God Himself. Possibly, the Phaedran stable could be deemed a midway station where we might, figuratively, prepare for the final stage in the ascent, but not a haven to which, as divine souls dominated by our intellects, we would need to return. We might accept the "refoddering" as something necessary for a soul fallen to earth, whose ecstasies are occasional and brief, but not for celestial beings. Ficino tries to circumvent the problem by interpreting the return home as an opportunity for the charioteer to exercise jovian providence. Even so, he cannot explain why it is needful for the charioteer to "descend" in order to do this, particularly as this descent implies logical if not temporal sequentiality, however much we may affirm the simultaneity of the uranian, saturnian, and jovian activities.

Inevitably, Ficino is encountering here the central strains not only in Plato's figure but in the Neoplatonic system: the tension between optimistic belief in the return of all things to the pleroma, the fullness of the One, and the pessimistic awareness of the extent of cosmic emanation, of the universal descent from the enfolded absolute, the origins of which present man with the impenetrable mystery of his fall into limitation, earthy corporeality, and mortality. Though the descent of the divine soul down through the dome and concavity of the intellectual heaven, and thence to its "proper" station in the celestial realm, is superficially explicable in terms of Neoplatonic ontology and epistemology, it suggests nevertheless the more precipitous descent of the human soul and the final agonizing loss of flight which ensues upon the rebellion of the black steed and its surrender to appetitive lusts. It is to this further, wholly tragic descent of souls other than gods, souls who do not contemplate intelligibles with their utmost "attention" and "desire" (*affectus*), that the next three summae address themselves.

Chapter Seven: The Soul's Descent

While Ficino suspended his commentary midway through his analysis of the charioteer myth at 247E on the life of the gods, the summae covering the rest of the mythical hymn, 23 to 33, are sufficiently ample for us to trace the main lines of his interpretation and to reconstruct the shells of what might have been two or more subsequent commentary chapters. For methodological convenience I have grouped these eleven summae under two heads: 23, 24, and 25 I shall consider under the general theme of the soul's descent, and 26 to 33 under that of Beauty and the appetite. Both groups tackle some of the darker aspects of the myth and cover its climax and resolution; for, leaving aside the important digressions on Theuth and the cicadas and the prayer to Pan which I have treated under the theme of Socrates' inspiration, the rest of the dialogue, from Ficino's viewpoint if not ours or Plato's, was primarily an oratorical extension on the theme of beauty, the dialogue's Neoplatonically ascribed *skopos* and its preoccupation from the beginning.

Summae 23 to 25 deal with 248A to 249C, paragraphs where Plato is especially ambiguous, especially figural, especially indebted to Orphic and Pythagorean notions, as Ficino recognized. Not unexpectedly, given the absence of a formal commentary chapter, they are three of his longest summae.

Of the two kinds of descent portrayed in the *Phaedrus,* the descent to the stable and the descent into corporeality, the one is a constantly recurring and justifiable event in the life of the gods, the other a tragic loss of power and knowledge on the part of man. While the first should be figured as repose, a moment of recuperation, of satiation even, the second is the result of weakness and failure: failure to maintain flight and to rule the darker horse, to keep the chariot on a steady, controlled career. At 248AC the

Phaedrus graphically depicts the struggle on the part of the weaker charioteers "to reach the heights" even for a moment. The confusion, conflict, and grievous sweat, the indiscriminate trampling, the vortical sucking down (*submerse*), the laming (*claudicare*) and the breaking of wings, all are attributed to the failure of the charioteers, or what Ficino translates as their vice or defect (*vitium*). Having failed to perceive the Ideas, they sink down at last to feed, not upon ambrosia and nectar and the memory of truth, but upon the food of opinion.[1]

The details of this passage summa 23 leaves aside to focus on the causes of the soul's descent, the aetiology of human weakness. Interestingly, Ficino ignores Plato's account of the host of souls who join the cavalcade only to fail to mount to the dome of the intellectual heaven, let alone to its convexity, and he assumes the pristine situation which the myth implies but does not itself embody, namely a host united in its ability to complete the various circuits dependent on the head Ideas. He omits analysis, that is, of the Homeric agony of the battle for vision, and concentrates on the first instance of failure, the inaugurative moment in the degenerative process.

Initially the soul starts with two sets of powers (the *Cratylus*'s orientation formula has been laid aside): one to contemplate divine matters and the other to provide for inferiors; and "if it can always fulfill both tasks, for the good of all and then for itself, then it must do so." As long as the soul can live up to its dual status and perform both duties in the cosmic hierarchy, it is one with the gods, winging its way upwards with them to gaze upon the supercelestial place, and then "returning home" to the stable to feed its lower powers on ambrosia and nectar. Since, however, the human soul is at the bottom of the series of souls, at the bottom indeed of the scale of divinities, it finds the "governing of our body on earth most difficult" (notice Ficino's shift from providing to governing). Accordingly, since it cannot fulfill both its major duties at the same time (*simul prorsus*)—and this is its built-

---

1. *Phaedrus* 248B5: τροφῇ δοξαστῇ χρῶνται; Ficino renders this literally as *alimento utuntur opinabili*. For Plato's notion of "opinion" (δόξα) Ficino could turn to a number of texts, most notably to the *Gorgias* 454E ff.; *Republic* 5.476D ff.; 6.508D ff.; *Timaeus* 51D ff.; and *Theaetetus* 187A-210B.

in disadvantage compared with the other souls who can—it "probably fulfills them alternately, now pursuing the celestial life, now the earthly."

This would seem to suggest an oscillatory course or destiny fated from above. To admit this, however, would lead directly to determinism and all its unacceptable implications from a Christian, and certainly from a Christian-Platonist, viewpoint. Thus Ficino hastens to add, "Since the soul should not be forced by divine influence (*divinitus*) to come from heaven hither (*inde huc*), it descends, rather, as a result of a natural condition (*naturali quadam potius conditione*)." He further defines this "natural condition" as follows: "the circuit of the soul's understanding has its measures (*mensuras suas*), and these will last for certain intervals of time (*duraturas certis temporum curriculis*)"; and the vegetative action (*actio vegetalis*) also has its measures. Accordingly, "the activity (*actus*) of the soul's understanding is gradually in a while remitted, and similarly its desire (*affectus*)." Though *actus* and *affectus* are a complementary pair from scholastic Latin—*affectus* being almost synonymous here with *passio* or even *potentia*—it is hard to grasp what Ficino has in mind. Perhaps he means, "what the understanding actually does and what it would like to do or has the potentiality for doing." *Remittere* is a critical word choice, since it supposes the weakening of its opposite, *intendere*.[2] *Remissio* and *intentio* are the slackening and tensing or intensifying that together signify the two opposing forces, or directions of force, at the heart of Ficino's analysis of the Phaedran fall. For the remitting of the actual and potential states of the understanding is accompanied by the tensing of the lower powers, presumably all the biological; but Ficino specifically mentions the procreative (*genitalis*), the imaginative, and the discursive powers. Since "the remission of intention is soon the origin of future intermission (*intermissio*), and intermission is at length the cause of future abandonment (*dimissio*)," understanding must be abandoned at last for the lower activities.

---

2. In scholasticism they were a standard pair. See Anneliese Maier, *Zwei Grundprobleme der scholastischen Naturphilosophie: Das Problem der intensiven Grösse, die Impetustheorie,* 2d ed. (Rome, 1951), pp. 3-109: "De intensione et remissione formarum."

While the triadic formula, *remittere, intermittere, dimittere,* is traditional, it begs the question here. Why is remission necessarily the "origin" of intermission and intermission the "cause" of abandonment? The three terms seem to signify qualitative stages in a descent, but actually signify degrees on the same scale. Again, if remission at one end of the scale results in intensifying at the other, the reverse should also be true: were the understanding absolutely intensified, then the other activities should be absolutely remitted. But this would run counter both to the integral image of the chariot with all its powers intensified and to the predication of providential powers for the charioteer. However, Ficino's utilization of the three terms does point to his sense of the gradual surrender of power over the horses, of neglect degenerating slowly into criminal omission. Specifically, he is glossing the sequence of the charioteer's errors established by Socrates: the remission of contemplation that gives rise to troublesome behavior by the horses; the temporary intermission of contemplation that occasions in turn their outright rebellion; and finally the permanent abandonment of contemplation that leads to their overpowering their lord completely. Ficino underscores the fact that it is the charioteer who fails first: the steeds can only take advantage of his errors, the first and fatal one being the weakening of his commitment to contemplation. He does not add as a corollary that this weakening occurs because the charioteer turns to providing, but he has implied it in the opening sentences. That is, in human souls the commitment to providing for inferiors, which divine souls can administer in their stride, leads to the eventual abandonment of contemplation. But this abandonment is bound to happen, at least temporally, because human souls find it well-nigh impossible to exercise both contemplative and providential powers simultaneously.

A fuller analysis might further refine the stages from *intentio* to *dimissio* by distributing them through the human faculties, each undergoing in turn the same triadic process; but Ficino makes the summary judgment that the remission of understanding means that all the lower powers are correspondingly intensified, not sequentially but together. He sees the whole process implied by "the loss of wings" and the plummeting downwards to quicken (*vegetandum*) the lower body and to govern its earthly province.

The nadir of the flight is identified in the second paragraph of the summa. Plato means, Ficino says, by the poetic figure of the souls struggling in heaven (*certamina*) that the "contemplation" of supercelestials has now been abandoned for the "consideration" of celestials. This signals the second, intermediate stage, already hinted at in summa 22, between unhindered flight and uncontrollable descent. In other works, such as his proem to his commentary on St. Paul as we have seen, Ficino establishes a clear-cut distinction between contemplation and consideration as different kinds of mental activity, the one denoting the intuitive vision of the intelligibles or the intellectuals, the other the discursive comprehension of celestials and the animate world.[3] Accompanying the consideration of celestials is the arousal (*excitari,* presumably a variant of *intendere*) both of the concupiscible (or appetitive) power, which is directed towards subcelestials as we might expect, and of the irascible power in what must be its debased form; for instead of the spirited mettlesomeness we admire in the warrior or warhorse we now have "warlike pride." It is difficult to know what to make of this, since the chariot model requires that there be one good, or at least better, horse, even if it is read allegorically at the lowest ontological level. Ficino probably assumed that Plato intended the good steed to be brought low by the bad.

The outcome of the exciting of the lower powers is that the souls in their disorder (*perturbate*) return from the cavalcade with opinion rather than knowledge (*scientia*) of divine things. Ficino concludes, however, "Because the soul retains a certain hidden memory of that [ideal] beauty, however, when it recalls it in a way, it chooses to recover it completely. Eventually it will receive that beauty from the meadow of truth [which Ficino again glosses as 'from the fullness of Ideas in the intelligible world']." Thus the soul "is always justly drawn to the knowledge of all things. Whenever it becomes liberated, it will strive for knowledge zealously (*studiose contendit*)." For Ficino's comment that truth and beauty are inseparable, see chapter 8 below.

Note that throughout summa 23 Ficino is not, like his ancient counterpart, the professorial Hermias, proceeding strictly lemma by lemma, but is striving for a general account of the causes of the

---

3. See chap. 6, nn. 22 and 31 above.

soul's descent as he can derive them from the wording of the myth. Utilizing the jovian motif of providing, he tries to interpret the original imagery of turmoil and confusion in terms of contained, if not exactly orderly, loss of altitude, of the Neoplatonic conversion towards the body, as contrasted say with Phaethon's spiraling plunge into the abyss. Though the black steed may be ultimately culpable, the more obvious culprit is the charioteer himself, whose negligence brings disaster on the whole chariot; for Ficino involves the whole soul in the fall, not just one part of it. He never suggests, moreover, that the biological, imaginative, and rational powers, which are intensified as the intellectual powers weaken, are bad in themselves; rather, that they are good if accompanied by the exercise of the understanding. This implies a mind at odds with the extremer manifestations of Plato's dualism, one drawn to envisaging the human condition not in the shadows of unending ἀγωνία, of ceaseless war between the animate prisoner and his inanimate bars, but rather in the light of intellect and body partaking together in a unitary reality.

In brief, the charioteer is solely responsible for the soul's descent, since he has it in him to govern the steeds to the summits of contemplation. What Ficino did not succeed in explaining here is how we might reconcile Plato's depiction of the return home to the stable with the onset of the understanding's remission. But then this would have entailed a definitive solution to the mystery of evil's, or at least of error's, origins in a universe governed by the One and the Good.[4]

The next two summae are both elaborate and suggestive, and in them Ficino confronts some of the pressing questions raised by Plato's introduction of innate differences in character, intelligence, and ethical commitment in men. Summa 24 asks the question: Does the remission of the understanding—remission marking the first stage in the degenerative as opposed to the providential descent—precede, accompany, or succeed the intensifying of the

---

4. For an excellent general account of Ficino's attitudes towards the physical world and towards evil, see Kristeller, *Philosophy,* pp. 64-66 and 351-401; also Tarabochia Canavero, "S. Agostino nella *Teologia Platonica* di Marsilio Ficino," p. 635.

lower powers? Plato and other Platonists, he observes, had suggested various solutions. Diplomatically, Ficino opts for the view that the remission and intensifying exactly correspond and occur concurrently on the following grounds. One cannot permit an inferior power to "distract" a superior "as long as it thrives in its native land (*patria*)"—a question-begging clause that may refer specifically to the stable but more generally, probably, to the circuits of contemplation (see for instance the heading of summa 22). Nor can one accept the possibility that the superior power would allow itself to be "diverted" from "so much good" unless its potentiality or actuality were remitted "naturally"—that is, of its own accord—and the potentiality of the lower power were concurrently intensified (but not, note, the actuality). Once again, the burden of responsibility lies entirely with the higher power. The concurrence itself is the result of "universal harmony" under the rule of Adrastia or Necessity, the goddess whom Ficino glosses as "an inescapable law of divine providence," and who decrees (*sancit*) the laws and distributes the orders for both the mundane and the supermundane realms.[5] Ficino is not saying that Necessity causes the onset of remission, for that would strip man of his essential freedom, but merely that Adrastia ensures the maintenance of cosmic balance—ensures that remission in one place is duly accompanied by intensification at another, the harmony of the universe requiring that both take place concurrently.

Ficino proceeds in the second paragraph to gloss Plato's enigmatic phrases describing the actual start of remission. Having followed in the train of its particular ruling deity, the soul rides to the highest point of supernal contemplation, where it gazes on the Idea at the head of a circuit. It then follows its god, "as long as it

5. Cf. Hermias, pp. 161.10-162.28 (ed. Couvreur); and Proclus, *Theologia Platonica* 4.17 (ed. Saffrey and Westerink, 4:51-53).

Ficino also introduces Adrastia in his commentary on the *Republic* 5: the ancient theologians, he says, thought of her as "the omnipotent queen of inevitable laws," but he defines her as "the divine providence" (*Opera*, p. 1405). In the *Timaeus* 47E-48A Plato had spoken of matter as necessity, and in the *Symposium* 195BC had argued that the reign of necessity preceded that of love. Cf. Ficino, *De Amore* 5.11 (ed. Marcel, pp. 195-196); and Pico, *Commento* 2.23 (ed. Garin, pp. 515-516).

Though Ficino makes no mention of them at this point, he must have also recalled the other great eschatological myths in Plato: in the *Gorgias* 523A-526D, *Phaedo* 107D-114D, and *Republic* 10.614B-621B.

encounters no impediment" (*impedimento procul*), round the circuit of "Ideas consequent on the head Idea"—that is, which depend, in continuous progression, on a particular supreme Idea like Justice or Fortitude. Having completed one circuit in this manner, it sets off again as soon as it sees the supreme Idea at the head of another circuit.[6] But whenever it completes the journey round the Idea at a circuit's head or summit a little too negligently (*paulo negligentius*)—and Ficino glosses Plato's reference to the soul's weakness (*inpotens*) simply as the state when "its higher power is now somewhat remitted and its lower simultaneously intensified" —then it sinks down from that stage to one a little worse; perhaps, Ficino adds, from the intelligible realm to the intellectual, thence to the rational (or animate), and thence to the imaginational and sense realms, but always from a higher to a lower sphere until it arrives at the elemental realm at the bottom.

Clearly, Plato's text is open to a number of interpretations. But one would like to know how Ficino thought of the relationship between the supreme Ideas (supposing one knew what all of them were) and their respective attendant circuits of "subsequent" or "consequent" Ideas, and how he conceived of the soul passing from one to the other. One envisages a Ptolemaic model of some kind with the highest spheres abounding in epicycles, each representing a circuit. As participant in any one of the Olympian gods' careers, each soul, with its pristine intellectual power, should be able to succeed in gazing on at least one of the supreme Ideas and its consequents—though Ficino nowhere suggests that the supreme Ideas are apportioned according to the characters of the twelve gods: Justice to jovians, Fortitude to martians, Beauty to venereans, and so on. Of course, the Phaedran myth raises in an acute form the problem of the connection between Plato's conception of the soul and his conception of an Idea. Ficino is content, however, to formulate the soul's contemplation of each Idea in terms of its highest power, the understanding, being intensified to the maximum degree, while the lower powers, though potentially operative, are relaxed or even abandoned totally. This still leaves us with the problem of why a soul should suddenly start to round the head

6. Cf. *Platonic Theology* 17.3 (ed. Marcel, 3:159; trans. Allen, *Charioteer,* pp. 230-231).

of a circuit—that is, approach a supreme Idea—"more negligently" than usual. Since there is no possibility of chance intervening as yet, it can only be natural that this should happen eventually. But if so, this itself needs explaining.

The final, catastrophic descent to the elemental world comes about when the soul has so constricted or constrained its wings (*iam coegerit in angustum*)[7]—and note again the emphasis on the soul's freedom—that it forgets divine matters entirely. Only at this point does Ficino turn to gloss Plato's mysterious mention of the soul's encounter with some mischance;[8] for on reaching the elemental world, the soul succumbs at last to its senses and therefore to sensory illusions. Thus Ficino can note that the soul forgets divine matters "especially if it has by some chance (*casu quodam*) fallen among those demons who turn away towards sensibles [MS sensuals]." Whereas Plato had accepted the possibility of chance playing a role from the beginning of the process of descent, Ficino confines its range of operation to the last and lowest stage, the incorporation into matter when sensation trammels the wings. Ficino's gloss also effectively restricts the operational range of the demons concerned with the sensible world: though they may inflict harm upon us if we are "unlucky" enough to fall into their hands, this cannot happen unless we succumb to our lower powers. Once we have liberated ourselves from sensibles and begun our flight back to the intelligibles, we escape from chance and thus from their realm entirely.[9]

At this juncture, Ficino mentions something he will elaborate in the next summa: the impossibility of supposing that Plato intended us to hold that a soul which has fallen from heaven is precipitated directly into the soul of a beast; for such could only happen after

---

7. At *Phaedrus* 248C8 Socrates refers to the soul as "shedding" or "molting" its wings (πτερορρυήσῃ); later at 249E and even more dramatically at 251B ff. he refers to the wings burgeoning again from their roots, the stumps swelling and then sprouting in plumage as the lover experiences the first flood of his passion for the beloved. On the other hand, at 248B3 he had referred to the "breaking" of the wings (πολλαὶ δὲ πολλὰ πτερὰ θραύονται). In his Latin translation Ficino uses *confringere* ("to wreck" or "to ruin") for both 248B3 and 248C8, ignoring Socrates' distinction.

8. *Phaedrus* 248C6: τινι συντυχίᾳ χρησαμένη; Ficino renders this as *casu aliquo usa*.

9. See chap. 1, pp. 18-20 above.

the soul has sinned still more—that is, further deviated from its heavenly condition to neglect human characteristics (*mores*) altogether and adopt those of savage brutes. Even then one must imagine such souls as purgatorially condemned to associate with beasts, not actually to become them (*in aliqua brutorum commertia tanquam ad purgatorium anime transmittuntur*). Plato's operative phrase at 248D1-2, "the soul shall not be implanted in her first birth in any brute beast," Ficino translates as *in aliquam brutalem ire naturam.* By choosing *natura,* he can skirt around the possibility that the human soul might subsequently enter into a brute soul absolutely.

He next turns to Plato's allotment of souls and the differing degrees of excellence in their lives. As long as they dwell in their native country (*patria* again) and use their intellects alone, sedulously contemplating the Ideas in the company of the mundane and the supermundane gods alike, then "they all see all things equally, although all things in different ways" (*illinc cuncte pariter omnia vident, etsi aliter et aliter omnia*). The final clause refers to the differing perspectives that each possesses by virtue of its being in the train of a particular god. Still, one would like to know the bases of these differing perspectives: how does a junonian soul, say, see Temperance or Fortitude or whatever differently from a martian soul?

The descent itself is graphed in terms of a radical change in mental functioning: from "contemplating" the intelligible realm with the intellect alone, to "considering" (note, again, the word shift) the celestial realm along with the mundane gods with the intellect accompanied by the reason.[10] This descent from true contemplation to discursive reasoning or consideration brings with it a similar restriction on what is seen; for all the souls no longer see all things (the Ideas and their consequents), but some souls see more (*plura*) and others less (*pauciora*). Ficino can thus describe Plato's nine lives as if they took their origin from nine differences of

10. At this juncture Ficino seems to be ignoring the intermediate stage of contemplating the "intellectuals"; see chap. 5, pp. 141-142, and chap. 6, n. 30 above. But in the previous paragraph he had clearly charted the descent as sinking from the intelligible to the intellectual and thence to the rational before ending with the imaginative and the sensual.

vision, which he can arrive at by assigning them to the seven planetary souls, to the soul of the fixed stars, and to the World-Soul;[11]
he makes no attempt, however, to dovetail the nine lives into the
dodecade of mundane gods.[12] From gazing at celestials instead of
intelligibles or even intellectuals (the concern of the supermundane
gods), the weakening souls must perforce submit to nine differing
limitations of vision which correspond in turn to their differing
innate dispositions (*ingenia*).

What he had formerly translated as *plurima* Ficino now glosses
as *plura* in the lemma at 248D2, "but the soul which has seen
most/more." Necessity bids such a soul in the future to be born as
either a philosopher, or a man desirous of beauty, or a lover, or a

11. This contradicts Ficino's decision in the *Platonic Theology* 17.3 (ed. Marcel, 3:159;
trans. Allen, *Charioteer,* pp. 230-231) to link the nine lives with the seven planets, and with
the higher elements of fire and air. In effect he is upgrading the nine lives; for he has replaced the two at the bottom, those linked with fire and air, with two at the top, those
linked with Uranus and "great" Jove. Consequently, the nine lives are no longer associated
with the elemental spheres at all and are exclusively celestial.
    Elsewhere, as in the *Platonic Theology* 17.2 (ed. Marcel, 3:155), the *De Amore* 6.4 (ed.
Marcel, p. 204), and the *De Vita* 2.20 (*Opera,* p. 528), Ficino works with the theme of
man's seven lives, the stages through which he passes from birth to death. Each of these
stages is assigned to a different planet, and a man is subject therefore to them all in sequence as well as being subject to his own predominant planet; thus, at any moment, he is
subject to two planets except in the stage when his own planet and the one presiding over
that stage coincide. The seven gifts of the seven planets are (from the Moon outwards): the
power to grow and generate; subtlety; love; clearsightedness and prophecy; magnanimity
and courage; authority; contemplation; see de Gandillac, "Astres, anges et génies," p. 101,
and Maurice de Gandillac, "Neoplatonism and Christian Thought in the Fifteenth Century
(Nicholas of Cusa and Marsilio Ficino)," in *Neoplatonism and Christian Thought,* ed.
Dominic J. O'Meara (Albany, N.Y., 1982), pp. 143-168 at 161. In the *De Vita* 2.15 (*Opera,*
p. 521) he also toys with the notion of the five stages in men's lives. For the possible bearing
of these and a Proclan source, the *In Alcibiadem* 196 (ed. Westerink, pp. 90-91), on our
understanding of Jaques' famous speech in *As You Like It,* see Michael J. B. Allen,
"Jaques against the Seven Ages of the Proclan Man," *Modern Language Quarterly* 42.4
(1981), 331-346.
    Of related interest is the theory that Ficino expounds in his *Philebus* Commentary 1.25
(ed. Allen, pp. 232-233), namely that each soul has nine companions: a star god, an airy
and a watery demon, a charioteer (the reason), two horses (the rational and the sensual
appetites), an "impulse to the good," a "desire that draws the soul towards the enjoyable
good," and finally an "opinion that leads the soul towards the honorable good." Ficino
makes no attempt, however, to link these nine "companions" with the nine celestial gods.
12. Commentators on the pseudo-Dionysius had managed to reconcile nine as the number of the heavenly choirs with twelve as the number of the cosmic spheres by adding the
triad of Innocents, Martyrs, and Confessors; see Heninger, *Cosmographical Glass,* pp.
116, 117, 122.
    Ficino regarded the "supercelestial" gods as equivalent to the dionysian choirs rather
than as twelve subdivisions merely of the lowest choir, the angels.

man of music and poetry. *Plura,* he observes, means not only numerically more, but qualitatively more: the souls had seen more and "comprehended with more reasons and with more ardent study." But more what? Plato surely intends Ideas, but Ficino's introduction of reasons (*rationes*) raises the possibility that he thought of it—perhaps additionally—as more celestials, though his comment says vaguely "whatever they may have seen" (*quodcunque viderint*).

The nine lives themselves offer a few interesting variations.[13] The lover and the poet-musician are subdivisions of the philosopher, defined as the lover of wisdom and abstract beauty; for, whereas the lover loves visual beauty and the musician audible beauty, the philosopher is born to examine all beauty. The king administers the universal providence among men while the philosopher contemplates the sources of that providence in heaven. Thus Ficino sets up the king as the active counterpart of the contemplative philosopher. Plato says nothing of the king wielding (*gerere*) "universal providence," merely that he rules while attended by the general and the judge (appointed for life). Ficino's translation, incidentally, glosses this as "a lawful king" possessed of the warrior powers of a general (*virum imperatorium*). The less the souls have seen of the Ideas,[14] the more restricted their spheres of providential activity, themselves subdivisions of Jove as the provider. So we descend, along with Plato, to the local politician, businessman, and merchant, whose "prudence" is more restricted (*angustior*) than the king's "providence"; to the athletic coach and doctor, "whose providence is constrained within even more narrow limits"; to the mercenary diviner and fortune-teller, who draws upon traditional lore and luck (*consuetudine quadam nititur atque sorte*), not knowledge or genuine skill (*ars*); to the imitative, derivative poet; to the craftsman and farmer, whose concern is with "providing" for matter; to the sophist and demagogue, who deliberately misuse their reason; to the tyrant, finally, who supplants

13. He will make no attempt, however, to assign Plato's list of nine lives to their respective deities, for the difficulties are insuperable.

14. As Hackforth judiciously notes (*Phaedrus,* p. 102), ascertaining the identity of one's god is inseparable from, though not strictly the same as, reacquiring knowledge of the Ideas.

reason altogether with the arbitrary will. Implicit in this entire scheme, in Ficino's eyes, are both the concept of providence already analyzed in treating of Jove, and the related concept of the reason as a faculty confined to increasingly restricted areas of operation until it is first abused and then eventually abandoned. Little of this appears in Plato; and it points to Ficino's Neoplatonic need for, and attraction to, systematizing. At the same time, it focuses on his major tenet: that man's peculiar faculty is the reason.

Summa 25 deals with the difficult passage at 248E to 249C where Plato plays with numbers Orphically.[15] Ficino's opening paragraph is preoccupied with the symbolism underlying Plato's choice of ten and three as his integers to apportion the time stints of the philosopher and of his fellow men. We must not read them literally, but see them as symbols, because of their intrinsic perfection, for the time it takes to perfect the soul through purgation and restoration (*restitutio*). Three is "the first complete number"— and Ficino, understandably, has the Trinity in mind—and thus three cubed can be called the *solid* number (as the *Timaeus* had proposed at 32B and 55B-E) and used to represent the earth itself, and/or, Ficino hastens to subjoin, the earthy body. Ten is the universal number and ten cubed is the number we must work with to signify the perfection of the whole, the universal, man. As the universal number cubed or "earthed," a thousand signifies the span allotted a soul to pass from one generation in an earthy body to another. The philosopher only needs three thousand years, for he passes, not from one earthy body to another, but from an earthy body to one of impure air (foggy air, air heavy with water) to a third of pure air.[16] He can speed back to heaven more quickly than

15. Of several possible sources here Ficino was probably especially indebted to Proclus's *In Rempublicam* 13 (ed. Kroll, 2:21-22, 52-54, 66-70; trans. Festugière, 2:126, 159-161, 178-182).

16. Origen had argued that we submit to three bodies (though he had in mind the aethereal, the airy, and the earthy) as to three kinds of punishment (*apud* Jerome, *Liber contra Joa. Hierosol.* [Migne, *PL* 23.368]; cf. Augustine, *De Genesi ad Litteram* 12.32 [Migne, *PL* 34.481]). This thesis was of course condemned by the orthodox; see Klein, "L'enfer de Ficin," pp. 57-59. Even so, it received support from Macrobius and the Arabs, who conceived of the soul as falling through the planetary spheres, its *spiritus* submitting to their influences and receiving their gifts (ibid., p. 64). In his *De Amore* 6.4 (ed. Marcel, p. 204)—

other men, there to be awarded wisdom as his prize; and he will
speed the more quickly and effectively (*melius*) if he joins his
study not only to the love of divine goodness but also from the
beginning to the acknowledgment and ardent love of its wonderful
beauty. Plato's note at 249A1-2 is quite different, since he offers
as alternatives either the soul "who has sought after wisdom un-
feignedly" or the soul who "has conjoined his passion for a loved
one with that seeking" (which Ficino translates, incidentally, as
"or who has loved beauty along with the study of wisdom"!).

For men other than philosophers—those destined to live the full
ten thousand years since they either neglected to take up philosophy in their initial descent or abandoned it thereafter—there is another arrangement. Logically one might suppose that instead of
ten millennia there would be a peel-off system, those who were
kings requiring a millennium to become philosophers, statesmen
and merchants requiring two millennia, and so forth. Each would
then need three additional millennia as philosophers. But Plato's
description prevents this, and Ficino has to reconcile the nine lives
with ten incarnations. He manages to do so by insisting that men
are first born as philosophers and do badly at it, thereby setting
themselves on the downward path towards demagoguery and tyr-
anny; they thus have to be born again at the end, in a tenth life, as
philosophers (though one might argue that the other lives could
also be similarly duplicated). Presumably, the three philosophical
incarnations in the three kinds of body (the earthy, the impurely
aerial, and the purely aerial) are all squashed into this last life.
After the tenth life, the soul immediately returns, Plato says at
248E5-6, to "the same." Ficino glosses this as follows: First the
soul returns to the *same* planetary sphere and celestial god whose
train it was in originally (and this dovetails with the stable image).
Then, after some time perhaps has elapsed, it returns to the *same*
Idea and to the *same* superlative degree of contemplation and hap-

cf. *Platonic Theology* 18.5 (ed. Marcel, 3:196-197)—Ficino describes the soul's journey
from the Milky Way via Cancer and its acquisition there of "celestial" and "transparent"
bodies, "veils" that are "thicker than the soul" but "purer than the [ordinary] body."
Ficino seems to be implying that Plato means us to ascend via these same stages, though
naturally in reverse order, and starting, apparently, from Capricorn. Cf. Macrobius, *In
Somnium Scipionis* 1.12 and Porphyry, *De Antro Nympharum* 22. The whole question
hinges on the nature and function of the "aethereal" or "celestial" vehicle, for which see
chap. 4, nn. 20, 28, and 29 above.

piness it had formerly enjoyed when it journeyed with the celestial god to the outer surface of the intellectual heaven to gaze upwards at the Idea. Ficino makes no attempt to reconcile the notions that a soul cannot switch gods or their trains and that philosophers always look to Jove as their patron with the notion that all souls must eventually live their lives as philosophers even as they had lived their very first lives, and are, accordingly, jovian first and last.

Before they can ascend after each life, the souls must undergo judgment. If they have lived justly—and, like Plato, Ficino insists that you can live a just life in any of the nine categories—they are dispatched to "one of heaven's places" (249A7-8), which Ficino interprets as the air (our first heaven),[17] and endowed accordingly with an aerial body (presumably of the same kind as the purely aerial body in which the philosopher spends his third life). If they have lived unjustly, they are imprisoned "under the earth" (249A6). Since he has already interpreted "earth" to mean "the earthy body," Ficino is more inclined to argue that men are imprisoned in their own corporeal "inclinations," even though he admits the existence of actual subterranean places set aside for punishment (for which of course he had both Platonic and biblical authority).[18] The souls, moreover, are led to these "places of punishment" because they are "appropriate" (*convenientia*), meaning, presumably, adapted to the souls' particular "inclinations."

Plato's comments at 249B, "then does a man's soul enter into the life of a beast...and the beast's soul, which was once in a man, returns to a man," had suggested to Plotinus that Plato was adverting to the Pythagorean dogma of radical metempsychosis.[19]

17. Presumably it is also the habitation of the aerial demons and where we too become demonic.

18. For an analysis of Ficino's conceptions of Hades and Hell, see Klein, "L'enfer de Ficin," pp. 47-84 (with a particular emphasis on Ficino's *Platonic Theology* 18.10 [ed. Marcel, 3:227-243]); also Chastel, *Arte e umanesimo,* p. 209; and Kristeller, *Philosophy,* pp. 359-364.

19. *Enneads* 3.4.2; 4.3.9, 12, 15, 17; 5.2.2; 6.7.6, 7. In the course of discussing the immortality of the soul in his *Platonic Theology* Ficino reviews various Pythagorean theories and refutes those treating of reincarnation and particularly of metempsychosis. Even so, Pythagoras himself he revered as a great pre-Platonic sage, and the *Phaedrus* he seems to have thought of as being more deeply indebted to Plato's Pythagorean training than any of the other dialogues. See Allen, "Two Commentaries," pp. 127-128; Michael J. B. Allen, "Marsilio Ficino on Plato's Pythagorean Eye," *MLN* 97.1 (1982), 171-182.

Ficino argued, however, that Plato never believed in metempsychosis (Plato's teachings being in harmony, ultimately, with Christianity), though he apparently accepted, at least for a time, that Plotinus had misread Plato, and that his successors, notably Proclus and Hermias, had successfully refuted him on this one point (otherwise Ficino admired Plotinus even more fervently perhaps than he did Plato).[20] Ficino maintains that the phrase "enter into the life of a beast" does not mean that the rational soul of a man actually becomes the irrational soul of a beast, but rather that it associates with beasts (*in bestiarum commertia*) in the sense that it surrenders to beastly passions (*affectus*) and habits (*habitus*); it may even, if the divine judgment has so decreed, superimpose itself (*se desuper applicat*) on the souls of beasts, but never to the extent that it becomes *the* soul of a beast's body. This solution depends, as he immediately recognized, on maintaining the radical separation of the rational from the irrational soul as species of soul—a separation he thinks Socrates himself is making when Socrates subsequently remarks that only originally human souls can return to human form after their sojourn in the life of beasts, since they alone "had formerly gazed on the truth itself" (249B5-6). The impossibility of the rational human soul serving as the form (in the Aristotelian sense now) of a brute body and vice versa presents in actuality an arresting argument for upholding the dignity and appropriateness of the human body for the human soul. For when a man descends to the brute life, he not only imprisons his soul but deforms his body. Living the life of a brute, therefore, must be taken either figuratively to mean surrendering to one's lower nature or, if literally, then in the sense that we are condemned to live and feel like beasts but not to become beasts totally, as metempsychosis implies.

---

20. For a general account of Ficino's engagement with Plotinus, and especially for the view that it passed through at least two stages, see Eugenio Garin, "La rinascita di Plotino," in his *Rinascite e rivoluzioni*, pp. 89-112. Garin fails to note, however, that on several occasions Ficino voiced certain reservations about Plotinus's (and Proclus's) overly literal interpretation of some aspects of the *Phaedrus*'s myth, even though he had chosen Plotinus as his principal guide to that myth. The aspects in question apparently concerned details of "the circuit of the souls" (*de animarum circuitu*); see the *Platonic Theology* 17.1 and 4 (ed. Marcel, 3:148-149, 165-166). In his *Oratio* (ed. Garin, pp. 140-143), Pico refers to Plotinus's "learned indirectness" (*docta sermonis obliquitas*) and to Proclus's "Asiatic fertility" (*Asiatica fertilitate luxurians*).

Finally, in tackling the well-known cruces at 249BC, "man must needs understand the language of Forms, passing from a plurality of perceptions to a unity gathered together by reasoning; and such understanding is a recollection of those things our souls once beheld as they journeyed with their god," Ficino argues that Plato means we assemble one universal concept from the many particulars we see (a concept we usually name the *species*). Through this species we arrive at a universal formula (the *formula ideae*) implanted in us from birth, and thence at an Idea itself, a true species that truly exists (as opposed to the universal concept we abstracted and which had only a limited existence in our reason). This epistemological ascent, indebted both to Thomist and to Augustinian systems, is obviously impossible for the irrational soul of the beast, since the latter was never endowed with the formulae of the Ideas in the first place.[21] Though an irrational soul can abstract a universal concept from particulars (like the concepts of food or danger), it cannot then make the critical referral back to formulae and thence to the authentically existent intelligibles. For, Ficino's gloss continues, to use the formulae to arrive at the Ideas, which is the office of the rational as opposed to the irrational soul, is "nothing other than" to recall the intelligibles the soul has already seen antenatally in heaven in the train of its mundane god. To "regain one's wings" is thus to recollect at last the antenatal vision. Once it has been recollected, the philosopher returns not only to his god but to the point where he can gaze beyond celestials and intellectuals at the intelligibles themselves. Since this gazing precisely distinguishes a divinity from inferiors, the philosopher can reacquire his own divinity.

Throughout these remarks on the fall, we can see Ficino constantly thinking in terms of the soul's ascent: he is not interested in

---

21. The irrational soul does possess, however, "replicas" of the Ideas in their lower manifestation as forms; see for instance Ficino's remarks in chap. 11, par. 2 of the *Phaedrus* Commentary (ed. Allen, pp. 120-123): "for the universal forms exist in a way in the soul's vegetative nature and in its imagination, reason, and intellect." Since the irrational souls of beasts consist of the nature plus the *idolum* (that is, the imagination, sense, and vital force together) plus the spirit, they can possess the forms on the two levels of the nature and of the imagination. We should note by contrast that the irrational souls in men consist of the nature alone. Cf. *Philebus* Commentary 1.20 (ed. Allen, pp. 198-199, 542 n. 98). See Kristeller, *Philosophy*, pp. 108, 370-371, 385. The subject awaits further exploration.

the theology of sin for its own sake or on its own terms. The descent was a complex problem for him to deal with philosophically for several reasons, not least of which were the intrinsic contradictions, or better perhaps paradoxes, in the Plotinian system. As Émile Bréhier,[22] A. H. Armstrong,[23] J. M. Rist,[24] and others have demonstrated, the emanatory process is open to both an optimistic and a pessimistic interpretation, paralleled to some extent in Christianity by the coexistence of the doctrines of original sin and the fortunate fall. When we also adduce Ficino's own basic philosophical optimism,[25] which drew upon both Christian and Plotinian argumentation to underscore man's potential for ascent and apotheosis, we can understand how the whole question of the fall might not be congenial to him. Indeed Robert Klein, on the evidence of a range of passages and not just from the *Platonic Theology,* has persuasively argued that Ficino was oriented by the structure and direction of his own thought to adopt what are, in some key respects, neo-Origenist positions on the themes of hell, damnation, and the everlastingness of punishment.[26]

While Ficino's preoccupation with ascent clearly entailed treating of the descent also, the two being reciprocal aspects of the soul's relationship to the absolute as well as a Platonic given, his temperamental affinities seem to have led him away from theodicean and eschatological analysis, except insofar as he could dwell on them as part of an examination of the emanation process in ancient Neoplatonism—that is, as part of an ontological and aetiological rather than an ethical system. Though metaphysics and ethics are interdependent for a Platonist, Ficino seems never to have been particularly inspired by the problems of sin, the infected will, the necessity of prevenient grace, and other dogmas associated with Pauline and/or Augustinian views on the Atonement and its theology. To the contrary, as one with a professional medi-

---

22. *Philosophy of Plotinus.*

23. A. H. Armstrong, *The Architecture of the Intelligible Universe in the Philosophy of Plotinus* (Cambridge, 1940; reprint, Amsterdam, 1967).

24. J. M. Rist, *Plotinus: The Road to Reality* (Cambridge, 1967).

25. See chap. 4, nn. 15, 16 above.

26. "L'enfer de Ficin," pp. 51, 56-59. See also Kristeller, *Philosophy,* pp. 359-364 and Edgar Wind, "The Revival of Origen," in *Studies in Art and Literature for Belle da Costa Greene* (Princeton, 1954), pp. 412-424.

cal training and the son of a doctor to boot, he habitually adopts a physiopsychological rather than a radically ethicoreligious approach to man's unhappiness and failings, attributing them to dispositional melancholia, to the baleful influences of particular stars and of the objects associated with them,[27] to bad diet and bad regimen, and to mistaken goals for otherwise essentially good faculties, such as the natural appetite, the desire for success (the old Platonic mettlesomeness), the striving for felicity, and the will's ardor for the one good. Not that he denied the reality of sin, but he tends to ignore it except in works of an avowedly penitential nature, works which do not call upon his peculiar or original insights as a philosopher-thinker-sage. When he does treat of eschatological issues, as here, he seems to predicate (as the *Phaedrus* itself suggests) the final assumption of all men to the heights of the mystical contemplation they enjoyed before the fall, however far they may have subsequently fallen into bestial oblivion.

To conclude, the three summae project a charioteer who descends only to rise again in the due process of time: one who has

---

27. There is considerable disagreement over Ficino's attitudes towards astrology. At one extreme are those who contend that Ficino was always under the sway of the astrological world-view, despite his occasional protestations to the contrary; see Lynn Thorndike, *A History of Magic and Experimental Science,* 8 vols. (New York, 1923-1958; reprint, New York, 1964-1966), 4:562 ff.; and, more interestingly, Zanier, *Medicina,* pp. 5-60. In between are those who judiciously accept genuine vacillations and contradictions in Ficino's thought; see Hans Baron, "Willensfreiheit und Astrologie bei Marsilio Ficino und Pico della Mirandola," in *Kultur- und Universalgeschichte: Festschrift Walter Goetz* (Leipzig and Berlin, 1927), pp. 145-155; Cassirer, *Individual and Cosmos,* pp. 73-122; Kristeller, *Philosophy,* pp. 310-312; and Eugenio Garin in four important studies: "Recenti interpretazioni di Marsilio Ficino," *Giornale critico della filosofia italiana* 21 (1940), 299-319; "Le 'elezioni' e il problema dell'astrologia," in *Umanesimo e esoterismo,* ed. Enrico Castelli (Padua, 1960), pp. 17-37, reprinted in *L'età nuova,* pp. 421-447; "Magia ed astrologia nella cultura del Rinascimento," in his *Medioevo e Rinascimento: Studi e ricerche* (Bari, 1954; 2d ed., 1961), pp. 150-169; and, most recently, *Lo zodiaco della vita,* pp. 63-92, esp. 69-86. At the other extreme are those who argue, subtly, that while Ficino certainly believed in astral influences and in the "astral magic" to which man can turn in order to manipulate and utilize these influences, he nevertheless rejected divinatory or judicial astrology, as his 1477 treatise *Disputatio contra Iudicium Astrologorum* (ed. Kristeller, *Sup. Fic.* 2:11-76) and various letters, e.g. *Opera,* p. 958.1, testify. See Heitzman, "La libertà e il fato," passim; Walker, *Magic,* pp. 12-24; and Yates, *Bruno,* pp. 60, 114-115, 126. Of note is Pico's observation in his own *Disputationes adversus Astrologiam Divinatricem* 1.1 (ed. Garin, 2 vols. [Florence, 1946, 1952], 1:60) that Ficino had written against the astrologers in his Plotinus commentaries; he may have had in mind such a comment as: *liberum vero in nobis arbitrium Plato in decimo de Repub. et in Phaedro atque Timaeo absque dubio ponit* (*Opera,* p. 1731.1, commenting on the *Enneads* 4.3.1). The work of Garin and Walker seems to me to be particularly authoritative here.

suffered from an inexplicable but somehow "natural" kind of inadvertency, or loss of concentration, or even from an excess of concern for those aspects of lower life committed to his care and providence. Throughout Ficino's analyses, brief though they are, there are a buoyancy and an expectancy which effectively belie Plato's account of the soul's failure to attain the head of a circuit and to gaze upon a supreme intelligible. This will become more dramatically pronounced in the eight summae which follow on the final sections of Socrates' mythical palinode to Amor.

Chapter Eight: The Idea of Beauty

The difficult problem of the relationship between three major concepts, Goodness, Truth, and Beauty—only two of which are the traditional transcendentals[1]—had already been broached by summa 21. In the list at 247D which singles out three Ideas, Plato includes none of them, though he does seem to think of Beauty as an Idea at 250B ff.: "Beauty it was ours to see in those days in all its brightness... beauty shone bright amidst these visions." In treating of noumenal as opposed to phenomenal beauty,[2] Ficino had two separate schemes to hand: the Platonic realm of Ideas and the Plotinian ontological hypostases. Mediating the two schemes is the concept of Being which Plotinus had identified with Beauty in his great treatise "On the Intellectual Beauty," *Enneads* 5.8.9. The Platonic Ideas are the supreme beings, and the Plotinian, or at least Neoplotinian, system of the five hypostases[3] is in essence an elaboration of the notion that being is manifested at various levels or stages. Since both the One and Mind, the first two hypostases in all the Neoplatonic variations, exist prior to the Ideas, we cannot suppose that there are Ideas of them, but rather that they themselves are in a way the two supreme Ideas or meta-Ideas. Whether there are Ideas of the subsequent hypostases, particularly of Soul, or of being itself, is an even more complicated question.

Whereas Plato (whose views changed radically in the course of his career) had argued that the Ideas were absolutely supreme with

---

1. In medieval philosophy the three transcendentals predicated of God were *unum, verum, et bonum*. See Kristeller, *Philosophy*, pp. 45-46, 64; and, for beauty, Henri Pouillon, "La beauté, propriété transcendantale, chez les scholastiques (1220-1270)," *Archives d'histoire doctrinale et littéraire du Moyen Âge* 15 (1946), 263-329; and Beierwaltes, *Ficinos Theorie des Schönen*, pp. 30 ff.

2. Panofsky, *Studies in Iconology*, p. 133 and n. 10; see also Erwin Panofsky, *Idea: Ein Beitrag zur Begriffsgeschichte der älteren Kunsttheorie* (Leipzig, 1924). Cf. Ficino's *Platonic Theology* 11.4 (ed. Marcel, 2:121 ff.).

3. Kristeller, *Philosophy*, pp. 75, 106-108, 167-169, 266, 400; Allen, "Ficino's Theory of the Five Substances," passim.

the Idea of the Good at their head, and transcended the capacity of any soul or even of the Timaean Demiurge to comprehend them fully,[4] the Middle Platonists, in postulating the concept of a prime intellect thinking the Ideas, were forced to reassess their status as absolute beings. Finally, when Plotinus identified the *Republic*'s Idea of the Good with the One, his prime hypostasis, Platonists then had to differentiate between different kinds of Ideas: not only between the Ideas of *zoa*, living things, to which the Demiurge looks as models for fashioning the universe, and moral Ideas such as the *Phaedrus*'s own Justice and Temperance, but also between qualitatively higher and lower Ideas, and in particular between the Ideas linked with the Idea of Goodness and all other Ideas.[5] Linked with Goodness are not only Unity but Truth and Beauty, which, by virtue of the Good's primacy, exist prior to (logically if not temporally) all other Ideas. What then is their mutual relationship?

Ficino was consistent in accepting Plotinus's thesis that Goodness was absolutely identifiable with the One, at least with the One as we can think about it in its immanence, the One in its transcendence being, traditionally, beyond all predication, even of goodness.[6] Truth he defines as the "light" from the Good irradiating Mind, the first Being, and irradiating the Ideas in Mind (for the

---

4. *Timaeus* 28A ff., 30C ff., 38B ff. In Plato the Demiurge looks up at the Ideas, which are superior to him. For the Christian Platonists the situation was more complicated in that the Ideas were deemed to exist in the Mind of God (often identified with Christ) and therefore in the Mind of the Creator, the supreme Demiurge. Ficino was also faced with the problem of Proclus's apparent subordination of the Ideas to the Demiurge, whom he identified with Mind; see Proclus, *In Timaeum* 91E-97D (ed. Diehl, 1:299.10-319.21; trans. Festugière, 2:151-177), and Zeller-Mondolfo, *Filosofia*, p. 155n.

5. This problem is distinct from the somewhat less complicated one of differentiating between manifestations or replicas of the Ideas at lower ontological levels. The problem of hierarchizing the Ideas was present almost from the onset and connected with another issue: how to determine what did not have an Idea, an issue which soon occupied the Middle Platonists; see Dillon, *Middle Platonists*, pp. 28, 280-281.

6. The theological *via negativa* had alerted Ficino to the theoretical impossibility (and even, to some minds, absurdity) of attributing characteristics to God univocally, and perhaps analogically too; and his studies of Plotinus and the Areopagite immediately prior to his final stint at the *Phaedrus* Commentary had certainly accustomed him to handling the consequent paradoxes. He seems never to have committed himself to the *via negativa* as a working method, however; and, though utilizing it on particular occasions, customarily he employed propositions that argued for God's essence and existence in terms of His being the keystone of Plato's metaphysics. In other words, Ficino remained throughout his life a rationalist who believed that, in certain real senses, one could indeed "know" God and

One is beyond Being for all the classical Neoplatonists and Ficino, though for others, like Pico, coincident with it).[7] The irradiation results in a "splendor" which is prime Beauty. Ficino is again drawing upon an analogy with light conceived of in its three manifestations as unradiated, radiating, and radiated, the latter designated as "splendor."[8] From this viewpoint Beauty is not so much an Idea in Mind as the splendor resulting from the irradiation of all the Ideas in Mind by Truth, the light from the Good.[9] Parallel, therefore, to the ontologically descending series, One, Mind, Idea, is the epistemologically descending series, Good, Truth, Beauty.

This account is too simple, however, in that it ignores Plato's commitment, in the *Republic* at least, to the theory that the Good is an Idea. Thus, while Ficino habitually thinks of the One, Mind, and indeed Soul, Quality, and Body, as hypostases, he thinks of the Good, Truth, and Beauty as Ideas, even though the One as hypostasis and the Good as Idea are identical. So Beauty emerges, paradoxically, as both the splendor in Mind resulting from the Good's irradiation of all the Ideas with Truth, and as a single, autonomous Idea, though one linked to Truth, which is itself both an Idea and yet the light of the Good in all the Ideas. Hence response to Beauty is simultaneously response to an Idea, to Truth as all the Ideas, and ultimately to Goodness as an Idea above all

---

predicate his attributes. Like many other distinguished thinkers, that is, he continued to entertain contradictory positions with regard to the profounder questions of philosophy and theology.

7. The two major texts in this intriguing controversy were Pico's *De Ente et Uno* of 1491 (ed. Garin, 1:385-441) and Ficino's *Parmenides* Commentary of 1492-1494 (*Opera*, pp. 1136-1206).

8. These distinctions between various kinds or states of light derive in the main from Augustine; see, for instance, the notable passage on "morning" and "evening" knowledge of the Good in his *De Civitate Dei* 11.29. Chastel gives a preliminary but useful account of Ficino's "light" metaphysics in his *Ficin et l'art*, pp. 103-104; see also Yates, *Bruno*, p. 120; but more work needs to be done.

9. Beierwaltes, *Ficinos Theories des Schönen*, pp. 31-32. Panofsky, *Renaissance and Renascences*, pp. 184-185, claims that Ficino, in reacting to Aquinas, is "reinstating the identity of the beautiful with the good"; and he calls our attention to the wordplay in Greek, of which Ficino was certainly aware (e.g. *Opera*, p. 1927.2), between "beauty" ($\kappa\acute{\alpha}\lambda\lambda o\varsigma$) and "calling" ($\kappa\alpha\lambda\epsilon\hat{\iota}\nu$) the soul to God (p. 185). This identity is correctly denied by Saitta, *Marsilio Ficino e la filosofia dell'umanesimo*, pp. 210-211. See too Kristeller, "The Modern System of the Arts," in his *Renaissance Thought II* (New York, 1965; reprinted as *Renaissance Thought and the Arts*, Princeton, 1980), pp. 166-167. The great meditation in the *Enneads* at 1.6.6-9 is open to several interpretations.

the other Ideas and above Truth. Such a response commences as an epistemological ascent and soon becomes an ethical and ontological ascent also.[10]

Plato had supplied various clues for this elevation of Beauty, and notably in the *Symposium, Phaedrus,* and *Hippias Major,* clues used by Plotinus to full advantage.[11] Still, it is the Renaissance Neoplatonists under the leadership of Ficino, as Cassirer,[12] Panofsky,[13] Chastel,[14] and Garin[15] especially have stressed, who raised Beauty to the status of being the highest artistic and even moral and intellectual abstraction (for this was implicit in the Greek term τὸ καλόν). It was also one endowed for them with a unique power,[16] a power which supplanted in various unexpected ways the power of another Idea of extraordinary significance for Plato and the Greeks, the Idea of Justice and its cognate, Temperance. Though Ficino appreciated Plato's reverence for Justice, as both intellectual historian and translator, he could not share the ancient Greek conception of it as the ordering principle of the world, the principle underlying the gradations and hierarchies and distributed values extending through man, society, nature, and the universe.[17] To his Christian sense of the contingency of all things,

10. For the interdependence of epistemology and ontology in Ficino's metaphysics, see Kristeller, *Philosophy,* pp. 48-59; also, more speculatively, Schiavone, *Problemi filosofici,* pp. 259-324.

11. Of particular significance for Ficino were Plotinus's treatises 1.6 (on Beauty), 3.5 (on Love), and 5.8 (on Intellectual Beauty); they provided him with his working assumptions about its nature. See Ficino's commentaries on these treatises, *Opera,* pp. 1573-1578, 1713-1717, 1767-1769; also his *De Amore* 2.3, 5, 9; 5.1, 3, 4; 6.17, 18 (ed. Marcel, pp. 147-149, 152, 159; 178-179, 182-186; 233-239) and his epitome for the *Hippias* (*Opera,* pp. 1270-1272).

12. *Individual and Cosmos,* pp. 63-67, 134-135, 163 ff.

13. *Studies in Iconology,* chap. 5, esp. pp. 141-148; *Renaissance and Renascences,* pp. 184-185: "Ficino, defining beauty as 'the splendor of the face of God,' restored to its 'radiance' the metaphysical halo which it had lost at the hands of Thomas Aquinas" (p. 185).

14. *Ficin et l'art,* pp. 69n, 81-114. Chastel argues that, whereas the *Timaeus* seeks an "intellectual" definition of beauty, the *Phaedrus* seeks an "affective" definition (p. 69 n. 1).

15. *Lo zodiaco della vita,* pp. 69-86.

16. For a preliminary note on the *power* of beauty in Ficino, see Michael J. B. Allen, "Tamburlaine and Plato: A Colon, a Crux," *Research Opportunities in Renaissance Drama* 23 (1980), 21-31 at 24-26.

17. Edgar Wind, "Platonic Justice, Designed by Raphael," *Journal of the Warburg Institute* 1 (1937), 69-70: Platonic justice is not a "particular virtue juxtaposed to Prudence, Fortitude and Temperance...[but] that fundamental power in the soul which assigns to each of them their particular function."

however great, on God, and of God's mysterious gifts of providence, grace, and love, Justice must perforce give way to another touchstone: the spiritual beauty perceived in a man's soul, in the created world, in Christ. It is Beauty which inspires love in man, more so than Truth or Goodness directly, let alone Justice and Temperance, whose "earthly likenesses" have "no luster" (250B) and to behold which we need dialectic and syllogisms. Why is this? The answer is at the core of summae 26 to 33's account of the final sections of Socrates' mythical hymn. Though adumbrations perhaps of what Ficino might have written on the abstract Phaedran beauty, still they are sufficiently informative for us to appreciate why Ficino accepted the decision of Iamblichus and his followers to posit Beauty as the dialogue's *skopos,* its primary and all-embracing theme.[18] As the first dialogue, the *Phaedrus* treated of the Idea we first encounter in this world if not on the Phaedran flight; it is also, mysteriously, the splendor of all the Ideas and therefore of Truth itself. We encounter it first, moreover, because it alone of the Ideas is made manifest, Plato says at 250D, to the "keenest" of our senses, our eyes. The most accessible to man of the intelligibles, it is equally the cause of the soul's soaring towards the dome of the intellectual heaven, and of the tormenting desire in the black steed for physical union and generation.

Working from the epistemological position outlined in summa 25, summa 26 argues that the philosopher, as soon as he has perceived the Ideas and the divine wisdom and goodness through them, should venerate and worship them immediately, and thereby submit to the hieratic madness in order to be "completely filled with divinity" (249CD). Essentially Ficino is glossing the phrase at 249C7-8, τελέους ἀεὶ τελετὰς τελούμενος (the stem, τέλος, ensures that "perfect," "initiate," and "mystery" are cognates in Greek). He had already said a number of interesting things in his commentary chapter 4 about the close relationship between the philosopher and the priest, the former devoted to the intellect, the latter to the will (with all the attendant complications), and about

---

18. Hermias, *In Phaedrum,* pp. 8-11 (ed. Couvreur). Cf. Bielmeier, *Phaidrosinterpretation,* pp. 22-23; Larsen, *Jamblique,* pp. 363-366; Dillon, *Iamblichi Fragmenta,* pp. 248-249; Allen, *Charioteer,* pp. 9-11.

their eventual union in the contemplation and love of the Good. Again he singles out the philosopher-priest (and he could have added poet) as the ideal recipient of the amatory fury on the grounds that he alone has become accustomed to recalling Ideas from sensibles and is thus most prepared to recollect divine Beauty from sensible beauty.[19] This recollecting is itself the height of the amatory madness, which excels the other divine madnesses, Ficino observes, on two counts: it is inspired by the most excellent "Ideas" or "meta-Ideas" of all, Goodness and Truth witnessed in their splendor as Beauty; and it "unites us more effectively and more firmly with God" (glossing Plato's reference at 249E1-2 to "best in itself and in its sources"—in Ficino's Latin translation, *optima atque ex optimis sit*). Hence as lover the philosopher-priest-poet is the lover of Beauty. Ficino is elaborating Plato's statements at 249DE that the "lover of beauty" who beholds the beauty of this world is "reminded" of true beauty (hence the importance of memory in loving); thereupon he begins to grow his wings, though unable as yet to lift them. Inherently, of course, the love of such Beauty is also the love of Good and of Truth.

But not all saw Beauty in its plenary form. Summa 27, which treats of 249E-250B, focuses on the difference between the souls who saw more Beauty—that is, more Ideas—more fully, and who then received a philosophical education and nurturing consonant with their philosophical genius (*ingenium*), and those who saw less Beauty—that is, who saw neither so many Ideas nor so well—and who did not receive, therefore, the appropriate education. In other words, Ficino reads the educational theme into Plato's description at 250A of those who "consorted unhappily with such as led them to deeds of unrighteousness," which he glosses as "unfortunate and depraved by certain daily habits" (*quibusdam consuetudinibus depravate*). Ideas other than Beauty we can recall (tardily if at all) only by means of syllogisms (which Ficino defines as "certain hidden instruments"), because they have imparted "their like-

19. In his article, "Von Plotin, Proklos und Ficinus," *Deutsche Vierteljahrsschrift für Literaturwissenschaft und Geistesgeschichte* 19 (1941), 407-429, Oskar Walzel focuses on this recollective process. However, his accounts of the views of all three thinkers (and thus of the relationships between them) are as controversial as they are brief, and have been superseded by Beierwaltes's work.

nesses to souls, but not to bodies" and consequently have no "splendor" in their images and cannot be recollected through sensibles. Beauty, on the other hand, "the splendor of the Good sparkling in the series of the ideas," not only "propagates its images" (*imagines*) to our souls but also to "sensible forms"; and it is unique in doing so. Earlier, when Plato had maintained at 249BC that a soul passes "from a plurality of perceptions to a unity assembled by reasoning," he must have been talking, therefore, of our sense perceptions of beauty, since Beauty has "more light" than other Ideas, is "more accessible," and can excite and inflame us more through the sight, the "keenest of our senses." That sight is the acutest sense does not necessarily contradict, incidentally, the earlier thesis that hearing has priority;[20] for clearly priority and acuity are not necessarily interdependent. Beauty has the advantage too in that when it reveals itself to our sight, it does so as a totality, not as a part—a notion based on the classical theory that beauty depends on due proportion, on the harmonious balancing of all the parts that make up a whole that alone is truly beautiful.[21] Surprisingly, Ficino here compares beauty's rapturous effect upon us with the "total" pleasure experienced in sex. Insofar as Beauty alone reaches down to sensibles, its power corresponds, in a way, to Jove's as the provider for inferiors; but insofar as it is the splendor of all the Ideas at the same time, it reaches directly up to Truth.

20. See chap. 2, pp. 51-55 above.
21. Ficino did not always espouse the harmony theory even in treating of sensible beauty. Most notably he was drawn at times to the Plotinian notion that beauty could be pure and uncompounded: contrast, for instance, the views in his *De Amore* 5.3 (ed. Marcel, p. 183) with those in the *De Amore* 1.4 or 5.6 (ed. Marcel, pp. 142, 188-190) or in the *Phaedrus* Commentary, chap. 3 (ed. Allen, pp. 80-81). He also refers to sensible beauty as the outward form of inner goodness (*De Amore* 5.1 and 6.2 [ed. Marcel, pp. 178-179, 200-201]), and occasionally as the "congruence" between what we see and the "reason" (*ratio*) in our mind (*De Amore* 5.5 [ed. Marcel, p. 187]). The issue at stake was not so much the natures of sensible and of ideal beauty as the relationship between them. It was here that Ficino explored a number of formulae as did Pico, his fellow Platonist but not always his disciple in these matters (see the *Commento* 2.8-11 [ed. Garin, pp. 494-499]). See N. Ivanoff, "La beauté dans la philosophie de Marsile Ficin et de Léon Hébreux," *Humanisme et Renaissance* 3 (1936), 12-21; Kristeller, *Philosophy*, pp. 265-266; Chastel, *Ficin et l'art*, pp. 87-91, 99-106; G. Solinas, "Sull'estetica di Marsilio Ficino," *Annali della Facoltà di Lettere, Filosofia, e Magistero dell'Università di Cagliari* 18 (1951), 365-380; and Beierwaltes, *Ficinos Theorie des Schönen*, pp. 32-36.

In dealing with 250B-D, summa 28 comments on the pristine vision of Beauty on the part of the philosophers in the train of Jove as the World-Soul; "for the most ample contemplation and providence pertain to the World-Soul and to the philosopher." Not only the supreme contemplator among men and the highest on the scale of human souls, the true philosopher is also the greatest provider in that he governs and cares for the whole man as less philosophical souls are incapable of doing. Astrologically, it means that primarily he is under Jove and only secondarily under Saturn. Though the planet Saturn "corresponds to" the higher, "the pure, separated intellect," and thus enables the philosopher to escape the world,[22] Ficino notes that Plato does not approve of men, who are by nature ensouled, becoming such purely saturnian philosophers and thus abandoning their primary allegiance to Jupiter.[23] For this sets them apart from their fellows and may either make them vulnerable to the melancholia and depression that do not afflict the pure saturnian intellects but can certainly affect the impure ones joined to souls, or else may encourage them to abandon their providential duties for unalloyed contemplation and thus cut them off before their time from the lower world. The

22. Cf. Ficino's *De Vita* 1.6 (Opera, p. 498): "[Saturnus] omnium planetarum altissimus investigantem evehit ad altissima. Hinc philosophi singulares evadunt praesertim cum animus, sic ab externis motibus atque corpore proprio sevocatus et quam proximus divinis, divinorum instrumentum efficiatur. Unde divinis influxibus oraculisque ex alto repletus, nova quaedam inusitataque semper excogitat et futura praedicit." ("As the highest of all the planets, [Saturn] lifts the seeker up to the highest realms. Hence philosophers are alone in escaping; this happens especially when the soul, having been separated from external movements and from its own body and brought as close as possible to divine things, is rendered an instrument of the divinities. Then, made full from on high with divine influences and oracles, it always ponders new and unfamiliar matters and predicts future events.")

23. The *locus classicus,* from Ficino's viewpoint, of the doctrine that Saturn gives the soul the power of thought and discernment whereas Jupiter gives it the power to act is Macrobius, *In Somnium Scipionis* 1.12; but Ficino clearly thought of both powers as *vires intelligendi,* as a passage in a letter to Jacopo Antiquario demonstrates: "Sane Platonici, cum animam in tres praecipue distinguant vires, intelligendi videlicet et irascendi atque concupiscendi, primam partiuntur in duas, scilicet in mentem vel contemplationi vel actioni praecipue deditam. Mentem quidem contemplatricem nomine Saturni significant, mentem vero actionibus occupatam nominant Iovem." ("The Platonists, in distinguishing the powers of the soul into three, those of understanding, of indignation, and of desire, divide the first power into two and arrive at the mind dedicated to contemplation on the one hand, to action on the other. The contemplating mind they signify under the name of Saturn; but the mind preoccupied with activities they call Jupiter.") (*Opera,* p. 860.3; cf. *De Vita* 3.22 [*Opera,* p. 565].) Insofar as philosophers are ruled by the *vis intelligendi,* they are therefore ruled by both of the highest planets.

jovian philosopher, by contrast, strives both to contemplate and to act, to temper his saturnian powers with those that are preeminently Jove's.[24] Thus he strives to achieve the jovian ideal, which is the ideal for man.

The gloss is interesting, therefore, in that it vindicates the *Phaedrus*'s elevation of Jupiter over his progenitors in the Plotinian but not in the Iamblichean or the Proclian interpretation. Given Ficino's familiarity with classical mythology, and given the compatibility of the jovian syndrome with Christianity's view of God as both the universal father and ruler and the provider alike, this elevation might seem unremarkable. But Neoplatonism had been responsible for upgrading Saturn's role by identifying him with Mind,[25] the hypostasis that is absolutely critical to Plotinus's entire system of both metaphysics and ethics. Moreover, as Panofsky, Saxl, Klibansky, and others have emphasized, in the revival of interest in Saturn and things saturnian during the Renaissance, a revival that eventually became a major intellectual vogue, Ficino himself played the key role.[26] His psychosomatic treatise, *De Vita,* emerged as the most popular and seminal of the texts,[27] and he

24. Cf. *Platonic Theology* 18.8 (ed. Marcel, 3:204-205), and *De Vita* 3.2, 12, 22 (*Opera,* pp. 533, 547, 564). See Chastel, *Ficin et l'art,* pp. 71, 164, 167 n. 9; and Raymond Klibansky, Erwin Panofsky, and Fritz Saxl, *Saturn and Melancholy,* rev. ed. (London, 1964), pp. 140, 181 n. 173, 254-274 (esp. pp. 260, 271-272)—this is a revised edition of Panofsky and Saxl's *Dürers "Melencolia I": Eine quellen- und typengeschichtliche Untersuchung* (Leipzig and Berlin, 1923).

Of particular significance was Plato's myth in the *Statesman* 269-274.

25. Of interest here are two etymologies: the "old" one, *sacer nus,* that Ficino derived from Boccaccio, *Genealogia Deorum* 8.1; and the "new" one, *saturnus nous,* that in fact he derived from Varro, *Lingua Latina* 5.64, and used in a letter to Pico (*Opera,* p. 889.4) in the course of a pun on Pico and the Picus in Vergil's *Aeneid* 7.189 and Ovid's *Metamorphoses* 14.320 who is the son of Saturn (cf. *Opera,* pp. 892.2 and 901.1). See Klibansky, Panofsky, and Saxl, *Saturn and Melancholy,* pp. 177, 251 n. 28.

26. *Saturn and Melancholy,* chap. 2, pp. 241-274. See also Erwin Panofsky, *The Life and Art of Albrecht Dürer,* 4th ed. (Princeton, 1955), pp. 165-171; Kristeller, *Philosophy,* pp. 208-214; Chastel, *Ficin et l'art,* pp. 163-171; André Chastel, "Le mythe de Saturne dans la Renaissance italienne," *Phoebus* 1.3-4 (1946), 125-134.

27. For an excellent account of its *fortuna,* see Alessandra Tarabochia Canavero, "Il *De Triplici Vita* di Marsilio Ficino: Una strana vicenda ermeneutica," *Rivista di filosofia neoscolastica* 69.4 (1977), 697-717. The work is variously referred to as the *De Vita,* the *De Vita Triplici* and the *De Triplici Vita;* but Kristeller, *Sup. Fic.* 1:lxxxiii-lxxxvi, establishes the case for *De Vita* as Ficino's intended title, and I have followed him.

The only English translation of this work to date, Charles Boer's *Marsilio Ficino: The Book of Life* (Irving, Texas, 1980), is entirely inadequate; see my review in *Renaissance Quarterly* 35.1 (Spring 1982), 69-72. However, a critical edition with accompanying translation by John R. Clark and Carol V. Kaske is forthcoming.

himself took pride in his saturnian connections, cultivated on
occasions his saturnian melancholia,[28] and interested the Medici
circle generally in saturnian imagery and themes.[29] In this *Phaedrus* Commentary, however, his emphasis is fairly and squarely on
Saturn's rebellious son and successor; logically so, given the Platonic text and given that Jove is much more suited to Ficino's
abiding concern with the soul's nature and powers as "the bond
and knot" of the world,[30] for he, not Saturn, best symbolizes the
soul's intermediary position on the cosmic ladder, its providential
as well as its contemplative duties. Jove is the philosopher's—is
man's—true divinity, therefore; and total submission to the medi-
tative planet is to be shunned as a separation from our humanity.[31]

In the company of "great" Jove,[32] philosophic souls will con-

28. Like Plato, he possessed a saturnian horoscope (*Opera*, pp. 732-733, 763; trans. *Letters* 2:31-34, 3:33) and dwelt on "the saturnian hill," Montevecchio (*Opera*, pp. 843.4-844).
See Chastel, *Arte e umanesimo,* pp. 234 ff.; idem, *Ficin et l'art,* p. 12; Klibansky, Panofsky, and Saxl, *Saturn and Melancholy,* pp. 256-258.

29. Ficino described Lorenzo as "the first among the Saturnians" (*Opera*, p. 888.2). See
Chastel, *Ficin et l'art,* p. 12. Klibansky, Panofsky, and Saxl even go so far as to claim that
"the élite among the Italian humanists turned to Saturn rather than to Jupiter" and that
Saturn "eventually became the chief patron of the Platonic Academy at Florence" (*Saturn
and Melancholy,* pp. 254 and 273). I seriously doubt this, since each of the chief classical
deities was accorded primacy on particular occasions, and the Florentines were continually
ringing the changes in what was always a kind of game. Klibansky, Panofsky, and Saxl
themselves draw our attention to the extraordinary importance attributed to Mercury (p.
260 n. 56), and Wind has stressed the central place occupied by Venus in the Orphic pantheon so crucial to Ficino's understanding of Platonic mythology (*Pagan Mysteries,* pp.
36-41).

30. As such he is the patron of friendship, *casti amoris ac firmioris amicitiae pater*
(*Opera*, p. 959). See Alessandra Tarabochia Canavero, "L'amicizia nell'epistolario di Marsilio Ficino," *Rivista di filosofia neo-scolastica* 67.3 (1975), 422-431 at 429.

31. Despite their special concern with the new "contemplative" Saturn of the Renaissance Neoplatonists, Klibansky, Panofsky, and Saxl fully acknowledge his "dangerous bi-
polarity" (*Saturn and Melancholy,* p. 261). Of Ficino, the high priest of Renaissance Sat-
urnism, they even observe: "despite all his familiarity with Dante and ancient Neoplatonism, he regarded Saturn as an essentially unlucky star, and melancholy as an essentially
unhappy fate" (p. 256). They also admit to the countervailing importance of Jupiter, quoting from the *De Vita* 3.22 (*Opera*, pp. 564-565): "Jupiter arms us against Saturn's influence, which is generally foreign to, and somehow unsuitable for, mankind" (p. 272). In
fact the *De Vita* praises Jove throughout book 3, especially chaps. 4-6 and 22 (*Opera*, pp.
536-538, 564-565).

32. That is, of the World-Soul. The later Renaissance's interest in the World-Soul, and,
concomitantly, in nature mysticism, panentheism, and pantheism was much indebted to
Ficino, and thus to his fascination with the mythology and metaphysics of Jupiter. A history of the World-Soul in the Renaissance will therefore have to include, perhaps even commence with, an account of the role of Jupiter in Ficino's thought. See Beierwaltes, *Ficinos
Theorie des Schönen,* pp. 36-38; de Gandillac, "Neoplatonism and Christian Thought,"
pp. 165-166; and Yates, *Bruno,* pp. 65-67, 132, 137, 243, 309-310, 350-351, 436.

template "the blessed spectacles" of the Ideas and be initiated into the sacred mysteries as both beholders and celebrants; for the Ideas will enable them "to look up at higher things and to grasp hold of them [*or possibly* than they can grasp]" (*superiora suspiciunt atque capiunt*). As Ficino is now referring to the future philosopher-priest, he speaks of contemplation in the sense not of the intellect's vision alone but also of the feelings associated with the will, "a desirable appetite belonging to [our] nature...love, joy, veneration, and providence." All of them will be granted man when he is bathed in the light proceeding from the Good, in the Beauty that, Ficino says, will join man's intellect and will with the Ideas; "for alone of divine things beauty manifestly goes forth through all and advances into the sight there and here likewise as eagerly as a liquid." Thus Beauty inspires both vision and love in man. At the same time, of all the heavenly Ideas it alone enables him to achieve the union between his own intellect and the intelligibles in the prime intellect by granting him truth and the love of truth, and by restoring him to his original identity as lover-philosopher-priest, as a jovian being.

Hackforth comments on 250E to 252C, "This powerful analysis of the nature of sublimated παιδεραστία may be left for the most part without comment" (*Phaedrus,* p. 98). Ficino's response in summa 29 is identical. It is almost as if the passion of this, one of the most magnificent arias in ancient literature, had already been anticipated by, or Freudianly displaced to, earlier summae. His only comments are to insist once more on beauty's twin gifts of vision and inspiration to love, affecting our nature "with heat and motion" as well as our sight with light, as he glosses the lemma at 252B9 that Love must be "winged by necessity." Obviously, he could see nothing requiring philosophical analysis that he had not already dealt with elsewhere—most notably, since he refers to it directly, in the *De Amore.*[33]

Covering 252C-253C, summa 30 is somewhat technical and introduces two topics I have discussed already: the relationship of

---

33. I have decided that Ficino's reference here in summa 29 to *in libro de amore* probably refers to his own *De Amore* rather than to the *Symposium* (which was, nevertheless, subtitled *De Amore*). My translation and index in *Charioteer,* pp. 180 and 267, should be emended accordingly. Passages in the *De Amore* where Ficino deals with the effects of physical passion include 6.9, 10, and 7.2-12 (ed. Marcel, pp. 212-223, 242-256).

the demons to their planetary rulers, and of men to their gods and demons; and the iconology of Venus and Juno. Additionally, however, it concentrates on the way we may recognize our psychological type and our particular god and demon and the beloved who best reflects them. We have a natural "instinct" for things, people, and actions under the aegis of a particular deity—that is, we find them especially beautiful—and this informs our character (*ingenium*). If we nurture this instinct, which is in fact a kind of love, by study and practice, it will first lead us to know, then to imitate, and finally to attain, our patron deity. For we must know before we imitate; and in order to know we must inquire from external circumstances, but even more importantly from introspection (as our thoughts and feelings are the best guides) in whose train we journeyed before the fall. "Whatever you love beyond all else and whatever you naturally delight in most," Ficino writes, "such usually is your genius and god"—presumably *genius* refers both to our demon and to our *ingenium*. The same goes for our beloved, for we love "nothing more fervently in a man than the beauty of the body and soul." Having been drawn to the beauty of someone in the same planetary train as ourselves,[34] our duty is to instruct them in the affairs of our mutual god and his demons. When we have both been thus converted, we may attain love's end, which is the mutual worship of our god and a common union with him (*communiter copulari*). While this rule applies to all the planetary gods, Ficino confines himself to Jove and to jovian men and jovian beloveds.

Surprisingly, in the light of his own *De Amore,* he underplays the importance of the beloved in effecting one's conversion to one's god, perhaps because the beloved is less crucial for jovian than for martian, junonian, or apollonian souls. In effect, however, all the various classes of souls have, in the famous phrase of

34. The kinship or identity that exists between two friends as a result of their sharing a star is known as synastry. Cf. Ficino's *De Amore* 2.8; 6.4-6; 7.9, 10 (ed. Marcel, pp. 155-158, 203-208, 253-255); *De Vita* 3.22, 23 (*Opera,* pp. 564-568). See Klibansky, Panofsky, and Saxl, *Saturn and Melancholy,* p. 261; and especially Wind, *Pagan Mysteries,* pp. 8n, 64-65.

De Amore 6.5 (ed. Marcel, p. 205) states that four astrological types are particularly subject to love: jovians, apollonians, martians, and junonians (that is, venereans of a particular kind).

the *Theaetetus* 176B, a unitary ὁμοίωσις θεῷ as their goal, a becoming like god—not just any god, but the universal god, Jove. Vulcan or Neptune—to take two of the least revered Olympians in Ficino's interpretation of Plato's scheme—are just preliminary stages to becoming Jove. Ficino's postulation of a personal demon from the same cosmic train also works against the importance of the beloved. Whereas the demon represents the internal or spiritual presence of what we recognize as our patron deity, the beloved—at least in terms of his physical presence—represents the corroborative manifestation of that deity in the outer world (and this parallels in a way the division between the demon's role in hearing as opposed to the beloved's beauty informing our sight).

Plato's account at 253C to 254E of the taming of the appetite for physical beauty symbolized by the crooked steed with its short neck, snub nose, swart skin, and gray eyes is another vividly descriptive passage. The taming climaxes when the charioteer "spatters the horse's jaws and tongue with blood, forcing him down on his legs and haunches and delivering him over to anguish" (254E). Ficino reacts to this Homeric image in summa 31 not only by ignoring much of it, as we might expect, but also by adverting to the ludic, fanciful surface of Plato's style: "Plato rejoices and plays like a youth with poetical figures and with a rhetorically studied description of horses and of loves." This description Ficino in turn "medievalizes": the reason becomes the prince in the castle of the head; the white steed, the irascible power, is the knight in the heart; the black steed, the concupiscible power, is the mass of peasants and artisans in the liver. We arrive at Plato's three-tier sociopsychological system as outlined in the ninth book of the *Republic* (580D ff.) but translated into feudal terms and paralleled microcosmically.

Apart from footnoting, paraphrase, and pedestrian commentary, however, Ficino does introduce in summa 31 one major interpretative distinction critical for our understanding of his varying responses to the Phaedran myth. He pounces on Plato's use of εἶδος at 253C8, "In the beginning of our story (μύθου) we divided each soul into three parts, two being *like* steeds, the third *like* a charioteer." He sees it alerting us to the fact that Socrates now turns away from depicting the "separated" soul in its discarnate,

godlike state, before the allotment of the various earthly lives, to
treat, again though in terms of the charioteer myth, of the soul
"joined" with the body, the incarnate, passion-tormented soul in
its oyster-shell of earth. The transition is all-important. Whereas
formerly the charioteer had signified the soul's unity, the white
horse its intelligence (*mens*), and the black horse, the will, they
now signify respectively the reason (*ratio*), the irascible power, and
the concupiscible power.[35] The myth, that is, can refer to either the
risen or the fallen soul, the soul in love with Beauty or with beau-
ties; its details accordingly signify different human faculties and
goals. While the correspondence theory led Ficino to see the lower
reflected in the higher—the reason in the unity, the irascible power
in the intelligence, the concupiscible in the will—not all the myth's
components could be so duplicated. The wings, for instance, can
only come into the picture when we treat of the separated soul
(even if this separation is the outcome of a merely temporary
ecstasy); and the soul's unity similarly.[36]

Perhaps the truly anomalous position in this new model is the
white horse's. From being the symbol of the intellect's contemplative pursuit of truth, it has now become the honor-driven, irascible
power that sends men out into the world of competitive action.
This is not surprising in itself in that, whereas the winged chariot is
paradigmatic of the contemplative life whatever its constituent
powers, the earthbound chariot is impelled by the three powers
which we call upon, like Paris, to choose between the lives of contemplation, action, and pleasure. In actuality we must choose all
three lives for the chariot to remain intact, as Ficino had urged
Lorenzo to do in his proem to the second version of the *Philebus*
Commentary.[37] However, the irascible power does not dominate
the earthbound chariot as we might expect, as it has no especial

35. Cf. Ficino's letter to Giovanni Nesi of 1 July 1477: "Proinde rationem in Phaedro
nominat aurigam, quoniam naturali quodam ordine dux est partium reliquarum. Adiungit
huic geminos equos, album quidem alterum, alterum vero nigrum. Quantum vero ad pro-
positum spectat equi sunt cordis vires et iecoris, quia rationi debeant tanquam aurigae
par[e]re. Sed magnanimitas, quae accommodatur cordi, equus dicitur albus; est enim rationi propinquior. Iecoris autem concupiscentia, quoniam a rationis excellentia remotior est,
equus est niger" (*Opera*, p. 775; trans. in *Letters* 3:61).
36. See chap. 9 below.
37. Ed. and trans. Allen, pp. 480-483; cf. Wind, *Pagan Mysteries*, pp. 82, 197-198.

goal of its own. Whereas the reason longs for intelligible beauty and the concupiscible power for sensible beauty, the irascible power is merely a partisan in the fundamental struggle between the reason and the appetite. In this struggle for beauty at different ontological levels—for the reproduction of beauty physically (which makes sense only in the context of heterosexual union) and for the contemplation of intelligible beauty—the white steed might be expected not simply to ally itself with the charioteer but to have animate beauty as its peculiar goal. For that matter, the charioteer as reason should have not intelligible but intellectual beauty as his goal, since the former is unattainable to the soul in its embodied state. But Ficino aims merely to contrast the black steed with its companions, and thus establishes a stark division between love of sensible beauty at one end of the scale and of intelligible beauty at the other.[38] Consequently, the role of the white steed, and of irascibility per se, is overshadowed.

Though the charioteer and the white horse have been transposed in this new model to a lower key, still the black horse alone has truly fallen; and worthwhile parallels might be drawn not only with the *Symposium*'s presentation of the cacodemon Penia[39] but also with the *Republic*'s analysis of desire. In book 4 of the latter at 439D-441C Plato had insisted that only the third and lowest faculty of the soul, τὸ ἐπιθυμητικόν, has desire, while later in book 9 at 580D ff. he had attributed to all three faculties their own individual desires. He could thus afford to be much harsher in assessing the lowest desire, having salvaged the best elements in the notion of desire for the two higher faculties. In the *Republic,* accordingly, his emphasis shifts away from the nature of desire itself towards the differing objects of desire: wisdom, honor, political power, and money.[40] Without utilizing this material in the *Republic* directly, Ficino achieves a workable compromise for the problems raised by the dark horse and its desire for beauty. In the winged chariot the horse is intrinsically good, but in the earthbound chariot, potentially depraved. His optimism prevents him,

38. See chap. 2, n. 74 above.
39. Cf. Ficino's *De Amore* 6.7, 8 (ed. Marcel, pp. 208-212) and Pico's *Commento* 2.13, 21 (ed. Garin, pp. 501-504, 513).
40. As noted by Hackforth, *Phaedrus,* p. 107.

that is, from following through on Plato's decision that the fallen
horse is completely evil (κακός);[41] for he cannot reject desire, even
to the degree Plato had selectively rejected it in the *Republic,* given
the connections he perceived between it and the will and love. Indeed the concupiscible power is actually closer to being transformed into the love of wisdom than the irascible power,[42] and in
itself it is good as long as it obeys the dictates of reason. As the last
link in the downward extension of Jove's providence, its longing
to acquire and transform sensible beauty even has its own legiti-
macy; for, after it ceases to "recollect" the intelligible splendor
which is all beauty's source, beauty still remains its object as a
providential goal.

Ficino's dual interpretation of the Phaedran charioteer accounts, perhaps, for his lack of interest in, or of analytical commitment to, what he thought of as Plato's sections on the earthbound charioteer and the toiling for mastery over the appetitive
nature and its passionate intractability. In his view the dialogue's
true mysteries concerned the soul in flight, borne aloft on the
plumes of its intelligence and will to St. Paul's third heaven,[43]
rather than the all too human contest between restraint and lust,
between moral steadfastness and indulgence in physical possession. This view might also explain summae 32 and 33's sidestep-
ping of the lemmata in 255A to 257A. Summa 32 even avoids ade-
quate paraphrase, merely contenting itself with sketching the
theory that the beloved reciprocates his lover's love eventually because he succumbs to the reflection of his own beauty in the lover,
a theory elaborated in the *De Amore.* Ficino also eschews the
opportunity to enlarge on Plato's memorable suggestion at 255D,
later to be echoed by Augustine in the opening to the third book of
The Confessions,[44] that the beloved in love does not know what he

41. *Phaedrus* 247B3, 253D3; cf. 266A5 (σκαιός ἔρως).
42. For the idea that the concupiscible power is more closely linked to the contemplative
life than the irascible power, see the third excerpt appended to Ficino's *Philebus* Commentary in its first and second versions (ed. Allen, pp. 452-455). As in the proem to Lorenzo
accompanying the second version (ibid., pp. 480-483), Ficino is adverting to the Judgment
of Paris and to the choices explored in the *Philebus.*
43. 2 Cor. 12:2-4. See Ficino's comments on these verses entitled *De Raptu Pauli ad Tertium Coelum* (*Opera,* pp. 697.2-706.3).
44. "To Carthage I came, where there sang all around me in my ears a cauldron of un-
holy loves. I loved not yet, yet I loved to love, and out of a deep-seated want I hated myself
for wanting not. I sought what I might love, in love with loving.... To love then, and to be
beloved, was sweet to me" (trans. Pusey).

loves; and he neglects too the birth of ἀντέρως, the counterlove which mirrors the lover's love.[45]

Similarly summa 33 concerns itself almost exclusively with the lemma at 256B4-5, "the three rounds of the Olympic struggle," a lemma which Ficino interprets in the light of the philosopher's three lives. In the first the philosopher subjugates his lower powers to his understanding (*intelligentia,* not *ratio*); in the second he attains wisdom by way of divine madness (presumably via all four *furores*); and in the third he actually recovers his wings and soars with the celestials. The three stages are equivalent to turning away from corporeal to moral beauty, thence to intellectual, and finally to intelligible beauty. But in fact there are only two major steps: the black steed's subjugation and the recovery of the wings. Philosophy alone obtains the latter, though the lover of earthly beauty reaches the state of being ready for his wings.

As we have seen, Ficino, like Plato, is at pains to insist on the kinship of the philosopher and lover. At this point, however, we are not meant to see the lover as yet another aspect of the philosopher like the prophet, priest, and poet, but as the philosopher's separate companion. While prophets, priests, and poets have their degenerate, parodic counterparts in the prognosticator, haruspex, and versifier, the true lover's counterpart is not the man obsessed with physical beauty, but the nonlover of Lysias's speech. He relies on skill and machination to achieve his sensual ends totally unaware of beauty, and never uses his "knowing" powers, even misdirectedly, being subject to the basest sense of all, touch. He is indeed the villain of the dialogue in that just as the sequence of *prisci theologi* mounts upwards from prophet to lover, so the inverse sequence sinks downwards from false prophet to false lover—that is, to himself; and he is lowest precisely because he had access to the greater madness as a mature human being and refused its gifts. On the other hand, even if it is bound to corporeal beauty alone, a soul has its foot on the Diotiman ladder and is potentially capable of the divine madness, all love being in some sort a madness, as Plato says at 256D. Insofar, therefore, as we may think of the lover alone, we think of someone in love with sensible beauty; but insofar as we may think of him as the philosopher's companion,

---

45. See Panofsky, *Studies in Iconology,* pp. 126-128.

we think of someone in love with moral, intellectual, and intelligible beauty. In both instances beauty, not wisdom per se, is the lover's goal, while the nonlover is insensitive to beauty in any of its forms.

Again we must recall that for Ficino and his readers the *Phaedrus* served as the prolegomenon not just for the *Symposium,* the dialogue on love, but for all the dialogues. Ficino agreed with the ancient Neoplatonists that the *Phaedrus*'s *skopos* was beauty in all its forms,[46] and beauty as the aggregate glory of all the Ideas in the prime intellect eventually emerges as the motive force behind his presentation of the figure of the charioteer. While we can agree with Alicja Kuczyńska that Ficino had no formal system of aesthetics, nevertheless both his metaphysical and his ethical system are incomprehensible without the Idea of Beauty.[47] As the first, in the sense of most accessible, Idea for man, it may be loved in sensibles initially in the way that no other Idea can be. Without the lure of beauty, the charioteer would never commence his forward career, let alone his flight; for, though the goal of the enlightened philosopher might be goodness, the first goal of the earthbound soul is beauty. Since all beauty participates in an Idea, however, which is also the splendor of all the Ideas, the soul's love for beauty intensifies the nearer it reaches the goal of its flight, the beauty of all-embracing Truth, which is itself the light of the Good.

Thus beauty dominates the *Phaedrus,* as even its name suggests,[48] and unless we interpret the dialogue with an eye to this domination, we shall fail to understand the major reason for its impact on the Renaissance Florentines. It was as close to the hearts of many quattrocento poets, musicians, painters, and philosophers as the *Symposium* precisely because it vindicated their own apotheosis of beauty as one of the seminal abstractions of the

46. Hermias, p. 9.9-10 (ed. Couvreur): περὶ τοῦ παντοδαποῦ καλοῦ. See Allen, *Charioteer,* pp. 9-11.

47. *Filozofia i teoria piękna Marsilia Ficina* (Warsaw, 1970). Since I cannot read Polish, I am grateful to Professor E. B. Fryde of the University College of Wales at Aberystwyth for his special kindness in working through some of this study with me. Cf. Kristeller, *Philosophy,* pp. 305 ff.

48. φαιδρός means "bright" or "beaming"; see Allen, *Charioteer,* pp. 11 and 38 n. 42, for this and other associations.

epoch, the idea or Idea to which they could instinctively and continuously turn in order to formulate a vision of the ideal.[49]

Admittedly, Ficino had explored other Platonic Ideas in the course of his work on Plato and Plotinus, but the fact that he postponed commenting on the *Phaedrus* till the last decade of his life, and yet repeatedly cited its more famous dicta and figures, bears witness to the hold that its controlling Idea had upon him. The experience of intelligible beauty—the experience, that is, of the Phaedran charioteer at the apogee of his flight—is something that Ficino shared with many of his contemporaries but to which he gave a uniquely compelling philosophical and, we might add, mythological formulation. This is not the same, of course, as formulating an aesthetic system in the modern sense.[50] For Ficino saw the experience of intelligible beauty primarily in terms of the broadly introspective, philosophical, religious, and mystical life rather than the narrowly aesthetic (if such exists). More than refining his sensibility—and we should recall his considerable musical skills—beauty shaped his understanding of the noumenal and, in part, of the phenomenal worlds; and the summae he composed for the *Phaedrus* provide us, however waywardly and fragmentarily, with some penetrating insights into this shaping, this poetic, process.

49. The most eloquent articulation of this view is still part 4 of Burckhardt's *The Civilization of the Renaissance in Italy*.

50. Tigerstedt, "The Poet as Creator," p. 474: "Ficino's term [*ars*] has the old, large, classical and medieval sense: it means human activity, productivity in general, whether the fine arts, or techniques.... For this reason, there is no aesthetics in the modern sense in Ficino's philosophy. Ficino sees no fundamental difference between an artist and an artisan; he calls both of them *artifex* and their products *artificia*." Cf. Kristeller, "The Modern System of the Arts," pp. 163-227; and Beierwaltes, *Ficinos Theorie des Schönen*, pp. 43-56. Certainly Chastel is fully aware of the distinction Tigerstedt is making but sometimes loses sight of it in his *Ficin et l'art*. If Ficino clung to the "old" conception of *ars*, however, he was exploring some fundamentally new conceptions of beauty, and of beauty in *ars;* and this Chastel has very properly emphasized.

Chapter Nine: Ficino's Earlier Analyses

Though the *Phaedrus* Commentary provides Ficino's most elaborate and definitive treatment of the dialogue, material from it appears throughout his work. This is of three kinds. First are the *obiter dicta,* the wise saws, the pithy golden sayings, such as "the gods feel no envy" and "first of the host of gods and demons Zeus proceeds, ordering all things and caring for them," that like their counterparts from other dialogues Ficino uses as philosophical tags on any or all occasions. Easily, though from our viewpoint dangerously, extracted from their context, they constitute a skein of sapiential insights amounting at times almost to definitions which he can cite along with other dicta not only from Plato but from pre- and post-Platonic sages. Second are various equally extractable "proofs," particularly those from 245C to 246A on the soul's self-motion and priority in motion, and from the section on the four divine furies. These Ficino deploys as perennially valid blocks of argumentation like geometrical proofs. A list of occasions, for instance, where Ficino refers, implicitly or explicitly, to the immortality arguments would cover a number of pages and involve many of his works including his letters. But from early in his career, these proofs, like the dicta, had become part of his intellectual arsenal, basic counters in his thinking; and while they surely indicate the impact the *Phaedrus* had upon him, they do not, in themselves, constitute an interpretation, since "proofs" from other dialogues function just as independently and are evidence rather of his syncretistic methodology. Still, the *Phaedrus* certainly served as a primary source for both concepts and arguments and obviously would have continued to do so even if Ficino had never commenced a *Phaedrus* commentary or attempted any kind of individual evaluation of the dialogue or of its controlling myth.

The third kind of Phaedran material in Ficino's works is concerned specifically with this myth. Apart from numerous passing references,[1] and apart from the Commentary itself, Ficino analyzes the myth in some detail in five earlier works, though in one instance the analysis is merely repeated. The analyses constitute not so much alternative accounts of the material in Ficino's seventh commentary chapter as preliminary stabs at some of the interpretational possibilities. The first dates from late 1457 before Ficino had translated Plato, and is found in the opening chapter of the *De Voluptate*. The second dates from 1466-1468 and occurs in the *Ion* argumentum and then again in the *De Amore* of 1468-1469. The others date from the particularly generative period of 1469-1474, and occur in the *Philebus* Commentary and in the *Platonic Theology*. Though none are as elaborate or as satisfactory as the analysis in the *Phaedrus* Commentary, each provides its own calibrations to the final measure of interpretation. Together they demonstrate Ficino's expertise as a mythologist and an allegorist in evaluating the various components in the charioteer myth differently for different occasions, and they alert us to the dangers of assuming that Ficino had a fixed, or even habitual, set of readings for the myth, as some previous scholars, who have turned to one or other of the accounts in isolation, have too easily supposed.

On the evidence of its postscript, the *De Voluptate* (*Opera,* pp. 986-1012) was completed by the 29th or 30th of December 1457, when Ficino was just twenty-four, and hardly a month after he had written his important little epistolary tract, the *De Divino Furore* (*Opera,* pp. 612-615). The analysis of the charioteer myth, which Ficino must have read at this time in Bruni's 1424 translation, occurs in the very first chapter and serves as an exordium for the entire work. He begins by distinguishing between the various kinds of pleasure before describing the principal ancient philosophies of pleasure on the basis of the secondary sources available to him, primarily Cicero's *De Finibus, De Officiis,* and *Tusculanae.*[2]

---

1. For instance in the *Opera,* pp. 612.2, 742.2, 775 ff., 1027.2, 1031.1, 1412, 1423.2, 1431, 1731.1, 1914.2, 1921.3, 1925.5 ff. See also n. 17 below.
2. The history of Ficino's (youthful?) attraction to philosophical hedonism, and particularly to its poetic masterpiece, Lucretius's *De Rerum Natura,* has yet to be written. But see the four letters published by Kristeller in his *Sup. Fic.* 2:81 ff., 82 ff., 84 ff., and 86 ff.; and some important preliminary observations by Eugenio Garin, "Ricerche sull'epicureismo

In differentiating between the noetic and sensual pleasures, he refers joy (*gaudium*) and gladness (*laetitia*) to the former, and then distinguishes between the joy we experience when we actively contemplate the truth or God, or exercise the various virtues, and the gladness we experience intellectually when we passively partake of some good—gladness being the inferior.[3]

Ficino maintains that the Phaedran myth is concerned with portraying joy, thus differentiated from both gladness and sensual pleasure, and is therefore a model not for the fallen soul but for the soul in its risen, or what Plato had called its "divine," state in "the first, the true life" of active contemplation. The charioteer, chariot, horses, and wings in their totality signify the soul contemplating truth. Ficino proceeds to interpret them, he says, in the "Pythagorean manner" since Socrates was especially indebted to the Pythagoreans in his presentation of the myth.[4] The charioteer represents the reason; and the wings (whether the charioteer's, the horses', or both, is not specified) represent the two powers lifting the soul to heaven, the contemplative and moral (the latter refers back to "exercising the various virtues"). The wings are nourished by the pasturage growing on the plain or meadow of truth—that is, by contemplation; and from truth and its contemplation comes joy, which is the mind's nourishment and food. We lose our wings, or at least our ability to use them, by desiring earthly delights rather than the truth. Having, apparently, reached the meadow of truth without the wings, truth enables us to recover them so we may fly back to the heights (*ad superos*), which is Ficino's reading

---

del Quattrocento,'' in his *La cultura filosofica del Rinascimento italiano* (Florence, 1961), pp. 72-92. See also various comments by Kristeller, *Philosophy*, pp. 23-24, and *Studies*, p. 49; by Yates, *Bruno*, pp. 224-225; and by Wind, *Pagan Mysteries*, pp. 48 ff., 55, 61, 68 ff., 70, 79, 141, 274.

Especially fruitful, I believe, would be a comparison with Lorenzo Valla, whose work first appeared in 1431 with the title *De Voluptate* but was subsequently thrice revised, attaining its final form between 1444 and 1449, when it was retitled, less provocatively, *De Vero Falsoque Bono*. This fourth, definitive version has been edited critically by Maristella De Panizza Lorch (Bari, 1970) and also translated into English, with the Latin *en face*, by her and A. Kent Hieatt as *Lorenzo Valla: On Pleasure: De Voluptate* (New York, 1977).

3. See Cicero, *De Finibus* 2.4.13-14; 3.10.35; and *Tusculanae* 4.6.11-14; 4.31.66. Later, in his *Philebus* Commentary at 1.7 (ed. Allen, p. 117) and also in a letter to Mercati (*Opera*, p. 611.1; trans. *Letters* 1:39), Ficino again carefully distinguishes between them.

4. As Ficino was to make clear in his *Platonic Theology* 17.2, 3, 4 (ed. Marcel, 3:156-174). See p. 217 below.

for returning "home" to the "stable." There the soul receives two rewards, the ambrosia of contemplating the divine, and the nectar of "the perfect, absolute joy which it fully experiences in the very knowledge of God." Contemplation of the truth, the meadow's pasturage, thus nourishes the wings and enables the charioteer to rise above the meadow to the knowledge and enjoyment of God himself, twin goals symbolized by the gifts of ambrosia and nectar.[5]

Plato had depicted the charioteers, however, first gazing upon the ultimate realities in the meadow of truth and not upon any God existing beyond them, and then descending into the interior of heaven. Thence they return home to the stable far below and provide their horses with food and drink; they themselves meanwhile have already partaken of their nourishment from the meadow. Thus Ficino makes three important misreadings of, or modifications to, his original text. He locates the stable "above" the meadow of truth; he has the charioteer therefore climb the interior of heaven in order to return "home"; and he gives the soul in its entirety rather than the horses individually the gifts of ambrosia and nectar. Additionally, since he has interpreted the charioteer as reason (*ratio*) rather than as intuitional intelligence (*mens/intellectus*)—perhaps because he had not yet fully worked out their relationship—he has to subordinate him to the wings—that is, to the contemplative and moral powers. The horses are entirely subordinated too as the soul's inferior "parts and natures" and remain undifferentiated. In brief, Ficino is less concerned with the myth as a paradigm of the soul's structure than he is with it as a paradigm of the soul's sequence of activities. He is led, significantly, to ignore the notion of descent entirely, the descent not only to earth but even to the soul's "proper sphere" after the ecstatic vision.

Interestingly, he concludes his chapter by quoting, in a slightly garbled form, from the hymnlike epilogue of the Hermetic *Asclepius* where Trismegistus thanks the Most High for his gifts. This has only come down to us in a Latin translation then attributed to Apuleius,[6] and Ficino seems to have had access to a better text

---

5. Wadsworth, "Landino's *Disp. Camal.*," p. 25; see chap. 6, n. 32 above.
6. See Nock and Festugière, *Corpus Hermeticum* 2:259.

than the editors of his own *Opera Omnia* (who included the *Asclepius* after Ficino's *Pimander* translation). Since Ficino would not have known the *Pimander* in 1457, however, the *Asclepius* constituted for him Hermetism's primary document. Even so, he has to fiddle with the original in order to accommodate it to the charioteer myth. Not only does he transpose *sensu* and *ratione* in the opening phrase, but *sensus* has to be interpreted, unusually, to mean "contemplating" rather than "sensing,"[7] and *intellegentia* to mean not so much "understanding" as "enjoying what the *sensus* has already understood." Clearly the Apuleian phrasing of the prayer corresponds exactly neither to the "Pythagorean" allegorizations adopted by Ficino for the Phaedran myth nor to the meanings that certain key terms habitually carry in his lexicon. However, it is interesting that the climactic moment of the *Asclepius* should be thus juxtaposed with the *Phaedrus* material. For both describe the soul in ecstasy at the uppermost limits of its flight, where the image of a winged angel has been superimposed on that of the Platonic charioteer.

The *Symposium* Commentary was completed by July 1469, though Ficino revised it subsequently.[8] It analyzes the charioteer myth in chapter 14 of the final speech, Marsuppini's presentation of Alcibiades' contribution to the banquet, though in doing so it borrows almost verbatim from the analysis Ficino had already arrived at in his *Ion* epitome (*Opera,* pp. 1281-1284) of a few years

7. Interestingly, *sensus* seems to be equated with *intellectus* in the Latin version of the medieval Arab magic manual, the *Picatrix;* see Garin, *L'età nuova,* pp. 406-408, with citations. We now know that Ficino had read this version; see Daniela Delcorno Branca, "Un discepolo del Poliziano: Michele Acciari," *Lettere italiane* 28 (1976), 470-471; also Eugenio Garin, "Postille sull'ermetismo del Rinascimento," *Rinascimento,* 2d ser., 16 (1976), 245-246.

8. Kristeller, *Sup. Fic.* 1:cxxiii-cxxv, 86-87; and Marcel, ed. cit., pp. 41 and 45; also his *Marsile Ficin,* p. 339.

For Ficino's later revisions, see James A. Devereux, "The Textual History of Ficino's *De Amore,*" *Renaissance Quarterly* 28.2 (1975), 173-182.

For a thorough reappraisal of the MS tradition and of the exact status of the autograph text edited by Marcel, see Sebastiano Gentile, "Per la storia del testo del 'Commentarium in Convivium' di Marsilio Ficino," *Rinascimento,* 2d ser., 21 (1981), 3-27.

A new edition of Marcel's Latin text and Karl Paul Hasse's German translation, with introduction, notes, and a select bibliography by P. R. Blum, has been announced by Meiner of Hamburg for 1984.

earlier.[9] The preceding chapter had dealt with the four species of divine love on the basis of four Plotinian hypostases it had interposed between the One and Body—namely Intelligence, Reason, Opinion, and Nature. This constitutes a different series, we should note, from that adopted for what Kristeller has referred to as his "mature" metaphysical scheme in the opening books of the *Platonic Theology*.[10] Chapter 14 begins, therefore, with this corollary: just as the soul descends through four degrees, it must ascend through four: and it must do so via the series of the four divine madnesses (*furores*), starting with the poetic, and then traversing the hieratic and the prophetic to arrive at the amatory.[11] At this climactic moment, from the viewpoints both of the dialogue and of Ficino's commentary upon it, Ficino turns to the Phaedran charioteer as the ultimate paradigm for the ecstatic soul and its ascent. The Phaedran myth supplies the crowning image, that is, for the *Symposium*'s love theory.

9. The material in the *De Amore* 7.13 and 14 constitutes in fact the opening half of the *Ion* argumentum; in the second half Ficino deals more specifically with the themes of the *Ion:* the poetic madness, the nature and function of the rhapsode, Homer, the Muses and their respective poets.

The date of the *Ion* argumentum or epitome is uncertain. I am adhering to Kristeller's view that the various argumenta were composed by Ficino at the same time as he translated their respective dialogues (*Sup. Fic.* 1:cxvi-cxvii). In this case the *Ion* epitome would date from the same period as the *Ion* translation. If we assume, with Kristeller (*Sup. Fic.* 1:cxlvii ff.), that the order in which the dialogues were translated is the same as that in which they appear in the 1484 edition of the *Platonis Opera Omnia,* then this period can be established as falling between July 1464, when Ficino had only completed ten dialogues, and April 1st, 1466, when he had completed twenty-three, the *Ion* appearing as the fourteenth. Thus the *Ion* epitome would precede the drafting of the *De Amore* by some three to four years and would therefore be the source of the material in *Oratio* 7.13 and 14; see Sheppard, "Influence of Hermias," pp. 107-108; also Yates, *French Academies,* p. 81. We should note, however, that the contrary view that the Plato argumenta were composed together around 1475-1476, after the translations of their respective dialogues had been completed and revised, has been put forward by both della Torre, *Accademia Platonica,* pp. 606-607, and Marcel, *Marsile Ficin,* pp. 457-458 (but see Kristeller's refutation in "Marsilio Ficino as a Beginning Student of Plato," *Scriptorium* 20 [1966], 41-54).

Further discussion of the relationship between the *Phaedrus* material in the *Ion* epitome and that in the *De Amore* will clearly have to depend upon advances in our perception of the dating of the Plato argumenta. From our present viewpoint, however, the two versions may be treated as one: both proffer the same interpretation of the *Phaedrus*'s myth and of its theory of the divine madnesses, the only significant difference being that Ficino's use of the myth in the *De Amore* is itself of considerable interest.

10. Kristeller, *Philosophy,* pp. 106-108, 167-169, 266, 370, 384, 400-401; Allen, "Ficino's Theory of the Five Substances," pp. 19-22, 41-44.

11. For analyses see Gombrich, *Symbolic Images,* pp. 168-170; Sheppard, "Influence of Hermias," pp. 101-103; Yates, *French Academies,* pp. 81-82.

Though chapter 14 contains much that has a bearing on chapter 4 of Ficino's *Phaedrus* Commentary, I shall leave consideration of that for some future occasion and concentrate entirely on the allegorization of the myth. The charioteer is now interpreted as the intelligence (*mens*), and his head or crown as the soul's unity (*unitas*). The good horse is reason and opinion, the bad horse the confused phantasy and the appetite. The chariot is the soul's nature (*natura*) with its wheels returning on themselves. One wing is the intelligence's pursuit of truth, the other the will's desire (*desiderium*) for the good. The four madnesses mark the stages by which the charioteer achieves perfect mastery: first by distinguishing between the horses, then by subjugating the bad horse to the good and both to himself, then by turning himself towards his head or crown, and finally by turning his crown to the crown of all things. In the final, the amatory, madness, the charioteer stops his horses at the stable of divine beauty and gives them the vision of beauty as ambrosia, and the gladness (*laetitia,* not *gaudium*) deriving from that vision as potable nectar. As befits a *Symposium* commentary, the ultimate goal is neither the intellect's Truth, nor the will's Goodness, but Beauty, the goal of the fully integrated and harmonious soul. With Beauty comes the *gladness* it occasions, not the *joy* derived from the contemplation of Truth. Though this account introduces the soul's unity and does full justice to the role of Beauty in Plato's presentation of the myth, it avoids all mention of the pasturage and still depicts the stable as the ultimate home and goal, the divine beauty which occasions vision and gladness. Its most notable contribution, however, concerns the stages of integration and their dependence on the doctrine of the divine madnesses.

Having completed his intricate commentary on the *Symposium*, Ficino probably turned to earlier lecture notes to work up his next long commentary, again on a major dialogue, the *Philebus*.[12] In

12. The dating of this work continues to excite controversy. In my edition I argued for the latter half of 1469 as the most likely date for the composition of the first written version (pp. 48-56). In a generous review Manfred Lentzen drew attention to some weaker links in my chain of reasoning (*Archiv für das Studium der neueren Sprachen und Literaturen* 216 [1979], 218-220). Even so, I believe he failed to take into sufficient account the evidence I had adduced from the various positions occupied by Zoroaster in Ficino's discussions of

the next six months or so he managed, before setting the commentary aside in order to compose his magnum opus, the *Platonic Theology*, to finish one book of thirty-seven chapters and four chapters of a second book as well as some other material that was either appended to the commentary or incorporated into later letters. He makes a number of references to the *Phaedrus*, but the most important occurs in chapter 34, where he discusses the simplicity of man's ultimate end, a simplicity compounded primarily from understanding and secondarily from pleasure. Having introduced the myth in order to amplify his analysis of the "highest part of ourselves," the soul's unity, he turns in chapter 35 to an extended examination of the roles of truth, proportion, and beauty in effecting the proper compound of wisdom and pleasure in the highest good for man.

Again, Ficino gives us some intriguing variations. It is not the charioteer as either the reason, the intelligence, or the soul, but his unity that is raised by the two wings towards the One and the Good. The two wings represent the intellect and the will, the former explores and looks around (*explorare et circumspicere*), the latter searches out (*petere*); but this distinction is redefined as that between seizing hold (*rapere*) and retaining (*retinere* and *adhaerere*), the former constituting wisdom or understanding, the latter pleasure (*voluptas*). Ficino proceeds to gloss two selected lemmata: "The souls who were about to be blessed raised [their] head[s] above the heavens" and "When the charioteer has stopped his horses at the stable, he provides them with ambrosia and also potable nectar" (247E). He identifies the charioteer with his head or crown, and the horses with their wings. The goal of the flight is the Good above heaven: the charioteer's unity stops his horses, "the intellect's pursuit and the will's ardor," at the stable, at the

---

the genealogy of the six Platonic sages. For Ficino's conception of Zoroaster in his *Philebus* Commentary is essentially that which also appears in his *Platonic Theology* 6.1 (ed. Marcel, 1:224), and it is a more mature conception than the one present in the *De Amore*. Indeed, it was Marcel's failure to note the Zoroaster evidence in the *Philebus* Commentary which permitted him to entertain the notion that it preceded the *De Amore*.

Recently I discovered that the passage in the *In Philebum* 1.5 (ed. Allen, pp. 109-111) which I paralleled to one in the *De Amore* 2.2 (ed. Marcel, pp. 146-147) can also be paralleled to one at the end of Ficino's *Hippias* epitome (*Opera*, pp. 1271-1272). An analysis might resolve their mutual relationship and thus their comparative dating.

Good. Ficino interprets the ambrosia as vision, equating it presumably with the wisdom or understanding of the preceding paragraph; and the nectar as joy, equating it similarly with the pleasure. At this point he is careful to argue that the soul's unity is not as such the first "faculty" to see or to rejoice, since the understanding is the first to see and the will is the first to rejoice, and the unity is above both these faculties. But by virtue of the fact that the unity is the soul's prime "faculty," it bestows vision on the understanding and joy on the will. Hence it is above the wings and is the supreme power in the charioteer-chariot complex, the part corresponding to and reflecting the One itself.[13] There are therefore two steps in the flight: the conversion of the intellect and will to higher things and their "being informed" respectively by wisdom and pleasure; then, upon completion of this process, the "plunging" of the soul's unity totally into the universal One, and its identification with it.[14] Thus the goal of the intellect and will is "to become one act for the One's sake."

Ficino next introduces three degrees of happiness which enable him to relate the aims of the *Philebus* and *Phaedrus.* The *Philebus* treats of the first and lowest degree of true happiness, when the soul, still busy ruling the body in this life, converts the intellect and will to higher things and thus enjoys wisdom and pleasure (*voluptas* identified with *gaudium*). The *Phaedrus,* on the other hand, treats of the two higher degrees of happiness: the soul, having abandoned the earthy body in a state of ecstasy or as a hero or demon even, first becomes wholly identified with its intelligence and with the joy, the inner pleasure (*interior voluptas*), that it experiences in being whole. It then becomes divine when its intelligence is wholly identified with its unity, its own image of the absolute One. Ficino makes no attempt to reconcile this, however, with the theory of the four divine madnesses.[15]

13. On this one within the soul in ancient Neoplatonism, see Werner Beierwaltes, "Der Begriff des 'unum in nobis' bei Proklos," *Miscellanea Medievalia* 2 (1963), 255-266; idem, *Proklos: Grundzüge seiner Metaphysik* (Frankfurt, 1965), pp. 367-382; also Wallis, *Neoplatonism,* p. 153. Cf. chap. 6, n. 4 above.

14. Cf. Plotinus, *Enneads* 5.3.14; 5.5.8; 6.7.35; 6.9.3; also J. M. Rist, "Mysticism and Transcendence in Later Neoplatonism." *Hermes* 92 (1964), 213-225.

15. It might, however, be satisfactorily linked with the notion of the three "Olympian" contests that Ficino analyzes in summa 33 of his *Phaedrus* Commentary (ed. Allen, pp. 190-191); for there all four divine furies are confined to the second contest, which is concerned with attaining wisdom and turning away from the soul's moral beauty to its intellectual beauty.

Thus Plato's moving portrait of human weakness and the un-ruliness of passion has become transformed into a myth of the final stages in the ecstatic ascent of the soul not just to the Ideas but to the One. In the process, the original distinctions both be-tween the charioteer and his head or unity, and between the wings and the horses, have become blurred. Once again, moreover, Ficino has ignored the meadow of truth and the nourishment derived from its pasturage in order to concentrate exclusively on the ambrosia and nectar as the supreme gifts, not from a human charioteer to his horses, but from God to an angelic charioteer. The latter has become, virtually, a head separated not only from its body but from all its parts and faculties, lifted up by two cheru-bic wings like the putti heads in a della Robbia frieze to be lost in the blaze of the divine sun. In short, the *Philebus* Commentary contains the most ecstatic and transcendental, and at the same time reductive, version of the Phaedran myth. For it ignores its complexities and details to insist upon its sublimity, its concern with the ultimate, wholly mystical flight of the *Parmenides* beyond the intelligible world of Mind into identification and oneness with the One,[16] the flight which Ficino was later to doubt, if not abso-lutely deny, was the *Phaedrus*'s central mystery.

The last four analyses occur in the second and third chapters of book 17 and in chapters 4 and 8 of book 18 of Ficino's *Platonic Theology,* written between 1470 and 1474.[17] They reveal a more careful scrutinizing of the myth and an awareness at the same time of new possibilities.

Having established the basic postulates of his theory of the soul and its immortality in the earlier books, Ficino turned in books 15, 16, and 17 to "five questions" concerning the soul, questions stim-ulated by the controversial views of Averröes on the unity of the intellect and involving consideration of a number of heresies con-

16. Kristeller, *Philosophy,* pp. 250-251, 368. Cf. chap. 6, n. 4 above.

17. Other references in the *Platonic Theology* specifically to the *Phaedrus* occur at 3.1; 12.3; 13.2, 4; 15.5; 16.7; 17.4; 18.8 (ed. Marcel, 1:135; 2:159, 202, 203, 205, 236; 3:37, 139, 170, 205). In addition, sundry passages quote from, allude to, or imply the *Phaedrus:* e.g. 9.1, 5; 10.2; 13.2, 5; 16.6, 7; 17.3; 18.8 (ed. Marcel, 2:9, 31, 37, 56-58, 206, 210, 242; 3:130, 132, 134, 164, 220). All these references, incidentally, are limited to the *Phaedrus* 244 to 249 —that is, to the sections on the four madnesses, the immortality syllogisms, and the open-ing half of the palinode.

cerning the soul found in "ancient" theology. Book 17 concentrates entirely on the fifth and last question, "What was the soul's condition before its entry into the body, and what will it be when it has departed thence?" Chapter 1 introduces the question and the ancient context generally. Chapter 2 discusses the views of the "last two academies" on the soul's composition, and chapter 3 their views on the various kinds and circuits of souls. The final chapter discusses some of the correct interpretations of Plato as preserved by the "first four academies" and particularly by the first and fourth. Of the six post-Platonic academies chapter 1 lists three Greek and three non-Greek: the old Greek academy under Xenocrates, the middle under Arcesilaus, and the new under Carneades; the Egyptian under Ammonius, the Roman under Plotinus, and the Lycian under Proclus.[18] The three Greek and the Egyptian "interpreted everything Plato had written on the souls' journey" (*circuitus*) in a sense that did not reflect the literal meaning of the text (*aliter quam verba sonarent*). The Roman and Lycian, by contrast, "followed the literal sense (*faciem ipsam*) of the words more strictly (*curiosius*)." The first four, despite their mutual disagreements, had all admitted that much of what Plato had written was entirely poetical. Nevertheless Xenocrates and Ammonius in particular had argued—correctly, Ficino feels—that Plato had propounded certain truths, notably those concerning God's providence and the soul's immortality. In chapter 4 Ficino makes a careful commitment:

So we, following in the footsteps of Xenocrates and Ammonius, do not deny that Plato affirmed some things about the soul. Many things by him, however, which concern the soul's circuit, we think poetical, and we

18. Did Ficino ever mean to suggest a parallel between the hexad of *prisci theologi* and the six post-Platonic academies? As E. N. Tigerstedt has noted in his *The Decline and Fall of the Neoplatonic Interpretation of Plato: An Outline and Some Observations,* Commentationes Humanarum Litterarum: Societas Scientiarum Fennica, vol. 52 (Helsinki, 1974), pp. 19-20, Ficino, like the ancient Neoplatonists themselves, did not conceive of the history of Platonism in terms of Old, Middle, and New. Middle Platonism he largely ignored, and the New he regarded as the direct and legitimate heir to the Old. Even so, he did find a legitimate place, as we can see, for the Skeptical Academy under Arcesilaus and Carneades; and he was well aware of the general development and the schools (*scholae*) of what we now know as Neoplatonism, as chap. 38 of his *Parmenides* Commentary (*Opera*, pp. 1155-1156) demonstrates. See Allen, "Ficino's Theory of the Five Substances," pp. 34-36.

understand them in other than the literal sense. We are emboldened to do so, moreover, since Plato did not discover the soul-circuits himself, but reported the views of others: in the first instance the circuits which the Egyptian priests symbolized in the figure of the purging of souls, and then those chanted only in their hymns by Orpheus, Empedocles, and Heraclitus.[19] And we leave aside the fact that Pythagoras always introduced the transmigrations of souls in his customary discussions and in his symbols.[20]

Predictably, Ficino wishes to avoid the notion that Plato himself believed in reincarnation in either its conservative or its more radical form.[21] While Plotinus, for instance, is a reliable, indeed eminent, authority on nearly every aspect of interpreting Plato, he was wrong to espouse metempsychosis on the basis of an overly literal reading of certain remarks in the *Phaedo* (113A), the *Phaedrus* (249B), and the *Republic* (10.620A-D). The same might be said of Pythagoras, an otherwise unimpeachable ancient theologian whose system Plato, after his youthful search for enlightenment, chose to espouse as "the more probable."[22]

19. In his edition, 3:165-166, Marcel identified these references as follows: Orpheus, *Hymns* 4.9 and 87.3-5 (Abel); Empedocles, frag. 115 (ed. Hermann Diels and Walther Kranz, *Die Fragmente der Vorsokratiker,* 3 vols., 11th ed. [Zurich and Berlin, 1964], 1:356-358); Heraclitus, frag. 15 (Diels-Kranz, 1:154-155). The Egyptian reference remains unaccounted for but probably refers to passages in Iamblichus's *De Mysteriis* and/or in the *Corpus Hermeticum.*

20. Marcel refers us to Ficino's translation of the *Symbola* (*Opera*, p. 1979); but it would be interesting to know what particular gnomes Ficino had in mind, probably the last, no. 39: *Ab animalibus abstine.* Heninger notes in his *Sweet Harmony,* pp. 66 n. 54, 274, that Ficino used the collection of *symbola* in Iamblichus's *Protrepticae Orationes ad Philosophiam* 21 as the text for his Latin translation, but we should note that he has additions to nos. 13 and 15 and that no. 21 is out of order. Ficino would also have turned to Diogenes Laertius's account in his *Lives* 8.17-18, 34-35, and possibly to Porphyry, Plutarch, Clement of Alexandria, St. Jerome and others (see Heninger, *Sweet Harmony,* pp. 57-58). His own commentary on the *Symbola,* which is extant only in MS Vat. lat. 5953, fols. 316ᵛ-318ᵛ (reprinted in Kristeller, *Sup. Fic.* 2:100-103), deals with just seven of the gnomes and with none concerning transmigration.

21. That is, in traducianism, reincarnation proper, and metempsychosis. See Allen, "Two Commentaries," p. 127; also chap. 10, pp. 241 ff. below.

22. *Platonic Theology* 17.4 (ed. Marcel, 3:168): "meminisse debemus Platonem pythagoricam sapientiam, quae a Zoroaste manaverat, ab Archyta, Euryto, Philolao didicisse, et cum peragrasset orbem aliasque omnes philosophorum opiniones examinavisset, pythagoricam denique sectam tanquam verisimiliorem prae caeteris elegisse." Cf. Apuleius, *De Platone et Eius Dogmate* 1.3 (ed. Thomas, 3:84). See Allen, "Marsilio Ficino on Plato's Pythagorean Eye," pp. 173-174.

Three pieces of evidence alert us, Ficino says, to Plato's reservations about certain Pythagorean theories. First, Plato presents the same people who had formulated these theories as still in the process of debating them. Next, he presents Socrates as referring doubtfully to what he has heard others say. Finally, he never ultimately confirms in the *Laws,* which included for Ficino the *Epinomis* as its thirteenth book, and which was the one work apart from the *Letters* in which he spoke *in propria persona,* what he had written earlier. Indeed, Ficino continues, the evidence of the second and seventh *Letters* (314C and 341C) makes it clear that Plato had never intended to reveal publicly his inmost thoughts on theological matters, and had contented himself with expounding the views of others. There were two exceptions, however. Plato had affirmed God's concern with human affairs, and also God's rewarding or punishing the actions of the immortal soul. (The *Timaeus* also argues—and this would be a third exception—for the world's creation, as opposed to its existence from all eternity.) In short, Ficino accepts some of the important caveats developed by the earlier academies over and against the too literal readings of certain figurative passages by Plotinus, Proclus, and their followers, particularly of passages involving theological speculation about the soul's flight and fall.

The Phaedran myth is just such a passage, however. Hence Ficino's remark in the preceding, the third, chapter of the *Platonic Theology,* book 17, the chapter specifically concerned with the views of the Roman and Lycian academies on the souls and their circuits: "undoubtedly many of Plato's comments are poetical here rather than philosophical."[23] Hence too his curiously guarded formulae for introducing his analysis of the soul's composition in chapter 2, formulae such as "I won't go into" and "I'll leave aside." He assumes that the following views are those of Pythagoreans and Platonists of the Roman and Lycian schools rather than of Plato himself. It is they, not Plato, who call the soul a chariot and attribute to it a straight line, a lower, closed circle, and a

---

23. Ed. Marcel, 3:159; trans. Allen, *Charioteer,* p. 230. Cf. *Platonic Theology* 18.5 (ed. Marcel, 3:196): *delectat tamen cum antiquis interdum poetice ludere:* this means "yet it is pleasant sometimes, as the ancients do, to play poetically" (*contra* Walker, *Magic,* p. 40). Cf. too Pico, *Commento particolare* (ed. Garin, pp. 580-581).

higher, helical one, signifying by them a chariot's three possible paths: the straight path to the stars, the circular path of the seven planets, and the circular but helical path of the sphere of the fixed stars. The two schools also assign the following literally to the soul: two wings (the impulse of the intellect towards the Truth, and of the will towards the Good); a charioteer (the *mens*);[24] a head for the charioteer (the divine unity); two superior and two inferior horses (interpreted in the light of the *Sophist* as identity and rest, difference and motion);[25] and a good and a bad horse (the irascible and concupiscible natures or powers). Ficino makes it clear that we are treating of a complex of notions developed by Pythagorean sages such as Plato's own teachers, Archytas, Eurytus, and Philolaus, but then worked up poetically by Plato into the charioteer myth.[26] Plato was fully aware, that is, of the figurative nature of much of what he was writing, even though he was subsequently taken too literally by the last two ancient academies. At all events, the Pythagorean myth can still serve as a model for all rational souls, angelic, demonic, heroic, and human in both unfallen and fallen states.

In chapter 3 Ficino returns to the *Phaedrus* as interpreted by the literalists in order to describe the meaning of the nine lives and the nine divine companies. Interestingly, the companies no longer gaze solely upon the meadow of truth but on all things: on the Ideas above heaven, on the celestials within it, and on the naturals below it, heaven being simply the abode of the celestials and not yet the realm of the intellectual gods. In their many circuits they repeat the journey from cause to effect to cause again (compare the earlier reference to the helical, circular, and straight lines). The fall occurs because the concupiscible power "turns away from contemplating to generating" and does not return to the Idea at the

---

24. Ficino seems to have wavered between identifying the charioteer with the *mens* and identifying him with the *ratio;* see p. 223 below.

25. Here Ficino is obviously working with the image of the *quadriga* rather than the *biga;* but this seems to be an isolated case. Cf. chap. 4, n. 3 above.

26. Cf. Ficino's Latin translation of the conclusion to Pythagoras's *Aurea Verba (Opera,* pp. 1978-1979): "Optimam deinde sententiam tibi velut aurigam praepone: Corpore deposito cum liber ad aethera perges, / Evades hominem, factus Deus aetheris almi." Hierocles' commentary on these verses specifically refers to Plato's *Phaedrus,* but Ficino never mentions Hierocles in his works.

circuit's head. What exactly precipitates this turning is undetermined, except that the concupiscible power is excited by the generative power, which is one of the "natures" included in it and which "has been waxing stronger now its time has come." The many subsequent transformations described by Plato in 294A-C are largely, though Ficino is careful not to say exclusively, poetical.

Book 18 treats of opinions concerning the soul common to all theologians, Jewish, Christian, and Moslem.[27] It deals with issues such as: Are souls created daily? When is the soul joined to the body? Whence does it enter the body and whither depart? What is the nature of its incorporeal state? and so forth. The *Phaedrus*'s myth is referred to twice: in chapter 4 Ficino treats of the chariot as the soul's vehicle and in chapter 8 of the two circuits.

Chapter 4 is particularly notable for its extended analysis of the life of the soul's aethereal body, "its immortal garment," which is naturally circular in shape though molded on earth to man's mortal likeness.[28] Man must have a body, given his midway status between the beasts with their irrational souls and the angels with their pure intelligences, but he has various kinds of body. The purest is the aethereal "vehicle" or "chariot," the *igneus spiritus*; less pure is the aerial body, the *aereus spiritus*;[29] and least pure is the

27. Judaism, Christianity, and Islam were of course *the* three world religions for Ficino. Just as they had a common monotheistic core, so each could be reconciled with the universal philosophy of Orphic-Pythagorean Platonism, the "religion" of antiquity. It was precisely the Renaissance Neoplatonists' ecumenism, syncretism, and irenicism that George of Trebizond found so contemptible and dangerous; see Garin, *Rinascite e rivoluzioni,* pp. 113-120: "A ogni spirito di concordia, di tolleranza, di conciliazione; all'appello insistente per l'unità della cultura, le *Comparationes* [del Trapezunzio] oppongono, con l'antitesi durissima fra Platone ed Aristotele, la guerra implacabile fra l'Oriente islamico e l'Occidente cristiano" (p. 119).

The importance of Renaissance Neoplatonism in the history of religion has yet to be explored; but see de Gandillac, "Neoplatonism and Christian Thought"; Garin, *Cultura filosofica,* pp. 127-142; Balbino Giuliano, *L'idea religiosa di Marsilio Ficino e il concetto di una dottrina esoterica* (Cerignola, 1904); and Giuseppe Anichini, *L'umanesimo e il problema della salvezza in Marsilio Ficino* (Milan, 1937).

28. For the history of this concept, see Dodds, *Proclus: The Elements of Theology,* app. 2; Robert Christian Kissling, "The ὄχημα-πνεῦμα of the Neo-Platonists and the *De Insomniis* of Synesius of Cyrene," *American Journal of Philology* 43.4 (1922), 318-330; Paul Moraux, "Quinta Essentia," in Pauly-Wissowa-Kroll, *Realencyclopädie der classischen Altertumswissenschaft* 24.1 (1963), 1171-1263 at 1251-1256: "Das ätherische Vehikel der Seele"; Verbeke, *L'évolution de la doctrine du pneuma,* esp. chap. 6; Walker, "Astral Body in Renaissance Medicine"; idem, *Magic,* pp. 38-40. Cf. chap. 4, nn. 28 and 29 above.

29. See chap. 1, n. 29 and chap. 4, n. 29 above.

body of all four elements. Until he commences the ascent to godhead, man occupies all three bodies, as we have seen. To the aethereal chariot the soul imparts "a vivifying act," known in the technical language of Neoplatonism as the soul's *idolum,* "an irrational but immortal life."[30] Similarly the soul gives "an irrational but long-lasting life" to the aerial body, and "an irrational but mortal life" to the elemental body. The *idolum* is not, note, the irrational soul (normally identified in man with the *natura*) but an irrational "act of life" bestowed in the first place on the aethereal body by the rational soul as its image.[31] How the *idolum* of the aethereal body and its lower equivalents for the aerial and elemental bodies are mutually related, or whether the various bodies possess potentialities of some kind to receive the *idolum* and its lower equivalents—these and related questions Ficino leaves unexplored. Since the soul never actually loses its aethereal body (for it would then be a pure intelligence), the idol never vanishes; so it too has a de facto immortality and will accompany the aethereal body and the rational soul to heaven. Apart from the obvious theosophical and theurgical dimensions, the postulation of the idol, which Ficino further defines, following the *Timaeus* 69C, as "the soul's mortal form (*species*)," begs for an explanation in terms of

---

30. Of particular significance was frag. 158 (ed. Des Places) from the *Chaldaic Oracles,* which Ficino quotes from here and which he almost certainly knew from Psellus's important commentary (ed. Des Places, in *Oracles chaldaïques,* app., pp. 162-164): "but the idol also has its part in the region bathed in light." Cf. chap. 4, n. 27 above.

31. Ficino also deals at length with the *idolum* in his *Platonic Theology* 13.2 (ed. Marcel, 2:207-210), where he carefully distinguishes it in man from the *natura:* "Animae quippe rationales non modo vim illam habent intelligendi, per quam angelicae sunt et in ordine providentiae numerantur, verumetiam vim illam vivificam rectricemque corporis, quae alit corpus in corpore, sentit corporalia per corpus, movet corpus per locum regitque in loco, quam vim idolum, id est simulacrum rationalis animae Platonici nuncupant. In hoc idolo insunt semina motionum et qualitatum omnium quae in corpore explicantur ab anima.... Sequitur natura. Nam in quolibet corpore animato est certa quaedam eius affectio sive complexio efficax atque vitalis, quam virtus animae suae vivifica corpori tribuit. Hanc volunt esse Platonici naturam corporum, quasi quoddam vestigium animae in corpore sive umbram" (p. 207). See Heitzman, "La libertà e il fato," p. 359; Garin, *Lo zodiaco della vita,* pp. 79-80; and above all Kristeller, *Philosophy,* pp. 369-378 and 385.

Juxtaposed, the passages in 13.2 and 18.4 are, however, difficult to reconcile; for 13.2 treats both the *idolum* and the *natura* as faculties, following Plotinus in the *Enneads* 1.1.5-12, while 18.4 treats of the *idolum* as "an act of life" imparted to the aethereal body alone, the *natura* presumably being the act of "irrational and mortal life" imparted to the earthly body. Ficino's notion of the *idolum* and the nature of his indebtedness to Plotinus and others require in fact a full-length study. Fortunately, he avoided the term *idolum* altogether in his *Phaedrus* Commentary, as we have seen.

Ficino's general theory of what constitutes a species; it cannot be reconciled, superficially at least, with Ficino's statement in chapter 46 of his *Sophist* epitome that "just as the species itself is called εἶδος in Greek, so too can the efflux from the species' body be called the εἴδωλον, the specimen as it were from the species or the attenuated species."[32] At all events, it suggests that Ficino's views on the dogma of the resurrection of the body may contain other, unexpected dimensions.

The idol is not only, however, the life of the aethereal chariot, but embraces in the Plotinian tradition "the irrational and confused phantasy,"[33] and also the sense or senses which enable a soul to hear the heavenly harmonies and to hear and see demons. In the aethereal body these senses are "common"[34] and "impassible"— that is, unlocalized, incorruptible, and infallible; in the aerial body "common" and "passible"—that is, unlocalized but corruptible and fallible; and in the elemental body both localized—that is, distributed among the individual organs—and "passible." This raises a number of interesting problems concerning the need for, and the quality of, sensation among rational souls.

Finally, in chapter 8 of book 18 of the *Platonic Theology,* in discussing the condition of the pure soul, Ficino claims that the souls

---

32. *Opera,* p. 1293: "sicut species ipsa Graece dicitur εἶδος, sic et effluxus e corpore speciali εἴδωλον appelletur, quasi ex specie specimen speciesve tenuis." For a long and complex analysis of the metaphysical status of the species, see Ficino's *Philebus* Commentary 1.13-14, 17-22, 27 (ed. Allen, pp. 144-159, 176-215, 248-261); see also Kristeller, *Philosophy,* pp. 81-83.

33. Ficino seems to have distinguished, at least on particular occasions as in the *Platonic Theology* 8.1 (ed. Marcel, 1:285-286), between the imagination and the phantasy, in contradistinction to many, like Aquinas, who considered them identical. Whereas the imagination merely unites sense perceptions, the phantasy formulates preliminary judgments of them and thus forms "intentions"; in a way it is "the gatherer-together of the five senses," in the words of the *Platonic Theology* 13.2 (ed. Marcel, 2:210). See Heitzman, "L'agostinismo avicennizzante," pp. 309-319; Kristeller, *Philosophy,* pp. 234-236, 369; and, most importantly, Klein, "L'imagination comme vêtement de l'âme." Klein insists upon the part played by both Avicenna and Albertus Magnus in the formation of Ficino's psychology and argues that for all of them the imagination is a faculty of the sensitive soul, the phantasy of the rational (p. 24).

Here, however, as in the extract quoted above from the *De Amore* 7.14 (ed. Marcel, p. 259), Ficino refers to the "confused" phantasy; the addition of the epithet may signify that it now means the same as the imagination.

34. Ficino is not referring to the Aristotelian notion of the "common sense," which he customarily, *more Platonico,* identified with the imagination. Cf. *Sophist* epitome, chap. 46 (*Opera,* p. 1293): "cognosces animam primo quidem efficaciterque imaginationem in coelesti vehiculo exercere, sensumque prorsus omnem per totum vehiculum expedire."

first take part in the celestial circuit with the celestial gods and then in the supercelestial circuit with the supercelestial gods. The first entails accompanying various stars and heavenly beings in the celestial (aethereal) vehicle, and taking part with them in the dual activities of "governing" the lower world and "discoursing" with the reason through the species of things. The second entails accompanying the angels in gazing at the Ideas in an instantaneous act of intellectual intuition. Clearly, Ficino believes at this point that the *Phaedrus* describes or intends these circuits as two separate events: having followed the celestial gods, as in Plotinus's interpretation, we then leave them to follow the supercelestial gods, as in Iamblichus's and Proclus's interpretation.[35] Later, as we have seen, Ficino decided that the *Phaedrus* was not directly concerned with the supercelestial cavalcade, here identified explicitly with the angels, but with the jovian celestial cavalcade, which was itself capable of traversing the realm of the intellectual heaven, thence to gaze upwards at the intelligibles of its own accord. That is, it fulfilled independently the three functions of intellectual (intuitive) contemplation, rational discoursing, and providential governing or caring. This marked an absolutely critical advance.

The "ambrosia" he allegorizes as "the sweet, clear gazing at the truth," and the "nectar" as "the excellent providing." The latter reading particularly improves on those of the *De Voluptate,* the *De Amore,* and the *Philebus* Commentary, but still falls short of Ficino's eventual recognition that they must always be distinguished from the pasturage.

To conclude, in the *Platonic Theology* and notably in the last three books, where Ficino treats of the great aetiological and eschatological mysteries concerning the soul, the charioteer myth occupies a position somewhat different from its role in the earlier works. It is now the test case in the delicate issue of deciding how literally Plato meant us to read his poetic figures at large, and concomitantly how deeply indebted he was to Pythagoreanism (since he was more likely to have been indebted in his first work than in

---

35. Plotinus, we should recall, makes no distinction between the "intelligible" realm and the "intellectual"; for this was Iamblichus's innovation, though one adopted by all the later Neoplatonists and read back into Plotinus and Plato. See chap. 5, n. 14 above; and chap. 10, p. 240 below.

any other). That the dialogue had led both Roman and Lycian academies astray—had been the occasion, indeed, for their disagreement—has a bearing surely on Ficino's carefully distancing himself from his primary sources of ancient commentary on the *Phaedrus,* namely the scholia of Hermias and the various sections in Proclus's *Theologia Platonica,* particularly 4.4-26. Conceivably his closer scrutiny of some of the problems in the course of writing his own *Platonic Theology* might have induced an onset of skepticism, or mistrust in his ability to interpret the myth correctly, especially since it involved major theological issues such as the role of the soul's aethereal vehicle and its idol (the *Platonic Theology*'s most signal innovation). For, however unintentionally at the time, Ficino was not to embark on another extended analysis of the myth until the *Phaedrus* Commentary itself many years later.

In reviewing these four earlier interpretations of the myth, along with the two separate interpretations in the *Phaedrus* argumentum and in the commentary proper, two contrasting aspects strike us immediately. First is their vertical integrity, their independently coherent portraits or visions of the Phaedran charioteer; for none of the accounts depends directly on another, though they do sometimes share details of exegesis. Second, however, is the horizontal development and mutation of individual features as Ficino adapts the myth to differing contexts and subjects it to varying interpretations. In this respect the Phaedran myth is, I believe, unique. No other figurative episode in Plato engaged Ficino's attention so constantly and so generatively: not the Cave, not Er, not Aristophanes' androgyne, not even the *Phaedrus*'s own story of Theuth, favorite though it was.

With the parts of the chariot and charioteer, certain allegorizations stayed unchanged either from the very beginning or from the time a particular component was first interpreted. For instance, the charioteer's head is always interpreted as the soul's unity after its first appearance in the *Ion* epitome and the *De Amore*; and the wheels, when allegorized at all, invariably signify the soul's self-motion, though the Commentary's seventh chapter introduces the further refinement that their twin motions simultaneously stand for the soul's turning upon itself and its movement forward towards higher things. Other components undergo slight but significant variation. For instance, the charioteer himself represents either the soul generally or one of its two faculties, the reason or the intellect; and the chariot, which the *De Voluptate* and the *Philebus* Commentary do not deal with, goes from being the soul's nature in the *De Amore* to being the celestial vehicle or body in the *Platonic Theology* and the *Phaedrus* Commentary, chapters 7 and 8.

Allegorization of the wings, on the other hand, is subject to greater change. In the *De Voluptate* they commence as the contemplative and moral powers and then become consistently defined either as the intellect and will themselves or as the "impulse" driving these faculties towards truth and goodness—the latter modification becoming necessary when the charioteer is defined as the intellect, as in the *Ion* epitome, the *De Amore,* and the *Platonic Theology*. But in the seventh chapter of the Commentary they are once again back to being simply "the powers lifting the soul," since Ficino has shifted his attention to the charioteer on the one hand and to the horses on the other, in contradistinction, say, to the *Philebus* Commentary, where the wings are accorded pride of place.

The most radical development occurs with the horses. Commencing as merely the "parts and natures" of the soul subject to reason and to the "contemplative and moral powers," and defined by the *Phaedrus* argumentum as the rational and irrational appetites, they become in the *Ion* epitome and the *De Amore* "reason and opinion" and either the "sense's appetite" (as in the *De Amore*) or the "nature" (as in the *Ion* epitome). In the *Philebus* Commentary—as we might anticipate, given its consistently reductive idealism—they reach their sublimest signification as the intellect's "pursuit" and the will's "ardor" and thus become in effect simply extensions of the wings as intellect and will. The *Platonic Theology* introduces a "Pythagorean" elaboration that suggests there are four higher horses, which Ficino sees in terms of the ontological categories in the *Sophist,* and two lower horses representing the irascible and concupiscible powers or natures. Finally the *Phaedrus* Commentary expands on and systematizes this division. The seventh chapter, using the myth as a model for the liberated soul, allegorizes the white horse as the rational power and the black horse as the appetite, the imagination, and the nature. Summa 31 contrariwise, using the myth as a model for the earthbound soul, defines them as the irascible and concupiscible powers. While the higher and lower models correspond, an interesting transference takes place in that the irascible power gets switched from the white to the black horse, as noted above. Of all the myth's parts or components, in short, the horses are most subject to variation and are the surest guides to the orientation of a particular interpretation, at one extreme being identified virtually with the wings, at the other with the lowest of the appetitive powers.

With the circuitous flight the situation is somewhat different, given the superficial treatment elsewhere and the extended and penetrating analysis of its various stages in the Commentary. Whereas gazing on the meadow of truth is interpreted in the *De Voluptate* and the *Platonic Theology* as contemplating "what truly exists," namely the Ideas, and receives no mention whatsoever in the *Ion* epitome, the *De Amore,* or the *Philebus* Commentary, it is not until the *Phaedrus* Commentary that Ficino really concerns himself with the location of the supercelestial place in terms of the intelligible world of late Neoplatonic ontology. Accordingly, "returning home to the stable" in all the earlier versions, bar the *Platonic Theology,* which omitted this detail, Ficino had always interpreted to mean *advancing* beyond the meadow of truth to the ultimate vision either of Beauty or Goodness or of God Himself. In the *Phaedrus* Commentary, however, he took a closer look at Plato's text, which speaks of the chariots *descending* the interior of heaven after the vision, and confronted and solved the interpretative crux by borrowing and then adapting the Neoplatonic and more particularly the Proclian distinctions between the intelligible, intellectual, and celestial realms.

In the earlier versions, similarly, the ambrosia and nectar, which Plato had the charioteer throw before the steeds after they descended home, Ficino consistently interprets as the contemplative vision of God, Beauty, Truth, or the One Good, and as the joy, gladness, or pleasure deriving from it (depending on his theoretical frames at the time). The one notable exception is the *Platonic Theology*'s allegorization of nectar as the "excellent and benevolent providence" which the soul extends to inferiors. Once again, the conceptual breakthrough comes with the *Phaedrus* Commentary. If the stable is lower than the summit of the dome of the intellectual heaven, then the ambrosia and nectar cannot symbolize man's immediate response to the vision of the intelligibles but must symbolize something subsequent and inferior to that vision. Hence Ficino's decision in the Commentary to allegorize ambrosia as "stopping the lower powers in the causes and in what is good for them" and nectar as "strengthening and inciting these powers to provide for inferiors." Ambrosia and nectar are thus the single most significant pointers to the Commentary's emphasis on the providential duties of all superiors towards their inferiors in the universal hierarchy.

Finally, the goal of the flight itself shifts from Truth to Beauty, to the One Good, to the Ideas, to the Ideas specifically of Justice, Temperance, and Knowledge, to the Idea of Beauty. This is partially because the theoretical frame shifts from being hedonism in the *De Voluptate* to being a concern respectively with the divine madnesses and primarily the amatory madness in the *Ion* epitome and the *De Amore,* with the human happiness in the *Philebus* Commentary, and with Pythagorean concepts of the afterlife in the *Platonic Theology.* Only the *Phaedrus* Commentary focuses on the structure and cosmological implications of the charioteer myth with no other goal but accurate exegesis. Each other version in a way distorts the myth by adapting it to its own theoretical ends. Admittedly, the shifting depiction of the cavalcade's goal may also reflect the stages in Ficino's understanding of and response to the myth, an understanding that was not fully matured until the 1490s. In short, we must admit the possibility of both external and internal reasons for the adaptations and mutations.

If nothing more, a genetic approach focuses our attention on the existence of two distinct layers of interpretation in the final version of the *Phaedrus* Commentary: the first embodied in its argumentum—and specifically chapter 2—written, as I have argued previously, along with other argumenta in the 1460s when

Ficino translated the Platonic corpus; the second embodied in the eight chapters of commentary proper and their corresponding summae, and also in summa 31.

As we might expect, the allegorization of the *Phaedrus* argumentum is much more closely allied, as is its orientation and language generally, to that of the *Ion* epitome and the *De Amore* (it is contemporaneous with the first and predates the second by only a year or so) than to the maturer allegorization of the commentary proper. Notably it defines the horses as "the rational and irrational appetites" (the latter including both irascible and concupiscible); and the goal of the flight seems to be Beauty as it is in the *Ion* epitome and the *De Amore*. On the other hand, the argumentum is confusing insofar as it fails to distinguish the model for the earthbound soul, as we find it later in summa 31, led by the charioteer as the reason, wingless still and drawn entirely by the steeds, from the model for the liberated soul, now lifted on the wings of the intellect's "impulse" for truth and the will's for goodness. It also fails to mention the soul's unity or its flight, though its definition of the two wings suggests that the *Platonic Theology* borrowed from it.

Though there from the onset in Plato, Ficino did not exploit the distinction between the winged and wingless charioteer until the *Phaedrus* Commentary. For he could only really do so after he had plotted both the descent to the stable and the descent to matter in terms of Neoplatonic ontology. To put it another way, while earlier analyses concentrated on the parts of the chariot and the charioteer and their mutual subordinations, later analyses not only elaborated on these but dealt in considerable detail with the flight itself, both ascending and descending. Still, even in the *De Voluptate* Ficino was aware of the Pythagorean nature of much of the *Phaedrus*'s material on the flight; and perhaps it was this that spurred him on to explore the interpretational possibilities of the myth's opening sections, while simultaneously making him pause before the later sections, those where he would have to argue *inter alia* that Plato never embraced the doctrine of metempsychosis.

While presenting a full-scale account in only five works besides the *Phaedrus* Commentary, Ficino used the charioteer myth as a leitmotiv throughout his career. In the *Apology* epitome, for instance, the spur, rein, wings, and chariot are not merely alluded to but function as basic modules in his argumentation.[36] This goes for other passages in his treatises and letters, where the myth has a subsurface life and colors the formulation and articulation of a number of arguments and proofs. Comparable to such running metaphors as the sun, light, shadow, fire, and so forth, in the philosophical discourse of Ficino and other Neoplatonists, ancient, medieval, Byzantine, and Renaissance, it does not have to be explicitly invoked to be operative as a controlling idea or image. While God, Truth, and Goodness are naturally figurable in terms of the sun or light, the charioteer is a fitting emblem for man, his amphibious nature and heroic quest, an emblem that may still be used apparently to body forth the three-tiered structure of the human brain,[37] even as it evokes the clash of fell and mighty opposites on the windy plains of Troy.[38]

The first, the most poetic, the most Pythagorean of Plato's works, the *Phaedrus* had thus transformed the traditional figure of martial prowess into one of spiritual struggle and self-transcendence, had endowed the maddened Achilles with a seraph's wings. From the onset of his career, therefore, it supplied Ficino with a difficult but supremely arresting symbol for man's ecstatic response to beauty in all of its varied forms, and for the mystical ascent that had borne Moses and Elijah, Parmenides and St. Paul, to the inmost heavens. At last, just three years before he died, he was moved to present it to a Florence already in the throes of political and religious turmoil at the close of its own Platonic century as Plato's truly definitive image both for fallen and for liberated man.

36. *Opera,* pp. 1386-1389, and esp. p. 1387. Earlier I suggested that translating the *Phaedrus* may have impelled him directly to the *Apology* (*Charioteer,* p. 16).

37. Carl Sagan, *The Dragons of Eden: Speculations on the Evolution of Human Intelligence* (New York, 1977), p. 79.

38. Or of Chicago: see Robert M. Pirsig, *Zen and the Art of Motorcycle Maintenance: An Inquiry into Values* (New York, 1974), esp. chap. 30.

Chapter 10: Sources

A scholar interested in the sources and background of Ficino's terms and propositions could approach the commentary chapters, and indeed many of the summae, from a number of angles and often at considerable length. Even so, an authoritative *index fontium* would still elude him; for this must depend on a comprehensive understanding of Ficino's reading. Though advances have been made in recent years in the area of identifying some of the manuscripts that he owned and annotated, or borrowed or had access to,[1] research is still in the preliminary stages. Apart from works he actually translated, and those he quoted from constantly (if frequently without acknowledgment) like Augustine's *De Trinitate, De Vera Religione,* and *De Civitate Dei* and Aquinas's *Summa contra Gentiles,*[2] we cannot be sure for the most part of what he read attentively or the order in which he did so, though we do

---

1. For example, see: for Plotinus, Paul Henry, "Les manuscrits grecs de travail de Marsile Ficin, le traducteur des Ennéades de Plotin," in *Association Guillaume Budé: Congrès de Tours et Poitiers* (Paris, 1954), pp. 323-328; for Iamblichus, Martin Sicherl, *Die Handschriften, Ausgaben und Übersetzungen von Iamblichos "De Mysteriis": Eine kritisch-historische Studie* (Berlin, 1957), pp. 22-37, 182-188; for Proclus, Saffrey, "Notes platoniciennes"; for Olympiodorus (Damascius), L. G. Westerink, "Ficino's Marginal Notes on Olympiodorus in Riccardi Greek MS 37," *Traditio* 24 (1968), 351-378; for Cicero and Macrobius, Alberti, "Ficino e il Codice Riccardiano"; for Julian's "Hymn to the Sun," Garin, "Per la storia della cultura filosofica del Rinascimento"; for the Latin version of the Arab *Picatrix,* idem, "Postille sull'ermetismo," pp. 245-246; for Hyginus, Paola Zambelli's discovery of notes scribbled on the flyleaf of MS 690 in Milan's Biblioteca Trivulziana (Castello Sforzesco)—though Hyginus is never mentioned, incidentally, in Ficino's works (private letter from Kristeller, March 1, 1981).

In general see Kristeller, *Sup. Fic.* 1:liii-lv, and *Studies,* pp. 158-174, 585.

2. For Ficino and Augustine, see Heitzman, "L'agostinismo avicennizante"; Eugenio Garin, "S. Agostino e Marsilio Ficino," *Bollettino storico agostiniano* 16 (1940), 41-47; Kristeller, *Studies,* pp. 355-372; Tarabochia Canavero, "Agostino e Tommaso"; eadem, "S. Agostino nella Teologia Platonica di Marsilio Ficino."

For Ficino and Aquinas, see Étienne Gilson, "Marsile Ficin et le *Contra Gentiles,*" *Archives d'histoire doctrinale et littéraire du Moyen Âge* 24 (1957), 101-113; Eugenio Garin, "Marsilio Ficino e la *Contra Gentiles,*" *Giornale critico della filosofia italiana* 39 (1959), 158-159; Cornelio Fabro, "Influenze tomistiche nella filosofia del Ficino," *Studia patavina* 3 (1959), 396-413; Kristeller, *Studies,* pp. 35-97; idem, *Thomisme,* pp. 93-104;

know he received a thorough Aristotelian training in his youth and considerable exposure to medical texts.[3]

As an eclectic, he accepted—and rejected—ideas wherever he found them. Since we are mainly ignorant, however, about his habits as a reader and notetaker, annotator and digester, we can rarely ascertain in a particular instance whether he was working from what we recognize as the primary source (in a good or bad text) or from a secondary source that was itself quoting, paraphrasing, epitomizing, or garbling either the primary source or yet another secondary source. Marcel has even suggested that we cannot always be sure that Ficino was utilizing his sources in what we would now regard as scholarly good faith. For at times he seems deliberately to have avoided identifying them in order perhaps not to alienate orthodox or intellectually timid readers.[4] And this is quite apart from carelessness, forgetfulness, repeating prior misquotations, or adapting them rather radically to his own needs. All we can safely say is that his philosophical background embraced an exceptionally wide range of classical, patristic, medieval, early Renaissance, and possibly Byzantine sources that no one yet is in a position to unravel, let alone evaluate, and that included writings we currently assume to be spurious or apocryphal or themselves derived from originals unknown to Ficino and his contemporaries, such as the *Liber de Causis*.

Tarabochia Canavero, "Agostino e Tommaso"; Ardis B. Collins, *The Secular Is Sacred: Platonism and Thomism in Ficino's "Platonic Theology"* (The Hague, 1974). For Ficino's unacknowledged borrowings from Aquinas and Augustine in his *Philebus* Commentary, see Allen's edition.

3. He was tutored by Niccolò Tignosi; see A. Rotondò, "Nicolò Tignosi da Foligno," *Rinascimento,* 2d ser., 9 (1958), 217-255. See also della Torre, *Accademia Platonica,* pp. 485-501; Kristeller, *Studies,* pp. 42-43, 46-50, 191-211; Garin, *Cultura filosofica,* p. 63n; and Samuel Jones Hough, "An Early Record of Marsilio Ficino," *Renaissance Quarterly* 30.3 (1977), 301-304.

4. Ed. *Théologie platonicienne* 1:29. In the preface to his Plotinus translations, *Opera,* p. 1537, Ficino speaks of providing "acute minds" (*acuta ingenia*) with a "philosophical lure" that will enable their reason to guide them back to Christianity. In his *Agrippa and the Crisis of Renaissance Thought* (Urbana, 1965), p. 239, Charles G. Nauert, Jr., observes rather nicely: "The practice of citing one's ancient authorities explicitly but at second-hand, while discreetly failing to mention the medieval sources from which one had really drawn information, was a standard practice of Renaissance authors." But Ficino was less culpable than many in this regard, since he was interested in and had access to the ancient authorities themselves.

In the following sections I propose to trace the contours of the general problem of Ficino's sources, concentrating on the charioteer myth rather than on individual dicta, syllogisms, or images, even such key ones as the "ambrosia" and "nectar" or "the plain of Truth." I leave it to others to supply the subtler details and shading. I shall assume, since the *Phaedrus* was unknown in the Latin West until Bruni's partial translation of 1424,[5] that Ficino went directly to antiquity in search of the Platonic consensus on the dialogue's correct interpretation, and in general for guidance and insight. If he knew of the *fortuna* of the *Phaedrus* in the Byzantine East—and he was certainly aware, however casually, of the controversies surrounding Pletho and of the polemics between George of Trebizond and Cardinal Bessarion[6]—nevertheless it was the ancient Neoplatonists in the main who obviously offered him the most succor and to whom he naturally turned for the keys to the dialogue's mysteries. After all, he had long been familiar with their commentaries and terminology, and he saw them as closer to the original fountains of Platonic inspiration than the Byzantines, even such distinguished ones as Psellus and Bessarion. Moreover, George of Trebizond and even Bessarion had focused rather narrowly on the themes of love and sensible beauty, as by all accounts had the Middle Platonists, instead of dealing with the metaphysical insights of a work which, for all its youthfulness of style and inspiration, such master Neoplatonists as Iamblichus, Syrianus, and Proclus had regarded as one of the keystones in the Platonic arch, a masterwork of Platonic "theology."[7]

Four authors certainly attracted Ficino's attention.[8]

In his *Phaedrus* Commentary Ficino never mentions Cicero (106-43 B.C.), but he was familiar with Cicero's Latin translation

5. Baron, *Leonardo Bruni Aretino*, pp. 125-128, 172.

6. See Allen, *Charioteer*, pp. 5-6, with further refs. Of especial note is Ficino's exchange of letters in 1469 with Bessarion, *Opera*, pp. 616-617 (trans. *Letters* 1:51-53).

7. In a way, Ficino effected the same kind of "revolution" in the interpretation of the *Phaedrus* for his century that Plotinus and Iamblichus had for theirs.

8. In the following survey I am deeply indebted to the recent masterly introduction by Saffrey and Westerink, *Proclus: Théologie platonicienne* 4:ix-xlv, though my aim and perspective is of course very different from theirs. I am indebted too to the earlier work of Bielmeier, *Phaidrosinterpretation*, and to Larsen's and Dillon's work on Iamblichus already cited.

of the *Phaedrus's* immortality syllogisms in the *Tusculanae* at 1.23.53-54, and again, more significantly, at the very end of the *De Re Publica* 6 during the finale of the so-called *Somnium Scipionis*. This last had had an extraordinary impact in itself and via the commentary of Macrobius (5th century A.D.) on the medieval and Renaissance worlds, and was the source of much speculation on astronomical matters as well as on the music of the spheres. It was thoroughly familiar to Ficino, and we have his notes on both Cicero's text and Macrobius's commentary.[9]

In 6.26.29 Scipio Africanus addresses his grandson in terms that unmistakably recall the cosmic flight of the *Phaedrus*: "sunt autem optimae curae de salute patriae, quibus agitatus et exercitatus animus velocius in hanc sedem et domum suam pervolabit; idque ocius faciet, si iam tum, cum erit inclusus in corpore, eminebit foras et ea, quae extra erunt, contemplans quam maxime se a corpore abstrahet."[10] Here Cicero brings the myth to bear in a context that cannot be Neoplatonic obviously, and is not concerned even with Platonic metaphysics, but rather is astronomical-astrological:[11] the flight is seen in terms of an ascent through the celestial spheres of the planets towards the sphere of the fixed stars, the firmament of heaven, *summus ipse deus*. This astronomical interpretation of the great myth was obviously widespread during antiquity, and Cicero was not its originator but a representative spokesman for it. Later Plutarch (c. 45-c. 125 A.D.) seems to have held a similar view,[12] and Hermias (fl. late 5th century A.D.) mentions it in his doxology as one of the several ways the myth had been customarily interpreted in the past.[13]

While Ficino followed Plotinus and his successors in unequivocally rejecting the notion that Plato had intended the "heaven" of the myth to be the firmament of the fixed stars, he was more con-

---

9. Alberti, "Ficino e il Codice Riccardiano," pp. 187-193, with accompanying plates. Saffrey and Westerink, however, make no mention of Macrobius, nor does Ficino in the Commentary.

10. A little earlier in the *Somnium*, at 6.17.17, Cicero refers to the outermost celestial sphere as *summus ipse deus, arcens et continens ceteros*. Ficino borrowed the phrase *summus ipse deus* to refer to "Heaven" in his *De Amore* 2.7 and 6.7 (ed. Marcel, pp. 154 and 208), an indication, surely, of his familiarity with the passage. Cf. chap. 5, n. 27 above.

11. See A.-J. Festugière, *La révélation d'Hermès Trismégiste* 2:441-459.

12. *Table Talk* 9.5 (*Moralia* 740B). See Saffrey and Westerink, 4:xiv-xv.

13. *In Phaedrum*, pp. 135-136 (ed. Couvreur); cf. Dillon, *Iamblichi Fragmenta*, p. 251.

cerned than they with accommodating the *Phaedrus*'s myth to the Chaldaean-Ptolemaic model of the universe, and with emphasizing the corresponding structures of the mundane and the supermundane worlds—the parallels, that is, between the realms of Soul and of Mind. Hence his important and original decision to have both the number and the names of the mundane and the supermundane "leader" gods correspond—that is, to have the lower dodecade be a mirror image of the higher. Cicero and Macrobius together provided him with one half of the solution: a moving evocation of the myth in terms of the soul's flight towards the heaven we actually see—the dwelling place, says Macrobius, of the pure souls (1.11; 2.17). As a Neoplatonist, Ficino was firmly to reject this astronomical interpretation of the myth, but its focus on the celestial spheres and on man's flight through them was to remain with him. Indeed, I suspect that Ficino's Phaedran charioteer was as deeply indebted to the dream vision of the younger Scipio as it was to the profounder and more intricate speculations of Plotinus and Proclus: necessarily so, for Cicero's evocation of the *Phaedrus*—both its immortality proofs and its flight of the soul—at the finale of the *Somnium Scipionis* constitutes one of the few genuinely "Platonic" moments in Latin letters. At the same time, many of its eloquent phrases must have been intimately familiar to Ficino and his educated contemporaries from the days when they first mastered their Tully.[14]

The situation with Plotinus (204-270 A.D.) is more fundamental and at the same time more technical since it involves key terms in Neoplatonic metaphysics and not just compelling imagery. This is not the occasion to discuss Plotinus's impact as a whole on Ficino, nor to trace the influence of his methodology on Ficino's goals as a commentator. Rather, we must concentrate specifically on what Ficino saw as Plotinus's view of the *Phaedrus*.

This view, however, is not easy to ascertain. Several scholars, most recently perhaps Jean-Michel Charrue,[15] have demonstrated

14. Ficino's perception of the importance for Dante of the *Somnium Scipionis* and of Macrobius's commentary upon it is a topic awaiting investigation.
15. Jean-Michel Charrue, *Plotin: Lecteur de Platon* (Paris, 1978), esp. pp. 158-183: "L'exégèse du *Phèdre*."

how difficult it is for us to assess Plotinus's understanding of an individual dialogue, given the absence of specific references and the elusiveness of many of his remarks, remarks that indicate he often has several dialogues or passages or images simultaneously in mind, or contrariwise particular quotations but not the works from which they derive. Nevertheless, with the help of the Henry-Schwyzer *index fontium*[16] and the new Sleeman-Pollet lexicon,[17] we can arrive at three general observations. First, the *Phaedrus* was one of Plotinus's favorite sources of reference, even though he usually alluded to it indirectly, sometimes so indirectly as still to occasion differences among scholars as to what precisely he was alluding to, or whether he intended the allusion at all[18] or was merely calling on the memory of a particular Platonic phrase or image to color his own phrasing or to help him shape the formulation of an argument that had no real connection with its source(s). Second, the *Phaedrus* clearly interested Plotinus mainly because of its charioteer myth and the immortality arguments that serve as its prologue (the thesis that "all soul cares for all that is soulless" being especially favored). Some scholars have even surmised that Plotinus, like others during the same period and afterwards, may have habitually worked from a handbook of selections from Plato, which included in this instance the syllogisms and the first part of the myth, and not directly from the original texts.[19] And third, Plotinus was not concerned with interpreting the *Phaedrus* or even the myth for its own sake,[20] but rather with drawing upon it for his own purposes, most often to utilize such images as the "nectar" and "ambrosia," the "decrees of Adrasteia," and the "plain of Truth," and with drawing upon it, furthermore, in the company of images and motifs from other dialogues. All this means that we

---

16. P. Henry and H. R. Schwyzer, eds., *Plotini Opera,* vol. 3 (Paris, Brussels, Leiden, 1973), p. 452.

17. J. H. Sleeman and Gilbert Pollet, *Lexicon Plotinianum* (Louvain and Leiden, 1980).

18. Contrast, for instance, the references suggested by MacKenna-Page with those suggested by Bréhier.

19. Hans-Rudolf Schwyzer, "Plotinos," in Pauly-Wissowa-Kroll, *Realencyclopädie der classischen Altertumswissenschaft,* suppl. vol. 15 (1978), 310-328 at 323.62-324.4.

20. Saffrey and Westerink, 4:xviii: "Jamais Plotin n'élabore une interprétation détaillée du mythe du *Phèdre.* . . . la péricope du mythe (246E4-248C2) ne totalise pas plus d'une quinzaine de références, le plus souvent purement décoratives. . . . il est bien évident que Plotin a utilisé ce discours dans son ensemble, avec sa signification globale."

can only approximate Plotinus's sense of the problems raised by our dialogue as a whole and by the myth at its center. Even so, Ficino found what he was looking for in the *Enneads*.

Ficino came to Plotinus with the preconception he derived from the later Neoplatonists that the major theme of the *Phaedrus* was beauty, and particularly the intelligible beauty or absolute Beauty that men once saw shining afar off in the superheavenly place. It would be logical then if he first turned to Plotinus's great treatise on Intelligible Beauty, the *Enneads* 5.8. After all, he had already used it repeatedly in the course of writing his own *Symposium* Commentary (so much so that its status as a source for that Commentary is on a par with that of the *Symposium* itself). Moreover, it is 5.8, and specifically chapter 10, that provided him with Plotinus's most memorable evocation of the jovian cavalcade in the *Phaedrus*.

Given the importance of this chapter for our understanding of Ficino's own interpretation, I have thought it best to cite it in full in Ficino's Latin translation as it appeared in his *Plotini Enneades* published in Florence by Antonio di Bartolommeo Miscomini in 1492.[21] The translation is preceded, as was his custom throughout, by commentary. This commentary, along with all his other Plotinus notes and commentaries, appeared unaccompanied by the Plotinus translation in his *Opera Omnia* of 1561, 1576, and 1641, where they were entitled *Epitomae seu Argumenta, Commentaria, et Annotationes*. Despite their diversity, they are now known collectively as Ficino's *Plotinus* Commentary. The commentary on chapter 10 begins:

Una cum Iove, id est anima mundi, omnes animae caelestes daemonicaeque et humanae iam purgatae toto fruuntur mundo divino.   Cap. X.

Etsi ibi singuli cunctas contemplantur ideas, alii tamen alias attentius et avidius ad quas praecipue caeteras quodammodo referunt. Ipsa pulchritudo ibi potissimum est universus ille splendor ex cuncta idearum quasi stellarum serie micans. Tota intelligentiae potestas nisi ardentissimus

---

21. I shall cite from the splendid copy in the Elmer Belt library at UCLA (which lacks, unfortunately, the errata on quire [*]), expanding all abbreviations and diacritics, keeping the u/v and ae/e distinctions, and repunctuating. This chapter and my other citations can be found on fols. kk v-kk [vii].

amor accesserit, hucusque fortasse pervenit ut pulchritudinem illam pro-
spiciat ut externam. Accedens amor contemplantem in eam transfert ac
vicissim usque adeo ut contemplator amator iam se ipsum inspiciat pulchrum, immo pulchritudinem evasisse. Annuit Plotinus quod ait Plato
philosophos cum Iove solos incedere ab Iove missos. Caeteri enim homines singulis proprie sunt addicti. Solus philosophus universum ambit,
universi vero anima Iupiter.[22]

The translation follows:

Superioribus de causis Iupiter ipse etsi aliorum antiquissimus deorum
quos ipse ducit primus incedit ad mundum intelligibilem contemplan-
dum. Hunc deinde sequuntur caeteri dii, daemones, animi, quicunque
haec cernere possunt. Divinus autem ille mundus desuper illis effulget ex
occulto quodam et ab excelso illis exoriens, illustrat omnia numina im-
plens singula lumine. Tum vero ad se inferiores animos excitat, qui deinceps convertuntur ad ipsum cernere non valentes ceu solem. Sed alii quidem perspiciunt erecti ab ipso eiusque intuitum facile perferentes; alii
vero turbantur quotcunque longius ab ipsius natura distant. Cum vero
quicumque possunt singuli videant, omnes quidem ipsum et quod ipsius
est suspiciunt, neque tamen specimen semper idem unusquisque reportat.
Sed dum attenti conspiciunt alius quidem splendentem cernit ipsius iusti
fontem atque naturam, alius autem abunde temperantiam intuetur, non
qualem penes se homines quando habent. Imitatur enim haec nostra
quodammodo illam. Illa vero in omnibus circa omnem quasi magnitudi-
nem ipsius se diffundens postrema discernitur, et quidem ab illis qui spectacula iam multa perspicua perviderunt. Proinde dii tum unusquisque
seorsum tum simul cuncti conspiciunt. Conspiciunt et animae quae illic
omnia vident, ex omnibusque tales evadunt ut ipsae quoque cuncta a
principio ad finem usque contineant. Hae quidem illic habitant et quantum inest eis quod illic naturaliter valeat habitare, et saepe totum quod
est in eis ibidem habitat quotiens inde minime segregantur. Haec igitur et
ipse Iupiter et quicunque nostrum una cum Iove haec amat feliciter con-
templatur. Postremamque omnium pulchritudinem universam ex
omnibus effulgentem et quod pulchritudinis illius est particeps. Rutilant
enim illic omnia spectatoresque illos splendore collustrant adeo ut ipsi
quoque pulchri prorsus efficiantur. Quemadmodum saepe accidit his qui
altissimos montes ascendunt ubi flavum terra colorem habeat. Colore

---

22. In Ficino's *Opera Omnia* these, and the comments on 5.8.12 and 13, all appear on
p. 1769.

namque illo statim inficiuntur facti similes terrae ad quam ascenderant. In mundo vero divino florens ille color ipsa est pulchritudo, immo vero quicquid ibi est totum color est et funditus pulchritudo. Non enim aliud quiddam pulchritudo illic extat quasi superficie florens. Verum apud illos qui non inspiciunt totum solum quod in superficie micat aspectui censetur nominaturque pulchritudo. Qui vero per totum quasi mero perfusi nectare prorsus implentur, cum per totam animam se infuderit pulchritudo non solum spectatores evadunt. Non enim ulterius hic quidem spectator extra est, ibi vero spectaculum similiter extra. Sed qui acute perspicit rem habet in seipso perspectam. Atqui et habens saepe habere se nescit. Nam qui tanquam externum aliquid aspicit iccirco velut externum, quia tanquam visibile respicit, et quia sic videre constituit. Quicquid autem aliquis intuetur ut spectandum extra videt. Verum operae pretium est in seipsum iam spectaculum transferre divinum ac velut unum prorsus inspicere et tanquam seipsum penitus intueri. Ceu siquis occupatus a deo seu Phoebo sive Musa potissimum aliqua raptus in seipso dei ipsius intuitum iam efficiat siquidem in seipso deum valeat intueri.

Of importance too for the light they cast on 5.8.10 are 5.8.12 and 13. Ficino's prefatory note to 12 reads:

Quicunque intellectum suum totus ingreditur per hunc ingreditur et divinum. Qui boni quidem ipsius filius est, pater autem animae mundi. Cap. XII. Generatur vero et intellectus a bono et anima mundusque simul ab intellectu, non consilio deliberante sed natura foecunda. Natura vero tum in bono voluntas est sive voluptas, tum in intellectu primo ipsa eius intelligentia. De voluntaria creatione mundi alibi.

The third sentence of the translation begins:

Nempe se Deum vidisse pulchrum filium et omnia in filio generantem, conceptumque absque labore in se habentem. Deus enim delectatus his quae genuit suosque partus amans penes seipsum cuncta continuit, tum sui ipsius tum suorum splendore congratulans. Cum vero haec omnia pulchra sint et quae intus permanent pulchriora, solus omnium Iupiter filius foras emicuit. Ex quo etiam ultimo filio videre licet tanquam ex quadam illius imagine quantus sit ille pater quantive Iovis fratres apud patrem perseverantes. Hic autem non frustra dixerit se a patre venisse. Esse namque se alterum ab eo mundum, qui pulcher sit effectus velut pulchri ipsius imago; nefas enim esse imaginem pulchri ipsius atque essentiae non esse pulchram.

This mention of Jupiter as the sole son of intellect who "shone outside" in a chapter but one below the specific evocation of the jovian cavalcade from the *Phaedrus* would surely have strengthened Ficino in the belief that Plotinus had understood Plato to be referring in the figure of Jupiter to the World-Soul or Soul.

At 5.8.13 Plotinus had treated, Ficino supposed, of the castration of Heaven and the binding of Saturn. His prefatory comments begin:

Intellectus divinus qui et Saturnus cognominatur castrat Caelium id est ipsum bonum. Cap. XIII. Dividit enim penes se in plures formas uniforme patris donum. Permanet vero in se absque motu et a commertio corporis segregatus. Nam mundanam dispensationem motus generationes Iovi id est animae mundi concessit, cuius natura genitalis apellatur Venus. Pulchritudo mundi corporei umbra quaedam est ad ipsam mundi incorporei pulchritudinem....

Note that here the Good (and therefore the One) is identified with Uranus, Saturn with Intellect, and Jove with the World-Soul. The castration of Uranus signifies Mind's division of "the uniform gift of the father" (uniform meaning the gift of Form in its undivided totality) into many Forms (the Platonic Ideas). Ficino's translation begins:

Deus igitur ille Saturnus, qui ligatus fingitur propterea quod penes seipsum eodem semper habitu perseveret, qui et traditur mundi huius imperium Iovi filio concessisse; neque enim ei consentaneum erat illud imperium dimittenti iuniorem posterioremque se prosequi principatum quippe cum pulchrorum omnium plenitudinem complectatur. Saturnus inquam his obmissis patrem suum Caelium in seipso firmavit et illuc usque se erexit in altum. Firmavit rursus quae deinceps inde sequuntur a filio iam exordium nacta post ipsum. Sic itaque tenet inter utrumque medium, tum quia alteritate quadam paterna secat, tum quia ab inferioribus abstinet in sublime consurgens, dum fingitur ab inferiori iura [iure?] vinculis cohiberi, medium certe gradum obtinens inter maiorem patrem filiumque minorem. Quoniam vero Caelius Saturni Iovisque progenitor maior admodum est quam ut esse pulchritudo dicatur, iccirco Saturnus, id est intellectus primo pulcher extat quamvis anima quoque sit pulchra. Ille tamen hac est pulchrior quoniam haec vestigium est illius....

Again the proximity of this passage to 5.8.10, as well as its importance for an understanding of the correct "Platonic" interpretation of Uranus, must have confirmed Ficino in the impression that
5.8.10 was concerned with the flight of Soul, along with all rational souls, up to the intellectual heaven, thence to gaze upwards still
further at the primally and primarily beautiful, Saturn or Mind.

In this series of extracts from 5.8.10, 12, and 13 Plotinus does
not mention the "supercelestial place" or the "subcelestial
vault,"[23] and he is not concerned with the interpretation of individual details. Equally obvious, however, is the fact that in writing
5.8.10 he had the *Phaedrus's* charioteer myth very much in the
forefront of his mind: it is shaping the process of his thought and
constitutes the source of his imagery.[24]

One of the absolutely critical questions from Ficino's viewpoint
concerned, as we have seen, the status of Zeus in the myth. Apart
from the sections 5.8.10-13, he could turn to several other passages in the *Enneads* for confirmation—at least to his own satisfaction—that Plotinus had interpreted the *Phaedrus's* Zeus as the
World-Soul and not as the higher Zeus in Mind. But Plotinus's
various references to Zeus are ambivalent if not contradictory,
and at 6.9.7 he actually identifies him with the Good and the
One.[25] Of prime significance was Plato's enigmatic observation in
the *Philebus* 30D: "And in the divine nature of Zeus would you
not say that there is the soul and mind of a king, because there is in
him the power of the cause?" Ficino interpreted this to mean that
Zeus possessed "a royal intellect" and "a royal soul"[26] and that
Plato was adverting to Zeus's dual ontological status as the leader
or embodiment of Soul[27] and as the downward-oriented, providential power in Mind, Soul as it were in Mind.[28] Plotinus had ex-

23. Saffrey and Westerink, 4:xviii.
24. On pp. xix-xx Saffrey and Westerink treat in detail of 5.8.10, italicizing the words
that echo Plato's text. They do not treat, however, of 5.8.12 and 13.
25. Wallis, *Neoplatonism,* p. 135. Cf. *Enneads* 2.3.13; 3.5.8; 4.3.12; 4.4.6; 4.4.9-10;
5.1.7; 5.5.3; 5.8.13; etc.
26. Plotinus alludes to this passage on a number of occasions, most notably at 3.5.8 and
4.4.9; see also Ficino's *Philebus* Commentary 1.11 (ed. Allen, pp. 136-137).
27. Wallis, *Neoplatonism,* pp. 69-70 and 126, alerts us to the distinction in ancient Neoplatonism between the World-Soul and Universal or Unparticipated Soul; this distinction
had little significance for Ficino, who tended to equate them.
28. Wallis, *Neoplatonism,* p. 135; cf. chap. 5, nn. 12 and 33 above.

plored this Phileban formula at some length in his *Enneads* at 4.4.6, 9, 10, as Ficino well knew;[29] and it helps us to comprehend a particularly challenging passage in 3.5.8 where Plotinus seems to be saying that, since Aphrodite is Soul in the *Symposium's* myth of Love's birth, then the Zeus there must be Mind.[30] Ficino had accorded this passage extended analysis, not in his Plotinus Commentary, where he omits all consideration of 3.5.7-9,[31] but in his *De Amore* at 6.7.[32] There he had arrived at the following identifications: Uranus signifies God; in the Angel Saturn signifies the essence and Jupiter the life; but in the soul—that is, the World-Soul—Saturn signifies the knowledge of higher things and Jupiter the movement of the celestial bodies. In other words, Ficino had used the *Philebus's* formula to arrive at the notion that Mind and Soul could each be subdivided into their saturnian and jovian parts, or, more properly in light of the *Cratylus's* orientation triad, into their powers.[33] This perception had enabled him to penetrate what seemed to the uninitiated to be Plotinus's equation at 3.5.8 of Zeus with Mind, when even there he was treating of Soul.

However, perhaps the two most illuminating passages in Plotinus for glossing 5.8.10 correctly are 4.3.7 and 4.8.2.[34] In 4.3.7, without even mentioning Zeus by name, Plotinus quotes from the *Phaedrus* 246BC and proceeds to link our soul with the World-Soul and thus by necessity, given the quotations, with Zeus. Having adverted to the famous lemma at 246B6, "All that is soul cares for all that is soulless," he proceeds to quote 246B7-C2 thus: " 'The perfect soul,' we read, that of the All, 'going its lofty journey,' operates upon the Cosmos not by sinking into it, but, as

29. See his comment in *Opera*, p. 1742.1. Cf. Plotinus, *Enneads* 5.1.7, with Ficino's comment, *Opera*, p. 1758.2; also chap. 6, n. 18 above.

30. And so interpreted by Saffrey and Westerink, 4:xx-xxi. In an earlier volume, however, at 2:xlvii, they seem to be suggesting that Plotinus here is treating of divisions within Soul and not of the distinctions between the prime hypostases, Mind and Soul. For Plotinus himself refers not only to *Letter* 2's mention at 312E of "the third" (which he elsewhere identifies with Soul) and the *Philebus's* allusion at 30D to "the royal intellect" and "the royal soul," but also to the *Phaedrus's* reference at 246E to Zeus as "the great leader of the gods." His enigmatic conclusion is that the Aphrodite of the *Symposium's* myth must be the soul of Zeus and thus identical with Hera.

31. The analysis would have occurred in the *Opera* at p. 1717.

32. Ed. Marcel, pp. 208-210. Presumably he omitted consideration of this myth in the Plotinus Commentary precisely because he had dealt with it in the *De Amore*.

33. *Cratylus* 396BC. See Ficino's epitome, *Opera*, p. 1311; also chap. 5, passim, above.

34. Saffrey and Westerink, surprisingly, make no mention of these.

it were, by brooding over it; and 'every perfect soul exercises this governance.'" Similarly in 4.8.2, where he is defining the relationship between the World-Soul and our soul, Plotinus again quotes from 246C1-2: "This is how we come to read that our soul, entering into association with that complete soul and itself thus made perfect, 'walks the lofty ranges, administering the entire Cosmos,' and that as long as it does not secede and is neither inbound to body nor held in any sort of servitude, so long it tranquilly bears its part in the governance of the All, exactly like the World-Soul itself." For Ficino these two explicit references to the Phaedran flight of the soul would have established beyond the shadow of a doubt that Plotinus understood Plato at 246E4 ff. to be invoking Zeus as the World-Soul and not as the Soul in Mind.

Ficino was also concerned with Plotinus's views on one other vitally important question. How are we to understand the meaning of the myth's several references to "heaven"? For its definition necessarily affected the definitions of the "superheavenly" place of 247C3 and the "subheavenly" vault of 247B1. Again 5.8 is a crucial treatise, for it answers the question, Is the "heaven" of the *Phaedrus* the celestial vault we see, or the higher, the intellectual, heaven? Plotinus seems to have been the first to insist on the second alternative. In 5.8.3 he had written, "for yonder all is heaven, the earth is heaven, the sea, animals, plants, men: all that pertains to that heaven is itself heavenly—the gods in it do not hate men nor any other beings there; when they traverse all that region and all that place yonder for them, it is rest."[35] This passage, occurring as it does just a few pages before Plotinus's unmistakable invocation of the *Phaedrus*'s ascent, would have confirmed for Ficino what he already knew to be the Neoplatonic tradition on this issue, namely that Plotinus had "revolutionized" the interpretation of the *Phaedrus* by insisting that its "heaven" was the world or realm of Nous.[36] Zeus as Soul rose into Mind and thus made the greatest of ontological leaps, the advance from one primal category of being to another.

35. As Saffrey and Westerink, 4:xix, observe, Porphyry seems to have gathered together a number of treatises on the intellect and Intellect in order to constitute book 5 of the *Enneads*.

36. Again, we should bear in mind that Plotinus's realm of *Nous* has not yet been subdivided into "intelligible" and "intellectual"; in his interpretation the *Phaedrus*'s "heaven" is therefore both known and knowing. Cf. Saffrey and Westerink, 4:xxiv, "[c'est] une interprétation globale du ciel du *Phèdre* dans le sens d'un ciel intelligible."

From Ficino's viewpoint Plotinus had therefore arrived at two major insights in his reading of the myth: he had correctly perceived the nature of the "heaven" and the status of the Zeus who leads the cavalcade of souls up to and through this "heaven." However allusive and elusive Plotinus's various references to the *Phaedrus,* and however much he may have declined to provide detailed interpretation for other elements in the myth, elements which came to fascinate the later Neoplatonists, Ficino saw him as the originator of these two absolutely fundamental interpretative decisions, though in the event, as we shall see, Iamblichus and his successors had rejected the Plotinian view of the *Phaedrus*'s Zeus, mistakenly in Ficino's view. In this, as in so many other ways, Plotinus hence emerged as the profoundest, the most perceptive interpreter of Plato; in the words of Ficino's preface to his Plotinus volume of 1492: "Plotinus tandem his Theologiam velaminibus enudavit, primusque et solus, ut Porphyrius Proculusque testantur, arcana veterum divinitus penetravit. Sed ob incredibilem cum verborum brevitatem tum sententiarum copiam sensusque profunditatem non translatione tantum linguae sed commentariis indiget."[37]

However, Plotinus had committed one major error despite the sublimity and correctness otherwise of his interpretation. From Ficino's viewpoint he had read Plato's rather cryptic comments on the soul's descent "into a brute beast" at 248D1 and 249B2-5 too literally and taken them to mean that Plato believed in the transmigration of souls into animals, in radical metempsychosis.[38] In this overliteralness Plotinus was almost certainly, Ficino felt, following the lead of the Pythagoreans, the most famous exponents of metempsychosis and of the soul's journey. Ironically, Plotinus's Neoplatonist successors, notably Syrianus and his two pupils Hermias and Proclus, were able to correct Plotinus on this one point, and to argue for limited, not radical, metempsychosis.[39] All

37. It also appears in his *Opera* at p. 1537.
38. Most notably in *Enneads* 3.4.2. Ficino has a long chapter of somewhat tortuous commentary on this chapter: *Opera,* pp. 1709-1711.
39. In his *Platonic Theology* 17.3 and 4 (ed. Marcel, 3:164, 167-168), Ficino attacks Plotinus while defending his Platonic successors on this issue. At p. 164 he writes: "Deposita denique figura hominis, eius bestiae subit corpus, cuius se moribus simillimam praestitit, seu inserat se ferino foetui fiatque propria ferini corporis anima, ut Plotinus, Numenius, Harpocratius, Boethus existimant, seu animae ferinae seipsam iungat atque ferae sit comes, ut placuit Hermiae Syrianoque et Proculo." Again at pp. 167-168 he openly lauds Iamblichus, Porphyry, Proclus, Syrianus, and Hermias in that order for their stand against

Ficino then had to do was to argue that Plato had intended metempsychosis figuratively and not literally.[40] But this one lapse was the only thing that vitiated Plotinus's otherwise correct interpretation of Plato's meaning in the *Phaedrus,* an interpretation that was not Christian, of course, but nonetheless perfectly compatible with a Christian interpretation. For Ficino it was further proof of the sublimity and uniqueness of Plotinus as the great interpreter of Plato. This said, it is still remarkable how little acknowledgment Plotinus receives in Ficino's own *Phaedrus* Commentary: just half a dozen references and then on specific points. This is not, I believe, because Ficino was determined to mask his indebtedness, but because he had worked through the interpretative problems so thoroughly himself that he felt, and in fact was, entirely independent of Plotinus, though eager to claim him as his best authority. We recall that Plotinus had never analyzed the myth systematically and that Ficino had had to turn to later Neoplatonists in order to see the extent and nature of many of the interpretative problems the dialogue posed. Indeed, we can surmise that it was in all probability Ficino's encounter with these later Neoplatonists that enabled him to decipher Plotinus correctly, since in many ways, as even this brief survey has no doubt demonstrated, Plotinus's interpretation of the *Phaedrus* is as difficult to unravel as Plato's own text. To decide on what Plotinus had meant, even in such vividly

---

metempsychosis, Plotinus being conspicuous by his absence. Cf. Ficino's *Phaedrus* Commentary, summa 25.

For Ficino the two most important rejections of the overly "literal" reading of Plato's texts here were probably Proclus's *In Timaeum* 329DE (ed. Diehl, 3:294-295) and Hermias's *In Phaedrum,* pp. 170-171 (ed. Couvreur); he must have been influenced too by Augustine's *De Civitate Dei* 10.30. See Wallis, *Neoplatonism,* p. 120.

40. In his *Platonic Theology* 17.4 (ed. Marcel, 3:170 and 172) Ficino had already observed: "In Phaedro non dicit animam hominis in bestiae corpus transire, sed in ferinam vitam, et in Timaeo in naturam ferinam, non in corpus ferae.... In quibus intelligitur habitus vitaeque potius quam speciei vel corporis permutatio" (p. 170). "Transitum animarum accipiamus non in varias species, sed in habitus.... Eadem in Phaedro Socrates comprobat dicens 'Ego itaque considero, utrum ipse sim bestia Thyphone multiplicior, sive divinius animal.' Et postea in libro eodem in anima aurigam ponit et geminos equos, bonum atque malum, rationem scilicet irascendique et concupiscendi potentiam. Ubi apparet in ipsis animae viribus et hominem et beluas esse" (p. 172). He concludes the chapter by arguing that even if Plato had in fact affirmed metempsychosis at various times, it was only for the purposes of discussion: "Ac si quis ea etiam Platonem affirmavisse contenderit, nos quoque affirmare forsitan disputationis gratia concedemus, verum longe aliter quam verba designent, exponenda esse censebiums" (p. 174).

Phaedran passages at 5.8.10, Ficino must have already arrived at his own decision as to what Plato had meant. Plato would then, ironically, have provided a key to Plotinus, rather than the reverse. The reason for this piquant situation was *ob incredibilem cum verborum brevitatem tum sententiarum copiam sensusque profunditatem [in Plotino]*. "Incredible brevity" was not, however, the problem Ficino confronted when he leafed through Plotinus's successors.

A number of ancient Neoplatonists after Plotinus seem to have written *Phaedrus* commentaries (whether on the whole dialogue or on the mythical hymn it is difficult to say), including Iamblichus, Syrianus, Hermias, and Proclus.[41] With the exception of Hermias's, however, none of these commentaries has survived, and Hermias's comes down to us as a compendium of notes (*scholia*) on Syrianus's lectures. We can garner a good deal of information about Proclus's views of the dialogue, however, from various comments in his *Theologia Platonica* and most notably in book 4.4-26.

Hermias's commentary is significant for two reasons. First and most obviously, Ficino found it worth taking the considerable pains to translate it into Latin in its entirety somewhere between 1474 and 1484, though he never published this translation, which survives today in only two manuscripts.[42] Second, whatever its degree of intrinsic interest, and here opinions differ,[43] it is extrinsically interesting as a guide to what Syrianus thought (and Syrianus was the master, we recall, of Proclus as well as of Hermias). It also furnishes us with some tantalizing glimpses of Iamblichus's views, as does Proclus's *Theologia Platonica*. From these two sources we can reconstruct the general outlines of the later Neoplatonists' consolidation and elaboration of Plotinus's revolutionary interpretation of the *Phaedrus*.

---

41. The Middle Platonist Harpocration (fl. c. A.D. 180) may have written a *Phaedrus* commentary too on the evidence of Hermias, *In Phaedrum,* pp. 32.3 and 102.14 (ed. Couvreur). But see Dillon, *Middle Platonists,* pp. 258-262.

42. Allen and White, "Ficino's Hermias Translation and a New Apologue."

43. One of the more suggestive articles on Hermias is Sheppard's "The Influence of Hermias on Marsilio Ficino's Doctrine of Inspiration."

According to Bielmeier, Dillon, and Larsen, Iamblichus (c. 250-c. 326 A.D.) initiated the second phase of this revolutionary interpretation, and his impact was in a way more dramatic than Plotinus's. For he mounted a counterattack on those who had previously assailed the dialogue's themes as being too youthful by determining that its *skopos* was "beauty in all its forms" and its genre "theological." Most notably, he seems to have insisted on the work's unity as well as on its complexity and profundity of vision.[44]

From Hermias Ficino could discover that Iamblichus had set about subdividing Plotinus's unitary world of Mind into two categories later to become standard in Neoplatonism: the higher, the intelligible ($\nu o\eta\tau\acute{o}\varsigma$), and the lower, the intellectual ($\nu o\epsilon\rho\acute{o}\varsigma$). In effect this was to hypostasize the distinction between the known and the knower. Iamblichus had brought his categories to bear on what we have already seen to be one of the critical problems, the meaning of "heaven" in the charioteer myth. In his *Theologia Platonica* at 4.5 Proclus writes: "If one declares that the 'heaven' towards which Zeus leads the way, and all the Gods follow, and along with them the daemons, is of the intelligible order, he will be giving an inspired interpretation of Plato in accordance with the facts, and he will be in agreement with the most renowned of the commentators. For Plotinus and Iamblichus consider this 'heaven' to be an intelligible entity." Similarly in 4.23 Proclus asserts that "great Iamblichus, having declared the great heaven to be an order of intelligible gods, which he has in some places identified with the Demiurge, takes the 'inner vault of heaven' as the order of creation situated immediately beneath it and as it were the membrane covering the heaven. This is what he said in his *Commentaries on the Phaedrus*."[45]

Iamblichus's decision to identify the *Phaedrus*'s "heaven" as intelligible led him, logically I believe, to interpret the Zeus who leads the way there as intellectual; for his subdivision of Mind effectively made room for an intellectual Zeus to rise to an intelli-

44. Bielmeier, *Phaidrosinterpretation*, pp. 19 ff.; Dillon, *Iamblichi Fragmenta*, pp. 92-99, 248-256; and Larsen, *Jamblique*, pp. 361-372. Saffrey and Westerink, 4:xxv-xxvii, also press the claims of Theodorus of Asine; but from our viewpoint he can be dismissed.

45. Ed. Saffrey and Westerink, 4:21 and 68. The translations are Dillon's, *Iamblichi Fragmenta*, pp. 95 and 97.

gible realm, whereas in the simpler metaphysics of Plotinus Soul could only rise to Mind. In rejecting Plotinus's identification of Zeus with Soul and asserting his status as Mind, Iamblichus was ignoring, however, what Ficino saw as Plato's careful decision at 246E4 to describe Jupiter as the great, but not the greatest, leader.

Iamblichus had thus introduced two basic innovations into the Plotinian interpretation of the *Phaedrus*'s myth: he had subdivided Plotinus's intelligible heaven into intelligible and intellectual; and he had elevated Zeus to the position of being intellectual, of being the Zeus in Cronus, not the immanent animate Zeus. Whether he saw Zeus's train as consisting of intellectual as well as of animate gods is not clear (we know it must include animate beings, since Plato specifically mentions the demons at 246E6). It will be remarked that Iamblichus made no mention of the superheavenly place.

One other view attributed to Iamblichus is interesting. Hermias writes: "The divine Iamblichus, drawing on the name 'Zeus,' refers the subject of the present passage [246E] to the single Demiurge of the cosmos, who is described also in the Timaeus."[46] From Ficino's perspective Iamblichus had made a significant connection between the *Phaedrus*'s Zeus and the *Timaeus*'s Demiurge,[47] the Zeus in Mind, a connection that was to become standard in late antiquity but that Ficino, who was uncharacteristically circumspect about the possibility of reconciling the *Timaeus* with Christianity,[48] could obviously not countenance.

Syrianus (died c. 437 A.D.), whom we shall accept as the authority behind Hermias and for whom Hermias and Proclus are the primary but not the only spokesmen,[49] introduced some further

---

46. P. 136.17 ff. (ed. Couvreur); trans. Dillon, *Iamblichi Fragmenta,* p. 95, with commentary on p. 251.

47. Saffrey and Westerink, 4:xxviii-xxix and 128 n. 6, point out that, as contrasted with Hermias, Proclus claims that Iamblichus had identified the *Timaeus*'s Demiurge with all the intelligible world, *In Timaeum* 94A-D (ed. Diehl, 1:307-309; trans. Festugière, 2:162-165).

48. See Garin, *Studi sul platonismo medievale,* pp. 8 ff., 46 ff.; Tigerstedt, "The Poet as Creator," pp. 460, 479n; and Klibansky, *Continuity,* pp. 28 ff., 36. Klibansky points out that Ficino definitely made use of William of Conches's commentary on the *Timaeus.*

49. Saffrey and Westerink, 4:xxix-xxxi. Syrianus's commentary on the *Phaedrus* (or on its myth) is lost, as is his Συμφωνία Ὀρφέως, Πυθαγόρου, Πλάτωνος πρὸς τὰ λόγια βιβλία δέκα.

notable refinements. In particular he defined and distinguished
between the superheavenly place, the heaven, and the subheavenly
vault. For Proclus he became indeed the master exegete of the
Phaedrus, its "veritable Bacchant."[50] In taking up Iamblichus's
distinction between intelligible and intellectual, he turned to the
Orphic succession of deities: Phanes, Night, Uranus and the Cyclopes, Cronus, Zeus, and Dionysus. Phanes he interpreted as the
splendor of the prime Beauty and thus of Mind in its unity as the
intelligible and the intellect, as the intelligible intellect. Night he
pluralized as the first triad of gods below Phanes. Uranus he determined as the second triad of these same gods and the Cyclopes as
the third. Cronus he established as the first intellect, totally separated now from the intelligible. Zeus he made into this same intellect, seen in its creative aspect as the Demiurge. Finally he nomi-
nated Dionysus as the intellect in the world, what Ficino would
have described, I believe, as the *mens* in the *anima mundi.*

In retrospect we can see that Syrianus created an intermediate
category of gods between Phanes and Cronus, namely the three
triads represented by the Nights, by Uranus, and by the Cyclopes.
Nevertheless, he did not define or differentiate this category in
philosophical terms and he had obviously not arrived at Proclus's
decision to designate it as intelligible-and-intellectual νοητὸς καὶ
νοερός.[51] Still, he was clearly postulating a transition from the
intelligible, of which Phanes is the lowest limit, to the intellectual,
of which Cronus is the upper limit and Zeus the lower. Moreover,
in terms of the *Phaedrus*'s myth it is to this middle group that Syrianus was the first to assign "the superheavenly place," "heaven,"
and "the subheavenly vault." Thus to these three loci must be
assigned respectively the three Orphic Nights and the triads represented by Uranus and the Orphic Cyclopes. The three Nights are
the Knowledge, Temperance (Σωφροσύνη), and Justice witnessed
in the superheavenly place. Uranus is the summit of heaven. The
Cyclopes are the subheavenly vault. These deities subsequent to

50. *Theologia Platonica* 4.23 (ed. Saffrey and Westerink, 4:69): "Why speak of our
Master [Syrianus], that veritable Bacchant, who, being inspired by the sovereign inspiration
of the gods on the subject of Plato, has ensured that we too are inflamed with admiration
and wonder at Plato's doctrine?"

51. Saffrey and Westerink, 4:xxxvi, attribute the creation of both the concept and the
term to Proclus.

Phanes, as well as Cronus and Zeus below them, are all still referred to as "intellectual" ġods by Hermias, and therefore presumably by Syrianus. Nevertheless, Syrianus was clearly introducing a distinction between what are in actuality the higher intellectual gods—the Nights, Uranus, and the Cyclopes—and the lower ones—Cronus and Zeus. Not only are the three Phaedran loci reserved for the higher intellectual gods alone (Cronus and Zeus being confined presumably to the interior of heaven far below the vault), but Syrianus also equates the higher intellectual gods with "life" and the lower ones with "intellect" in the fundamental triad "being-life-intellect" (Phanes, as the last monad among the intelligible gods, is logically associated with "being").

We can now see why Proclus regarded Syrianus as the great interpreter of the *Phaedrus*. He had properly differentiated between the three loci of the myth and had assigned them to the three triads that constitute the "higher" intellectual divinities, gods which Proclus himself was to designate the intelligible-and-intellectual. At the same time he had established nine as the number of gods assigned to the loci, a number that was to be integral to Proclus's system but that Ficino later rejected, committed as he was to maintaining a correspondence between the twelve cosmic spheres (the eight celestial and the four sublunary) and the intellectual "spheres" above them.

Curiously, given that Hermias was a disciple of Syrianus and given Damascius's profile of him as a rather unoriginal if pious and scholarly man,[52] Hermias's own distribution of the Orphic deities differs considerably from Syrianus's (and Proclus's). Since Ficino was familiar with it, however, it deserves a brief outline.[53] Hermias sees all the Orphic deities mentioned, with the exception of Dionysus, as intellectual gods (and perhaps it was Hermias's example which determined Ficino to call all the higher gods intellectual and to reserve the term "intelligible" for the Ideas alone; and this despite his familiarity with the contrary usage of Proclus).

52. *Damascii Vitae Isidori Reliquiae* §§74-76 (ed. Clemens Zintzen [Hildesheim, 1967]).
53. Saffrey and Westerink's fourth volume contains detailed notes on the points of agreement and disagreement between Hermias and Proclus. For a more detailed study of Ficino's indebtedness to Hermias, see Allen, "Two Commentaries on the *Phaedrus*," passim.

Thus Phanes becomes, in Saffrey and Westerink's words, "the lower limit of the intelligible gods and the beginning of the intellectual gods, but the beginning as transcendent."[54] The Nights become "the coordinated beginning" of the intellectual gods,[55] and Hermias associates them with the superheavenly place and with the three Ideas at 247D6-7, Knowledge, Temperance, and Justice.

Hermias makes a fresh start with the three categories of unqualifiedly intellectual gods. Of the higher category, first comes Uranus (who does not appear to be divisible into three); he occupies the heaven of the myth. Next come the three Cyclopes and below them another Orphic group, the three Hundred-Handed Giants;[56] these all occupy the subheavenly vault. The middle category of intellectual gods is led by Cronus and the lower category by Zeus; both these categories must occupy the "interior" of heaven below the vault. Hermias's assignment of these various deities to the being-life-intellect triad also differs from Syrianus's; for he associates the Nights alone with life, while Uranus, the Cyclopes, and all those under them, he associates with intellect. Finally, he subdivides Zeus into the demiurgic triad: Zeus, Poseidon, and Hades, and subordinates three further triads to them, the zoogonic (the life-bringing), the phrouretic (the preserving or guarding), and the epistreptic (the returning or converting). The deities assigned to these four triads probably correspond with those in what I have previously called the zodiacal dodecade.[57]

Hermias's scheme was, accordingly, peculiar to himself; and it differed markedly from that of his master Syrianus, the one adopted in essence by Proclus (and, incidentally, by Damascius). Ficino seems to have ignored it, however, though he may be indebted, as I have said, to Hermias's decision to think of all the higher gods in the Orphic pantheon as intellectual, not intelligible.

54. Saffrey and Westerink, 4:xxxiii-xxxiv.
55. P. 152.17 (ed. Couvreur): αἱ γὰρ Νύκτες ἀρχαὶ αἷς ὡς συντεταγμένη ἡ ἀρχή. The older account by Zeller (ed. Martano), p. 198n, identifies the Orphic Night (if not the triadic form "Nights") with the intelligible gods.
56. In "Two Commentaries," p. 122, I mistakenly described these Cyclopes and Giants as "intramundane" instead of "ultramundane."
57. See Allen, "Two Commentaries," p. 122. For the zodiacal dodecade, see chap. 5, p. 118 above.

Even so, Hermias's basic methodology must have impressed him as valid; how otherwise to account for the considerable labor he expended in translating him in his entirety?

In a way Proclus (412-485 A.D.) represents the end of the line in the elaboration of the later Neoplatonic exegesis of the *Phaedrus.* Nevertheless, he deserves special recognition here; for Ficino was intimately acquainted with most of his surviving major works and indebted to them on a number of issues. Indeed, I have suggested elsewhere that Ficino's analysis of the *Phaedrus's* myth was probably Proclian in basic inspiration, although he rejected much of Proclus's analysis on the triple grounds that he had read Plato "overliterally" (*ipsam verborum faciem curiosius observavit*); that he had made too little allowance for Plato's playfulness on the one hand and for his interest in Pythagorean notions on the other, notions to which Plato did not necessarily subscribe;[58] and that he had excessively multiplied his categories, particularly for the gods and angels. Thanks to the discoveries of H. D. Saffrey, we now know that Ficino had read all of Proclus's *Theologia Platonica* in the original Greek and that he had mastered its daunting complexities as few before him or since; as a testament to this we have sundry jottings and notes that he made in the course of his reading.[59] Of particular moment is book 4, where Proclus deals in some detail with certain aspects of the *Phaedrus's* myth and presents us in effect with the crowning Neoplatonic analysis of it, an analysis with which Ficino was demonstrably familiar, though he barely mentioned Proclus in the course of his own Commentary.[60]

58. *Charioteer,* pp. 7, 34-36, n. 26, and 39 n. 47. The theory that Plato "played" with Pythagorean notions, however seriously, and that he only really committed himself to certain dogmas in his last works, the *Letters* and the *Laws* (including the *Epinomis* as its epilogue), is to be found in his *Platonic Theology* 17.4 (ed. Marcel, 3:168-169, 174), in his epitome for the *Laws* 1 (*Opera,* p. 1488.2), and in his preface to his 1484 Plato edition (*Opera,* p. 766.2; trans. *Letters* 3:38).
59. "Notes platoniciennes," esp. pp. 171-172; cf. Allen, *Charioteer,* pp. 34-36 n. 26. Saffrey presents an edition of these in the course of his article and praises Ficino for having arrived at "a profound understanding of an extremely difficult text" (p. 181) and in particular for grasping the complexities of Proclus's methodology (p. 180).
60. He mentions him just twice: in chap. 10 and in summa 25 (ed. Allen, *Charioteer,* pp. 121 and 173). This surely indicates the degree to which he rejected the details of Proclus's interpretation, rather than any attempt to "conceal" an important but pagan authority.

Along with the *Parmenides,* the master dialogue in Proclus's view for an understanding of Plato's metaphysics, the *Phaedrus* seems to have been Proclus's main text for his examination of the intelligible-and-intellectual gods as a category mediating between the purely intelligible gods and the purely intellectual. These three categories of gods in his system are all transcendent or supracosmic—that is, unattached in any way to the cosmos. Strikingly, Proclus confines the intermediate category of intelligible-and-intellectual gods to the three Phaedran loci, and, like Syrianus apparently, associates them with life in the being-life-intellect triad. They are in their turn subdivided into three triads: the first, which is identified with the Orphic Nights, he assigns to the super-heavenly place; the second, identified with Uranus, he assigns to the heaven; and the third and lowest, identified with the Cyclopes, he assigns to the subheavenly vault. Above these intelligible-and-intellectual gods are the three triads of purely intelligible gods, who are designated by abstractions rather than by proper names. Below them are the purely intellectual gods, who do not constitute, curiously, an ennead, but rather a hebdomad consisting of the three parents—Cronus (their leader), Rhea, and Zeus—the three Curetes, and a seventh deity derived from Uranus's castration in the *Euthyphro* 6A.[61] This "parent" Zeus is the Demiurge of the *Timaeus* 28A, as well as the Zeus of the *Philebus* 30D, of the *Protagoras* 321D-322D, and of the *Statesman* 269E-270E and 272B. The two groups of nine plus the final group of seven make up the twenty-five intelligible and/or intellectual deities who head the transcendent gods in Proclus's system.

On the ontological level below, and this time appearing in groups of twelve, are the immanent or cosmic gods. They too are divided into three broad categories: hypercosmic, hypercosmic-and-encosmic, and encosmic. The twelve hypercosmic gods are divided in turn into four triads, as are the twelve hypercosmic-and-encosmic gods. Whether the encosmic gods were also to appear as twelve and be subdivided similarly is uncertain. Of the hypercosmic gods the triads are as follows: 1) Zeus-Poseidon-Pluto; 2) Ar-

---

61. For a schematic presentation of Proclus's system, see Saffrey and Westerink, 1:lxv-lxvii.

temis-Persephone-Athena; 3) a triad under Apollo; and 4) the triad of the Corybantes. By contrast, of the hypercosmic-and-encosmic gods the triads are: 1) Zeus-Poseidon-Hephaestus; 2) Hestia-Athena-Ares; 3) Demeter-Hera-Artemis; and 4) Hermes-Aphrodite-Apollo. This group corresponds to the twelve encosmic gods in Iamblichus's system and to Hermias's too, though the order is different.

In sum, Proclus has assigned the three loci of the myth to the mixed category of the intelligible-and-intellectual gods and to its three constituent triads. The Zeus of the *Phaedrus*'s myth is the "parent" Zeus, the third monad in the first triad of the lower category of purely intellectual gods. Among the gods who follow him must be the hypercosmic-and-encosmic twelve of immanent, not transcendent, beings.

However much it may have seemed in its systematic clarity and logicality to be the culminating achievement of the ancient Neoplatonic analyses, and however much he may have profited from it in terms both of general inspiration and of various details, Ficino nevertheless rejected Proclus's account, along with the later Neoplatonists' accounts, for at least half-a-dozen reasons.

First, he was dismissive of the sheer number of deities involved and of the scholastic intricacies of Proclus's scheme; for these rendered Proclus (quite apart from his supposedly anti-Christian stance) much more difficult to reconcile with Christianity—and notably with its angelology—than either Plato or Plotinus, if not impossible.[62]

Second, Ficino had little use for the category of the intelligible-and-intellectual, or what he called the "mixed," gods, since he thinks of all the higher gods—that is, angels—as intellectual. Interestingly, however, he does introduce it on one occasion to designate the middle six deities of the transcendent, the intellectual, gods; that is, he employs a Proclian category but not in the Proclian way.[63]

---

62. See particularly his objections in his *Parmenides* Commentary, chap. 94, *Opera*, pp. 1194^{r+v}.

63. Chaps. 10 and 11 (ed. Allen, *Charioteer*, pp. 113, 125-127). Cf. Ficino's *Parmenides* Commentary, chaps. 94 and 95 (*Opera*, pp. 1194^{r+v}).

Third, Ficino seems to have been especially concerned to establish a gulf between the superheavenly place and the heaven below it. Instead of treating them, as Syrianus, Hermias, and Proclus had done, as a triad of related loci, he assigned the superheavenly place to the Ideas, the pure intelligibles, while to the next and inferior ontological category, the pure intellectuals, he assigned the heaven, along with its back and its vault. In the process he thus created a new triad of his own: the heaven's back, the heaven itself, and its vault below. These three, as the three aspects of heaven itself, were obviously related loci and could be dramatically subordinated to the superheavenly place.[64] This subordination was essential, of course, to a Christian Platonic reading of the myth, given the equation of the Platonic Ideas with the Ideas in God's Mind.

Fourth, he clearly rejected the discrepancy between the use of nine as the base number for the various categories of transcendent gods, and of twelve as the base number for those of the immanent gods (though this discrepancy could be numerologically justified, given the traditional associations of three and four). Simplifying the whole system, he decided to retain twelve as the base number for both the transcendent and the immanent leader gods (despite the precedent for nine in the Pseudo-Areopagite); he thus maintained a strict correspondence between them.[65]

Fifth, he rejected the late Neoplatonists' identification of the *Phaedrus's* Zeus with the Demiurge of the *Timaeus* and insisted on his being the World-Soul and not a purely intellectual god. In a way he may be said to have adopted the Zeus in Proclus's category of the hypercosmic-and-encosmic twelve, but to have put him in command of the flight upwards into the realms of the supracosmic, the transcendent, gods.[66]

Finally, much of the astronomical tradition that derived from the *Epinomis,* from Cicero, from Macrobius, from Dante possibly —to name just a few of its more obvious spokesmen—continued to influence Ficino. Though anxious to support the nonmaterial-

---

64. Chap. 11 (ed. Allen, *Charioteer,* p. 123).
65. Chap. 11 (ed. Allen, *Charioteer,* pp. 125-127).
66. Chaps. 2, 10, 11, and summae 19 and 28 (ed. Allen, *Charioteer,* pp. 77, 113, 127, 149, 177-179).

ist, Plotinian view of the *Phaedrus*'s "heaven," he was mindful that our heaven and its deities, the realm of the higher souls, was led back ultimately into the intellectual heaven, the heaven of the empyrean. Accordingly, he felt compelled to substitute Uranus and Saturn for Demeter and Athena in what is in effect Proclus's hypercosmic-and-encosmic twelve; and this compelled him in turn into a trinitarian interpretation of Zeus as both his father Saturn and his grandfather Uranus, as indeed the triune god.

In short, Ficino arrived at a much simpler and in many respects more symmetrical interpretation of the myth. Though indebted to the ancient Neoplatonists in diverse ways, in the long run he remained (or perhaps became) independent of them. In part this was because he succeeded (from our point of view ironically) in incorporating into his own analysis certain fundamental aspects of the astronomical interpretation of the *Phaedrus*'s myth, the very interpretation which the ancient Neoplatonists had associated with their unenlightened predecessors and had rejected as too "materialist." In itself this was an interesting and original achievement, and it bears testimony to Ficino's powers as eclectic and as syncretist; for he had managed to integrate the two traditions of *Phaedrus* interpretation current in antiquity despite their seemingly irreconcilable opposition.

Yet the essence of Proclus's *o altitudo* remained: his conviction that the dialogue treated of the highest mysteries of theology and that the flight was ultimately through the realm of the purely intellectual up to the realm of the purely intelligible, and his belief that Plato had provided us with a lucid architecture for this flight by means of a myth that was profoundly but coherently metaphysical. On closer inspection, we may note a certain tentativeness on Ficino's part in actually rejecting Proclus's analysis. In paragraph 10 of his last chapter of commentary proper Ficino seems to hesitate: "Some have supposed that the dodecade celebrated in the *Phaedrus* along with its leader, Jupiter, is supermundane; but I think, with Plotinus, that it is probably mundane." Admittedly, he then proceeds to list several good reasons why he believes it to be mundane, but he was clearly apprised of the late Neoplatonic interpretation and of the prestige of the masters who had espoused it. Certainly, he shared their sense of the dialogue's significance and their rejection of the rhetoricians' obsession with its youthfulness, its "overwritten" style, and its oratorical themes. In a way we might think of him as borrowing the grandeur associated with the demiurgic Zeus in their account and transferring it to his own vision of Zeus as the World-Soul, the leader of the animate realm and the immanent gods.[67] For this "lower" Zeus does indeed lead enlightened souls to the summit of the intellectual heaven Neoplatonically conceived. Whereas Plotinus had thought of Soul rising to Mind, Ficino had access to the intricate gradations between the two hypostases introduced by the Neoplatonists and still chose to have Soul rise through them. In this he was again expressing his heightened vision of the powers of Soul and of its accompanying souls who can ascend to the peaks of contemplation others have reserved for the pure angelic intellects alone.

Thus both the Plotinian (or at least what Ficino saw as the Plotinian) and the later Neoplatonic interpretations played into his hands. While the later Neoplatonic interpretations, in postulating further intermediary steps between man and the Ideas, had emphasized the complexity and difficulty of the ascent, the Plotinian interpretation, as Ficino had refashioned it in its simplicity and anthropocentricity, had emphasized man's ability to rise with Zeus, the culmination and leader of all souls, to the ineffable vision which man could share with the angels but which did not depend upon them, as was the case in the later Neoplatonists' accounts.[68] Of all the pagan authorities, Plotinus therefore seemed to have come the closest in his recognition that it was Plato's intention to center the dialogue upon man, his soul,[69] and his ability to transcend all metaphysical limitations in his pursuit of the divine

67. Note that Ficino does not adopt Proclus's usage with regard to the terms "hypercosmic" (supermundane) and "encosmic" (mundane). "Supermundane" is the term he uses for all the transcendent gods and for the Ideas above them, "mundane" for the gods in the animate realm, the immanent gods, and for all that is subject to them. For Proclus, on the other hand, "hypercosmic" signifies the highest order of immanent, or what Ficino calls the mundane, gods.

68. See the passage in Ficino's *Platonic Theology* 18.8 (ed. Marcel, 3:204; trans. Allen, *Charioteer*, p. 236).

69. It was this same concern with the integrity of the soul, and not just his desire to remain within the confines of Christian orthodoxy, that led him to reject Plotinus's theory of metempsychosis and to praise other Neoplatonists for their rejection of it.

vision. But we can now see that it was a Plotinus fashioned very much in Ficino's own image and a Plotinus that he had arrived at, paradoxically, through the later Neoplatonists and particularly through Proclus.

There is one final twist. Ficino must have known other authors from antiquity who had referred to the *Phaedrus*'s myth, if only in passing, and who were not pagan philosophers. Amongst them Saffrey and Westerink adduce four: a Jew and three Christians.

Philo Judaeus (c. 30 B.C.-45 A.D.) imagines the Hebrew God conducting "the winged chariot, that is, the entire sky, with a sovereign and all-powerful authority," the sky being the place of the intelligible Ideas;[70] in interpreting the *Phaedrus*'s winged chariot as the firmament, he is suggesting that the Zeus is, or figures, God Himself. It is unlikely, however, that Ficino knew Philo's work in any detail or knew this particular comment, though he mentions Philo on a number of occasions elsewhere in his work.[71]

Tertullian (c. 160-225 A.D.), in his *Apology* at 24.3, compares Plato's image of "great Jupiter in heaven, escorted by an army of gods and of demons," to God accompanied by his ministers;[72] and Athenagoras (2d century A.D.), in his *Legatio* at 23.9, includes the *Phaedrus* 246E in a *florilegium* of Plato texts concerning God, though he insists that the Zeus there is not the son of Cronus but rather "the creator of the universe" (with the *Timaeus* 40A-B obviously in mind).[73]

---

70. *Quis Rerum Divinarum Heres Sit* §301, cited along with other texts by Saffrey and Westerink, 4:xii-xvi. They refer us to three important studies: Pierre Boyancé, "Sur l'exégèse hellénistique du *Phèdre*," in *Miscellanea di studi alessandrini in memoria di Augusto Rostagni* (Turin, 1963), pp. 45-53; Marguerite Harl, ed. and trans., *Philon d'Alexandrie: Quis Rerum Divinarum Heres Sit* (Paris, 1966), introd., pp. 103-129; and Willy Theiler, "Philo von Alexandria und der Beginn des kaiserzeitlichen Platonismus," in *Parusia: Festgabe für Johannes Hirschberger* (Frankfurt am Main, 1965), pp. 199-218.

71. *Opera*, pp. 25, 44, 47, 53, 73, 325, 459, 867, 1257, 1313, 1408, 1443; also Kristeller, *Sup. Fic.* 2:16. These and the following refs. are taken from Kristeller's *index auctorum* in the Italian (and German) versions of his *Philosophy*.

72. Ficino mentions Tertullian in his *Opera*, pp. 8, 12, 15 ff., 24 ff., 29, 44, 55 ff., 72 ff., 852.

73. Ficino mentions Athenagoras in his *Opera*, pp. 1817 ff., and in Kristeller, *Sup. Fic.* 1:4. He had translated excerpts from Athenagoras's *De Resurrectione, Opera*, pp. 1871-1873; see Kristeller, *Sup. Fic.* 1:cxxxii and *Studies*, p. 51; also E. Lupieri, "Marsilio Ficino e il *De Resurrectione* di Atenagora," *Studi storico-religiosi* 1 (1977), 147-163.

Finally, and by far the most significantly, since we know that
Ficino had read the work and often quoted from it, is the evidence
of the *Contra Celsum* by the Christian Origen (c. 185-c. 254 A.D.),
the ancient apologist whom Ficino and his fellow Florentine Platonists much admired.[74] In 8.4 Origen writes:

> The man who has ascended to the supreme God is he who, without any
> divided loyalty whatever, worships Him through His Son, the divine
> Logos and Wisdom seen in Jesus, who alone leads to Him those who by
> all means try to draw near to God, the Creator of all things, by exception-
> ally good words and deeds and thoughts. I think it is for this and for simi-
> lar reasons that the prince of this world, who is transformed into an angel
> of light, caused the words to be written—"A host of gods and daemons
> follow him, arranged in eleven divisions," where he says of himself and
> the philosophers, "We are with Zeus, but others are with the other dae-
> mons, some with one, some with another."[75]

The "prince of this world," as the quotation from 2 Cor. 11:14
makes clear, is Satan. Nevertheless, Origen is establishing the
equation (even if Satanically) between the *Phaedrus*'s Zeus and
Christ, the Logos.

Any one of these, or similar, suggestions might have spurred
Ficino to an interpretation of the *Phaedrus* which, if not explicitly
or even implicitly Christian (for Christian concepts he omitted
from the Commentary, probably deliberately and probably for
apologetic reasons),[76] was compatible nevertheless with Christian
dogmas. But even without such authorities, he, like other perceptive and sympathetic readers, would have been drawn quite natu-

74. Ficino mentions Origen on a number of occasions: in his *Opera*, pp. 8, 26, 46, 72,
147, 152, 205, 216, 219, 223, 309, 382, 422, 426, 475, 478, 489, 562, 855, 866, 875, 994,
1008, 1217, 1257, 1260, 1309, 1438 ff., 1441, 1485, 1487, 1553 ff., 1556, 1614, 1621 ff.,
1663, 1667, 1672, 1676, 1694, 1697; and in Kristeller, *Sup. Fic.* 1:8, 33 ff; 2:19, 21, 50, 133,
147.
75. This is the translation of Henry Chadwick, *Origen: Contra Celsum* (Cambridge,
1965), p. 456.
76. In his *The Kiss Sacred and Profane* (Berkeley and Los Angeles, 1969), p. 166, Nicholas J. Perella observes that "the most striking or shocking feature" of Ficino's *De Amore*,
particularly when read from the vantage point of some fifteen centuries of Christianity, "is
the absence of Christ." The same might be said of the *Phaedrus* Commentary. But this
"absence" must be understood in the context of Ficino's goals as an apologist; it is not, as
Perella would be the first to admit, an indication that Ficino was (crypto-) pagan.

rally to the possibility of comparing the Zeus who leads the cavalcade of souls to the Christ who leads the souls of the saved in tri-
umph into heaven, into the Mind which is Himself. After all, the
notion of identifying the pagans' Jupiter, the father of gods and
men, with Christ the Judge and the Redeemer had had a long if
controversial history from the beginning of the Christian era; and
Ficino himself with his expertise in Orphic theology had already
played an important part in writing the Renaissance pages of that
history.

To conclude, Ficino achieved a memorable twofold synthesis.
First, he dovetailed the astronomical-astrological interpretation of
the *Phaedrus*'s myth as he probably found it in Cicero (and Macrobius) into the basic framework of the Neoplatonic analysis as he
found it in the writings of Plotinus, Hermias, and Proclus. Obviously such dovetailing itself required him to introduce a number of
modifications, many of which we now see as original, but he remained convinced that his view of the myth was essentially Plotinian and thus authentically Platonic, Plotinus being the arch exegete of Plato. Second, whether or not he was actually inspired by
such notices as Saffrey and Westerink have uncovered in Philo
and Tertullian, Athenagoras and Origen, he successfully arrived at
an interpretation that was wholly compatible with Christianity,
and most notably with the great dogmas concerning the Fall, the
Incarnation, and the Redemption. Ironically, even the most enthu-
siastic admirers of the wisdom of the ancients had usually agreed
in the past that, while the pagan theologians had succeeded in
anticipating many of the fundamental truths about God and His
Creation, they had not succeeded in anticipating the story of
Christ's Redemption. But Ficino's "correct" and authentically
"Platonic" interpretation of the *Phaedrus* had come near to refut-
ing this major reservation on the part of those well-disposed to
pagan learning. For he had brought this extraordinary monument
of Greek poetry and mythmaking into direct alignment with the
anticipatory signs and prophecies in the Hebrew Old Testament,
where the redemptive scheme of Christ the Savior was thought to
be truly foretold. In this regard we are once again struck by the
force of Ficino's own analogy between the hermeneutical chal-

lenges posed by the *Phaedrus* and those posed by the Canticle of Canticles.[77]

However complex and controversial the nature of his many debts—and much basic research remains to be done—Ficino's achievement as an interpreter of the *Phaedrus* is therefore a signal one, peculiar to himself and his Renaissance Florentine context and yet cognizant of its relationships to the various contributions of antiquity. Indeed we may say that the range and caliber of Ficino's learning and the thoroughness of his acquaintance with the ancient commentary tradition make the essential independence of his own interpretation the more striking. The same has yet to be proved with regard to his work on other major dialogues such as the *Parmenides,* the *Philebus,* the *Timaeus,* and even the *Symposium;* but we can confidently predict that there too we will find a comparable independence from, though familiarity with, the commentary traditions of antiquity, and possibly, in the case of the *Timaeus* and the *Parmenides,* of the Middle Ages also.[78] Such an independence has, after all, its own kind of originality; it was the fruit certainly of difficult if fascinating humanistic scholarship.

77. Chap. 2 (ed. Allen, *Charioteer,* p. 79; see also introd., pp. 14, 43 n. 59). Cf. chap. 2, n. 72 above.
78. See M.-D. Chenu, *La théologie au douzième siècle* (Paris, 1957), pp. 118-128: "Le platonisme du Timée et de Boèce"; and Garin, *Studi sul platonismo medievale,* chap. 1.

Bibliography of Works Cited

Alberti, Giovan Battista. "Marsilio Ficino e il Codice Riccardiano 581." *Rinascimento,* 2d ser., 10 (1970), 187-193.

Allen, Don Cameron. *Image and Meaning.* Baltimore, 1960.

Allen, Michael J. B. "The Absent Angel in Ficino's Philosophy." *Journal of the History of Ideas* 36.2 (1975), 219-240.

———. "Cosmogony and Love: The Role of Phaedrus in Ficino's *Symposium* Commentary." *Journal of Medieval and Renaissance Studies* 10.2 (1980), 131-153.

———. "Ficino's Lecture on the Good?" *Renaissance Quarterly* 30.2 (1977), 160-171.

———. "Ficino's Theory of the Five Substances and the Neoplatonists' *Parmenides.*" *Journal of Medieval and Renaissance Studies* 12.1 (1982), 19-44.

———. "Jaques against the Seven Ages of the Proclan Man." *Modern Language Quarterly* 42.4 (1981), 331-346.

———. "Marsilio Ficino on Plato's Pythagorean Eye." *MLN* 97.1 (1982), 171-182.

———. "The Sibyl in Ficino's Oaktree." *MLN* 95.1 (1980), 205-210.

———. "Tamburlaine and Plato: A Colon, a Crux." *Research Opportunities in Renaissance Drama* 23 (1980), 21-31.

———. "Two Commentaries on the *Phaedrus:* Ficino's Indebtedness to Hermias." *Journal of the Warburg and Courtauld Institutes* 43 (1980), 110-129.

———, and Roger A. White. "Ficino's Hermias Translation and a New Apologue." *Scriptorium* 35 (1981), 39-47.

———. Review of *Marsilio Ficino: The Book of Life,* trans. Charles Boer. *Renaissance Quarterly* 25 (1982), 69-72.

———, ed. and trans. *Marsilio Ficino and the Phaedran Charioteer.* Berkeley, Los Angeles, London, 1981.

———, ed. and trans. *Marsilio Ficino: The Philebus Commentary.* Berkeley, Los Angeles, London, 1975. Reprint, 1979 (this reprint contains several substantive corrections).

Amandry, Pierre. *La mantique apollinienne à Delphes.* Paris, 1950. Reprint, New York, 1975.

Anastos, Milton V. "Pletho's Calendar and Liturgy." *Dumbarton Oaks Papers* 4 (1948), 185-305.

Anichini, Giuseppe. *L'umanesimo e il problema della salvezza in Marsilio Ficino.* Milan, 1937.

Armstrong, A. H. *The Architecture of the Intelligible Universe in the Philosophy of Plotinus.* Cambridge, 1940. Reprint, Amsterdam, 1967.

———, ed. *The Cambridge History of Later Greek and Early Medieval Philosophy.* Cambridge, 1970.

Baron, Hans. *Leonardo Bruni Aretino: Humanistisch-philosophische Schriften.* Leipzig and Berlin, 1928.

———. "Willensfreiheit und Astrologie bei Marsilio Ficino und Pico della Mirandola." In *Kultur- und Universalgeschichte: Festschrift Walter Goetz.* Leipzig and Berlin, 1927. Pp. 145-170.

Beierwaltes, Werner. "Der Begriff des 'unum in nobis' bei Proklos." *Miscellanea Mediaevalia* 2 (1963), 255-266.

———. *Marsilio Ficinos Theorie des Schönen im Kontext des Platonismus.* Sitzungsberichte der Heidelberger Akademie der Wissenschaften: Philosophisch-historische Klasse, Jahrgang 30, no. 11. Heidelberg, 1980.

———. *Proklos: Grundzüge seiner Metaphysik.* Frankfurt, 1965.

Bessarion. *In Calumniatorem Platonis.* Venice, 1469. Edited in vol. 2 of Ludwig Mohler's *Kardinal Bessarion als Theologe, Humanist und Staatsmann.* 3 vols. Paderborn, 1923-1942.

Bielmeier, P[ater] Amandus. *Die neuplatonische Phaidrosinterpretation.* Rhetorische Studien, no. 16. Paderborn, 1930.

Boccaccio. See under Romano.

Boer, Charles, trans. *Marsilio Ficino: The Book of Life.* Irving, Texas, 1980.

Boese, Helmut, ed. *Procli Diadochi Tria Opuscula.* Berlin, 1960.

Boyancé, Pierre. *Le culte des muses chez les philosophes grecs.* Paris, 1937.

———. "La religion astrale de Platon à Cicéron." *Revue des études grecques* 65 (1952), 312-350.

———. "Sur l'exégèse hellénistique du *Phèdre.*" In *Miscellanea di studi alessandrini in memoria di Augusto Rostagni.* Turin, 1963. Pp. 45-53.

Bréhier, Émile. *The Philosophy of Plotinus.* Translated by Joseph Thomas. Chicago, 1958.

Burckhardt, Jacob. *The Civilization of the Renaissance in Italy.* Translated by S. G. C. Middlemore. Revised and edited by Irene Gordon. New York, 1961.

Burnet, John, ed. *Platonis Opera.* Vol. 2. Oxford, n.d.

Calcidius. *In Timaeum.* See under Waszink.

Cassirer, Ernst. "Ficino's Place in Intellectual History." *Journal of the History of Ideas* 6.4 (1945), 483-501.

———. *The Individual and the Cosmos in Renaissance Philosophy.* Translated by Mario Domandi. New York and Evanston, Ill., 1963.

Cassuto, Umberto. *Gli Ebrei a Firenze nell'età del Rinascimento.* Florence, 1918.

Castelli, Enrico, ed. *Umanesimo e esoterismo: Atti del V Convegno Internazionale di Studi Umanistici.* Padua, 1960.

Chadwick, Henry, trans. *Origen: Contra Celsum.* Cambridge, 1965.

Charrue, Jean-Michel. *Plotin: Lecteur de Platon.* Paris, 1978.

Chastel, André. *Arte e umanesimo a Firenze al tempo di Lorenzo il Magnifico.* Translated by Renzo Federici. Turin, 1964.

———. *Marsile Ficin et l'art*. Geneva and Lille, 1954.

———. "Le mythe de Saturne dans la Renaissance italienne." *Phoebus* 1.3-4 (1946), 125-134.

Chenu, M.-D. *La théologie au douzième siècle*. Paris, 1957.

Cherniss, Harold. *The Riddle of the Early Academy*. Berkeley, 1945.

Cody, Richard. *The Landscape of the Mind: Pastoralism and Platonic Theory in Tasso's Aminta and Shakespeare's Early Comedies*. Oxford, 1969.

Collins, Ardis B. *The Secular Is Sacred: Platonism and Thomism in Ficino's Platonic Theology*. The Hague, 1974.

Comito, Terry. *The Idea of the Garden in the Renaissance*. New Brunswick, N.J., 1978.

Cornford, Francis M. *Plato's Cosmology: The "Timaeus" of Plato Translated with a Running Commentary*. London, 1937.

———. *Plato's Theory of Knowledge: The "Theaetetus" and "Sophist" of Plato*. Translated with a Running Commentary. London, 1935.

———. *Principium Sapientiae: A Study of the Origins of Greek Philosophical Thought*. Cambridge, 1952.

Couvreur, P., ed. *Hermiae Alexandrini in Platonis Phaedrum Scholia*. Paris, 1901. Reprint, Hildesheim, 1971.

Craven, William G. *Giovanni Pico della Mirandola: Symbol of his Age*. Geneva, 1981.

Cumont, Franz. *Recherches sur le symbolisme funéraire des Romains*. Paris, 1942.

Damascius. See under Zintzen.

Dannenfeldt, Karl H. "Hermetica Philosophica" and "Oracula Chaldaica." In *Catalogus Translationum et Commentariorum*, vol. 1, edited by Paul Oskar Kristeller. Washington, 1960. Pp. 137-151, 157-164.

———. "The Pseudo-Zoroastrian Oracles in the Renaissance." *Studies in the Renaissance* 4 (1957), 7-30.

Delcorno Branca, Daniela. "Un discepolo del Poliziano: Michele Acciari." *Lettere italiane* 28 (1976), 470-471.

Delcourt, Marie. *L'oracle de Delphes*. Paris, 1955.

Des Places, Édouard, ed. and trans. *Jamblique: Les mystères d'Égypte*. Paris, 1966.

———, ed. and trans. *Oracles chaldaïques*. Paris, 1971.

Devereux, James A. "The Object of Love in Ficino's Philosophy." *Journal of the History of Ideas* 30.2 (1969), 161-170.

———. "The Textual History of Ficino's *De Amore*." *Renaissance Quarterly* 28.2 (1975), 173-182.

Diehl, Ernst, ed. *Procli Diadochi in Platonis Timaeum Commentaria*. 3 vols. Leipzig, 1903-1906. Reprint, Amsterdam, 1965.

Diels, Hermann, and Walther Kranz, eds. *Die Fragmente der Vorsokratiker*. 3 vols. 11th ed. Zurich and Berlin, 1964.

Dihle, Albrecht. *The Theory of Will in Classical Antiquity*. Berkeley, Los Angeles, London, 1982.

Dillon, John M. *The Middle Platonists.* Ithaca, N.Y., 1977.
——, ed. *Iamblichi Chalcidensis in Platonis Dialogos Commentariorum Fragmenta.* Leiden, 1973.
Diogenes Laertius. *Lives of the Philosophers.* Edited and translated by R. D. Hicks. 2 vols. Cambridge, Mass., and London, 1959.
Dodds, E. R., ed. and trans. *Proclus: The Elements of Theology.* Oxford, 1933. 2d ed., 1963.
Dress, Walter. *Die Mystik des Marsilio Ficino.* Berlin and Leipzig, 1929.
Fabro, Cornelio. "Influenze tomistiche nella filosofia del Ficino." *Studia patavina* 3 (1959), 396-413.
Fauth, Wolfgang. "Pythia." In Pauly-Wissowa-Kroll, *Realencyclopädie der classischen Altertumswissenschaft* 24.1 (1963), 515-547.
Festugière, A.-J., trans. *Proclus: Commentaire sur la République.* 3 vols. Paris, 1970.
——, trans. *Proclus: Commentaire sur le Timée.* 5 vols. Paris, 1966-1969.
——. *La révélation d'Hermès Trismégiste.* 4 vols. Paris, 1950-1954.
See also under Nock.
Ficino, Marsilio. *Commentaria in Platonem.* Florence, 1496.
——. *Opera Omnia.* Basel, 1576. Reprint, Turin, 1959, 1983.
——. *Platonis Opera Omnia.* Florence, 1484. 2d ed., Venice, 1491.
——. *Plotini Enneades.* Florence, 1492.
See also under Allen, Boer, Kristeller, Marcel, and Members.
Flacelière, Robert. *Devins et oracles grecs.* Paris, 1961.
——, ed. and trans. *Plutarque: Sur la disparition des oracles.* Paris, 1947.
Flamini, F. *Peregrino Allio: Umanista, poeta e confilosofo del Ficino.* Pisa, 1893.
Frutiger, Perceval. *Les mythes de Platon.* Paris, 1930.
Gandillac, Maurice de. "Astres, anges, et génies chez Marsile Ficin." In *Umanesimo e esoterismo* (see under Castelli in this Bibliography), pp. 85-109.
——. "Neoplatonism and Christian Thought in the Fifteenth Century (Nicholas of Cusa and Marsilio Ficino)." In *Neoplatonism and Christian Thought,* edited by Dominic J. O'Meara. Albany, N.Y., 1982. Pp. 143-168.
Garin, Eugenio. *La cultura filosofica del Rinascimento italiano: Ricerche e documenti.* Florence, 1961.
——. "La 'dignitas hominis' e la letteratura patristica." *La Rinascita* 1.4 (1938), 102-146.
——. "Le 'elezioni' e il problema dell'astrologia." In *Umanesimo e esoterismo* (see under Castelli in this Bibliography), pp. 17-37. Reprinted in Garin's *L'età nuova* (q.v. in this Bibliography), pp. 421-447.
——. *L'età nuova: Ricerche di storia della cultura dal XII al XVI secolo.* Naples, 1969.
——. "Magia ed astrologia nella cultura di Rinascimento." *Belfagor* 5.4 (1950), 657-667. Reprinted in Garin's *Medioevo e Rinascimento* (q.v. in this Bibliography), pp. 150-169.

————. "Marsilio Ficino e la *Contra Gentiles.*" *Giornale critico della filosofia italiana* 39 (1959), 158-159.

————. *Medioevo e Rinascimento: Studi e ricerche.* Bari, 1954. 2d ed., 1961.

————. "Per la storia della cultura filosofica del Rinascimento." *Rivista critica di storia della filosofia* 12.1 (1957), 3-21.

————. *Portraits from the Quattrocento.* Translated by Victor A. Velen and Elizabeth Velen. New York, 1972.

————. "Postille sull'ermetismo del Rinascimento." *Rinascimento,* 2d ser., 16 (1976), 245-249.

————. "Recenti interpretazioni di Marsilio Ficino." *Giornale critico della filosofia italiana* 21 (1940), 299-319.

————. "Ricerche sull'epicureismo del Quattrocento." In *La cultura filosofica del Rinascimento italiano* (q.v. in this Bibliography), pp. 72-92.

————. *Rinascite e rivoluzioni: Movimenti culturali dal XIV al XVIII secolo.* Bari, 1975.

————. "Ritratto di Marsilio Ficino." *Belfagor* 6.3 (1951), 289-301. Revised as "Immagini e simboli in Marsilio Ficino" in Garin's *Medioevo e Rinascimento* (q.v. in this Bibliography), pp. 288-310. English translation in Garin's *Portraits from the Quattrocento* (q.v. in this Bibliography), pp. 142-157.

————. "S. Agostino e Marsilio Ficino." *Bollettino storico agostiniano* 16 (1940), 41-47.

————. *Studi sul platonismo medievale.* Florence, 1958.

————. *Lo zodiaco della vita: La polemica sull'astrologia dal Trecento al Cinquecento.* Rome and Bari, 1976. Translated by Carolyn Jackson and June Allen (the translation revised by Clare Robertson in conjunction with the author) as *Astrology in the Renaissance: The Zodiac of Life.* London, 1983.

————, ed. and trans. *G. Pico della Mirandola: De Hominis Dignitate, Heptaplus, De Ente et Uno, e scritti vari.* Florence, 1942.

————, ed. and trans. *Pico della Mirandola: Disputationes adversus Astrologiam Divinatricem.* 2 vols. Florence, 1946, 1952.

Gentile, Giovanni. "Il concetto dell'uomo nel Rinascimento." In his *Il pensiero italiano del Rinascimento.* Florence, 1940. Pp. 47-113.

Gentile, Sebastiano. "Per la storia del testo del 'Commentarium in Convivium' di Marsilio Ficino." *Rinascimento,* 2d ser., 21 (1981), 3-27.

Gersh, S. E. Κίνησις ἀκίνητος: *A Study of Spiritual Motion in the Philosophy of Proclus.* Leiden, 1973.

Gilson, Étienne. "Marsile Ficin et le *Contra Gentiles.*" *Archives d'histoire doctrinale et littéraire du Moyen Âge* 24 (1957), 101-113.

Giuliano, Balbino. *L'idea religiosa di Marsilio Ficino e il concetto di una dottrina esoterica.* Cerignola, 1904.

Gombrich, Ernst H. "*Icones Symbolicae:* The Visual Image in Neoplatonic Thought." *Journal of the Warburg and Courtauld Institutes* 11 (1948), 163-192.

————. *Symbolic Images: Studies in the Art of the Renaissance.* Oxford and New York, 1972. 2d ed., 1978.

Gundel, W. *Dekane und Dekansternbilder: Ein Beitrag zur Geschichte des Sternbilder der Kulturvölker.* Studien der Bibliothek Warburg, no. 19. Glückstadt and Hamburg, 1936.

Guthrie, W. K. C. *A History of Greek Philosophy.* 6 vols. Cambridge, vol. 1, 1962; vol. 2, 1965; vol. 3, 1969; vol. 4, 1975; vol. 5, 1978; vol. 6, 1981.

Hackforth, R., trans. *Plato's Phaedrus.* Cambridge, 1952. Reprint, 1972.

Hadot, Pierre. "Être, vie, pensée chez Plotin et avant Plotin." In *Les sources de Plotin.* Fondation Hardt, Entretiens sur l'antiquité classique, vol. 5. Geneva, 1960. Pp. 107-157.

Harl, Marguerite, ed. and trans. *Philon d'Alexandrie: Quis Rerum Divinarum Heres Sit.* Paris, 1966.

Harvey, E. Ruth. *The Inward Wits: Psychological Theory in the Middle Ages and the Renaissance.* London, 1975.

Heitzman, Marian. "L'agostinismo avicennizzante e il punto di partenza della filosofia di Marsilio Ficino." *Giornale critico della filosofia italiana* 16 (1935), 295-322, 460-480; 17 (1936), 1-11.

———. "La libertà e il fato nella filosofia di Marsilio Ficino." *Rivista di filosofia neo-scolastica* 28 (1936), 350-371; 29 (1937), 59-82.

Heninger, S. K., Jr. *The Cosmographical Glass: Renaissance Diagrams of the Universe.* San Marino, Calif., 1977.

———. *Touches of Sweet Harmony: Pythagorean Cosmology and Renaissance Poetics.* San Marino, Calif., 1974.

Henry, Paul. "Les manuscrits grecs de travail de Marsile Ficin, le traducteur des Ennéades de Plotin." In *Association Guillaume Budé: Congrès de Tours et Poitiers.* Paris, 1954. Pp. 323-328.

———, and Hans-Rudolf Schwyzer, eds. *Plotini Opera.* Vol. 3. Paris, Brussels, Leiden, 1973.

Hermias. See under Couvreur.

Hieatt, A. Kent. See under Lorch.

Hillman, James. "Plotinus, Ficino, and Vico as Precursors of Archetypal Psychology." In *Loose Ends: Primary Papers in Archetypal Psychology.* Irving, Texas, 1978. Pp. 146-169.

———. *Re-Visioning Psychology.* New York, 1975.

Hough, Samuel Jones. "An Early Record of Marsilio Ficino." *Renaissance Quarterly* 30.3 (1977), 301-304.

Hutton, James. "Some English Poems in Praise of Music." *English Miscellany* 2 (1951), 1-63.

Iamblichus. See under Des Places, Dillon, and Larsen.

Ivanoff, N. "La beauté dans la philosophie de Marsile Ficin et de Léon Hébreux." *Humanisme et Renaissance* 3 (1936), 12-21.

Jābir ibn Hayyān. See under Kraus.

Jackson, B. Darrell. "The Prayers of Socrates." *Phronesis* 16.1 (1971), 14-37.

Jayne, Sears R. *John Colet and Marsilio Ficino.* Oxford, 1963.

Joannou, Perikles-Petros. *Démonologie populaire—démonologie critique au*

XIe siècle: La vie inédite de s. Auxence par M. Psellos. Schriften zur Geistes-geschichte des östlichen Europa, no. 5. Wiesbaden, 1971.

Jowett, Benjamin, trans. *The Dialogues of Plato.* 4th ed. 4 vols. Oxford, 1953.

Kaske, Carol V. "Marsilio Ficino and the Twelve Gods of the Zodiac." *Journal of the Warburg and Courtauld Institutes* 45 (1982), 195-202.

Kenny, Anthony. *Aristotle's Theory of the Will.* London and New Haven, 1979.

Kieszkowski, Bohdan. *Studi sul platonismo del Rinascimento in Italia.* Florence, 1936.

————, ed. *Giovanni Pico della Mirandola: Conclusiones sive Theses DCCCC.* Paris, 1973.

Kissling, Robert Christian. "The ὄχημα-πνεῦμα of the Neo-Platonists and the *De Insomniis* of Synesius of Cyrenc." *American Journal of Philology* 43.4 (1922), 318-330.

Klein, Robert. "L'enfer de Ficin." In *Umanesimo e esoterismo* (see under Castelli in this Bibliography), pp. 47-84.

————. "L'imagination comme vêtement de l'âme chez Marsile Ficin et Giordano Bruno." *Revue de métaphysique et de morale* 61 (1956), 18-39.

Klibansky, Raymond. *The Continuity of the Platonic Tradition during the Middle Ages.* London, 1939. Reissued together with Klibansky's *Plato's Parmenides in the Middle Ages and the Renaissance,* and accompanied by a new preface and four supplementary chapters. Munich, 1981.

————, Erwin Panofsky, and Fritz Saxl. *Saturn and Melancholy.* Rev. ed. London, 1964. See also under Panofsky and Saxl.

Klutstein-Roitman, Ilana. "Les traditions latines des Oracles chaldaïques et des orphiques." Diss., Hebrew University, Jerusalem, 1981.

Kraus, P., ed. *Jābir ibn Hayyān: Essai sur l'histoire des idées scientifiques dans l'Islam.* Paris and Cairo, 1935.

Kristeller, Paul Oskar. "Augustine and the Early Renaissance." *Review of Religion* 8 (1944), 339-358. Reprinted as chap. 17 of Kristeller's *Studies in Renaissance Thought and Letters* (q.v. in this Bibliography).

————. *Iter Italicum.* 3 vols. to date. London and Leiden, 1963, 1967, 1983.

————. "Marsilio Ficino as a Beginning Student of Plato." *Scriptorium* 20 (1966), 41-54.

————. "Marsilio Ficino e Lodovico Lazzarelli: Contributo alla diffusione delle idee ermetiche nel Rinascimento." *Annali della R. Scuola Normale Superiore di Pisa: Lettere, storia e filosofia,* 2d ser., 7 (1938), 237-262. Reprinted as chap. 11 of Kristeller's *Studies in Renaissance Thought and Letters* (q.v. in this Bibliography).

————. "The Modern System of the Arts." *Journal of the History of Ideas* 12.4 (1951), 496-527; 13.1 (1952), 17-46. Reprinted in Kristeller's *Renaissance Thought II* (q.v. in this Bibliography), pp. 163-227.

————. *The Philosophy of Marsilio Ficino.* Translated by Virginia Conant. New York, 1943. Reprint, Gloucester, Mass., 1964. Italian version, Florence, 1953. German version, Frankfurt am Main, 1972.

————. *Renaissance Thought II: Papers on Humanism and the Arts.* New York, 1965. Reprinted as *Renaissance Thought and the Arts.* Princeton, 1980.

————. "The Scholastic Background of Marsilio Ficino: With an Edition of Unpublished Texts." *Traditio* 2 (1944), 257-318. Reprinted as chap. 4 of Kristeller's *Studies in Renaissance Thought and Letters* (q.v. in this Bibliography).

————. *Studies in Renaissance Thought and Letters.* Rome, 1956. Reprint, 1969.

————. *Le thomisme et la pensée italienne de la Renaissance.* Montreal, 1967.

————. "A Thomist Critique of Marsilio Ficino's Theory of Will and Intellect: Fra Vincenzo Bandello da Castelnuovo O.P. and His Unpublished Treatise Addressed to Lorenzo de' Medici." In *Harry Austryn Wolfson Jubilee Volume, English Section,* vol. 2. Jerusalem, 1965. Pp. 463-494.

————, ed. *Catalogus Translationum et Commentariorum: Mediaeval and Renaissance Translations and Commentaries: Annotated Lists and Guides.* Vol. 1. Washington, D.C., 1960.

————, ed. *Supplementum Ficinianum.* 2 vols. Florence, 1937.

Kroll, G., ed. *Procli in Platonis Rem Publicam Commentarii.* 2 vols. Leipzig, 1899, 1901.

Kuczyńska, Alicja. *Filozofia i teoria piękna Marsilia Ficina.* Warsaw, 1970.

Kuhn, Reinhard C. *The Demon of Noontide: Ennui in Western Literature.* Princeton, 1976.

Landino, Cristoforo. See under Lohe.

Larsen, Bent Dalsgaard. *Jamblique de Chalcis: Exégète et philosophe.* Plus supplement, *Testimonia et Fragmenta Exegetica.* Aarhus, 1972.

Lentzen, Manfred. Review of *Marsilio Ficino: The Philebus Commentary,* ed. and trans. Michael J. B. Allen. *Archiv für das Studium der neueren Sprachen und Literaturen* 216 (1979), 218-220.

Leonicus, Nicolaus. *Nicolai Leonici Thomaei Dialogi.* Lyons, 1542.

Lloyd, A. C. "The Later Neoplatonists." In *The Cambridge History of Later Greek and Early Medieval Philosophy,* edited by A. H. Armstrong. Cambridge, 1970. Pp. 272-325.

Lloyd, A. K. "Primum in Genere: The Philosophical Background." *Diotima* 4 (1976), 32-36.

Lohe, Peter, ed. *Cristoforo Landino: Disputationes Camaldulenses.* Florence, 1980.

Lorch, Maristella De Panizza, ed. *Lorenzo Valla: De Vero Falsoque Bono.* Bari, 1970.

————, and A. Kent Hieatt, trans. *Lorenzo Valla: On Pleasure: De Voluptate.* New York, 1977.

Lubac, Henri de. *Pic de la Mirandole.* Paris, 1974.

Lupieri, E. "Marsilio Ficino e il *De Resurrectione* di Atenagora." *Studi storico-religiosi* 1 (1977), 147-163.

MacKenna, Stephen, trans. *Plotinus: The Enneads.* 3d ed. Revised by B. S. Page. London, 1962.

Macrobius. *In Somnium Scipionis.* See under Willis.

Mahoney, Edward P. "Metaphysical Foundations of the Hierarchy of Being According to Some Late-Medieval and Renaissance of Philosophers." In *Philosophies of Existence, Ancient and Medieval,* edited by Parviz Morewedge. New York, 1982. Pp. 165-257.

Maier, Anneliese. *Zwei Grundprobleme der scholastischen Naturphilosophie: Das Problem der intensiven Grösse, die Impetustheorie.* 2d ed. Rome, 1951.

Marcel, Raymond. "L'apologétique de Marsile Ficin." In *Pensée humaniste et tradition chrétienne aux XVe et XVIe siècles.* Paris, 1950. Pp. 159-168.

————. *Marsile Ficin.* Paris, 1958.

————, ed. and trans. *Marsile Ficin: Commentaire sur le Banquet de Platon.* Paris, 1956.

————, ed. and trans. *Marsile Ficin: Théologie platonicienne de l'immortalité des âmes.* 3 vols. Paris, vols. 1 and 2, 1964; vol. 3, 1970.

Marley, Clyde. "Plato's *Phaedrus* and Theocritean Pastoral." *Transactions of the American Philological Association* 71 (1940), 281-295.

Martins, José V. de Pina. *Jean Pic de la Mirandole: Un portrait inconnu de l'humaniste, une édition très rare de ses "Conclusiones."* Paris, 1976.

Members of the Language Department of the School of Economic Science, London, trans. *The Letters of Marsilio Ficino.* 3 vols. London, vol. 1 (Liber I), 1975; vol. 2 (Liber III), 1978; vol. 3 (Liber IV), 1981.

Merlan, Philip. "Greek Philosophy from Plato to Plotinus." In *The Cambridge History of Later Greek and Early Medieval Philosophy,* edited by A. H. Armstrong. Cambridge, 1970. Pp. 14-132.

Mohler, Ludwig. *Kardinal Bessarion als Theologe, Humanist und Staatsmann.* 3 vols. Paderborn, 1923-1942.

Moore, Thomas. *The Planets Within: Marsilio Ficino's Astrological Psychology.* Lewisburg, Pa., 1982.

Moraux, Paul. "Quinta Essentia." In Pauly-Wissowa-Kroll, *Realencyclopädie der classischen Altertumswissenschaft* 24.1 (1963), 1171-1263, esp. 1251-1256.

Napoli, Giovanni di. *Giovanni Pico della Mirandola e la problematica dottrinale del suo tempo.* Rome, 1965.

Nauert, Charles G., Jr. *Agrippa and the Crisis of Renaissance Thought.* Urbana, 1965.

Nock, A. D., and A.-J. Festugière, eds. and trans. *Corpus Hermeticum.* 4 vols. Paris, 1945-1954.

Origen. See under Chadwick.

Panofsky, Erwin. *Idea: Ein Beitrag zur Begriffsgeschichte der älteren Kunsttheorie.* Leipzig, 1924.

————. *The Life and Art of Albrecht Dürer.* 4th ed. Princeton, 1955.

————. *Renaissance and Renascences in Western Art.* Stockholm, 1960. Reprint, New York, 1972.

————. *Studies in Iconology: Humanistic Themes in the Art of the Renaissance.* New York, 1939. Reprint, 1962.

————, and Fritz Saxl. *Dürers "Melencolia I": Eine quellen- und typengeschichtliche Untersuchung.* Leipzig and Berlin, 1923. See also under Klibansky, Panofsky, and Saxl.

Parke, Herbert William. *Greek Oracles*. London, 1967.

———. *The Oracles of Zeus: Dodona, Olympia, Ammon*. Oxford, 1967.

———, and D. E. W. Wormell. *The Delphic Oracle*. 2 vols. Oxford, 1956.

Parmenides. See under Tarán.

Parry, Adam. "Landscape in Greek Poetry." *Yale Classical Studies* 15 (1957), 3-29.

Pasquali, G., ed. *Procli in Platonis Cratylum Commentaria*. Leipzig, 1908.

Perella, Nicholas J. *The Kiss Sacred and Profane*. Berkeley and Los Angeles, 1969.

———. *Midday in Italian Literature*. Princeton, 1979.

Pézard, André. "Nymphes platoniciennes au paradis terrestre." In *Medioevo e Rinascimento: Studi in onore di Bruno Nardi*. Florence, 1955. 2:543-594.

Philo Judaeus. See under Harl.

Pico della Mirandola, Giovanni. See under Garin and Kieszkowski.

Pirsig, Robert M. *Zen and the Art of Motorcycle Maintenance: An Inquiry into Values*. New York, 1974.

Plato. See under Burnet; also under Cornford, Ficino, Hackforth, Jowett, Robin, and Vicaire.

Plotinus. See under Henry and Schwyzer; also under Ficino and MacKenna.

Plutarch. See under Flacelière.

Poliziano, Angelo. *Opera Omnia*. Basel, 1553.

Pollet, Gilbert. See under Sleeman.

Portus, Aemilius, ed. and trans. *Procli Successoris Platonici in Platonis Theologiam Libri Sex*. Hamburg, 1618. Reprint, Frankfurt am Main, 1960.

Pouillon, Henri. "La beauté, propriété transcendantale, chez les scholastiques (1220-1270)." *Archives d'histoire doctrinale et littéraire du Moyen Âge* 15 (1946), 263-329.

Proclus. See under Boese, Diehl, Dodds, Festugière, Kroll, Pasquali, Portus, Saffrey, and Westerink.

Riccioli, Giovanni Battista. *Almagestum Novum*. Bologna, 1651.

Rist, J. M. "Mysticism and Transcendence in Later Neoplatonism." *Hermes* 92 (1964), 213-225.

———. *Plotinus: The Road to Reality*. Cambridge, 1967.

Robin, Léon, ed. and trans. *Phèdre*. Paris, 1933.

Romano, Vincenzo, ed. *Giovanni Boccaccio: Genealogie Deorum Gentilium Libri*. 2 vols. Bari, 1951.

Rosán, Laurence Jay. *The Philosophy of Proclus: The Final Phase of Ancient Thought*. New York, 1949.

Rotondò, A. "Nicolò Tignosi da Foligno." *Rinascimento* 2d ser., 9 (1958), 217-255.

Russell, D. A. *Plutarch*. London, 1973.

Saffrey, H. D. "Notes platoniciennes de Marsile Ficin dans un manuscrit de Proclus, Cod. Riccardianus 70." *Bibliothèque d'humanisme et Renaissance* 21.1 (1959), 161-184.

———, and L. G. Westerink, eds. and trans. *Proclus: Théologie platonicienne*.

4 vols. to date (6 planned). Paris, vol. 1, 1968; vol. 2, 1974; vol. 3, 1978; vol. 4, 1981.

Sagan, Carl. *The Dragons of Eden: Speculations on the Evolution of Human Intelligence.* New York, 1977.

Saitta, Giuseppe. *Marsilio Ficino e la filosofia dell'umanesimo.* 3d ed. Bologna, 1954.

Saxl, Fritz. See under Klibansky and Panofsky.

Schiavone, Michele. *Problemi filosofici in Marsilio Ficino.* Milan, 1957.

Schmitt, Charles B. "Perennial Philosophy: From Agostino Steuco to Leibniz." *Journal of the History of Ideas* 27 (1966), 505-532.

Schwyzer, Hans-Rudolf. "Plotinos." In Pauly-Wissowa-Kroll, *Realencyclopädie der classischen Altertumswissenschaft,* suppl. vol. 15 (1978), 310-328, esp. 323-324.

See also under Henry.

Seznec, Jean. *The Survival of the Pagan Gods.* Translated by Barbara F. Sessions. New York, 1953. Reprint, 1961.

Sheppard, Anne. "The Influence of Hermias on Marsilio Ficino's Doctrine of Inspiration." *Journal of the Warburg and Courtauld Institutes* 43 (1980), 97-109.

Sicherl, Martin. *Die Handschriften, Ausgaben und Übersetzungen von Iamblichos "De Mysteriis": Eine kritisch-historische Studie.* Berlin, 1957.

Sleeman, J. H., and Gilbert Pollet. *Lexicon Plotinianum.* Louvain and Leiden, 1980.

Soldati, B. *La poesia astrologica nel Quattrocento.* Florence, 1906.

Solinas, G. "Sull'estetica di Marsilio Ficino." *Annali della Facoltà di Lettere, Filosofia e Magistero dell'Università di Cagliari* 18 (1951), 365-380.

Soury, Guy. *La démonologie de Plutarque.* Paris, 1942.

Svoboda, K. *La démonologie de Michel Psellos.* Opera Facultatis Philosophicae Universitatis Masarykianae Brunensis, no. 22. Brno, 1927.

Tarabochia Canavero, Alessandra. "Agostino e Tommaso nel Commento di Marsilio Ficino all'*Epistola ai Romani.*" *Rivista di filosofia neo-scolastica* 65 (1973), 815-824.

———. "S. Agostino nella *Teologia Platonica* di Marsilio Ficino." *Rivista di filosofia neo-scolastica* 70 (1978), 626-646.

———. "L'amicizia nell'epistolario di Marsilio Ficino," *Rivista di filosofia neo-scolastica* 67.3 (1975), 422-431.

———. "Il *De Triplici Vita* di Marsilio Ficino: Una strana vicenda ermeneutica." *Rivista di filosofia neo-scolastica* 69.4 (1977), 697-717.

Tarán, Leonardo, ed. and trans. *Parmenides: A Text with Translation, Commentary and Critical Essays.* Princeton, 1965.

Taylor, A. E. *Commentary on Plato's Timaeus.* Oxford, 1928.

Theiler, Willy. "Philo von Alexandria und der Beginn des kaiserzeitlichen Platonismus." In *Parusia: Studien zur Philosophie Platons und zur Problemgeschichte des Platonismus: Festgabe für Johannes Hirschberger.* Frankfurt am Main, 1965. Pp. 199-218.

Thorndike, Lynn. *A History of Magic and Experimental Science.* 8 vols. New York, 1923-1958. Reprint, 1964-1966.

Tigerstedt, E. N. *The Decline and Fall of the Neoplatonic Interpretation of Plato: An Outline and Some Observations.* Commentationes Humanarum Litterarum: Societas Scientiarum Fennica, vol. 52. Helsinki, 1974.

———. "*Furor Poeticus:* Poetic Inspiration in Greek Literature before Democritus and Plato." *Journal of the History of Ideas* 31.2 (1970), 163-178.

———. *Plato's Idea of Poetical Inspiration.* Commentationes Humanarum Litterarum: Societas Scientiarum Fennica, vol. 44, no. 2. Helsinki, 1969.

———. "The Poet as Creator: Origins of a Metaphor." *Comparative Literature Studies* 5.4 (1968), 455-488.

Torre, Arnaldo della. *Storia dell'Accademia Platonica di Firenze.* Florence, 1902.

Trinkaus, Charles. *Adversity's Noblemen: The Italian Humanists on Happiness.* New York, 1940. Reprint, 1965.

———. *In Our Image and Likeness: Humanity and Divinity in Italian Humanist Thought.* 2 vols. London and Chicago, 1970.

———. "The Unknown Quattrocento Poetics of Bartolommeo della Fonte." *Studies in the Renaissance* 13 (1966), 40-122.

Valla, Lorenzo. See under Lorch.

Verbeke, G. *L'évolution de la doctrine du pneuma du stoïcisme à saint Augustin.* Paris and Louvain, 1945.

Vicaire, Paul, trans. *Phèdre.* Paris, 1972.

Vicari, Patricia, and John Warden. Review of *Marsilio Ficino and the Phaedran Charioteer,* ed. and trans. Michael J. B. Allen. *Spenser Newsletter* 13.2 (1982), 29-34.

Vries, G. J. de. *A Commentary on the Phaedrus of Plato.* Amsterdam, 1969.

Wadsworth, James B. "Landino's *Disputationes Camaldulenses,* Ficino's *De Felicitate,* and *L'altercazione* of Lorenzo de' Medici." *Modern Philology* 50.1 (1952), 23-31.

Walker, D. P. *The Ancient Theology: Studies in Christian Platonism from the Fifteenth to the Eighteenth Century.* London, 1972.

———. "The Astral Body in Renaissance Medicine." *Journal of the Warburg and Courtauld Institutes* 21 (1958), 119-133.

———. *Spiritual and Demonic Magic: From Ficino to Campanella.* London, 1958. Reprint, Notre Dame, 1975.

Wallis, R. T. *Neoplatonism.* London, 1972.

Walzel, Oskar. "Von Plotin, Proklos und Ficinus." *Deutsche Vierteljahrsschrift für Literaturwissenschaft und Geistesgeschichte* 19 (1941), 407-429.

Warden, John. See Vicari.

Waszink, J. H., ed. *Calcidius: In Timaeum.* Corpus Platonicum Medii Aevi: Plato Latinus, edited by R. Klibansky, vol. 4. London, and Leiden, 1962. 2d ed., 1975.

Westerink, L. G. "Ficino's Marginal Notes on Olympiodorus in Riccardi Greek MS 37." *Traditio* 24 (1968), 351-378.

———, ed. and trans. *Anonymous Prolegomena to Platonic Philosophy.* Amsterdam, 1962.

———, ed. *Proclus: Commentary on the First Alcibiades.* Amsterdam, 1954. See also under Saffrey.

White, Roger A. See under Allen, Michael J. B.

Willis, J., ed. *Macrobius: In Somnium Scipionis.* 2d ed. Leipzig, 1970.

Wind, Edgar. *Pagan Mysteries of the Renaissance.* New York, 1958. Rev. ed., 1968.

———. "Platonic Justice, Designed by Raphael." *Journal of the Warburg Institute* 1 (1937), 69-70.

———. "The Revival of Origen." In *Studies in Art and Literature for Belle da Costa Greene.* Princeton, 1954. Pp. 412-424.

Wittkower, R. "Transformations of Minerva in Renaissance Imagery." *Journal of the Warburg Institute* 2 (1938-39), 194-205.

Wormell, D. E. W. See under Parke.

Yates, Frances A. *The French Academies of the Sixteenth Century.* London, 1947.

———. *Giordano Bruno and the Hermetic Tradition.* London and Chicago, 1964. Reprint, New York, 1969.

Zambelli, Paola. "Platone, Ficino e la magia." In *Studia Humanitatis: Ernesto Grassi zum 70 Geburtstag,* edited by Eginhard Hora and Eckhard Kessler. Munich, 1973. Pp. 121-142.

Zanier, Giancarlo. *La medicina astrologica e la sua teoria: Marsilio Ficino e i suoi critici contemporanei.* Rome, 1977.

Zeller, E., and R. Mondolfo. *La filosofia dei Greci nel suo sviluppo storico.* Part 3, vol. 6. Edited by Giuseppe Martano. Florence, 1961.

Zintzen, Clemens, ed. *Damascii Vitae Isidori reliquiae.* Hildesheim, 1967.

Index

Abandonment, 167, 168. *See also* Descent; Understanding
Academies, 6-7, 87, 214; on Phaedran myth, 216-217, 222
Achelous, 5, 6
Adrastia, 171
Aeneid, 4
Aesthetics, 202, 203. *See also* Beauty
Aether, 11-12, 93. *See also* Bodies, aethereal
Agli, Peregrino, 47
Air: cicadas in, 24; demons in, 12, 13; divisions of, 11-12; impure, 13, 177; pure, 13, 177
Alcibiades, 34
Alcibiades I, 21
Alcmaeon, 71
Alienation, 42, 59, 65, 66
Ambrosia and nectar, 108, 163, 166, 207, 210, 211, 212, 213, 221, 224-225. *See also* Meadow of truth
Ammon, 37, 38. *See also* Jove
Ammonius, 214
Anadyomene, 130
Angels, 141, 221; guardian, 19-20; as highest demons, 9; as intellectual gods, 251; Judaeo-Christian, 15-16; as supermundane gods, 101
Aphrodite. *See* Venus
Apollo, 7, 23, 29, 118, 129, 132, 134, 149, 251; and Bacchus, 31, 66-67; as beauty, 132; and Dionysus, 33, 34; inspires Socrates, 8, 34; and Muses, 30-31; as Socrates's personal god, 21-22, 34
Apology, 21, 24, 226
Apology epitome, 226-227
Appetite, 88, 89, 90, 197; black horse as, 199, 200, 210, 217-218, 223, 224, 226; irrational, 210, 223, 224,

226; rational, 223, 224, 226; v. reason, 198-199
Apuleius, 9, 11, 15, 20 n. 46, 207
Aquinas, 80, 82, 228
Arcesilaus, 214
Archytas, 217
Areopagite, 90, 252
Ares. *See* Mars
Aristotle, 103-104, 105
Armstrong, A. H., 73-74, 182
Artemis. *See* Diana
Ascent: to beauty, 55, 57; of soul, 144-164, 178-179, 181-184
Asclepius, 207, 208
Astrology, 34, 93, 98-99, 183 n. 27, 257
Astronomy, 118-119 n. 17, 231-232, 252-253, 257
Athena/Athene. *See* Minerva
Athenagoras, 255, 257
Augustine, 9, 16, 90, 228
Averröes, 213

Bacchus, 33; and Apollo, 31, 66-67. *See also* Dionysus
Beauty: as apex of universe, 146, 147; Apollo as, 132; ascent to, 55, 57; and being, 185; black horse desires, 199; corporeal, 201; divine, 190; in divine nature, 107, 108-109, 110, 111; and education, 190; as goal, 49, 57, 199, 202, 210, 226; of God, 56-57, 108-110; and harmony, 191; idea of, 185-203; intellectual, 56, 201, 202; as intelligible, 56, 65, 189, 199, 201, 202, 234; lover of, 190; moral, 56, 201, 202; Neoplatonists on, 188; noumenal, 185; phenomenal, 185; physical, 197; Plato on, 185, 188, 197; Plotinus

Designer:	UC Press Staff
Compositor:	Janet Sheila Brown
Printer:	McNaughton & Gunn, Inc.
Binder:	McNaughton & Gunn, Inc.
Text:	11/13 English Times
Display:	English Times